NORTON
UTILITIES® 5.0
An Illustrated Tutorial

Richard Evans

Dedication
Psalm 118:29
To Steve and Jessica, Bill and Sharon, and Tim and Gloria,
who are miles away but close at heart. May they continue
to do God's will and bring His Word to those in most need.

FIRST EDITION
FIRST PRINTING

Library of Congress Cataloging-in-Publication Data

Evans, Richard 1938-
    Norton utilities 5.0 : an illustrated tutorial / by Richard Evans
      p. cm.
    Includes index.
    ISBN 0-8306-7720-8 (pbk.)   ISBN 0-8306-0525-8
    1. Norton Utilities (Computer programs) I. Title.
QA76.76.U84E94 1991   90-19612
005.4'3—dc20   CIP

TAB Books offers software for sale. For information and a catalog, please contact
TAB Software Department, Blue Ridge Summit, PA 17294-0850.

Questions regarding the content of this book should be addressed to:

Reader Inquiry Branch
Windcrest Books
Blue Ridge Summit, PA 17294-0850

Acquisitions Editor: Ron Powers
Book Editor: David M. McCandless
Production: Katherine G. Brown
Series Design: Jaclyn J. Boone
Cover Design: Lori E. Schlosser
Cover Illustration: Greg Schooley

Contents

Acknowledgments   xi
Preface   xiii
Introduction to the New Edition   xiv
Introduction to the First Edition   xv

Chapter 1. Getting started   1
 Making a backup copy   *2*
 Installing version 5.0   *2*
 Installing version 4.5   *7*
 What's new in 5.0   *8*
 System requirements   *11*
 Version directories 4.0, 4.5, & 5.0   *11*
 Getting help   *14*

Chapter 2. Batch Enhancer   15
 New in version 5.0   *15*
 ASK   *16*
  BE ASK   *16*
  Batch file definitions   *19*

BEEP *27*
    BE BEEP *27*
    Comments *27*
BOX *28*
    BE BOX *28*
    BE CLS *29*
    BE DELAY ticks *29*
    PRINTCHAR *29*
    ROWCOL *30*
    WINDOW *30*
Screen attributes *31*
    BE SA *31*

Chapter 3. Calibrate 41
Command line use *41*
Network considerations *42*
Compatibility *42*

Chapter 4. DiskEdit 51
Command line usage *52*
Network considerations *52*
The heart *52*
The Norton Utility (NU) version 4.0 & 4.5 *61*

Chapter 5. Disk Monitor 75
Command line usage *75*
Network considerations *76*

Chapter 6. DiskReet 81
Command line usage *82*
Network considerations *82*
Other considerations *82*

Chapter 7. Disk Tool 87
Command line usage *87*
Network considerations *87*

Chapter 8. FileFind 93
Command line usage *93*
Network considerations *95*
File Attributes version 4.0 & 4.5 *100*
FileDate version 4.5 *105*

FileFind version 4.0 & 4.5 *108*
File Informaton version 4.0 & 4.5 *112*
FileSize version 4.0 & 4.5 *116*
List Directory verson 4.0 & 4.5 *120*
TextSearch version 4.0 & 4.5 *124*

Chapter 9. Filefix   127
Command line usage *127*
Network considerations *128*

Chapter 10. FileSave   131
Command line usage *131*
Network considerations *132*

Chapter 11. Image   137
Command line usage *137*
Network considerations *138*

Chapter 12. LinePrint   139
More on the setup file *144*

Chapter 13. Norton Change Directory   147
Command line usage *147*
Network considerations *148*
Version 4.0 & 4.5 *148*
Volume label *154*

Chapter 14. Norton Control Center   157
Command line usage *157*
    The stop watches *158*
Network considerations *159*
Version 4.0 & 4.5 *164*
TimeMark *173*

Chapter 15. Disk Cache   177
Command line usage *178*
    NCACHE-F specific *181*
Network considerations *181*
Configuration considerations *182*

Chapter 16. Disk Doctor   185

Command line usage *185*
    Limitation *186*
    Compatibility *186*
Network considerations *186*
Disk Doctor II *186*
Norton Disk Doctor *191*
DiskTest *197*

Chapter 17. Norton   203

Command line usage *203*
Network considerations *204*
Menu expansion and modification *204*
Norton Integrator version 4.5 *207*

Chapter 18. SafeFormat   211

Command line usage *211*
Network considerations *212*
SafeFormat version 4.0 & 4.5 *213*

Chapter 19. SpeeDisk   219

Command line format *220*
Network considerations *220*
SpeeDisk version 4.0 & 4.5 *229*
Directory Sort version 4.0 & 4.5 *236*

Chapter 20. System Information   243

Command line usage *243*
Network considerations *244*
A typical SysInfo report *255*
System Information version 4.0 & 4.5 *264*
Disk Information version 4.0 & 4.5 *270*

Chapter 21. UnErase   275

Command line usage *275*
Network considerations *275*
Quick UnErase version 4.0 & 4.5 *280*
Unremove Directory version 4.0 & 4.5 *283*

Chapter 22. UnFormat 285
Command line usage *285*
Network considerations *285*
Format Recovery version 4.0 & 4.5 *287*

Chapter 23. WipeInfo 291
Command line usage *291*
Network considerations *292*
WipeDisk version 4.0 & 4.5 *295*
WipeFile verson 4.0 & 4.5 *298*

Chapter 24. READ ME 303
Late additions to the Norton Utilities Version 4.5AE *304*
Welcome to the Norton Utilities Version 5.0 *306*
General information *306*
Additional program information *307*
Compatibility issues and additional considerations *313*
Manual corrections and changes *314*
Problems, error messages, and solutions *314*

Chapter 25. Questions & answers 317
Questions on new edition *317*
Questions from earlier editions *319*

Chapter 26. The dissected disk 325
Discussing the dissected disk *325*
Version 5.0 update *330*

Appendix 333

Epilogue 335

Index 337

Contacting Peter Norton Computing, Inc.

Peter Norton Computing, Inc.
100 Wilshire Blvd., 9th Floor
Santa Monica, CA 90401-1104

Customer Svc: (213) 319-2010 [voice]
Tech Support : (213) 319-2020 [voice]
Hours   : 7:00 AM to 5:00 PM Pacific Time
Days   : Monday thru Friday
FAX   : (213) 458-2048
MCI   : 331-7813

Acknowledgments

I must say a special word of thanks to Clayton Lamm and D. Kraig Lane for their assistance during the preparation of this manuscript. They were able to maintain their sense of humor through numerous questions. They also endured a few tirades during the Beta test period that should have tried the patience of a stone. In spite of all of this, they continued to smile and provide information in a timely manner.

Preface

Version 5.0 of the Norton Utilities surpasses many of the various utility programs available. The continuing excellence of the programming and the programmers' awareness of the users' limitations ensures that these Utilities perform as advertised. When you see the advertisements for the various Peter Norton products, however, you will notice a change. The company, Peter Norton Computing, Inc., has been purchased by another firm.

Symantec Inc. is a large, publicly held corporation. They have been most active in the Apple/Macintosh software arena. Their acquisition of the Peter Norton Group should improve the position of the Utilities. To some, bigger is not necessarily better. With a broader product base and wider distribution potential, however, the Utilities should profit from being part of a larger organization.

Other additions to the Norton Utilities line are the new versions for MAC and UNIX users. Until now, these users could only dream of having the power and help available to DOS users. Developing the Norton Utilities for the MAC and UNIX systems was more than just a simple porting of the existing code to these different operating systems. Included in the differences are the file structures themselves and file handling. Combine these changes with the differences when crashes or deletions occur, and you have a whole new set of Utilities behind the same familiar name.

If you have friends and associates who use these systems, be sure to tell them that tutorial books will be published that will assist them in the near future. Look for these books to be broader in scope and more along the lines of disaster recovery tutorials than just Norton Utility tutorials.

Introduction
to the New Edition

Version 5.0 contains more visible changes than any of the past versions. You could almost run any of the Utilities without ever breaking the shrink wrap on the manual; but by doing so, you will miss much of the speed and power of these new Utilities.

Every "needed" Utility is now menu-driven. In essence, you can read the screen and work your way through the features. Also, a few more safety features are present in those utilities that can cause the most trouble. (Utilities cause trouble only when misused anyway.) These Utilities are actually among the most powerful utilities available to the PC, XT, AT, 386, etc.,-user today.

For those of you who are very familiar with previous versions of the Utilities, I must urge you to read at least the index of the new manual. Some of the old, familiar Utilities are gone, and a few have been relocated into new, more logical places.

Another addition to Norton is network-compatibility. Now the workstations and the file server can benefit from regular Norton housekeeping. Don't tell anyone that Peter does windows, but don't be surprised when you can run his Utilities under your Windows.

Introduction to the First Edition

The Norton Utilities are a group of programs that provide the user with many useful tools not found on a system disk. A few of these tools perform almost the same function; they are not duplicates, however, but improvements.

While the programs themselves are very useful and powerful, the documentation that accompanies them is not the easiest to understand. Because of this, some frightened users refrain from using the Norton Utilities. Other users will work their way through the booklet only far enough to learn how to use a few of the programs. Once they have a basic understanding of the program's function, they put the book down, which leaves all of them without the full benefit of the programs that they have purchased.

Documentation is a stepchild. Programmers don't usually want to take the time to write it properly, and writers usually do not know enough about the program to do the job right. Then, the user must either become a programmer (in order to read the programmers' notes), or he must hope that the documentation isn't really necessary to use the programs. Hopefully, this manual will walk the narrow line between these two extremes and be both readable and useful.

PC/MS-DOS is a basic (read "bare-bones") operating system. It provides a limited number of utilities and very little help to the user attempting to use a micro-computer to efficiently do other tasks. A good interface or means of connecting the user to his programs should be as transparent as possible. DOS fails this first test. When a user makes a mistake. the interface should provide a clear message that an error has been made and some equally clear suggestions on how to correct the problem. DOS fails to do this also.

The Norton Utilities cannot eliminate all of the problems and shortcomings present in DOS, but it can provide us with a number of ways to avoid contact with DOS. Thus, many of DOS's pitfalls can be smoothed over. The suggestions and examples presented here have been carefully constructed to provide simple, clear, and easily used bypasses. They do not portend to be an exhaustive listing but are presented in such a manner that, hopefully, the reader will be able to adapt and expand these listings into useful individual applications.

If additional support or assistance is desired, I can be found on-line most evenings after 9 PM Eastern time. The place is DELPHI and my username is ELLISCO. Among other things, I am an assistant manager for a number of the Special Interest Groups (SIGs,) if you don't find me immediately, leave an electronic mail message. For those who don't know how to access DELPHI, you must start by making a local phone call. DELPHI is a host on both the TYMNET and TELENET Public Switching Networks.

You can get the number of your nearest TYMNET access point by contacting their Customer Service personnel at 800-336-0149. TELENET's Customer Service number is 800-336-0437. There are people on duty at these numbers all the time. Try to limit your requests for service to normal East Coast business hours, because the late-night service personnel are mostly tech types.

DELPHI is modem-accessible in over 65 foreign countries and over 600 U.S. cities. For those of you in the Boston area, call them direct at (617) 576-0802 (modem) or (617) 491-3393 (voice). Call the DELPHI Customer Service Section at 800-544-4005, during normal East Coast business hours to get help. You will need a modem and communications software to take full advantage of the DELPHI system.

1
CHAPTER

Getting started

Being prepared is half the battle of staying out of trouble. Computers are wonder-ful tools; however, they are just tools. Like all other tools, they are subject to wear and failure. Wear and failure aren't "if" conditions; they are "when" realities.

The hardware manufacturers continue to progress, introducing faster and more powerful systems almost daily. Some systems contain well-proven technol-ogy that will continue to work for many years to come. Some of this new technol-ogy has worked in the laboratory and during tests, but will it survive the user? There are no unqualified and unlimited promises.

Experience teaches that you must make backup copies of important data. Your Norton Utilities program disks are important, so make backup copies before you need to use them. Hard-disk users should also make a backup set of disks. The copies installed on the hard disk and the distribution disks may not always be adequate protection against a total loss of programs.

Making a backup copy

Your first step with any software disk should be to make a backup copy. Backing up these Utilities will take a few minutes, so while the computer does the work, continue reading.

Some of the program files of version 5.0 are compressed, which means that you will need more disks than normal to make a working floppy copy of all of the Utilities. Hard-disk users may want to install the Utilities and then make an uncompressed copy of the program files only on floppies. In version 5.0, the Utilities total over two megabytes of files.

Using freshly formatted disks, DISKCOPY the programs on the Norton Utility disks to the same number of your disks, even if you plan to install the Utilities on a hard disk. If your system allows you, format the disk while copying. I know it takes a bit longer, but I'm trying to give you more reading time before you start playing with all of the goodies available on those distribution disks.

The compression, or archiving, utility used to create the NU5_ ARC?.EXE files is called PKZIP. PKZIP is a shareware utility available on many of the free and subscription bulletin boards. If you have a copy of the current PKZIP (version 1.03), you can extract (-x) any of the compressed Utilities individually. The Norton Utility distribution diskettes are write-protected, so you will not be able to use any of PKZIP's recovery tools on those diskettes. I do not recommend that you use one of those "notching" tools to remove the little square of the plastic carrier. Should your distribution diskettes become unreadable, you can return them to Peter Norton Computing and get replacements. Be sure that you contact Norton Computing before you mail your diskettes. The phone number for Customer Service is listed in the front of this book. The representatives at Peter Norton are always ready to assist registered owners. Be sure that you mail in the registration form found in the box containing your manuals and software.

To make a backup, do the following:

1. Boot your system using PC/MS-DOS.
2. Place a Norton Utility disk in drive A.
3. Place a blank formatted disk in drive B.
4. Type DISKCOPY *.* B: at the A> prompt, then press RETURN.
5. When copying is complete, store the original disk(s) in a safe place. You should run the Utilities from the copies.

Installing version 5.0

You might want to review all of these screens before actually beginning the installation. There are more and different questions than have been asked by the earlier versions. To install the Utilities on a hard disk, do the following:

1. Place the disk containing the INSTALL program in drive A. Look at the

last disk first. This differs from all of the previous versions, but there is some method in the madness.

2. At the C> prompt, type A:INSTALL.

3. After loading itself into your system, the INSTALL program will go looking for earlier versions of the Norton Utilities. While it's doing that, you can monitor its progress by watching the Install opening panel, illustrated here in Fig. 1-1.

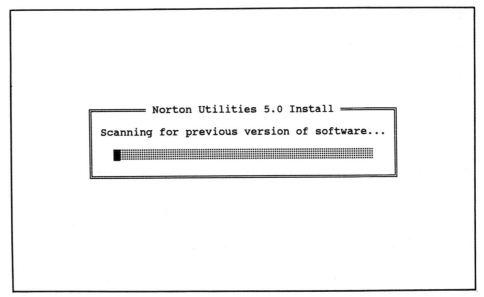

1-1 The Opening INSTALL screen.

Once the INSTALL program has all of the information it needs, the next screen will display. As illustrated in Fig. 1-2, your choices are to do a new installation, adjust what you have previously done, or quit and return to the C> prompt.

The New Install choice sets up to copy the files from your software package disks onto your hard disk. It will also delete or overwrite the programs of the previous version if you let it. You can elect to make backup copies of the old Utilities, just in case. The compressed files are *self-extracting* archives, which means that it is possible to decompress the Utility programs in these files without using the INSTALL program. If you must work this way, make a copy of the NU5_ ARC?.EXE file and then run the file like you would any .EXE file.

Should any of the compressed .EXE files be corrupted, you may be able to recover them by copying the corrupted files to another disk(ette). When these files are not on a write-protected diskette, the recovery tools in PKZIP may be able to salvage the information. If PKZIP fails, program replacement is the only other legal solution.

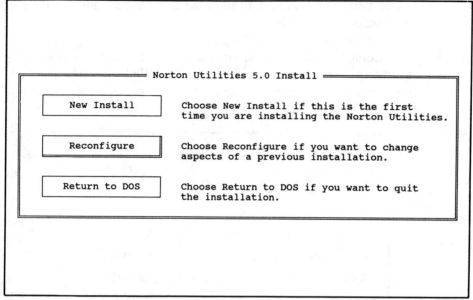

```
╔═══════════════ Norton Utilities 5.0 Install ═══════════════╗
║                                                             ║
║  ┌─────────────────┐   Choose New Install if this is the    ║
║  │   New Install   │   first                                ║
║  └─────────────────┘   time you are installing the Norton Utilities. ║
║                                                             ║
║  ┌─────────────────┐   Choose Reconfigure if you want to change ║
║  │   Reconfigure   │   aspects of a previous installation.  ║
║  └─────────────────┘                                        ║
║                                                             ║
║  ┌─────────────────┐   Choose Return to DOS if you want to quit ║
║  │  Return to DOS  │   the installation.                    ║
║  └─────────────────┘                                        ║
║                                                             ║
╚═════════════════════════════════════════════════════════════╝
```

1-2   The installation options for Norton Utilities 5.0.

The New Install option will tell you which disks to place in the A drive at the proper time. You will need to wait a few moments while the programs are decompressed. When this finishes, you will then be returned to the first options menu.

The Reconfigure option makes changes to things that are already in your system. It will not let you control the way files are copied from the distribution disks to your hard disk.

The Return to DOS option is just what it says. You quit the INSTALL program and return to the C> prompt.

Consider protecting the power of these Utilities if more than one user will be on the system with version 5.0.

Behind each of the options illustrated in Fig. 1-3, there are several other options. They should appear as follows: Password (a way to limit access to your Utilities), Norton Program (a way to disable the editing feature), Hardware (which offers choices between screen colors and graphics), and File Change (which lets you edit your AUTOEXEC.BAT or CONFIG.SYS files).

The Password feature is illustrated in Fig. 1-4. Each of the main programs that other people could use to damage your system or information can be protected with a password. If you protect any or all of these programs, however, it will be almost impossible to run the protected ones without the password. For this reason, you should be very careful in the selection of the word you use.

As an added measure of security, the INSTALL program doesn't transfer to your hard disk. In order to change or delete the password protection, you will have to run INSTALL from the distribution diskette—not a good idea—or from the backup copy you should make before you consider this installation complete.

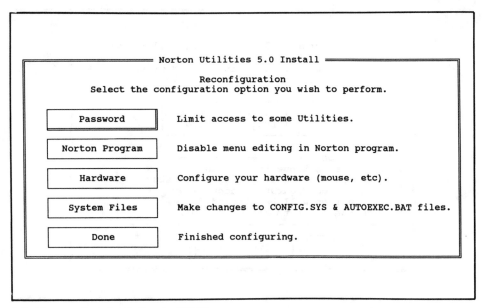

```
============= Norton Utilities 5.0 Install =============

                         Reconfiguration
              Select the configuration option you wish to perform.

      ┌─────────────────────┐
      │      Password       │      Limit access to some Utilities.
      └─────────────────────┘
      ┌─────────────────────┐
      │    Norton Program   │      Disable menu editing in Norton program.
      └─────────────────────┘
      ┌─────────────────────┐
      │      Hardware       │      Configure your hardware (mouse, etc).
      └─────────────────────┘
      ┌─────────────────────┐
      │    System Files     │      Make changes to CONFIG.SYS & AUTOEXEC.BAT files.
      └─────────────────────┘
      ┌─────────────────────┐
      │       Done          │      Finished configuring.
      └─────────────────────┘
```

1-3 The reconfiguration options for NU 5.0.

```
============= Set Password Protection =============

          Select programs which require a password to run

      [ ] Calibrate                [ ] Safe Format
      [ ] Disk Editor              [ ] Speed Disk
      [ ] Disk Monitor             [ ] UnErase
      [ ] Disk Tools               [ ] UnFormat
      [ ] FileFix                  [ ] WipeInfo
      [ ] Norton Disk Doctor II

      ┌─────────────┐   ┌─────────────┐   ┌─────────────┐
      │  Continue   │   │  Go Back    │   │   Abort     │
      └─────────────┘   └─────────────┘   └─────────────┘
```

1-4 Protecting various Utilities with a password.

If you want to be the only one able to use the editing power of the Norton Program (also known as the Norton Utility program), then you need to Disable Editing (shown in Fig. 1-5). Just remember that you will have to reset this feature before you can do any editing yourself. You shouldn't have much trouble because you will have the diskette with the INSTALL program on it.

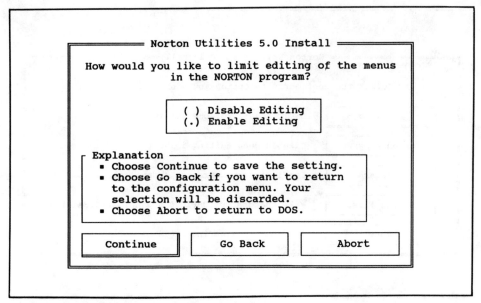

1-5 Protecting the Norton program from unauthorized users.

The Hardware menu is where you tell the Utilities about your system. The first four Screen Color options are for different types of monitors. The last one changes the color combination that the Utilities display when you run them. The default is bright white on blue. If you don't like this combination, try the other one—bright white on cyan. The Graphics options, shown in Fig. 1-6, relate to

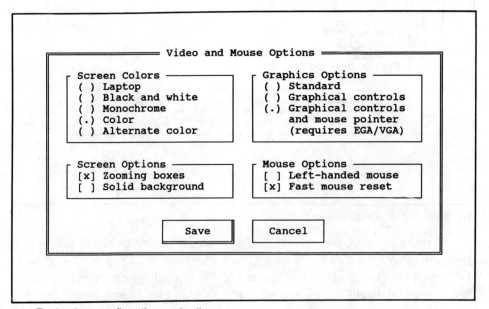

1-6 The hardware configurations and options.

your means of getting around in each of the menus. A mouse can make things a bit faster but isn't necessary. Using the TAB key and the ARROW keys usually can be just as fast.

Whether or not you make any changes in your CONFIG.SYS or AUTOEXEC.BAT files is up to you. If you are going to use the cache or encrypting features, then the CONFIG.SYS file must be changed. It would also seem reasonable to change the AUTOEXEC.BAT file to include the subdirectory with the Utilities in your PATH statement. This may not be necessary if you already have it there. Figure 1-7 illustrates this menu.

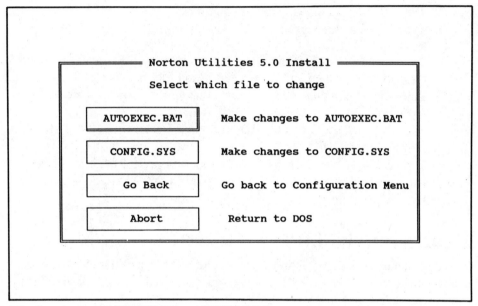

1-7 Changing your AUTOEXEC.BAT and CONFIG.SYS files.

When you exit the original configuration menu, all of the selections you have made will be saved—assuming that you didn't Abort any menus. There are additional configuration menus in a number of the other utilities that will be covered as that utility is explained.

By now you are at the DOS prompt and ready to explore all of the new features of this version. Enjoy.

Installing version 4.5

Version 4.5 contains an INSTALL.BAT program that will overwrite your existing .EXE Utility programs and add all of the new ones, which makes things much easier. While you may not want to retain the DEMO programs, you really should try them at least once. The procedure for installation is as follows:

1. Boot your system and place diskette 1 in drive A.

2. At the C> prompt, type A:INSTALL.
3. Follow the instructions as they appear on the screen.
4. After installation is complete, be sure you have a good working copy of the Utilities. Then store the distribution disks in a safe place.
5. Don't delete the DEMO files until you've tried them at least once. They will provide you with some interesting information.

Installing version 4.0

1. Place disk 1 of the Norton Utilities disk in drive A.
2. Type MD\NU at the C> prompt and press RETURN.
3. Type CD and then press the F3 key at the C> prompt. Then press RETURN.
4. Type COPY A:*.EXE at the C> prompt and press RETURN. Version 4.0 through 5.0 Standard and Advanced Edition files use the .EXE extension. Thus, copying in this manner ensures that unnecessary files are not transferred to the hard disk.
5. Type DEL NUDEMO.* at the C> prompt and press RETURN. That's **NU-DEMO**, not **NUDEMO**!
6. Type COPY A:*.HLP at the C> prompt and press RETURN. These last two steps will remove the DEMO program from the hard disk and add the helpfile program.

What's new in 5.0

Fewer filenames doesn't mean that you are getting fewer Utilities. With the reorganization of everything, several Utilities are combined. All of the old Utility names will be listed so that you can find your favorites.

There are actually 20 new or improved Utilities in version 5.0. If you are a version 4.5, Advanced Edition user, you know this means that almost everything has been worked on; there were only 24 Utilities in that version. One of the reasons that some of the version 4.5 Utilities weren't improved is that they have been dropped. I will list these for you.

Shown below are the positive changes:

- Norton Disk Doctor is now Norton Disk Doctor II, capable of more and better repairs at even faster speeds, automatically.

- UnErase still recovers deleted files. Now it can also recognize 1-2-3 and dBASE file formats.

- UnFormat used to be part of the Format Recover Utility. Now it has an improved file recovery capability in the case of accidental hard-disk format.

- A new Utility, Image, replaces the FRECOVER.IDX file that was hidden and read-only at the end of your hard disk. It contains the information needed by UnFormat, UnErase, and Norton Disk Doctor II to do their "thing."

- Another addition is the FileFix Utility. It is helpful in recovery operations and recognizes corrupted 1-2-3 and dBASE data files.

- FileSave is used to protect deleted files from being overwritten. Thus, UnErase will be able to find all of the sectors of a deleted file. In the past, it was possible that portions of a deleted file would be overwritten before recovery was started. If this happened, that portion of the file was lost forever. Using FileSave means that you will be using more disk space because this Utility will not allow the deleted file to be overwritten until there is no more disk space available for new files.

- The Disk Editor is also new. Many of its features were in the Norton Utility (NU) program of earlier versions. The split-screen clipboard and quick links make it much more usable. The Editor also has more safeguards. Like NU, this Utility can access every byte of your hard disk or diskette and make changes. It will also allow you to create an UNDO log that can be run if one of your changes causes more problems than it solved.

- Disk Tools is really a collection of Utility programs. With it, you can revive almost any defective diskette. (The qualifier is still there because it cannot perform miracles.) Another very useful feature is the "rescue diskette.") Disk Tools will write lots of useful and necessary information to a floppy for you. Then, when disaster strikes, you will have at least one more ace to play before defeat may become a fact.

- SpeeDisk has been improved, too. It has more options and will also recommend which optimization process should be used to gain the greatest improvement with the least change.

- If you thought you knew how well your hard disk was running, be prepared to learn even more. Calibrate tells you almost more than you really want to know about the operation and health of your hard disk. It will also suggest changes to improve performance. I'd suggest that you take its advice: so far, Calibrate has been correct on every change suggested.

- The buzzword "cache" means many things to many people. In some cases it means problems: not every system is built to use a caching utility. The Norton Utilities understands this and evaluates your system before recommending which, if any, cache Utility you install.

- There may be more words in print about viruses in computers than there are about the HIV or AIDS virus. Both types require understanding so that they can be protected against. Version 5.0 has its own protection scheme, one that is compatible with all of the other Utilities, so you shouldn't have any of the problems that can come from incompatible Terminate and Stay Resident (TSR) programs. The head-parking feature is just another way of protecting your disk and your data.

- Do you insist on total privacy of your information? Have you had problems with others being able to read things they shouldn't? Check out the DiskReet Utility. When it is in full operation, only the information on your screen can be read. Everything else is encrypted, and how it is encrypted is your choice. There are the PNCI and DES methods. Normally the PNCI method will be adequate; but if it's really "top secret," then the DES method will be required.

- It used to be that you had to choose between WipeFile and WipeDisk to be sure that things were completely erased from your disk(ette)(s). These programs have been combined into WipeInfo for version 5.0.

- Formatting disks used to mean that all data would be lost. This was true until SafeFormat (SF) appeared. The improved combination Utility (SFormat) still does everything that the old programs did, but just does it faster and more automatically. The safeguards are still there to try and ensure that you don't accidentally lose something necessary forever.

- One of the expanded capabilities of FileFind is its ability to search across a network for a filename. There are also searches using dates, owners, attributes, etc. If you know anything about the lost file, you should be able to uncover its hiding place. FileFind retains its capability to display filenames that do not display when the DOS DIR command is issued.

- The Norton Control Center (NCC), new in version 4.5, has been updated to give you control over more settings. It has also been expanded to include the capabilities of the newer systems that have been introduced since version 4.5 was released.

- The System Information (SI) Utility provided almost everything most of us needed to know about what was in the "box" and how well our system compared with the rest of the microcomputer world. The new SysInfo Utility now writes a 10-page report on your system's health and well being. The presentation formats have been enhanced, and the total quantity of quality information has been expanded.

- One more change that you must be aware of before you get into these new Utilities is that some of the programs are compressed. You cannot run them before you run the INSTALL program. The important Utilities, however, such as Disk Doctor II, UnErase, UnFormat, Disk Tools, and the Disk Editor, are not compressed and may be used even before you install the balance of the package.

Unchanged is the fact that even though there is some network compatibility, the Utilities still do not do everything that many network managers need done.

System requirements

Now that you are ready to install version 5.0, you'd better make sure your system will hold all of its power and programs. You will need the following:

- An IBM XT, AT, PS/2 or 100%-compatible.
- MS/PC-DOS 2.0 or later.
- 512 kilobytes of available Random Access Memory (RAM).
- At least 3 megabytes of free space on your hard disk.

It is possible to use version 5.0 on a system without a hard disk. If this is necessary, it would be best to install the Utilities on a hard disk first. Then the programs can be copied onto floppies. Once they are on floppies, they can be used as needed. Just be sure that all of the information each one needs is available.

Version 5.0 supports the large hard-disk partitions that may be created when you have DOS 4.x or Compaq 3.31. There are other hardware and software combinations that are compatible. This also implies, however, that there are still some incompatible combinations.

If you discover an incompatible combination, be sure to give the Technical Support team at Peter Norton all of the details. I can't promise that they will provide you with a solution, but they are continuously working to ensure that the Utilities have maximum compatibility. A copy of SysInfo's report would be great if you can get one from the system. The address is printed on the software manual.

Version directories 4.0, 4.5, & 5.0

The listings in Table 1-1 are for the Utility programs only. They do not include the various DEMO programs that are in the later versions. The byte count at the end of each column is for information only. Over the life of each version, it has been necessary to distribute fixes to correct problems that were not discovered during the Beta test period. The byte count of these programs may vary from those which I received.

Normally all of the Utility programs will share the same time/date stamp information. If you have any questions about the size or creation date of any of your Utility programs, please contact the Technical Support Group of Peter Norton Computing, Inc. Their telephone, FAX, and MCI mail numbers are listed near the front of the book.

Table 1-1 Comparing the contents of Norton Utilities versions 4.0, 4.5, and 5.0.

Version 4.0		Version 4.5		Version 5.0	
ASK	.EXE.	—		—	
BEEP	.EXE.	—		—	
—		BE	.EXE	BE	.EXE
—		—		CALIBRAT	.EXE
—		DI	.EXE	—	
—		—		DISKMON	.EXE.
—		—		DISKREET	.EXE
—		—		DISKREET	.SYS
DS	.EXE	DS	.EXE		
DT	.EXE	DT	.EXE		
FA	.EXE	FA	.EXE		
—		FD	.EXE		
FF	.EXE	FF	.EXE	FILEFIND	.EXE
FI	.EXE	FI	.EXE	—	
—		—		—	
FR	.EXE	FR	.EXE	IMAGE	.EXE
FS	.EXE	FS	.EXE	—	
—		INSTALL	.EXE	INSTALL	.EXE
LD	.EXE	LD	.EXE	—	
LP	.EXE	LP	.EXE	—	
MARY		MARY		MARY	
—		—		NCACHE-F	.EXE
—		—		NCACHE-S	.EXE
—		NCC	.EXE	NCC	.EXE
NCD	.EXE	NCD	.EXE	NCD	.EXE
—		NDD	.EXE	NDD	.EXE
—		—		NORTON	.CMD
NI	.EXE	NI	.EXE	NORTON	.EXE
—		—		NORTON	.OVL
NU	.EXE	NU	.EXE	DISKEDIT	.EXE
NU	.HLP	NU	.HLP	—	
QU	.EXE	QU	.EXE	UNERASE	.EXE
—		—		PCSHADOW	.SYS
READ	.ME	READ	.ME	READ	.ME
SA	.EXE	—		BE	.EXE
SD	.EXE	SD	.EXE	SPEEDISK	.EXE
—		SF	.EXE	SFORMAT	.EXE
SI	.EXE	SI	.EXE	SYSINFO	.EXE
TM	.EXE	TM	.EXE	NCC	.EXE
TS	.EXE	TS	.EXE	—	
UD	.EXE	UD	.EXE	UNERASE	.EXE

Table 1-1 Continued					
VL	.EXE	VL	.EXE	–	
WIPEDISK	.EXE	WIPEDISK	.EXE	WIPEINFO	.EXE
WIPEFILE	.EXE	WIPEFILE	.EXE	WIPEINFO	.EXE

total bytes, by version

388,310	882,225	2,637,227

The dashes (-) in the various columns indicate that there isn't a comparable program in another version. It was difficult to hold this strictly true with version 5.0 because it contains so many changes.

Roughly speaking, version 4.5 was 2.27 times larger than version 4.0. Version 5.0 continues the expansion trend in that it is 2.99 times larger than version 4.5. Almost three megabytes of space is a lot of room just for a set of Utilities, even if they are the Norton Utilities.

For those of us with limited hard disk capacity, I'm going to suggest that some of the Utilities be kept on a floppy close at hand. This should reduce the amount of space needed to hold the remaining Utilities.

I think the following Utilities are a must:

DISKEDIT .EXE	216,074
DISKTOOL.EXE	123,198
FILEFIX .EXE	136,414
IMAGE .EXE	11,734
NDD .EXE	179,769
SFORMAT .EXE	94,598
SPEEDISK .EXE	110,400
UNERASE .EXE	170,342
WIPEINFO.EXE	67,678
Subtotal	1,110,207

The balance of the Utilities will hold more or less importance to each user based on the way that they employ their system. The Utilities won't all fit on a single diskette, so you will have room on one of your diskettes to make a rescue disk.

Remember that Image makes a couple of files that will also require space. This is in addition to the .INI files that are made to hold your default configurations of some of the Utilities.

Getting help

Getting help while you are in the Norton Utilities has never been too difficult. Still, there may have been times when there just wasn't any help when you needed it. On almost every screen you will see the notation "F1=HELP" in the upper right corner. By pressing the function key F1, you will bring up a helpfile. These helpfiles are context-sensitive, which means that they should provide you with useful information on how to get yourself out of the mess you are in—or the converse, how to get deeper into the Utility and the chance for an even bigger mess.

My use of the word "mess" was not a slip; I chose it for the purpose of getting your attention. My first reaction would be to say that I would NEVER make a "mess" of my hard disk. With the next breath, I would also have to admit that I learn more from my mistakes than I do from my successes.

After you make a backup copy of your hard disk, go ahead and play. The helpfiles will tell you enough to let you find your way through any of the Utilities. The more useful they can be for recovery, the greater the chance of making changes that may cause serious problems. Whenever the Utility gives you the opportunity to make an "undo" file, take it. If you don't need it, all well and good. If you do make a serious change that proves to be wrong, the undo file can eliminate many hours of frustrating work.

2
CHAPTER

Batch Enhancer

Version 4.5 & 5.0 directory name   **BE.EXE**

BE was a new addition to the Norton Utilities, version 4.5, collection of programs. Now it is not totally new because it contains some of the Utilities which
had been present in earlier versions. BE also has a few little features that have not
been present in any earlier version.

New in version 5.0
GOTO (used with BE ASK)
Format: GOTO label
          .....
          .....
          : label

Use: Use the GOTO command in BE just like you would in any other programming language. It allows you to skip or loop sections of code so that your program has added flexibility. These commands are not case-sensitive, so either case may be used.

ASK

BE ASK

This is the Norton ASK Utility from version 4.0. All of the information on how to use it is in the section on ASK.

Version 4.0 directory name   **ASK.EXE**
Version 4.5, included in the Batch Enhancer utility

Although this Utility has been incorporated into the Batch Enhancer utility in version 4.5, all of the features available in version 4.0 are still available. A new feature, Color, has been added in version 4.5 so that you can now select a specific color for the prompt. Incidentally, the use of different colors for the ASK prompt at different levels could be used as a reminder of where you are. It's a great help if interruptions call you away from your system.

ASK is a simple program-writing feature that allows the building of interactive batch files. These batch files would contain the command strings that are used to move to the drive, directory, subdirectory, and filename of a selected application.

Format: BE ASK prompt[,keys] [DEFAULT=key] [TIMEOUT=n] [ADJUST=n] [color]

prompt   is the character string displayed when ASK runs.

keys   An optional list of keys (characters, symbols, or numbers), one of which the user will enter as a response.

DEFAULT=key
        If no key is pressed within the time-out period, or if the user merely presses RETURN, then return to this key.

TIMEOUT=n
        Time in seconds before the default key is returned. If n is zero, or no TIMEOUT is specified, ASK will wait forever.

color   Optional color specification for the text of the prompt. See the chapter called Screen Attributes for information on specifying colors. SA is another of the Utility programs which has been combined into the BE Utility in version 4.5.

ASK provides the means for building a very user-friendly interface to the applications programs that are available. Although this may not be one of the highest priorities for a "power user" who never allows their system to be used by anyone else, it can make life much easier for those of us who cannot afford the luxury of an exclusive system. Experts can help new users by installing ASK. It is much easier to explain how to use the menu than to teach a person all of the necessary DOS commands.

ASK is an improvement on the DOS batch file capability in that ASK permits real-time interaction; the user is not locked into the previously written batch. This added flexibility can be expanded into providing a greater variety of options for task completion. The first benefit of ASK could be the integration of many small batch files into one larger interactive ASK file, which would tend to simplify operation and would also save time and disk space.

For those who have never written a batch file, ASK isn't demanding. Writing an ASK batch file is much like writing a macro or script in application programs. In the batch file shown in Fig. 2-1, the REM statements are the documentation for the program file.

2-1 A simple menu-generating batch file using Norton ASK.

```
ASK "Run the (D)atabase, (W)ord processor, or (Q)uit?", dwq
REM      the letters "dwq" after the comma are the acceptable
REM      inputs from the keyboard. If no characters are
REM      present, any keyboard entry is acceptable
  if errorlevel 3 goto quit
REM      branching instructions (if/then/elseif) are placed
REM      in reverse order to the ASK listing.
  if errorlevel 2 goto words
  if errorlevel 1 goto base
REM      this last branch is not necessary if the database
REM      commands follow immediately, as they do here.
:base
    c:\lotus\123
    goto quit
:words
    c:\wp\ewii
    goto quit
REM      the last goto line is unnecessary since "quit"
REM      follows immediately.
:quit
```

If no "key-list" is present, any key pressed is accepted.

Using the same logic that is shown above, writing a much more extensive ASK batch is possible, as Fig. 2-2 suggests. ECHO OFF prevents the display of unwanted information lines. CLS allows a full screen of information to be displayed before scrolling starts.

A variation of this could be to have all programs return to ASK rather than quitting. Then Quit could run Housekeeping before actually returning to the DOS prompt.

```
echo off
cls
rem    CLS follows ECHO OFF so that the  full screen is
rem    cleared. If they are reversed ECHO OFF is displayed.
echo Enter the first letter of the choice run next.
echo Programs or tasks available are:
echo
REM       An ASCII 255 character is placed on the line after
REM       the last "echo" as a spacer. To enter this
REM       character, press the ALT key and enter the numbers
REM       255 from the numeric keypad.
echo (B)asic
echo (C)ommunications
echo (E)ditor, Norton
echo (G)raphics
echo (H)ousekeeping
echo (I)nfo, File
echo (L)otus
echo (M)ultiMate
echo (N)orton Utilities
echo (P)ascal
echo (S)uperCalc
echo (Q)uit
echo
REM       ASCII 255 on previous line
ASK "Your request: ", bceghilmnpsq
   if errorlevel 12 goto quit
   if errorlevel 11 goto super
            .
            .
   if errorlevel 1 goto basic
:basic
      c:\bas\basic
      goto quit
:commo
      c:\comm\term
      goto quit
            .
            .
:super
      c:\cal\sc5
:quit


:housekeeping
   c:\nu\fr /save>a:
   goto quit
REM      this writes/overwrites the FRECOVER.DAT file on
REM      the disk in the A: drive.
REM          This isn't really necessary with the later versions
REM       of the Utilities since there is an automatic update
REM       feature. Also with Version 5.0 there is a filename
REM       change.

:quit returns you to the DOS prompt of the default drive.
```

If ASK is on a floppy disk in A:, remember to place the drive letter as well as the path in the instructions under each choice. Also, remember to use the drive letter to return to ASK after completing the selected task.

You could also change the screen colors for different applications programs: Simply incorporate the SA command line into any or all of the code segments being used.

Some purists may consider interposing a program between them and their chips a sacrilege. For most of us, having an easy-to-read menu instead of the DOS prompt is an encouraging start.

The programs provided by the Norton Utilities are not toys or gadgets. They are useful tools which become more valuable as you learn more about each one of them.

Batch file definitions

Here are the definitions of the MS-DOS batch file commands used in Figs. 2-1 and 2-2:

echo	Displays the balance of this line on the monitor.
echo on	Displays everything following on the monitor.
echo off	Does not display anything following on the monitor.
rem	A remark, or a means of providing internal documentation. These lines may or may not display. It depends on the setting of the echo on/echo off switch.

How can I prevent everybody, including me, from reformatting my hard disk?

The quickest way is to eliminate the FORMAT.COM program from the DOS directory. Another way is to rename the format program.

Assume that we rename FORMAT.COM to XQWZ.COM. Then we can establish a .BAT file called FORMAT.BAT with the single line

    XQWZ A:

Since this is a fixed file, we would lose the /S option which formats bootable floppy disks.

If a second .BAT file were called FORSYS.BAT and contained the line

    XQWZ A:/S

the problem would be solved. Floppy disks can still be formatted, but the hard disk cannot. To reformat the hard disk, it would be necessary to use a backup copy of the DOS system disk.

Now that I've done that, how do I remember the batch filenames?

They are good candidates for an ASK interactive file.

The list of options I want available exceeds a full screen. How do I resolve that problem?

An ASK file that allows you to select other ASK files might be one solution. For example, look at Fig. 2-3.

2-3 An example of an extensive menu structure using nested ASK batch files.

```
        ASK (main)
(A)pplications
(C)ommunications
(D)atabases
(U)tilities
(Q)uit


        ASK (A)pplications
(A)da
(B)asic
(C) "C"
(D)base
(F)ortran
(G)raphics
(L)isp
(M)asm
c(O)bol
(P)rolog
(R)eturn to main
(S)nobol4+
(T)urbo Pascal
(Q)uit


        ASK (D)atabases
(1)23
(D)base
(E)asyWriter
(F)ramework
(M)ultimate
(R)eturn to main
(S)ymphony
s(U)perCalc
(W)ordstar
(Q)uit


        ASK (U)tilities
(B)ackup
(D)os
(E)ditor, Norton
(F)ormat a floppy
(N)orton Utilities
f(O)rmat a bootable floppy
(R)eturn to main
(T)ape backup
(Q)uit
```

The (C)ommunications selection could go directly to the single communications program you use, or another ASK menu program could let you select the program for the occasion. Now that we have all of this laid out, how does it code up? Without consuming too much space in details, the first ASK program file and a portion of the ASK utilities files are shown in Fig. 2-4. These are source code files and may be used "as is" only if everything else is the same. Check the pathnames and filenames before attempting to use them.

2-4 A batch file that implements the structure shown in Fig. 2-3.

```
code file
ASK main

echo off
cls
echo The following selections are available
echo (255)
echo (A)pplications
echo (C)ommunications
echo (D)atabases
echo (U)tilities
echo (Q)uit
echo (255)
ASK "Your choice: ",acduq
    if errorlevel 5 goto quit
    if errorlevel 4 goto util
    if errorlevel 3 goto data
    if errorlevel 2 goto comm
:appl
    ASK appl
    goto quit
:comm
    ASK   comm
    goto quit
:data
    ASK data
    goto quit
:util
    ASK util
:quit

code file
UTIL
echo off
cls
echo The following utilities are available
echo(255)
echo (B)ackup
echo (D)os
echo (E)ditor, Norton
echo (F)ormat a floppy
echo (N)orton Utilities
echo f(O)rmat a bootable floppy
```

```
echo (T)ape backup
echo (Q)uit
echo(255)
ASK "Your choice: ",bdefnotq
   if errorlevel 8 goto quit
   if errorlevel 7 goto tape
   if errorlevel 6 goto boot
   if errorlevel 5 goto nort
   if errorlevel 4 goto form
   if errorlevel 3 goto noed
   if errorlevel 2 goto syst
:back
   c:\nu\fr/s
   goto quit
:syst
   c:\dos\dir/w
   goto quit
:noed
   c:\nu\ne
   goto quit
:form
   c:\dos\forsys.
   goto quit
:nort
   c:\nu\ni
   goto quit
:boot
   c:\dos\format
   goto quit
:tape
   backup.
:quit
```

Note that all of the selections exit to DOS after the running of just one application program. It is possible to cause the system to loop back into one of the ASK menu programs by changing the GOTO QUIT line to ASK MAIN or any of the other ASK menus.

If looping menus are going to be used, just remember to leave an exit somewhere. All of the Norton Utilities have an exit that will return control to the ASK program, so don't depend on those for your only exits.

How can I know that the character after an ECHO OFF is 255d?

Follow the steps and screens shown below and look at what has been written to the file.

Figure 2-5 shows the first screen or main menu of the NU program and, as such, is our gateway to everything on a disk. What we want to do is look at the actual characters that have been written to the disk when we created the ASK file. To do this, we will select the Explore Disk option. The reverse video block is already there, so it is only necessary to press the RETURN key.

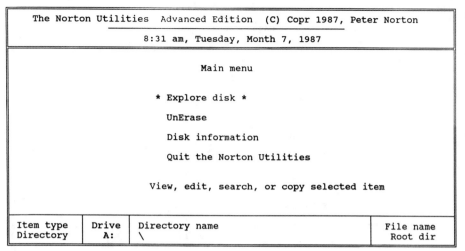

```
┌──────────────────────────────────────────────────────────────────────┐
│  The Norton Utilities  Advanced Edition  (C) Copr 1987, Peter Norton   │
│                 8:31 am, Tuesday, Month 7, 1987                        │
├──────────────────────────────────────────────────────────────────────┤
│                                                                        │
│                             Main menu                                  │
│                                                                        │
│                        * Explore disk *                                │
│                                                                        │
│                          UnErase                                       │
│                                                                        │
│                          Disk information                              │
│                                                                        │
│                          Quit the Norton Utilities                     │
│                                                                        │
│                  View, edit, search, or copy selected item             │
│                                                                        │
├──────────────┬────────┬─────────────────────────────┬─────────────────┤
│ Item type    │ Drive  │ Directory name              │ File name       │
│ Directory    │ A:     │ \                           │ Root dir        │
└──────────────┴────────┴─────────────────────────────┴─────────────────┘
```

2-5 The Main menu of NU.

Menu 1, shown in Fig. 2-6, assumes that we will want to select a specific item to explore. The reverse video is over the item we are interested in. Thus, pressing RETURN again takes us to Menu 1.1, shown in Fig. 2-7, which defaults to File Selection.

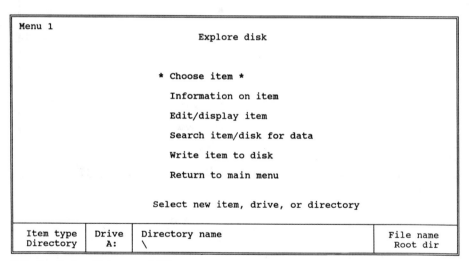

```
┌──────────────────────────────────────────────────────────────────────┐
│  Menu 1                                                                │
│                          Explore disk                                  │
│                                                                        │
│                                                                        │
│                      * Choose item *                                   │
│                                                                        │
│                        Information on item                             │
│                                                                        │
│                        Edit/display item                               │
│                                                                        │
│                        Search item/disk for data                       │
│                                                                        │
│                        Write item to disk                              │
│                                                                        │
│                        Return to main menu                             │
│                                                                        │
│                   Select new item, drive, or directory                 │
│                                                                        │
├──────────────┬────────┬─────────────────────────────┬─────────────────┤
│ Item type    │ Drive  │ Directory name              │ File name       │
│ Directory    │ A:     │ \                           │ Root dir        │
└──────────────┴────────┴─────────────────────────────┴─────────────────┘
```

2-6 The Explore Disk menu of NU.

Another press of the RETURN key displays Menu 1.1.3, shown in Fig. 2-8, which is the file or subdirectory menu. Since the ASK codefile is on a floppy disk, there are only a few files and no subdirectories. Pressing RETURN after positioning the reverse video over the filename CODEFILE.ASK returns us to Menu 1. Now we want to Edit/Display the data in file CODEFILE.ASK. Pressing the E key takes us directly to the beginning of that file.

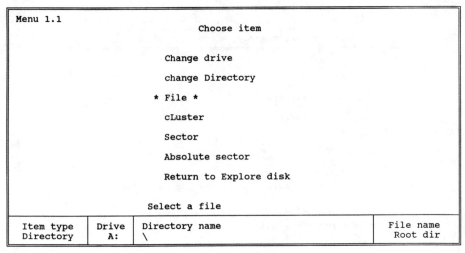

```
Menu 1.1
                          Choose item

                       Change drive

                       change Directory

                     * File *

                       cLuster

                       Sector

                       Absolute sector

                       Return to Explore disk


                    Select a file
```
Item type	Drive	Directory name	File name
Directory	A:	\	Root dir

2-7 The Choose Item menu for NU.

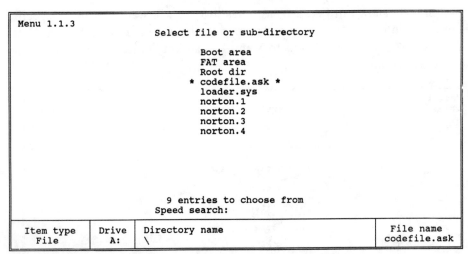

```
Menu 1.1.3
                    Select file or sub-directory
                          Boot area
                          FAT area
                          Root dir
                        * codefile.ask *
                          loader.sys
                          norton.1
                          norton.2
                          norton.3
                          norton.4




                     9 entries to choose from
                   Speed search:
```
Item type	Drive	Directory name	File name
File	A:	\	codefile.ask

2-8 The Select File menu of NU.

The HEX display of CODEFILE.ASK is shown in Fig. 2-9. Along the top edge of the screen window are the filename and the format being used to display this sector. By pressing the F3 key, we can change the format into something more readable to us, notably what is shown in Fig. 2-10.

In this format we can easily locate the characters we are interested in. They are the dots or periods after each of the words ECHO on the lines by themselves. However, we cannot tell what those character values are in this format. Pressing the F2 key returns us to the HEX format. Pressing the TAB key once moves the blinking cursor to the text half of the screen. Then, using the ARROW keys, we can place the blinking cursor over the dot after the last ECHO. Can't find the dot? Maybe you didn't enter the ASCII character value 255 after the second ECHO.

```
┌ codefile.ask ═══════════════════════════════════════════════ Hex format ═┐
│ Cluster 22   Sectors 52-53                        File offset 338, hex 0152│
│6563686F 206F6666 0D0A6563 686F2045 6E746572 20746865  echo off12echo Enter the│
│20666972 7374206C 65747465 72206F66 20746865 2063686F   first letter of the cho│
│69636520 746F2072 756E206E 6578742E 0D0A6563 686F2050  ice to run next.12echo P│
│726F6772 616D7320 6F722074 61736B73 20617661 696C6162  rograms or tasks availab│
│6C652061 72653A0D 0A656368 6F20FF0D 0A656368 6F202842  le are:12echo .12echo (B│
│29617369 630D0A65 63686F20 2843296F 6D6D756E 69636174  )asic12echo (C)ommunicat│
│696F6E73 0D0A6563 686F2028 45296469 746F722C 204E6F72  ions12echo (E)ditor, Nor│
│746F6E0D 0A656368 6F202847 29726170 68696373 0D0A6563  ton12echo (G)raphics12ec│
│686F2028 48296F75 73656B65 6570696E 670D0A65 63686F20  ho (H)ousekeeping12echo │
│2849296E 666F2C20 46696C65 0D0A6563 686F2028 4C296F74  (I)nfo, File12echo (L)ot│
│75730D0A 6563686F 20284D29 756C7469 6D617465 0D0A6563  us12echo (M)ultimate12ec│
│686F2028 4E29296F72 746F6E20 55746469 69746965 730D0A65  ho (N)orton Utilities12e│
│63686F20 28502961 7363616C 0D0A6563 686F2028 53297570  cho (P)ascal12echo (S)up│
│65724361 6C630D0A 6563686F 20285129 7569740D 0A656368  erCalc12echo (Q)uit12ech│
│6F20FF0D 0AB66DB6 6DB66DB6 6DB66DB6 00B66DB6 6DB66DB6  o .12 m m m m m . m m m m│
│6DB66DB6 6DB66DB6 6DB66DB6 6DB66DB6 6DB66DB6 6DB66DB6  m m m m m m m m m m m m m-│
│00B66DB6 6DB66DB6 6DB66DB6 6DB66DB6 6DB66DB6 6DB66DB6  . m m m m m m m m m m m m-│
│6DB66DB6 6DB66DB6 00B66DB6 6DB66DB6 6DB66DB6 6DB66DB6  m m m m . m m m m m m m m-│
│6DB66DB6 6DB66DB6 6DB66DB6 6DB66DB6 00B66DB6 6DB66DB6  m m m m m m m . m m m m m-│
│6DB66DB6 6DB66DB6 6DB66DB6 6DB66DB6 6DB66DB6 6DB66DB6  m m m m m m m m m m m m m-│
│00B66DB6 6DB66DB6 6DB66DB6 6DB66DB6 6DB66DB6 6DB66DB6  . m m m m m m m m m m m m-│
│6DB66DB6 6DB66DB6          Press Enter to continue     m m m m│
│1Help  =2Hex   =3Text  =4Dir   =5FAT   =6Partn =7      =8        =9Undo  =10QuitNU│
```

2-9 The HEX display of CODEFILE.ASK. ODh represents a carriage return, while OAh represents a line feed. The numbers 1 and 2 are used in the code representation to allow for proper printing of the screen.

```
┌ codefile.ask ═══════════════════════════════════════════════ Text format ═┐
│ Cluster 22   Sectors 52-53                          File offset 0, hex 00  │
│  ►echo off◄                                                                │
│  ►echo Enter the first letter of the choice to run next.◄                  │
│  ►echo Programs or tasks available are:◄                                   │
│  ►echo .◄                                                                  │
│  ►echo (B)asic◄                                                            │
│  ►echo (C)ommunications◄                                                   │
│  ►echo (E)ditor, Norton◄                                                   │
│  ►echo (G)raphics◄                                                         │
│  ►echo (H)ousekeeping◄                                                     │
│  ►echo (I)nfo, File◄                                                       │
│  ►echo (L)otus◄                                                            │
│  ►echo (M)ultimate◄                                                        │
│  ►echo (N)orton Utilities◄                                                 │
│  ►echo (P)ascal◄                                                           │
│  ►echo (S)uperCalc◄                                                        │
│  ►echo (Q)uit◄                                                             │
│  ►echo◄                                                                    │
│  ►m6m6m6m6m6m6.m6m6m6m6m6m6m6m6m6m6m6m6.m6m6m6m6m6m6m6m6m6m6m6m6m6m          │
│   6.m6m6m6m6m6m6m6m6m6m6m6m6.m6m6m6m6m6m6m6m6m6m6m6.m6m6m6m6m6m6m            │
│   6...more                                                                 │
│                         Press Enter to continue                            │
│1Help  =2Hex   =3Text  =4Dir   =5FAT   =6Partn =7      =8        =9QuitNU    │
```

2-10 The Text display of CODEFILE.ASK.

Look again at the information displayed in Fig. 2-10. The fifteenth line, first block, reads F6200D0A. This is much different than the fifth line, fourth block, which reads 6F20FF0D. The 0A begins the next block. When the TAB key was pressed, the cursor on the left half of the screen went from a blinking block over one letter to a solid reverse video block over two letters. It's possible to edit the data in either form. Just remember that it is the data under the blinking cursor block that is being changed.

Some data can only be edited in the HEX portion of the screen. 0Dh (Carriage Return) and 0Ah (Line Feed) are two of those characters. In fact, you will note that these characters have been changed completely in the screen dumps. They caused the printer to perform those actions when the computer dumped them.

The sequence of characters and HEX values at the end of the first echo is

```
  0          1   2   (in text)
 6F  20  FF  0D  0A  (in HEX)
```

The 1 normally displays on the screen as a musical note. The 2 normally displays on the screen as a reverse video block with a diamond centered in it.

You can verify these values by moving the cursor with the ARROW keys. Set the blinking cursor to the right side so that the solid block highlights the two HEX values that make up that character. Try making some changes. Toggle between the TEXT (F3) format and the HEX (F2) format. Also notice that all of the characters that have been changed are either bold or yellow.

You have two ways to end your edit. You can either cancel the changes you made by pressing the F9 key, or you can press ESC to leave the editor. Pressing RETURN will take you to the last portion of the file which is in the next sector. If you have not canceled the changes, pressing ESC or RETURN will take you to the Save/Discard menu, seen here in Fig. 2-11.

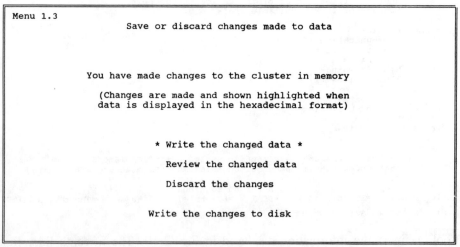

```
Menu 1.3
                    Save or discard changes made to data




            You have made changes to the cluster in memory

             (Changes are made and shown highlighted when
              data is displayed in the hexadecimal format)


                   * Write the changed data *

                    Review the changed data

                    Discard the changes


                  Write the changes to disk
```

2-11 The Save/Discard Changes menu of NU.

This menu gives you three choices: Save the changes you've made, Discard them, or Return to the previous screen to review them. If you're not sure that you have made proper corrections, then you should either review or discard. Once you are positive of the changes you've made, choose the Save option.

BEEP
BE BEEP

Again, this is the BEEP Utility from the previous version. The information in this chapter on the BE Utility program has been updated to reflect the features that have been added in version 4.5 and version 5.0.

BEEP sounds a tone, a series of tones, or plays a tune (IBM or 100%-compatibles only). For computers that are not fully compatible, BEEP will sound the standard tone once or many times, and the frequency and duration switches will not operate.

Format:	BE BEEP [switches] or [drive/path/filename] [/E] switches
/Dn	The duration in 1/18 of a second that the tone sounds.
/Fn	The frequency (hertz or cycles per second) of the tone.
/Rn	The repetitions or numbers of times the tone should be sounded.
/Wn	A wait or pause in 1/18 of a second between tones.
[drive/path/filename] **/E**	Echo the text in the file specified. The text to be echoed will be the text in the tonefile which is enclosed in quotes. Characters on lines beginning with a semicolon will be ignored.

A *tonefile* is where the parameters of a tune, or other tone sequence, play when called by BE BEEP. The filename may be any DOS-compatible filename, and an extension is not required. Also, the tonefile need not be on the same drive with BE BEEP.

Comments

When BEEP runs without any other parameters, the standard tone sounds once. Adding switch parameters to the command line calling BEEP will change the tone(s) sounded. Providing a complete drive, path, and filename to BEEP runs the tone sequence in the file. Wildcard characters cannot be used in the filename, nor is redirection of BEEP allowed. Having the printer attempt to act like a speaker could be disastrous. Print tonefiles using standard DOS commands.

The 1/18 of a second timing is based on the IBM PC clock speed of 4.77 megahertz. Higher clock speeds will reduce this fraction accordingly. Humans can normally hear tones between 20 hertz and 20 kilohertz. Some lower frequency tones can also be felt. Above 20 kilohertz the tones can be heard better by some animals, which may react when a human cannot even hear the tone being generated. For reference, the middle A on a piano is 440 hertz. See the Appendix for a full list of frequencies.

Write tonefiles using any ASCII editor. The tonefile segment listed in Fig. 2-12 is the first six lines of the file MARY found on the distribution disk.

2-12   The first six lines of the BEEP file MARY.

```
/F330 /D2                      ; Mar-
/F294 /D2                      ; -y
/F262 /D2                      ; had
/F294 /D2                      ; a
/R2 /F330 /D2                  ; little
/F330 /D4                      ; lamb
; put a semicolon before comments
; either on a separate line or after the switch listing
; as is shown above.
;
; Programmers are not accountable for their spelling.
; There is/was an error in line 28 of this file. ; Mary's
; lamb had a fleet as white as snow.
;
; APPENDIX 1 is a Chromatic Scale listing the Hertz values
; for 96 notes or 8 full octaves.
```

The / (slash) is optional in a tonefile. It is not optional when specifying switch parameters on the command line.

More than one set of tone parameters may be entered on a line. MARY was written in one tone lines to match the words. Your tune choices may require other arrangements.

For all not fully compatible computers, only the /R switch is operational. This reduces the flexibility of BEEP but it does not eliminate it as a useful utility.

Some possible uses for tonefiles are

- as progress indicators during the processing of batch files.
- as error or event indicators.
- as a novelty to enliven a demonstration.
- limited only by the imagination of the user.

BOX

BE BOX

BOX is a new program which draws a square or rectangle of a specified size in a specified location on the screen. The border may be either a single or double line.

Format: BE BOX parameters
BE BOX filespec

Parameters

Sequence: the corners (top, left, bottom, right); the line type (single, double); the color.

top ROW location of the box's upper left-hand corner.

left COLUMN location of the box's upper left-hand corner.

bottom ROW location of the box's lower right-hand corner.

right COLUMN location of the box's lower right-hand corner.

SINGLE Draw the box with a single width line.

DOUBLE Draw the box with a double width line.

color Color to be used to draw the box with. The format for this command comes from the Screen Attributes (BE SA) Utility.

filespec This is an ASCII text file that contains the various parameters for the box to be drawn. A number of files may be written to define different size/color boxes. Each must have a unique filename. These filenames do not require an extension. The extension .BOX might be a good way to identify these files. A filename which describes the box might also help in keeping track of the various boxes already defined. Another way to keep track of the contents of these box definition files might be to use the FI (File Information) Utility and add a more complete description than is provided there.

BE CLS

Clears the screen and returns the cursor to the home position. The home position is the upper left corner of the screen.

BE DELAY ticks

Permits the addition of a user specified delay. Each "tick" is 1/18 of a second.

PRINTCHAR

This is also a new feature in version 4.5. It displays a specified character a given number of times at the current cursor location.

Format: BE PRINTCHAR character, repetitions [color]

character

Which character is to be displayed.

repetitions

      The number of times the character is to be displayed. The limit is 80.

color   The color the character should be. The current foreground color is used if none is specified. See the section of SA for valid choices.

ROWCOL

Another addition in version 4.5. Positions the cursor at the specified row and column location, and optionally displays text.

    Format: BE ROWCOL row,column[,text] [color]

row   The row to move the cursor to. These are numbered from top (1) to bottom (25) on your screen. This utility will also work with a 43-row screen accurately.

column   The column to move the cursor to. These are numbered from left (0) to right (80) on your screen. **ROWCOL** works with 132-column screens as well.

WINDOW

The last addition to this utility program.

    Format: BE WINDOW top,left,bottom,right [color] [SHADOW] [ZOOM]

top   The row location of the window's upper left-hand corner.

left   The column location of the window's upper left-hand corner.

bottom   The row location of the window's lower right-hand corner.

right   The column location of the window's lower right-hand corner.

color   The color chosen to fill the window. Refer to the SA chapter for valid options.

SHADOW

      Draw the window with a see-through shadow. The shadow will appear along the bottom and right edges of the window as a see-thru gray.

ZOOM   Zoom the window while drawing it, which means that it will grow dynamically as it is being drawn. In other words, the window expands from a point to full-size right before your eyes.

Screen attributes

BE SA

This is the Screen Attributes Utility.

Some programs do not support color, even when the system is color-compatible. BE SA provides a means of adding some color to your session. There is no reason or capability to redirect the output of this Utility to the printer or a disk file.

Format: BE SA [prefix] main-setting [/N]
                BE SA main-setting [/N]
                BE SA [prefix] [foreground] [ON background] [/N]
                BE SA [intensity] [foreground] [ON background] [/N]

The optional [prefix] can specify the BRIGHT, BOLD, and/or BLINKING attribute.

The possible values for [main-setting] are:

    NORMAL
    REVERSE
    UNDERLINE

The value of [foreground] may be set to:

    WHITE   BLACK   RED   GREEN
    YELLOW   BLUE   MAGENTA   CYAN

The [ON background] may specify:

    WHITE   BLACK   RED   GREEN
    YELLOW   BLUE   MAGENTA   CYAN

The /N switch inhibits the border that matches the foreground color. Systems with an EGA or VGA graphics card will not be able to get the border to display.

Adding the /CLS switch will clear the screen after setting the newly selected color combination.

The results you get using BE SA will depend on the hardware you are using. Your system must be able to display colors or shades of the monochrome color of your screen (green or amber). Shading is a function of the video card, not the monitor. With any good graphics card installed, you should be able to see different shades on a monochrome monitor.

Some programs set their own screen attributes, but this will not interfere with the operation of SA. Some programs will replace the screen attributes, i.e., colors, upon termination, which others will not. Not all computers support all of the options that DOS supports. Experimentation will determine the limits of your system as well as the more pleasing combinations.

If the utility ANSI.SYS is required for SA to run properly, an error message will prompt you to install it. No harm will be done if you run SA before installing

ANSI.SYS. Your DOS manual will explain how to include the command DE-VICE = ANSI.SYS in the CONFIG.SYS file.

The /N switch is used by all computers that are not fully IBM-compatible. This is because SA uses IBM-specific means to produce a colored border for the screen. The border will be the same color as the background. The EGA card generates a borderless display, which means there will be no border regardless of the /N switch.

While the final choice of colors is yours, the following combinations have proven useful to many others.

```
BE SA WHITE ON BLUE
BE SA YELLOW ON BLUE
BE SA BLACK ON GREEN
```

Or how about

```
BE SA REVERSE
BE SA BRIGHT BLINKING RED ON BLUE
```

to attract attention used with BE BEEP? The BLINKING screen demands attention.

> *Note:* The REVERSE video switch may not work on some systems where the display is not fully IBM-compatible. The TI Professional is one of those that does not support the REVERSE switch.

Illustrations of the various color combinations will have to be provided by your system or that of a friend if yours does not support color. Peter Norton has used his favorite colors to good advantage within the Utilities.

BE SA may be included in batch files between various programs to restore colors, add color, or in ASK to change the display for specific programs.

Is there any way to check which color combinations look best?

There are two ways available: The "trial and error" method and the COLORS .BAT method. Using the trial and error method may work, but it may also take longer. Plus, in order to be sure that all of the possible combinations have been evaluated, you will at least duplicate the work done in the COLORS.BAT file.

COLORS.BAT, shown below as Fig. 2-13, is a simple fixed batch file that can be written to a disk using your favorite ASCII editor. It has few requirements. Simply boot your system with the ANSI.SYS program installed. COLORS.BAT and BE (Batch Enhancer) are in the same directory on the same disk.

2-13 A listing of the batch file COLORS.BAT, which automates the evaluation of all the possible SA color combinations.

```
;CODEFILE
COLORS.BAT                              ;the file name
CLS
BE SA WHITE on BLACK                    ;_____
PAUSE Evaluate this combination
```

```
CLS
BE SA BLACK on WHITE                    ;_____
PAUSE Evaluate this combination
CLS
BE SA RED on MAGENTA                    ;_____
PAUSE Evaluate this combination
CLS
BE SA BRIGHT RED on MAGENTA             ;_____
PAUSE Evaluate this combination
CLS
BE SA RED on BLUE                       ;_____
PAUSE Evaluate this combination
CLS
BE SA BRIGHT RED on BLUE                ;_____
PAUSE Evaluate this combination
CLS
BE SA RED on GREEN                      ;_____
PAUSE Evaluate this combination
CLS
BE SA BRIGHT RED on GREEN               ;_____
PAUSE Evaluate this combination
CLS
BE SA RED on CYAN                       ;_____
PAUSE Evaluate this combination
CLS
BE SA BRIGHT RED on CYAN                ;_____
PAUSE Evaluate this combination
CLS
BE SA RED on YELLOW                     ;_____
PAUSE Evaluate this combination
CLS
BE SA BRIGHT RED on YELLOW              ;_____
PAUSE Evaluate this combination
CLS
BE SA RED on WHITE                      ;_____
PAUSE Evaluate this combination
CLS
BE SA BRIGHT RED ON WHITE               ;_____
PAUSE Evaluate this combination
CLS
BE SA RED on BLACK                      ;_____
PAUSE Evaluate this combination
CLS
BE SA BRIGHT RED on BLACK               ;_____
PAUSE Evaluate this combination
CLS
BE SA MAGENTA on BLUE                   ;_____
PAUSE Evaluate this combination
CLS
BE SA BRIGHT MAGENTA on BLUE            ;_____
PAUSE Evaluate this combination
CLS
BE SA MAGENTA on GREEN                  ;_____
PAUSE Evaluate this combination
CLS
BE SA BRIGHT MAGENTA on GREEN           ;_____
PAUSE Evaluate this combination
```

```
CLS
BE SA RED on MAGENTA                    ;_____
PAUSE Evaluate this combination
CLS
BE SA BRIGHT RED on MAGENTA             ;_____
PAUSE Evaluate this combination
CLS
BE SA RED on BLUE                       ;_____
PAUSE Evaluate this combination
CLS
BE SA BRIGHT RED on BLUE                ;_____
PAUSE Evaluate this combination
CLS
BE SA RED on GREEN                      ;_____
PAUSE Evaluate this combination
CLS
BE SA BRIGHT RED on GREEN               ;_____
PAUSE Evaluate this combination
CLS
BE SA RED on CYAN                       ;_____
PAUSE Evaluate this combination
CLS
BE SA BRIGHT RED on CYAN                ;_____
PAUSE Evaluate this combination
CLS
BE SA RED on YELLOW                     ;_____
PAUSE Evaluate this combination
CLS
BE SA BRIGHT RED on YELLOW              ;_____
PAUSE Evaluate this combination
CLS
BE SA RED on WHITE                      ;_____
PAUSE Evaluate this combination
CLS
BE SA BRIGHT RED ON WHITE               ;_____
PAUSE Evaluate this combination
CLS
BE SA RED on BLACK                      ;_____
PAUSE Evaluate this combination
CLS
BE SA BRIGHT RED on BLACK               ;_____
PAUSE Evaluate this combination
CLS
BE SA MAGENTA on BLUE                   ;_____
PAUSE Evaluate this combination
CLS
BE SA BRIGHT MAGENTA on BLUE            ;_____
PAUSE Evaluate this combination
CLS
BE SA MAGENTA on GREEN                  ;_____
PAUSE Evaluate this combination
CLS
BE SA BRIGHT MAGENTA on GREEN           ;_____
PAUSE Evaluate this combination
CLS
BE SA MAGENTA on CYAN                   ;_____
PAUSE Evaluate this combination
```

```
CLS
BE SA BRIGHT MAGENTA on CYAN          ;_____
PAUSE Evaluate this combination
CLS
BE SA MAGENTA on YELLOW               ;_____
PAUSE Evaluate this combination
CLS
BE SA BRIGHT MAGENTA on YELLOW        ;_____
PAUSE Evaluate this combination
CLS
BE SA MAGENTA on WHITE                ;_____
PAUSE Evaluate this combination
CLS
BE SA BRIGHT MAGENTA on WHITE         ;_____
PAUSE Evaluate this combination
CLS
BE SA MAGENTA on BLACK                ;_____
PAUSE Evaluate this combination
CLS
BE SA BRIGHT MAGENTA on BLACK         ;_____
PAUSE Evaluate this combination
CLS
BE SA MAGENTA on RED                  ;_____
PAUSE Evaluate this combination
CLS
BE SA BRIGHT MAGENTA on RED           ;_____
PAUSE Evaluate this combination
CLS
BE SA BLUE on GREEN                   ;_____
PAUSE Evaluate this combination
CLS
BE SA BRIGHT BLUE on GREEN            ;_____
PAUSE Evaluate this combination
CLS
BE SA BLUE on CYAN                    ;_____
PAUSE Evaluate this combination
CLS
SA BRIGHT BLUE on CYAN                ;_____
PAUSE Evaluate this combination
CLS
SA BLUE on YELLOW                     ;_____
PAUSE Evaluate this combination
CLS
BE SA BRIGHT BLUE on YELLOW           ;_____
PAUSE Evaluate this combination
CLS
BE SA BLUE on WHITE                   ;_____
PAUSE Evaluate this combination
CLS
BE SA BRIGHT BLUE on WHITE            ;_____
PAUSE Evaluate this combination
CLS
BE SA BLUE on BLACK                   ;_____
PAUSE Evaluate this combination
CLS
BE SA BRIGHT BLUE on BLACK            ;_____
PAUSE Evaluate this combination
```

```
CLS
BE SA BRIGHT BLUE on RED              ;_____
PAUSE Evaluate this combination
CLS
BE SA BLUE on RED                     ;_____
PAUSE Evaluate this combination
CLS
BE SA BLUE on MAGENTA                 ;_____
PAUSE Evaluate this combination
CLS
BE SA BRIGHT BLUE on MAGENTA          ;_____
PAUSE Evaluate this combination
CLS
BE SA GREEN on CYAN                   ;_____
PAUSE Evaluate this combination
CLS
BE SA BRIGHT GREEN on CYAN            ;_____
PAUSE Evaluate this combination
CLS
BE SA GREEN on YELLOW                 ;_____
PAUSE Evaluate this combination
CLS
BE SA BRIGHT GREEN on YELLOW          ;_____
PAUSE Evaluate this combination
CLS
BE SA GREEN on WHITE                  ;_____
PAUSE Evaluate this combination
CLS
BE SA BRIGHT GREEN on WHITE           ;_____
PAUSE Evaluate this combination
CLS
BE SA GREEN on BLACK                  ;_____
PAUSE Evaluate this combination
CLS
BE SA BRIGHT GREEN on BLACK           ;_____
PAUSE Evaluate this combination
CLS
BE SA GREEN on RED                    ;_____
PAUSE Evaluate this combination
CLS
BE SA BRIGHT GREEN on RED             ;_____
PAUSE Evaluate this combination
CLS
BE SA GREEN on MAGENTA                ;_____
PAUSE Evaluate this combination
CLS
BE SA BRIGHT GREEN on MAGENTA         ;_____
PAUSE Evaluate this combination
CLS
BE SA GREEN on BLUE                   ;_____
PAUSE Evaluate this combination
CLS
BE SA BRIGHT GREEN on BLUE            ;_____
PAUSE Evaluate this combination
CLS
BE SA CYAN on YELLOW                  ;_____
PAUSE Evaluate this combination
```

```
CLS
BE SA BRIGHT CYAN on YELLOW          ;_____
PAUSE Evaluate this combination
CLS
BE SA CYAN on WHITE                  ;_____
PAUSE Evaluate this combination
CLS
BE SA BRIGHT CYAN on WHITE           ;_____
PAUSE Evaluate this combination
CLS
BE SA CYAN on BLACK                  ;_____
PAUSE Evaluate this combination
CLS
BE SA BRIGHT CYAN on BLACK           ;_____
PAUSE Evaluate this combination
CLS
BE SA CYAN on RED                    ;_____
PAUSE Evaluate this combination
CLS
BE SA BRIGHT CYAN on RED             ;_____
PAUSE Evaluate this combination
CLS
BE SA CYAN on MAGENTA                ;_____
PAUSE Evaluate this combination
CLS
BE SA BRIGHT CYAN on MAGENTA         ;_____
PAUSE Evaluate this combination
CLS
BE SA CYAN on BLUE                   ;_____
PAUSE Evaluate this combination
CLS
BE SA BRIGHT CYAN on BLUE            ;_____
PAUSE Evaluate this combination
CLS
BE SA CYAN on GREEN                  ;_____
PAUSE Evaluate this combination
CLS
BE SA BRIGHT CYAN on GREEN           ;_____
PAUSE Evaluate this combination
CLS
BE SA YELLOW on WHITE                ;_____
PAUSE Evaluate this combination
CLS
BE SA BRIGHT YELLOW on WHITE         ;_____
PAUSE Evaluate this combination
CLS
BE SA YELLOW on BLACK                ;_____
PAUSE Evaluate this combination
CLS
BE SA BRIGHT YELLOW on BLACK         ;_____
PAUSE Evaluate this combination
CLS
BE SA YELLOW on RED                  ;_____
PAUSE Evaluate this combination
CLS
BE SA BRIGHT YELLOW on RED           ;_____
PAUSE Evaluate this combination
```

```
CLS
BE SA YELLOW on MAGENTA                    ;_____
PAUSE Evaluate this combination
CLS
BE SA BRIGHT YELLOW on MAGENTA             ;_____
PAUSE Evaluate this combination
CLS
BE SA YELLOW on BLUE                       ;_____
PAUSE Evaluate this combination
CLS
BE SA BRIGHT YELLOW on BLUE                ;_____
PAUSE Evaluate this combination
CLS
BE SA YELLOW on GREEN                      ;_____
PAUSE Evaluate this combination
CLS
BE SA BRIGHT YELLOW on GREEN               ;_____
PAUSE Evaluate this combination
CLS
BE SA YELLOW on CYAN                       ;_____
PAUSE Evaluate this combination
CLS
BE SA BRIGHT YELLOW on CYAN                ;_____
```

I have placed a semicolon and a string of underscores (_) after each combination in the printed codefile. These are not required on the disk file but are there simply for your personal use. Record your comments on each as it displays. Be careful, as some of the combinations are very hard to read.

BRIGHT and BOLD are equivalent in effect, so only BRIGHT is used here. WHITE, as opposed to BRIGHT WHITE, looks gray on my monitor. Most of the other colors are harder to define in the foreground when they are not BRIGHT. By the way, BRIGHT BLACK is not a valid combination. If you try it, BE SA displays an error message.

For those of you who don't want to do all of this coding, just use the lines starting with BE, key them in one at a time, and then write your evaluation on the line in the book. You may never need most of these combinations, but evaluating them will give you an excellent reference for later.

For some people, collecting all of these Utilities (which are most used in batch file processing) into a single program will be a boon. For others, it will cause problems. If batch processing is your interest, you will learn these new command formats quickly. Those of us who seldom process in batches will have to consult the book when we need formats. The really smart users will remember that NI (Norton Integrator) has most of the basic formats listed with the more common options.

How can I make my own tonefile(s)?

Use your favorite editor to create an ASCII file, and then go for it. Name the tone-file something descriptive, without an extension, and then create the file. Below are sample lines for a tonefile. Both are equal, i.e., they will be read by BEEP exactly the same.

/F300 /D18 /R2 /W36

f300 d18 r2 w36

Both lines tell BEEP to play 300 hertz for 1 sec, pause for a sec, and then play 300 Hz again for 1 sec. The slash (/) is only required when the commands are issued on the same line that starts BEEP. They are not required within a tonefile. The semicolon separates comments from the code.

Great, but how do I translate my sheet music into tonefile frequencies?

You will need a translation table that gives the note names and their associated frequency. For your convenience, a full eight-octave chromatic scale is included in the Appendix of this book. Be sure that the tunes are simple; the computer plays only one tone at a time.

Can you give me an example of the BOX feature in use?

Boxes and windows are used extensively in the various Norton Utilities. They also could be used in developing an ASK program for less experienced users; these users could be given their choices from within a box or window rather than from a long laundry list of options. Using this technique would also force you, the developer, to think simply. Keeping user interfaces simple and clear is almost as important as keeping the underlying programming bug-free.

How do I code a BOX or WINDOW routine with text in it?

The following file, called EXAMPLE.BAT, opens a black hole in my blue screen, borders that hole with a double red line, and then prints the two lines of text (the double quotes) in bright white letters before redisplaying the DOS prompt twice.

```
EXAMPLE.BAT
ECHO OFF
CLS
BE WINDOW 4,18,10,47 RED ZOOM
BE ROWCOL 6,21,"This is an example of BE" BRIGHT WHITE
BE ROWCOL 8,20,"using both WINDOW & ROWCOL" BRIGHT WHITE
ECHO ON
```

> *Note:* The quotes around the text are necessary. If you forget them, only the first word will be displayed in the window. If ECHO OFF is not included, the lines of EXAMPLE.BAT will be displayed as the file runs. If ECHO ON is omitted at the end, the DOS prompt will display immediately after the last character of the last ROWCOL command line.

BOX can be substituted for WINDOW in the previous example if ZOOM is replaced with SINGLE or DOUBLE and transposed with RED. For example:

BE BOX 4,18,10,47 SINGLE RED

If you do not specify a color after the text in ROWCOL, it will use the same color as the BOX or WINDOW command line used. Thus, if BRIGHT WHITE is omitted from the ROWCOL command lines, the text would be displayed in RED. Any of the valid choices for a foreground color, in addition to the options BRIGHT, BOLD, or BLINKING, may be used in the ROWCOL command line. In fact, each command line can use a different color and option.

Using the BLINKING option on the BOX or WINDOW command line will cause everything to blink. Using BRIGHT in the ROWCOL command line doesn't stop the BLINKING. Therefore, if you want something to blink, include BLINKING only in the last line. I find it very difficult to read an entire window of blinking text.

Remember that you can also include BE BEEP command lines in a batch file link EXAMPLE.BAT. This will give you a combination of attention-getters.

Now that the ASK Utility has been incorporated into the Batch Enhancer Utility, will I still be able to use the files I developed with version 4.0?

Yes. The only changes will be in the way those files are called. Now you must use BE ASK rather than just ASK.

Where would I use the new BOX feature?

One possibility would be in the submenus that are called by a BE ASK routine. Since the called ASK lists are small, they would fit into a window or a BOX, and the main ASK menu would still be partially visible behind the new menu.

I don't see any value in the new features DEFAULT=KEY and TIMEOUT=n.

By providing you with the ability to specify a key as the default, Norton Utilities allows you to control the response of the program regardless of the user input. TIMEOUT permits you to limit the time between the display of the prompt and the next step in the program. One caution, however: a TIMEOUT=0 or failure to include TIMEOUT on the command will hang ASK. Then the system will have to be rebooted.

Are there any programs that I cannot run from an ASK file?

I don't know of any. This doesn't mean that there aren't any; it just means that I'm not aware of any. Since ASK and the Norton Utilities in general are very DOS friendly, I would not anticipate that any DOS-compatible program would cause problems if included in an ASK file.

3
CHAPTER

Calibrate

Directory name

Calibrate is a new Utility and can conduct a complete automated "physical" or just a special checkup for your hard disk when you suspect a problem.

Command line use

Format: CALIBRAT [d:] [/switch] [/switch] ...
                   d: The letter of the drive to be calibrated.

The following command-line switches are available:

/BATCH   Skips all of the prompts and exits to DOS when complete.

/NOSEEK   Do not perform the seek tests. Once the head-positioning mechanism is determined to be reliable, it is not necessary to run the seek tests every time Calibrate runs.

/NOFORMAT	Perform pattern testing only. Do not perform a low-level format.
/PATTERN:*n*	Perform pattern testing at level *n*. The only possible values for *n* are 0, 5, 40, and 80. Calibrate will reject all other values.
/R:*filename*	Generate a report and write it to the *filename*. This switch can only be used with the /BATCH switch.
/RA:*filename*	Generate a report and append it to the *filename*. If the filename doesn't exist, it will be created. This switch can only be used with the /BATCH switch.
/X:drives	Exclude drives from testing. This switch is for Zenith DOS users, meant to exclude allocated but nonexistent drives.

Network considerations

Calibrate doesn't work on network drives.

Compatibility

Calibrate is hardware and software dependent. It works at a very low level and is not as compatible as many of the other Utilities in version 5.0.

Back up your hard disk before you run Calibrate for the first time. Do not run Calibrate if you have

- an Iomega Bernoulli Box.
- a Novell file server.
- hard disk(s) with a logical sector size other than 512 bytes.

Also, Calibrate cannot perform low-level formatting of

- drives with SCSI or IDE controllers.
- drives that are not 100% IBM-compatible.
- controllers that perform "sector translation."
- hard-disk controllers with on-board disk cache.

The first time you run Calibrate, you might want to try it in the interactive mode. In other words, run it without any of the switches. Then you will be able to see just how many things it does, as well as understand just how deeply these new Norton Utilities dig. It almost seems like the sum of the reports provided is more information than you really need to operate a system.

When Calibrate says that it "optimizes the speed of your Disk System," as shown in Fig. 3-1, it doesn't mean that it is going to attempt to change the speed at

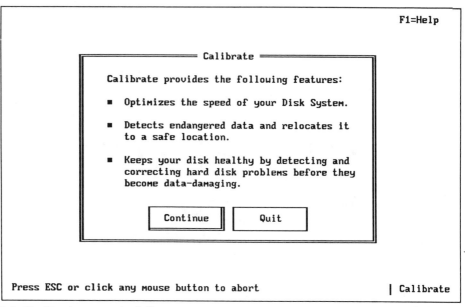

Calibrate

Calibrate provides the following features:

■ Optimizes the speed of your Disk System.

■ Detects endangered data and relocates it
  to a safe location.

■ Keeps your disk healthy by detecting and
  correcting hard disk problems before they
  become data-damaging.

Continue   Quit

Press ESC or click any mouse button to abort | Calibrate

3-1 The Opening screen for Calibrate.

which your hard disk runs. What Calibrate does mean is that it will change, with your permission, any of the operating parameters that it can to improve how and how fast your hard disk works.

On the Calibrate Select Drive panel, shown in Fig. 3-2, you can select the one drive that will be checked by Calibrate. The /BATCH mode of operation is the only mode that allows multiple disks to be tested. When using /BATCH, however, you can use the /X switch to limit Calibrate to a single drive.

Calibrate is not one of the Utilities which you should or must have on your hard disk at all times. If this is the way you decide to set up your copy of these Utilities, then you will most likely run Calibrate in the /BATCH mode more often than in the interactive mode. This, then, might be the only time you will see the Select Drive screen.

Just in case you have a system that wasn't mentioned previously in the list of incompatibles and yet is in fact incompatible, Calibrate makes its own check for compatibility. The Compatibility Test Information panel, shown here in Fig. 3-3, lists the tests that can be performed without harming your disk or your data. Also notice that, while only four tests are listed, more tests are actually conducted. This is true in many of the Utilities.

Assuming that your hard disk passed the first battery of tests, it will then be ready, with your permission, to take Calibrate's next batch (listed in Fig. 3-4). The dialog box on the right side provides a brief description of what's happening with each test. When Calibrate begins a test, it places a black dot (or "bullet") next to the test name. When the test is successfully completed, the dot changes to a check mark.

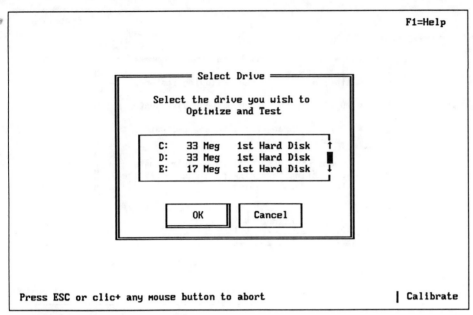

3-2 Selecting the drive you wish to calibrate.

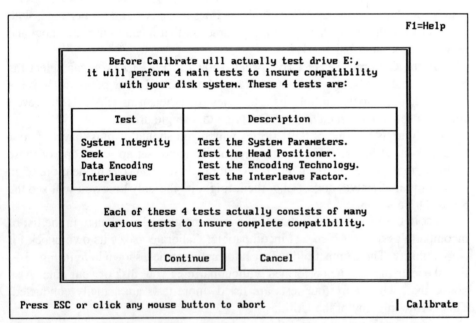

3-3 The many tests Calibrate will run on your disk.

If a cache program is discovered, you will receive the warning window shown here in Fig. 3-5. Because this was a software cache, Calibrate was able to continue testing. Had it been a hardware cache, Calibrate would not have been able to continue.

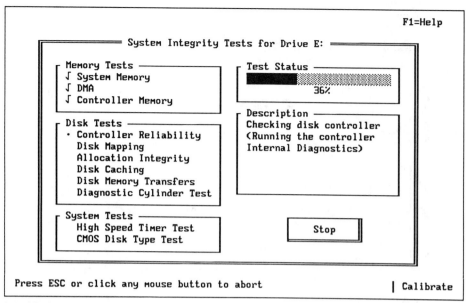

3-4 Monitoring the calibration process.

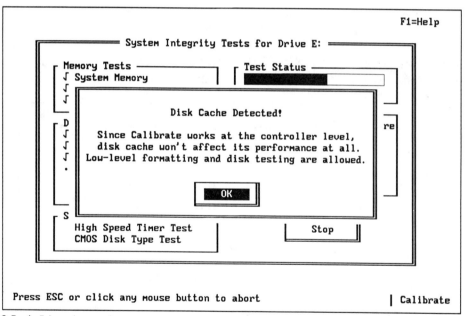

3-5 A disk cache warning.

Figure 3-6 shows a typical message screen when an error is detected during testing. The system being tested has an 85 megabyte SCSI hard disk installed. Because of this, Calibrate was not able to perform all of its tests on this disk. Thus, I've taken the illustrations of the tests it could not perform from another system.

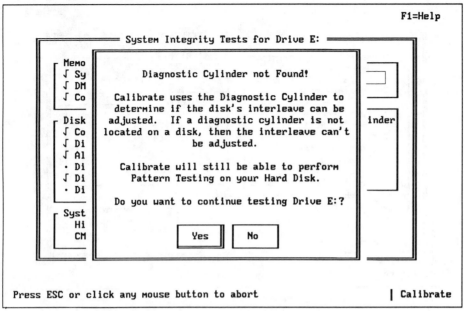

3-6 Other errors that may occur while testing.

Just how fast or slow your hard disk really operates has been the subject of many discussions, usually between manufacturers and their advertising types. When Calibrate gets to the Seek Test, shown in Fig. 3-7, it will determine the truth. Don't be alarmed by the noise or be distracted by the fast-moving graphics.

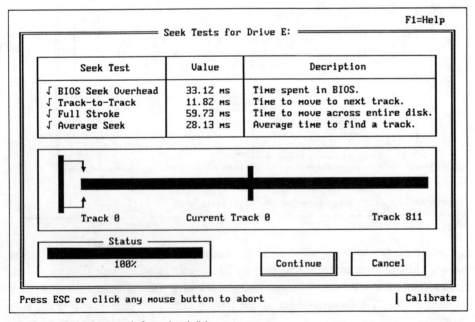

3-7 Determining the speed of your hard disk.

All of the noise is necessary to make the tests, and the graphics are just an attempt to give you a fair representation of what is happening inside the sealed container of your hard disk.

The design speed of a hard disk is 3,600 revolutions per minute (RPM). To a limited extent, how far away from this speed your hard disk runs isn't important. It's more important that it operate at its speed consistently. The disk being tested here in Fig. 3-8 is running a little slow (specifically, just over 10% slower than nominal).

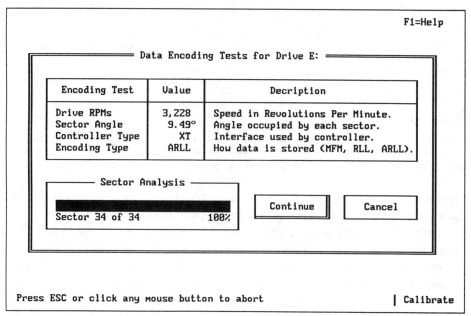

3-8   Determining the RPM of your hard drive, among other things.

Commercial power in most U.S. locations is subject to many variables. Despite this fact, however, the power entering your system is stable enough to drive a hard disk at a consistent speed. Still, low, high, and no voltage conditions will create problems for any system, which is why so many users with sensitive data are including a UPS (Uninterruptible Power Supply) in their basic configuration.

The encoding type (ARLL) is one of the types that is incompatible with this version of Calibrate. This hard disk has a SCSI interface controller.

There are actually two things happening when Pattern Testing is done. Calibrate does a nondestructive low-level format of the hard disk while it checks each sector's ability to hold information. The choice of 0, 5, 40 or 80 patterns, as indicated in Fig. 3-9, will have to be a balance of time and need. The more patterns used in testing, the longer it will take Calibrate to completely test the disk. For a large hard disk, this could mean hours. On a 33 megabyte hard disk, it will take

```
                                                                F1=Help


                  ═══════ Pattern test for drive E: ═══════

                     Pattern Testing will detect disk defects
                         before they become data-damaging.

                       Select the level of Pattern Testing
                               you wish to perform:

                  ┌─────────────────────────────────────────────┐
                  │  ○   No Pattern Testing                       │
                  │  ○   Minimal  Pattern Testing ( 5 patterns)   │
                  │  ○   Standard Pattern Testing (40 patterns)   │
                  │  ○   Rigorous Pattern Testing (80 patterns)   │
                  └─────────────────────────────────────────────┘


                       ┌──────────┐   ┌──────────┐
                       │    OK    │   │  Cancel  │
                       └──────────┘   └──────────┘



   Select OK to begin pattern testing, or CANCEL to abort    │ Calibrate
```

3-9 Selecting the level of pattern testing for Calibrate to do.

approximately one hour to do a complete 5-pattern test. A forty-pattern test of that same disk will take about 4 hours; and an 80-pattern test, almost 8 hours.

Only a simple read or write test is used if No Pattern Testing is selected. During routine maintenance, this might be an acceptable level of testing. At intervals, a more complete testing should be performed. If you are seeing intermittent errors, you should also consider doing a more complete test.

While testing is in progress, you can blank the screen by pressing the SPACE-BAR. The display will return when you press the SPACEBAR a second time. While the display is blanked, a floating window will be open which reports the progress of the testing. The window moves from place to place on the screen—so that no image burn-in occurs.

One of the things that determines the speed at which information transfers between memory and your hard disk is the interleave. An interleave of 1:1 means that the tracks are used sequentially. If the interleave is 1:2, then the tracks are used in an every-other scheme. For example, the track following track 1 will be track 3. The intervening tracks are also used, but only as they occur in the interleave scheme. As the interleave expands, the time needed extends, due to the addition of the time it takes the hard disk to read the information.

After Calibrate tests the various interleave schemes and determines the current interleave, it will recommend the best possible scheme. In Fig. 3-10, the current and optimal interleave are the same. If they weren't, you would have the option of changing either to the optimal or to any other interleave, or of making no change.

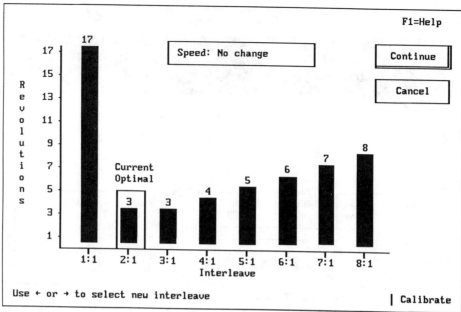

3-10 Viewing and changing the interleave.

As its last test, Calibrate checks the surface of your hard disk. As mentioned earlier, this can be a relatively short process, or it can take hours. The time necessary depends on the size of the disk under test and also on the extent of the test. Of course, if errors are found, then more time will be needed to make corrections.

The Pattern Testing panel, shown in Fig. 3-11, provides a significant amount of information. The upper portion of the screen shows the typical Norton display of the disk blocks. The ones with the white dots in them are in use, while the blank gray section is free disk space. As each block is tested, it changes color or is changed to a bold character. The current time and estimated time of completion together with the current testing location are also shown.

The legend in the lower right portion of the screen explains what the symbols in use mean. As each block is tested, you will see a progression of symbols displayed. Should all of this begin to get boring, you can always follow the instructions at the bottom of the screen and press the SPACEBAR. When you do, the display will change to a small block which travels around the screen and reminds you that testing is in progress as well as showing you the percentage completed. This same figure is also displayed at the bottom right corner of the bar graph in the lower left part of the full Pattern Testing screen.

Is there any order in which the various Norton Utilities tests should be performed?

There isn't any fixed order, but there may be some logic to selecting the appropriate test(s) to run.

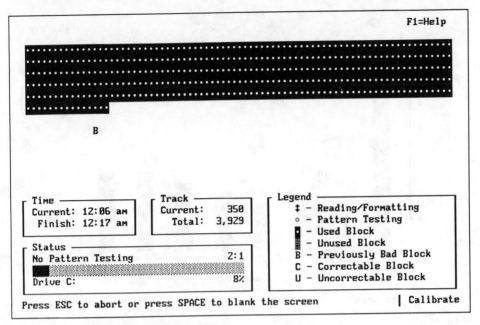

```
                                                            F1=Help
```

Time	**Track**	**Legend**
Current: 12:06 am	Current: 350	‡ - Reading/Formatting
Finish: 12:17 am	Total: 3,929	o - Pattern Testing
		▊ - Used Block
Status		▨ - Unused Block
No Pattern Testing 2:1		B - Previously Bad Block
		C - Correctable Block
Drive C: 8%		U - Uncorrectable Block

Press ESC to abort or press SPACE to blank the screen | Calibrate

3-11 Monitoring Calibrate through each disk block.

If SpeeDisk finds an error while it is optimizing your hard disk, it will recommend running Disk Doctor with the /COMPLETE switch. If Disk Doctor doesn't find any problems, it might be worth the extra time to run Calibrate and do at least a 5-pattern test. The refreshed format addressing data and the verification that all sectors can accurately hold your information should do at least two things. First, it should solve the problem SpeeDisk had, and then it should put your mind at ease about the safety of your data. It might also prompt you to remember when you did your last backup. If it was awhile ago, it might be time to do it again.

Do I have to run all of the tests in Calibrate every time?

No. There are keywords along the top line of the display when you run Calibrate, each being the key to a pull-down menu. Depending on which test(s) you feel are necessary, you can select it or them individually from these menus.

4
CHAPTER

DiskEdit

Directory name

DISKEDIT.EXE
or
DE.EXE

DiskEdit is a new Utility with version 5.0. The core of the program comes from the Norton Utility program of earlier versions and is now the heart of the Utilities. Thus, before you attempt to do anything with this program, **read the book!**

Every part of your hard disk or diskettes can be exposed and changed by this utility. Inappropriate changes can do serious harm. The Utility contains safeguards that attempt to prevent mistakes and accidents, but this does not imply that a dedicated user cannot create a problem that cannot be solved.

DE is not limited to just DOS disks or diskettes, either. When invoked in the maintenance (/M) mode, DiskEdit could allow you to view the contents of non-DOS disks. Being able to view the contents of a disk also implies the ability to edit the contents; and, in this case, it's true. DE will allow you to edit anything you can see without regard to the operating system involved.

A new term introduced with this program and this version of the Utilities is the word *object*. The context of use here is defined as any entity you select as the limits of your editing session, which means that you can define an object as a sector, or a cluster, or group of clusters as an object.

Command line usage

Format: DISKEDIT [d:] [path] [filename] [switches]

Drive, path and filename, if used, identify the first object.

Switches

/M invokes DE in the maintenance mode. This bypasses DOS and allows direct access to the disk or diskette.

/x:[d:][d:] Exclude drive [d:] and [d:], etc. This switch is for Zenith DOS uses.

Network considerations

Version 5.0 is not a multi-user program but is designed and sold as a single-user program to be installed on a stand-alone PC. Unless otherwise noted, all of the Utility programs are network-compatible and will not cause more problems than they solve when run in a network environment. Before running any of the Utility programs, check the Network Considerations section in the chapter on that Utility.

The heart

Disk Editor (DE) can display every part of a hard disk or diskette and make changes in it. This kind of power should not be used lightly. Safeguards are built into the program so that you will find it hard to make a fatal mistake. Of course, this does not imply in any way, shape, or form that such errors cannot be made. You can still destroy your access to any hard disk or diskette and also destroy data so that it cannot be recovered by any means. I guess that's enough scare tactics for now, however.

The basic unit of operation within DE is the *object*, which is the entity you have chosen to view and perhaps modify or delete. An object may vary in size from a single cluster (512 bytes) to an entire hard disk (? megabytes).

An object may be chosen by using a mouse to click an item, the ARROW keys can be used to move the reverse video bar to the desired object, or a combination keypress can be used. You can also move the reverse video bar to the desired item by pressing the bold uppercase letter/number (yellow uppercase for color-monitor users). The clipboard, shown in Fig. 4-1, serves the same function as the clip-

```
   Object   Edit   Link   View   Info   Tools   Quit              F1=Help
Na┌──────────────────────────┐    Time    Cluster Arc R/O Sys Hid Dir Vol
Se│ Drive...            Alt-D │                                          ↑
IB│ diRectory...        Alt-R │ 8  12:00 pm      2  Arc R/O Sys Hid
IB│ File...             Alt-F │ 8  12:00 pm     14  Arc R/O Sys Hid
Da│ Cluster...          Alt-C │ 0  12:52 am      0                    Vol
AR│ Sector...           Alt-S │ 0  12:22 pm     33              Dir
CA│ Physical sector...  Alt-P │ 0   2:18 pm     38              Dir
CW│                           │ 0  12:23 pm     32              Dir
DH│ partition Table     Alt-A │ 0  12:23 pm     30              Dir
HS│ Boot Record         Alt-B │ 0   7:46 am     41              Dir
LH│ 1st copy of FAT     Alt-F1│ 0  10:37 pm     42              Dir
MO│ 2nd copy of FAT     Alt-F2│ 0  12:28 pm     29              Dir
MT│                           │ 0   2:09 am     43              Dir
NC│ cLipboard                 │ 0  12:47 pm     47              Dir
PS└──────────────────────────┘ 0   1:53 pm     35              Dir
RW                           0  6-02-90   1:45 pm     51              Dir
SCAN                         0  6-02-90  12:23 pm     36              Dir
SPRINT                       0  6-02-90  12:22 pm     37              Dir
Sector 134
TEST                         0  6-02-90  12:23 pm     67              Dir
ZIP                          0  6-02-90  12:23 pm     34              Dir   ↓
 Root Directory                                          Sector 133
 C:\                                                     Offset 0, hex 0
 Select a disk drive                                     Disk Editor
```

4-1 Choosing the object you wish to view.

boards found in many other programs. With it, information can be transferred
from one location to another. The clipboard is not available, however, until after
the data to be transferred has been selected.

The screen under the pull-down menu is the opening screen of DE as well as
the Root directory of the default drive. Notice toward the bottom of the screen the
line reading "Sector 134." This type of notation is used throughout DiskEdit.
These "mile markers" make it much easier to find what you are looking for, if
you know the sector number they also make it easier to return to your previous
location. The amount of information displayed on any one screen is usually just
enough to ensure that one of these mile markers is always visible. When one isn't,
you can use the location information shown in the bottom right-hand corner of the
screen.

After selecting and locating the object you want to edit, you will probably
need some editing tools. Figure 4-2 shows you a list of some tools you can use.
The first tool listed, Undo, can be the most important one available. DE keeps a
file of the changes actually made, just like the Disk Doctor Utility. Using the
Undo function, you can cancel any change you have just made. Still, once new
data has been written to a disk location, the information that was there is lost forever. Because forever is such a long time, you should always make backup copies.

How often you see the link pull-down menu, shown here in Fig. 4-3, will
depend in part on how you have configured DE. The linking feature of DE automatically moves you from one related item to another if you have the Quick Link

```
    Object   Edit   Link   View   Info   Tools   Quit                    F1=Help
 Name     .E┌─────────────────────────┐ Cluster Arc R/O Sys Hid Dir Vol
 Sector 133 │ Undo           Ctrl-U   │                                      ↑
 IBMBIO   CO│─────────────────────────│ pm      2   Arc R/O Sys Hid
 IBMDOS   CO│ Mark           Ctrl-B   │ pm     14   Arc R/O Sys Hid
 Data_Dis k │ Copy           Ctrl-C   │ am      0                        Vol
 ARC        │ Paste Over     Ctrl-V   │ pm     33                        Dir
 CAL        │ Fill...                 │ pm     38                        Dir
 CW         │                         │ pm     32                        Dir
 DH         │ Write changes... Ctrl-W │ pm     30                        Dir
 HSG        │ Discard changes...      │ am     41                        Dir
 LHARC      └─────────────────────────┘ pm     42                        Dir
 MOUSE          0   6-02-90  12:28 pm     29                        Dir
 MTEZ           0   6-09-90   2:09 am     43                        Dir
 NC             0   6-02-90  12:47 pm     47                        Dir
 PS             0   6-02-90   1:53 pm     35                        Dir
 RW             0   6-02-90   1:45 pm     51                        Dir
 SCAN           0   6-02-90  12:23 pm     36                        Dir
 SPRINT         0   6-02-90  12:22 pm     37                        Dir
 Sector 134
 TEST           0   6-02-90  12:23 pm     67                        Dir
 ZIP            0   6-02-90  12:23 pm     34
 ┌─ Root Directory ──────────────────────────────────── Sector 133 ─┐
 │  C:\                                                 Offset 0, hex 0 ◆
 │ Undo last command                                    │ Disk Editor
```

4-2 Disk Editor's editing options.

```
    Object   Edit   Link   View   Info   Tools   Quit                    F1=Help
 Name     .Ext ┌─────────────────────────────────┐ r Arc R/O Sys Hid Dir Vol
 Sector 133    │ File...              Ctrl-F      │                           ↑
 IBMBIO   COM  │ Directory...         Ctrl-D      │ Arc R/O Sys Hid
 IBMDOS   COM  │ Cluster chain (FAT)... Ctrl-T    │ Arc R/O Sys Hid
 Data_Dis k    │ Partition...                     │                       Vol
 ARC           │                                  │                       Dir
 CAL           │ Window...                        │                       Dir
 CW            └──────────────────────────────────┘                      Dir
 DH             0   6-02-90  12:23 pm     30                        Dir
 HSG            0   6-04-90   7:46 am     41                        Dir
 LHARC          0   6-13-90  10:37 pm     42                        Dir
 MOUSE          0   6-02-90  12:28 pm     29                        Dir
 MTEZ           0   6-09-90   2:09 am     43                        Dir
 NC             0   6-02-90  12:47 pm     47                        Dir
 PS             0   6-02-90   1:53 pm     35                        Dir
 RW             0   6-02-90   1:45 pm     51                        Dir
 SCAN           0   6-02-90  12:23 pm     36                        Dir
 SPRINT         0   6-02-90  12:22 pm     37                        Dir
 Sector 134
 TEST           0   6-02-90  12:23 pm     67                        Dir
 ZIP            0   6-02-90  12:23 pm     34                        Dir
 ┌─ Root Directory ──────────────────────────────────── Sector 133 ─┐
 │  C:\                                                 Offset 0, hex 0 ◆
 │ View file's contents                                 │ Disk Editor
```

4-3 Moving from one related object to another.

option checked on the configuration screen. If the option is not checked, then you can use this menu to accomplish the same action.

The Configuration Window, presented in Fig. 4-4, is where you set your default features. If you have set DE to read-only during installation and also

```
   Object   Edit   Link   View   Info   Tools   Quit                    F1=Help
 Name     .Ext     Size    Date      Time      Cluster Arc R/O Sys Hid Dir Vol
 Sector 133                                                                     ↑
 IBMBIO  ┌════════════════ Configuration ════════════════┐              d
 IBMDOS  ║                                               ║              d
 Data_Dis║  □   Read Only    Prevent data from being modified. ║        Vol
 ANSI    ║                                               ║
 ARC     ║  □   Quick Move   Don't compute status line updates. ║       Dir
 CAL     ║                                               ║              Dir
 CW      ║  □   Auto View    Automatically choose the best view. ║      Dir
 DH      ║                                               ║              Dir
 FP      ║  □   Quick Links  Enable linking with the Enter key. ║       Dir
 HSG     ║                                               ║              Dir
 LHARC   ║        ┌──────── Character filters ────────┐  ║              Dir
 MOUSE   ║        │  □   Show all characters          │  ║              Dir
 MTEZ    ║        │  □   View Wordstar files          │  ║              Dir
 NC      ║        └──────────────────────────────────┘  ║              Dir
 PS      ║                                               ║              Dir
 RW      ║                                               ║              Dir
 Sector 13║  ┌─────────┐   ┌─────────┐   ┌─────────┐    ║
 SCAN    ║  │  Save   │   │   OK    │   │ Cancel  │    ║                Dir
 SPRINT  └══│─────────│═══│─────────│═══│─────────│════┘                Dir   ↓
 ┌─────────────────────────────────────────────────────────────────────────┐
 │    Root Directory                                             Sector 133
 │    C:\                                               Offset 0, hex 0
 │   Configure the Disk Editor for your use                    │ Disk Editor
 └─────────────────────────────────────────────────────────────────────────┘
```

4-4 Disk Editor's configuration default settings.

password protected it, you will have to use that same method to change it. Otherwise the check mark can be toggled here. I haven't included check marks in the illustration in order that you can mark the book to indicate your settings.

The short sentence following each option describes what selecting that option will do. Quick Move allows you to view a screen before the exact location is displayed. The display will be updated, but usually after the rest of the information is on the screen. The delay isn't overly long on an AT-class system. It might be useful to leave this option off when you are doing disaster recovery, in order to reduce the possibility of making an error.

Before the information is displayed on the screen, Auto View determines which of the viewing options will be employed. When you are just looking, having this option checked makes it easier to see things in the most easily read format. You will have to change to HEX format to do any editing in some areas. The Directory and Partition table areas have limited choices for editing. The choices are arranged so that using the SPACEBAR toggles them. Attempting to place invalid values in any of these areas will result in an error beep and no change in the information.

The Quick Links option makes moving around within DE much easier and faster. It also makes finding your place easier because it's automatic. Unless you have a specific reason for turning this option off, I'd leave it on.

The Character Filter is used for Wordstar files only. DE recognizes these files and can eliminate the extra characters that Wordstar uses for formatting and other purposes, leaving the resulting text files looking like ASCII text files. Unless you are going to try and print a DE screen, showing all characters makes it easier to view and edit the displayed information.

If you need a hard copy of a DE screen, it might be easier to use a "grabber" utility and convert the screen to a graphic file. These files can then be printed because the characters have been changed. They are no longer ASCII, Control characters etc., but are printable graphics. Conversion eliminates any possibility of confusing your printer.

The last three boxes are used to save the selections you have made. In other words, they become the defaults the next time you use DE. To avoid this, you can select OK, which will allow you to use the selected options for this session in DE only. When you run DE the next time, the original settings will still be the default settings. If you Cancel the window, you do not save or use any of the changes.

The View menu shows possible ways you can view the information on your hard disk or a diskette (Fig. 4-5). Most of these features have been part of the Norton Utility (NU) for the past few releases.

```
    Object   Edit    Link    View    Info    Tools    Quit              F1=Help
 Name      .Ext    Size   ┌──────────────────────────────────┐ R/O Sys Hid Dir Vol
 Sector 133                │   as Hex              F2         │                        ↑
 IBMBIO    COM     23591   │   as Text             F3         │ R/O Sys Hid          ▓
 IBMDOS    COM     30648   │ √ as Directory        F4         │ R/O Sys Hid          ▓
 Data_Dis k             0  │   as FAT              F5         │                  Vol ▓
 ARC                    0  │   as Partition Table  F6         │              Dir     ▓
 CAL                    0  │   as Boot Record      F7         │              Dir     ▓
 CW                     0  │                                  │              Dir     ▓
 DH                     0  │   Split window        Shift-F5   │              Dir     ▓
 HSG                    0  │   Grow window         Shift-F6   │              Dir     ▓
 LHARC                  0  │   sHrink window       Shift-F7   │              Dir     ▓
 MOUSE                  0  │   sWitch windows      Shift-F8   │              Dir     ▓
 MTEZ                   0  └──────────────────────────────────┘              Dir     ▓
 NC                     0   6-02-90  12:47 pm       47                       Dir     ▓
 PS                     0   6-02-90   1:53 pm       35                       Dir     ▓
 RW                     0   6-02-90   1:45 pm       51                       Dir     ▓
 SCAN                   0   6-02-90  12:23 pm       36                       Dir     ▓
 SPRINT                 0   6-02-90  12:22 pm       37                       Dir     ▓
 Sector 134
 TEST                   0   6-02-90  12:23 pm       67                       Dir     ▓
 ZIP                    0   6-02-90  12:23 pm       34                       Dir     ↓
 ├────────────────────────────────────────────────────────────────────────────────┤
 │  Root Directory                                                   Sector 133  ◆
 │  C:\                                                           Offset 0, hex 0  ◆
 ├────────────────────────────────────────────────────────────────────────────────┤
 │  View data in hex dump format                              │   Disk Editor
```

4-5 Choosing a method with which to view your disk.

The first viewing option is HEX. As indicated in the View pull-down menu, HEX and the other various modes can be called by using the function keys, by clicking the mouse, or by using the ARROW keys to move the reverse video block to the desired option. When the HEX mode is chosen, your screen will look similar to Fig. 4-6. Note that the full path with filename is shown in the bottom left corner of the screen while the cursor location is shown in the bottom right corner. Offset 0 and HEX 0 mean that the cursor is over the "54" in the upper left corner

```
   Object   Edit   Link   View   Info   Tools   Quit            F1=Help
Cluster 10,325, Sector 41,457                                          ↑
00000000:  54 52 4F 55 42 4C 45 53 - 48 4F 4F 54 49 4E 47 0D   TROUBLESHOOTING♪
00000010:  0A 50 72 65 76 65 6E 74 - 69 6E 67 20 69 73 20 62   ▓Preventing is b
00000020:  65 74 74 65 72 2F 65 61 - 73 69 65 72 20 74 68 61   etter/easier tha
00000030:  6E 20 63 75 72 69 6E 67 - 0D 0A 0D 0A 20 20 20 20   n curing♪▓♪▓
00000040:  54 68 65 72 65 20 61 72 - 65 20 74 77 6F 20 63 6F   There are two co
00000050:  6D 70 6F 6E 65 6E 74 73 - 20 74 6F 20 61 6E 79 20   mponents to any
00000060:  64 61 74 61 2F 64 69 73 - 61 73 74 65 72 20 72 65   data/disaster re
00000070:  63 6F 76 65 72 79 20 0D - 0A 6F 70 65 72 61 74 69   covery ♪▓operati
00000080:  6F 6E 2E 20 54 68 65 20 - 66 69 72 73 74 20 70 61   on. The first pa
00000090:  72 74 20 69 73 20 64 65 - 74 65 72 6D 69 6E 69 6E   rt is determinin
000000A0:  67 20 77 68 61 74 27 73 - 20 77 72 6F 6E 67 2E 20   g what's wrong.
000000B0:  0D 0A 54 68 65 20 73 65 - 63 6F 6E 64 20 70 61 72   ♪▓The second par
000000C0:  74 20 69 73 20 63 6F 72 - 72 65 63 74 69 6E 67 20   t is correcting
000000D0:  74 68 65 20 70 72 6F 62 - 6C 65 6D 2E 20 54 68 65   the problem. The
000000E0:  20 74 6F 6F 6C 73 20 0D - 0A 61 76 61 69 6C 61 62    tools ♪▓availab
000000F0:  6C 65 20 66 6F 72 20 64 - 65 74 65 72 6D 69 6E 69   le for determini
00000100:  6E 67 20 77 68 61 74 27 - 73 20 77 72 6F 6E 67 20   ng what's wrong
00000110:  61 72 65 3A 0D 0A 0D 0A - 20 20 20 20 20 20 20 20   are:♪▓♪▓
00000120:  20 43 48 4B 44 53 4B 20 - 28 20 41 20 44 4F 53 20    CHKDSK ( A DOS
00000130:  75 74 69 6C 69 74 79 29 - 0D 0A 20 20 20 20 20 20   utility)♪
File                                                  Cluster 10,325
C:\SPRINT\NU5\TXT\shoot.txt                           Offset 0, hex 0
Press ALT or F10 to select menus                    │ Disk Editor
```

4-6   HEX mode viewing in DE.

and also over the uppercase "T." This is the first byte of this sector. The cluster and sector numbers are also displayed.

The blinking underline under the HEX value or the letter determines which edit mode is active. If the underline is on the HEX side, then editing is done by changing HEX values. If it's on the text side, then editing is done in text mode. Just remember that some characters are very difficult to enter from the keyboard. For these characters, it's usually easier to change to HEX mode editing.

Figure 4-7 is the text display of the information shown in Fig. 4-6. More letters are shown in this mode because there is more space available for the text display. The HEX display is less than a full sector. The presence of two sector identifiers indicates that more than a single sector of information is displayed.

No editing is done in this mode. You can read and search for things quickly in this mode and then switch to HEX for editing. The condition of the elevator bar on the far right side of most DE screens indicates where you are in the object. The ARROW keys and the mouse can be used in addition to the HOME, END, and PAGE keys for moving around in the object.

The Directory Viewing mode is visible under all of the menu illustrations. You can edit the directory in this mode, as well as view other types of information. There are strict limits on the values that can be placed in the various fields of the directory. Where they are fixed to just a few, they are arranged as SPACEBAR toggles. The field length and value are monitored for filenames, file dates, and times. If you make a mistake, DE will tell you.

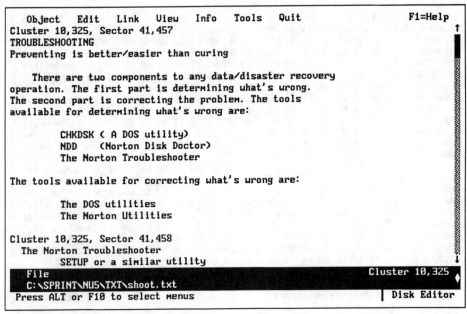

```
  Object   Edit   Link   View   Info   Tools   Quit              F1=Help
Cluster 10,325, Sector 41,457                                         ↑
TROUBLESHOOTING
Preventing is better/easier than curing


    There are two components to any data/disaster recovery
operation. The first part is determining what's wrong.
The second part is correcting the problem. The tools
available for determining what's wrong are:


        CHKDSK ( A DOS utility)
        NDD    (Norton Disk Doctor)
        The Norton Troubleshooter

The tools available for correcting what's wrong are:


        The DOS utilities
        The Norton Utilities

Cluster 10,325, Sector 41,458
  The Norton Troubleshooter
        SETUP or a similar utility                                    ↓
┌──────────────────────────────────────────────────────────────────────┐
│ File                                              Cluster 10,325      ◆
│ C:\SPRINT\NU5\TXT\shoot.txt                                           │
│ Press ALT or F10 to select menus                 │ Disk Editor       │
└──────────────────────────────────────────────────────────────────────┘
```

4-7 Text mode viewing in DE.

The File Allocation Table (FAT), shown in Fig. 4-8, indicates that this disk is almost full. The lack of End-Of-File markers, <EOF>, also indicates that most of the space is taken up by a single file.

```
  Object   Edit   Link   View   Info   Tools   Quit              F1=Help
  1932     1933   1934   1935    1936   1937    1938      1939        ↑
  1940     1941   1942   1943    1944   1945    1946      1947
  1948     1949   1950   1951    1952   1953    1954      1955
  1956     1957   1958   1959    1960   1961    1962      1963
  1964     1965   1966   1967    1968   1969    1970      1971
  1972     1973   1974   1975    1976   1977    1978      1979
  1980     1981   1982   1983    1984   1985    1986      1987
  1988     1989   1990   1991    1992   1993    1994      1995
  1996     1997   1998   1999    2000   2001    2002      2003
  2004     2005   2006   2007    2008   2009    2010      2011
  2012     2013   2014   2015    2016   2017    2018      2019
  2020     2021   2022   2023    2024   2025    2026      2027
  2028     2029   2030   2031    2032   2033    2034      2035
  2036     2037   2038   2039    2040   2041    2042      2043
  2044     2045   2046   2047    2048   2049
Sector 7
  2050     2051   2052   2053    2054   2055    2056      2057
  2058     2059   <EOF>  2061    2062   2063    2064      2065
  2066     2067   2068   2069    2070   <EOF>   0         0
     0        0      0      0       0      0    0         0
     0        0      0   <EOF>                                        ↓
┌──────────────────────────────────────────────────────────────────────┐
│ FAT (1st Copy)                                         Sector 7       │
│ Drive D:                                     Cluster 2,083, hex 823   ◆
│ Press ALT or F10 to select menus                 │ Disk Editor       │
└──────────────────────────────────────────────────────────────────────┘
```

4-8 FAT mode viewing in DE.

The system that generated Fig. 4-9 has only a single hard disk which is divided into two logical drives. One drive is more than 32 megabytes, as indicated by the BIGDOS notation in the System column. This particular hard disk has the capacity of being divided into more than two logical drives.

```
   Object   Edit   Link   View   Info   Tools   Quit              F1=Help

        |     | Starting Location  |  Ending Location  | Relative | Number of |
  System|Boot |Side Cylinder Sector|Side Cylinder Sector| Sectors  |  Sectors  |↑
  BIGDOS| Yes | 1       0      1   | 5    654     17   |      17  |    66793  |
  EXTEND| No  | 0     655      1   | 5    818     17   |   66810  |    16728  |
  unused| No  | 0       0      0   | 0      0      0   |       0  |        0  |
  unused| No  | 0       0      0   | 0      0      0   |       0  |        0  |↓




   Partition Table                          Cyl 0, Side 0, Sector 1
   Hard Disk 1                               Offset 450, hex 1C2
   Press ALT or F10 to select menus             Disk Editor
```

4-9   The Partition Table of a hard disk with two logical drives.

Now that you've seen a Partition Table, you may never see another one. One exists on every hard disk, but, unless there's trouble, you have no need to mess with it. The only exception to never messing around in the Partition Table area might be to make a hard copy of the information when the disk is new.

The last item of information that needs to be illustrated is the boot record. Figure 4-10 shows the boot record of my C drive. This drive is the larger partition of the single hard disk installed in my system. Note that the Utility and DOS reports are the same for the important items. At the time this illustration was made, this disk had not been formatted using the SafeFormat (SF) Utility.

Learning more about the object you have chosen can start with the Information menu shown in Fig. 4-11. The Map of Object choice will show you which cluster(s) hold the file or information you have chosen.

The Tools Pull-Down menu (Fig. 4-12) contains two very useful tools. The ASCII Table will display the decimal, HEX, and character values of all the IBM and compatible ASCII set from 1 to 255. The HEX Converter is a three-block window that is used to convert decimal to HEX and vice versa. You enter one value and DE calculates the other. The character representing this value will also be displayed in the bottom block and can be used to enter a character and have DE calculate the HEX and decimal values.

```
    Object    Edit    Link    View    Info    Tools    Quit              F1=Help
                    Description            Boot Record Data      DOS Reports
Sector 0                                                                       ↑
                          OEM ID: IBM  3.3
                  Bytes per sector: 512                        512
              Sectors per cluster: 4                           4
      Reserved sectors at beginning: 1                         1
                       FAT Copies: 2                           2
          Root directory entries: 512                          512
          Total sectors on disk: (Unused)
          Media descriptor byte: F8 Hex
                  Sectors per FAT: 66                          66
                Sectors per track: 17
                            Sides: 6
          Special hidden sectors: 17
      Big total number of sectors: 66793                       66793
          Physical drive number: (Unused)
      Extended Boot Record Signature: (Unused)
          Volume Serial Number: (Unused)
                     Volume Label: (Unused)
                   File System ID: (Unused)                                    ↓
┌──────────────────────────────────────────────────────────────────────────┐
│  Boot Record                                            Sector 0    ◆       │
│  Drive C:                                           Offset 3, hex 3 ◇       │
│  Press ALT or F10 to select menus                       │ Disk Editor      │
└──────────────────────────────────────────────────────────────────────────┘
```

4-10 The Boot record of a C drive.

```
    Object    Edit    Link    View    Info    Tools    Quit              F1=Help
Name      .Ext    Size      Date                            er Arc R/O Sys Hid Dir Vol
Sector 133                          ┌──────────────────────┐                        ↑
IBMBIO    COM    23591    5-27-      │  Object info...      │      Arc R/O Sys Hid
IBMDOS    COM    30648    5-27-      │  Drive info...       │      Arc R/O Sys Hid
Data_Dis k          0    6-18-       │  Map of object...    │                    Vol
ARC                 0    6-02-90     └──────────────────────┘ 33                Dir
CAL                 0    6-02-90    2:18 pm              38                Dir
CW                  0    6-02-90   12:23 pm              32                Dir
DH                  0    6-02-90   12:23 pm              30                Dir
HSG                 0    6-04-90    7:46 am              41                Dir
LHARC               0    6-13-90   10:37 pm              42                Dir
MOUSE               0    6-02-90   12:28 pm              29                Dir
MTEZ                0    6-09-90    2:09 am              43                Dir
NC                  0    6-02-90   12:47 pm              47                Dir
PS                  0    6-02-90    1:53 pm              35                Dir
RW                  0    6-02-90    1:45 pm              51                Dir
SCAN                0    6-02-90   12:23 pm              36                Dir
SPRINT              0    6-02-90   12:22 pm              37                Dir
Sector 134
TEST                0    6-02-90   12:23 pm              67                Dir
ZIP                 0    6-02-90   12:23 pm              34                Dir      ↓
┌──────────────────────────────────────────────────────────────────────────┐
│  Root Directory                                      Sector 133    ◆        │
│  C:\                                             Offset 0, hex 0   ◇        │
│  Get more information on the selected object         │ Disk Editor          │
└──────────────────────────────────────────────────────────────────────────┘
```

4-11 Getting information about an object of your choosing.

The Set Attributes and Set Time/Date tools can be used with any directory display. They function like the FA (FileAttribute) and FD (FileDate) Utilities of previous releases. To make changes, the file(s) must first be marked. Because only one block is active at any time, the files also must be adjacent. Separated files may be changed only one at a time.

```
  Object   Edit    Link     View    Info    Tools    Quit                F1=Help
Name      .Ext    Size     Date    T┌──────────────────────────────────┐r Vol
Sector 133                          │ Find...                   Ctrl-S  │      ↑
IBMBIO    COM     23591   5-27-88  12:│ find aGain                Ctrl-G  │
IBMDOS    COM     30648   5-27-88  12:│ Write to...                       │
Data_Dis k            0   6-18-90  12:│                                   │ Vol
ARC                   0   6-02-90  12:│ Recalculate Partition             │r
CAL                   0   6-02-90   2:│ Compare Windows...                │r
CW                    0   6-02-90  12:│ set aTtributes...                 │r
DH                    0   6-02-90  12:│ set Date/time...                  │r
HSG                   0   6-04-90   7:│                                   │r
LHARC                 0   6-13-90  10:│ Hex converter...                  │r
MOUSE                 0   6-02-90  12:│ ASCII Table...                    │r
MTEZ                  0   6-09-90   2:│                                   │r
NC                    0   6-02-90  12:│ cOnfiguration...         .        │r
PS                    0   6-02-90   1:└──────────────────────────────────┘r
RW                    0   6-02-90   1:45 PM       51              Dir
SCAN                  0   6-02-90  12:23 PM       36              Dir
SPRINT                0   6-02-90  12:22 PM       37              Dir
Sector 134
TEST                  0   6-02-90  12:23 PM       67              Dir
ZIP                   0   6-02-90  12:23 PM       34              Dir      ↓
┌─────────────────────────────────────────────────────────────────────────┐
│ Root Directory                                            Sector 133    ◆│
│ C:\                                                 Offset 0, hex 0      │
├─────────────────────────────────────────────────────────────────────────┤
│ Find a string or hex pattern in selected object          │ Disk Editor  │
└─────────────────────────────────────────────────────────────────────────┘
```

4-12 Choosing tools to use in DE.

After using the View menu (back in Fig. 4-5) to display two windows of information you will find the Compare Windows tool useful. Using it, you can find differences between the objects displayed in the windows. If you have different versions of the same program, you will be able to find the changes. This feature works on compiled as well as other types of files. In Fig. 4-13, two different view formats were chosen just for purposes of illustration.

You can exit DE in two ways. Use the Shell option shown in Fig. 4-14 if you are only leaving for a short period to perform a task which cannot be accomplished from within DE. Like other shell utilities, the bulk of the application program remains in RAM and you will have only a small window to work through. The other option, also shown in Fig. 4-14, allows you to leave DE on a more permanent basis. Leaving via the Quit option dumps the application (DE) from RAM and allows you to go on with normal computing tasks.

The Norton Utility (NU) version 4.0 & 4.5

Version 4.0 & 4.5 directory name   NU.EXE

NU is the heart of the Norton Utilities. This one program, when really needed, is worth the price of the entire package. With the enhancements that have been made over the years, NU continues to be a leader in the genre. This program has the ability to completely destroy your access to any disk. Care and following instructions are almost mandatory. The screen displays and the helpscreens will be useful only to those who take time to read them. Along with the format changes in the

```
   Object    Edit    Link    View    Info    Tools    Quit                      F1=Help
00000F60:  53 45 4C 45 43 54 20 20 - 43 4F 4D 20 00 00 00 00   SELECT  COM ....
00000F70:  00 00 00 00 00 00 E0 16 - 4C 0C 32 01 C3 07 00 00   ......α─L♀2⊡├·..
00000F88:  52 45 50 4C 41 43 45 20 - 45 58 45 20 00 00 00 00   REPLACE EXE ....
00000F90:  00 00 00 00 00 00 00 60 - 71 0E 33 01 FF 2D 00 00   .......`q♪3⊡.-..
00000FA0:  50 52 49 4E 54 45 52 20 - 53 59 53 20 00 00 00 00   PRINTER SYS ....
00000FB0:  00 00 00 00 00 00 00 60 - 71 0E 39 01 16 35 00 00   .......`q♪9⊡.5..
00000FC0:  4E 4C 53 46 55 4E 43 20 - 45 58 45 20 00 00 00 00   NLSFUNC EXE ....
00000FD0:  00 00 00 00 00 00 00 60 - 71 0E 40 01 F4 0B 00 00   .......`q♪@⊡∟δ..
00000FE0:  4D 4F 44 45 20 20 20 20 - 43 4F 4D 20 00 00 00 00   MODE    COM ....
00000FF0:  00 00 00 00 00 00 4A 7E - C7 08 42 01 BC 14 00 00   ......J~╟∘B⊡╝¶..
```
```
█ File                                           Cluster 3,120
  C:\CW\hhscand.sys                         Offset 4,080, hex FF0    ◆
.GI&è=Ç.0Ç.     w.GI&è.Ç.0Ç.     w.GI..Z...è.Z.Z...è.è.Z.è..&.       ↑
..&.
.Z[.......
u`&.G..tY....û.Ÿ.........è.J.=.mt
û..........3...%..ŵ.J.è.J.%..ú..J......"...<.u..6î..û........<..Ñè.â....»
è..........u......u          .....u..:.î.u.ë.ö....ö....ISK  SYS ........»
.SYS    COM ........sg
.....SELECT  COM ...........L.Z.....REPLACE EXE ...........`q.3..-..PRINTER »
.MODE    COM .........J~..B.....                                         ↓
█ File                                           Cluster 3,120
  C:\CW\hhscand.sys
  Press ALT or F10 to select menus                       │ Disk Editor
```

4-13 An example of split windows in DiskEdit.

```
   Object    Edit    Link    View    Info    Tools    Quit              F1=Help
Name       .Ext    Size    Date        Time                               ol    ↑
Sector 133                                    ┌──────────────────────────┐
IBMBIO   COM     23591    5-27-88   12:00 pm  │ Shell to DOS             │
IBMDOS   COM     30648    5-27-88   12:00 pm  │ Quit Disk Editor  Ctrl-Q │
Data_Dis k          0    6-18-90   12:52 am   └──────────────────────────┘
ARC                 0    6-02-90   12:22 pm        33              Dir
CAL                 0    6-02-90    2:18 pm        38              Dir
CW                  0    6-02-90   12:23 pm        32              Dir
DH                  0    6-02-90   12:23 pm        30              Dir
HSG                 0    6-04-90    7:46 am        41              Dir
LHARC               0    6-13-90   10:37 pm        42              Dir
MOUSE               0    6-02-90   12:28 pm        29              Dir
MTEZ                0    6-09-90    2:09 am        43              Dir
NC                  0    6-02-90   12:47 pm        47              Dir
PS                  0    6-02-90    1:53 pm        35              Dir
RW                  0    6-02-90    1:45 pm        51              Dir
SCAN                0    6-02-90   12:23 pm        36              Dir
SPRINT              0    6-02-90   12:22 pm        37              Dir
Sector 134
TEST                0    6-02-90   12:23 pm        67              Dir
ZIP                 0    6-02-90   12:23 pm        34              Dir    ↓
  Root Directory                                          Sector 133
  C:\                                               Offset 0, hex 0    ◆
  Access DOS and keep Disk Editor in memory               │ Disk Editor
```

4-14 Quitting DiskEdit.

screens themselves, version 4.0 and the Advanced Edition have on-line helpscreens.

Screen displays from more than one version will only be reprinted here when the changes are significant.

Format: NU [drive: \ path \ filename] [/switches]

d: Indicates which drive holds the disk where NU is to work.

The following command-line options and switches are available:

/Dn   Screen driver options available:
      $n = 0$ The default screen driver, for IBM PCs and fully-compatibles.
      $n = 1$ The screen driver to use with BIOS-compatible machines.
      $n = 2$ The screen driver to use with other MS-DOS machines that are not BIOS-compatible; requires ANSI.SYS.

Note: When using the /D2 option and the Advanced Edition, absolute sectors are not accessible.

/NOCOLOR
      The version 3.0 "no color" or monochrome option.

/NOC   The "no color" or monochrome option in version 3.1.

/TV   Makes special adjustments so that NU can work with IBM's Top-View program.

/Fn/Bn   Color control options available in Version 3.1.

      $n = 0$ to 15 permits the direct selection of a specific color

(ALT-F3)   Foreground color control. Successively pressing this key will cycle the screen through each of the 16 available colors. Version 4.0 & 4.5.

(ALT-F4)   Background color control. The color values for the numbers 0 thru 15 are those listed in the BASIC manual. Version 4.0 & 4.5.

/BW or (ALT-F1)
      Indicates that NU is running on a monochrome composite monitor from a CGA card. Version 4.0 & 4.5.

/P   The "display printable character" option, which is useful when trying to use PRNTSCR to get a hardcopy of the display. Version 3.1.

(ALT-F2)   This key combination toggles the IBM graphics character set on and off from within the NU program. It can be very useful when trying to print out HEX data. Version 4.0 & 4.5.

/EBCDIC The Extended Binary Coded Decimal Interchange Code used by mainframe computers. This option allows NU to read and write this code without attempting to display the many nonprintable characters. Version 3.1.

(ALT-F5)   Performs the same function as the /EBCDIC switch and is available from within the NU program. Version 4.0 & 4.5.

/EUR(opean)
Allows for the printing of the European character set. Version 3.1.

/EXT or **(ALT-F6)**
Allows NU to display the IBM extended character set (above ASCII 127). The ALT-F6 key combination can be used as a toggle from within the NU program. Version 4.0 & 4.5.

/M   Maintenance mode (available in the Advanced Edition only); bypasses the DOS logical organization, which you may need to do when working with badly damaged disks.

NU has always been a powerful utility for programmers and hackers. The Advanced Edition version is even more powerful now, which suggests that it has the potential to be much more useful and dangerous. With its new editing capabilities, NU can make or break your entire week (let alone, your day) almost instantly.

I cannot overstress the value of good housekeeping practices, such as regular hardware maintenance and proper backing up and storage of floppy disks and tapes. Having the power of QU (Quick UnErase) and NU (Norton Utility) never justifies poor operating techniques.

When you specify a filename on the command line while invoking NU, the program positions itself at the Explore Disk level. Beginning a filename with a question mark ("?") brings NU up to the UnErase feature with that file selected.

Access to disks with damaged directories is possible using the maintenance mode (/m switch), which is available only in the Advanced Edition. In this mode, clusters and sectors (or absolute sectors using an IBM or compatible system) are addressable; files are not. The UnErase feature, a file-oriented routine, is not usable in the maintenance mode.

You can make selections on the various menus either by pressing the UP ARROW or DN ARROW to position the reverse video block and then pressing the RETURN key, or by pressing the letter key corresponding to the capital letter that is highlighted and in a different color. Pressing the letter key causes NU to run that selection immediately; you will not need to press the RETURN key. This resembles pressing the "F"unction keys in earlier versions.

NU positions the reverse video block over the most likely response each time a new menu screen displays. This means that many tasks can be addressed by pressing RETURN a few times in succession.

Help is available in two forms throughout NU. One form consists of one-line comments on each menu, displayed as the reverse video block from selection to selection; the other can be called by pressing F1. The F1 helpscreens are full-screen displays that are context-sensitive, which means that the screen display is about the selection highlighted by the reverse video block. One other type of help is also available: the F9 key, also known as the "undo" key.

You can quit NU in two ways. Pressing the F10 key quits immediately and goes to the DOS prompt. Pressing the ESC key backs you out of NU one menu at a time. In either case, you will be warned to complete any unfinished tasks before quitting NU.

What will the Disk Information portion of the NU program tell me?

There are two different pieces of information available. The Map Disk, shown in Fig. 4-15, displays a graphic representation of where things are on the disk. This picture is similar to the one that is displayed by the SD (SpeeDisk) utility. The two main differences in the displays are the value of each of the "in-use" blocks and the fact that the display is static. Essentially, this means that you are not able to edit or change any of the information shown on this screen directly. The fixed X blocks and the bad B blocks are included in both displays.

```
Menu 3.1
                    Map of space usage for the entire disk

                      69% of disk space is free

                    Proportional Map of Disk Space
              · ·················································
 represents   ····················································
     space    ····················································
    in use



      Each position represents 34 clusters, 1/490th of the total disk space
                         Press any key to continue...


 Item type    Drive   Directory name                        File name
 Directory    C:      \EWT\BK2                               Dir area
```

4-15 The Space Usage map (version 4.5).

The Technical Information panel, pictured in Fig. 4-16, provides a text display which describes the capacity and logical organization of the disk. This selection is probably the only way to determine the format's cluster size (i.e., number of 512-byte sectors in the cluster). Older versions of DOS are formatted in 8-sector clusters (which is 4 kilobytes). DOS 3.x formats in 4-sector clusters (which is 2 kilobytes).

The most noticeable difference in this change is the reduction in slack or empty space on your hard disk when the majority of your files are relatively small. For example, a file of 5,500 bytes occupies a total of 11 sectors (actual).

```
  Menu 3.2
                             Technical information

         Drive C:

         Basic storage capacity:
              33 million characters (megabytes)
              69% of disk space is free

         Logical dimensions:
              Sectors are made up of 512 bytes
              Tracks are made up of 17 sectors per disk side
              There are 6 disk sides
              The disk space is made up of 655 cylinders
              Space for files is allocated in clusters of 4 sectors
              There are 16,657 clusters
              Each cluster is 2,048 bytes
              The disk's root directory can hold 512 files



                      Press any key to continue...
```

4-16 The Technical Information screen (version 4.5AE).

Under DOS 2.x, a total of 16 sectors or 2 clusters are assigned to that file. With DOS 3.x, only 12 sectors or 3 clusters are assigned to that file. Although the number of clusters assigned has increased, the actual amount of disk space assigned has decreased by 4 sectors (or 2 kilobytes). This means that these 4 sectors (1 cluster) can be assigned to another file.

The last line says that the Root directory can only hold 512 files. Am I limited to 512 files on my hard disk?

No. The limit is on the Root directory, not the hard disk. You may not have more than 512 files in the Root directory, but you may have a number of subdirectories. These files are not a part of the Root directory and therefore are not included in the 512-file total. Thus, the actual total number of files will be limited to the disk space available.

I've noticed a file called NU.HLP on the disk. What does it do?

The *.HLP files are the files called up when you press the F1 key to get help. Illustrations of some help screens that are part of the Norton Utility (NU) follow this text. Figure 4-17 and Fig. 4-18 show the Main menu.

Figures 4-19 and 4-20 help you Explore your disk.

Figures 4-21 and 4-22 lead you deeper into the Utility, showing you how to Choose Items.

Figures 4-23 and 4-24, Select File, may be your goal. With the exception of Sector editing, you can reach any part of your disk from here.

The difference in the information presentation between Fig. 4-25 and Fig. 4-26, both shown, is striking. If you try to compare the two, it's easy to get lost; the information, however, is actually the same. What you don't see is the support of the Utility.

Most of the areas that can be accessed within a disk by NU must be edited in the HEX mode. Figure 4-27 shows the on-line help screen that is immediately available to you when you are trying to edit. You can edit some things in the Text mode. Also, the Root directory, when it is in the Directory format, can be edited directly; there is no need to switch to the HEX mode.

```
┌──────────────────────────────────────────────────────────────────────────┐
│ The Norton Utilities, Advanced Edition 4.50, (C) Copr 1987-88, Peter Norton│
│                                                                            │
│                    10:22 pm, Sunday, April 30, 1989                         │
├──────────────────────────────────────────────────────────────────────────┤
│                              Main menu                                      │
│                                                                            │
│                           Explore disk                                     │
│                                                                            │
│                           UnErase                                          │
│                                                                            │
│                          *Disk information*                                │
│                                                                            │
│                           Quit the Norton Utilities                        │
│                                                                            │
│                    View, edit, search, or copy selected item               │
├────────────┬────────┬──────────────────────────────────┬──────────────────┤
│ Item type  │ Drive  │ Directory name                   │ File name        │
│ Directory  │ C:     │ \                                │ Root dir         │
└────────────┴────────┴──────────────────────────────────┴──────────────────┘
```

4-17   The Main menu for NU (version 4.5AE).

```
┌──────────────────────────────────────────────────────────────────────────┐
│                        ═══ Main Menu Help ═══                              │
│                                                                            │
│     Explore Disk            View or edit data                              │
│                             Edit FAT, Directory, Hex, and Partition Table  │
│                             Search for data                                │
│                             View information on item                       │
│                             Copy data from one area of disk to another     │
│                                                                            │
│     Unerase                 Recover lost or erased files                   │
│                                                                            │
│     Disk information        Map disk usage                                 │
│                             Report technical information on your disk       │
│  ───────────────────────────────── Keys ─────────────────────────────────│
│                                                                            │
│     Esc                     Back-up to the previous menu                   │
│     F10                     Exit to DOS                                    │
│     Enter                   Select a menu item                             │
│     Up arrow                Move highlight up                              │
│     Down arrow              Move highlight down                            │
│     letter                  You can select a menu by typing the letter shown│
│                             in bright, such as the D in "Disk information"  │
│                                                                            │
│                        Press any key to continue...                        │
└──────────────────────────────────────────────────────────────────────────┘
```

4-18   The Main menu helpscreen (version 4.5AE).

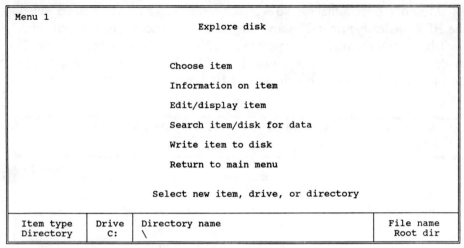

```
Menu 1
                              Explore disk


                       Choose item

                       Information on item

                       Edit/display item

                       Search item/disk for data

                       Write item to disk

                       Return to main menu


                  Select new item, drive, or directory

 ┌────────────┬───────┬──────────────────────────┬──────────────┐
 │ Item type  │ Drive │ Directory name           │ File name    │
 │ Directory  │ C:    │ \                        │ Root dir     │
 └────────────┴───────┴──────────────────────────┴──────────────┘
```

4-19 The Explore Disk menu (version 4.5AE).

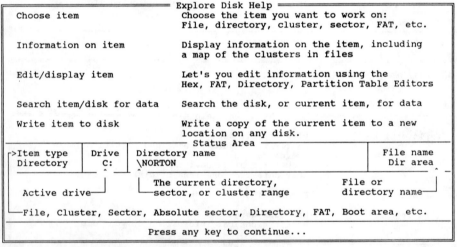

```
═══════════════════ Explore Disk Help ═══════════════
Choose item              Choose the item you want to work on:
                         File, directory, cluster, sector, FAT, etc.

Information on item      Display information on the item, including
                         a map of the clusters in files

Edit/display item        Let's you edit information using the
                         Hex, FAT, Directory, Partition Table Editors

Search item/disk for data  Search the disk, or current item, for data

Write item to disk       Write a copy of the current item to a new
                         location on any disk.
                  ─────── Status Area ───────
>Item type   │ Drive │ Directory name           │ File name
 Directory   │ C:    │ \NORTON                  │ Dir area

   Active drive┘        The current directory,    File or
                        sector, or cluster range  directory name┘

 └─File, Cluster, Sector, Absolute sector, Directory, FAT, Boot area, etc.

              Press any key to continue...
```

4-20 The Explore Disk helpscreen (version 4.5AE).

```
Menu 1.1
                              Choose item

                           Change drive

                           change Directory

                           File

                           cLuster

                           Sector

                           Absolute sector

                           Return to Explore disk


                     Select a file
┌──────────────┬───────┬─────────────────────────────────┬──────────────┐
│ Item type    │ Drive │ Directory name                  │ File name    │
│ Directory    │ C:    │ \                               │ Root dir     │
└──────────────┴───────┴─────────────────────────────────┴──────────────┘
```

4-21 The Choose Item menu (version 4.5AE).

```
═══════════════════════ Choose Item Help ═══════════════════════
Change drive            To select an item from another disk

change Directory        Change to another directory using a visual tree

File                    Select file or directory clusters (from the
                        current directory)

cLuster                 Select a single or range of clusters

Sector                  Select a single or range of sectors

Absolute sector         Select a single or range of absolute sectors

───────────────── Choosing special items ─────────────────

Dir area                Choose the "Dir area" pseudo-file

FAT and Boot areas      Change to the root directory ( \ ) and choose
                        the pseudo-files FAT area or Boot area

Partition Table         Select Absolute sector Side 0, Cylinder 0, Sector 1

                        Press any key to continue...
```

4-22 The Choose Item helpscreen (version 4.5AE).

DiskEdit **69**

```
Menu 1.1.3
                        Select file or sub-directory

        Boot area          capture.txt        spooler2.com
        FAT area           clock.bat          treeinfo.ncd
        Root dir           clock5.com
        ARC                command.com
        DH                 config.sys
        EWT                dh.bat
        GAME               flushot2.com
        NU_REF             flushot2.inf
        SPRINT             frecover.bak
        TEST               frecover.dat
        USA                frecover.idx
        ZIP                ibmbio.com
        ansi.sys           ibmdos.com
        autoexec.bat       sd.ini


                    30 entries to choose from
                    Speed search:
┌─────────────────┬──────────┬───────────────────────────────┬─────────────────┐
│ Item type       │ Drive    │ Directory name                │ File name       │
│ Directory       │ C:       │ \                             │ Root dir        │
└─────────────────┴──────────┴───────────────────────────────┴─────────────────┘
```

4-23 The Select File menu (version 4.5AE).

```
══════════════════ Select File Help ══════════════════

  Cursor keys          Move the highlight between file names

  Enter                Choose the file name under the highlight

  Esc                  Back up to the "Choose item" menu

  Speed search         If you start typing, the highlight will move to the
                       first name that matches the characters typed so far


  Other directories    Press Esc to back up to "Choose item" and use
                       "change Directory" to change directories

  FAT or Boot area     Choose the FAT area pseudo-file from the root
                       directory ( \ )

  Partition Table      Press Esc to back up to "Choose item" and select
                       the Absolute sector 0, 0, 1, 1


                       Press any key to continue...
```

4-24 The Select File helpscreen (version 4.5AE).

```
┌ Root dir ══════════════════════════════════════════════ Directory format ┐
║ Sector 133 in root directory                                Offset 0, hex 0
║                                                                  Attributes
║ Filename Ext      Size      Date      Time     Cluster  Arc R/O Sys Hid Dir Vol
║ ─────────────────────────────────────────────────────────────────────────────
║ IBMBIO   COM     23591    5-27-88   12:00 pm       2    Arc R/O Sys Hid
║ IBMDOS   COM     30648    5-27-88   12:00 pm      14    Arc R/O Sys Hid
║ Data Dis k                11-09-88   1:38 am                               Vol
║ ARC                        3-16-89  12:36 am      29                   Dir
║ DH                        10-26-88  10:18 pm      30                   Dir
║ EWT                       10-15-88   6:20 pm      31                   Dir
║ GAME                      10-15-88   7:30 pm      37                   Dir
║ NU_REF                    11-09-88  11:51 pm      38                   Dir
║ SPRINT                     3-23-89   9:35 pm      39                   Dir
║ TEST                      12-11-88  11:24 pm      40                   Dir
║ USA                        4-13-89   7:30 pm      43                   Dir
║ ZIP                        3-26-89   9:27 pm      44                   Dir
║ ANSI     SYS     1709    5-27-88   12:00 pm     2017
║ AUTOEXEC BAT      153    4-22-89    9:04 pm     2039    Arc
║ CAPTURE  TXT       96    1-12-89   10:54 pm     2040    Arc
║ CLOCK    BAT        9    3-11-89   11:24 pm     2041    Arc
║ ═══════════════════════════════════════════════════════════════════════════════
║          Filenames beginning with 'σ' indicate erased entries
║                       Press Enter to continue
1Help    2Hex    3Text    4Dir    5FAT    6Partn  7        8Choose 9Undo    10QuitNU
```

4-25 The Root directory in Directory format (version 4.5AE).

```
┌ Root dir ══════════════════════════════════════════════════════ Hex format ┐
║ Sector 133 in root directory                                    Offset 0, hex 0
║ 49424D42 494F2020 434F4D27 00000000 00000000 00000060 IBMBIO   COM'..........`
║ BB100200 275C0000 49424D44 4F532020 434F4D27 00000000 ***.'\..IBMDOS  COM'....
║ 00000000 00000060 BB100E00 B8770000 44617461 20446973 .......`***.*w..Data Dis
║ 6B202008 00000000 00000000 0000D20C 69110000 00000000 k  *.........**i*......
║ 41524320 20202010 20202020 00000000 00000000 00008C04 ARC       *.........**
║ 70121D00 00000000 44482020 20202020 20202010 00000000 p**......DH        *....
║ 00000000 000041B2 5A111E00 00000000 45575420 20202020 ......A*Z**.....EWT
║ 20202010 00000000 00000000 00008792 4F111F00 00000000 *.........**O**.....
║ 47414D45 20202020 20202010 00000000 00000000 0000D69B GAME      *.........**
║ 4F112500 00000000 4E555F52 45462020 20202010 00000000 O*%.....NU_REF    *....
║ 00000000 000070BE 69112600 00000000 53505249 4E542020 ......p*i*&.....SPRINT
║ 20202010 00000000 00000000 00006EAC 77122700 00000000 *.........n*w*'....
║ 54455354 20202020 20202010 00000000 00000000 00000BBB TEST      *.........**
║ 8B112800 00000000 55534120 20202020 20202010 00000000 **(.....USA       *....
║ 00000000 0000C39B 8D122B00 00000000 5A495020 20202020 ......****+.....ZIP
║ 20202010 00000000 00000000 00006AAB 7A122C00 00000000 *.........j*z*,.....
║ 414E5349 20202020 53595300 00000000 00000000 00000060 ANSI    SYS..........`
║ BB10E107 AD060000 4155544F 45584543 42415420 00000000 ******..AUTOEXECBAT ....
║ 00000000 000097A8 9612F707 99000000 43415054 55524520 ......*******...CAPTURE
║ 54585420 00000000 00000000 0000CBB6 2C12F807 60000000 TXT .........**,***`...
║ 434C4F43 4B202020 42415420 00000000 00000000 00000BBB CLOCK   BAT .........**
║ 6B12F907 09000000         Press Enter to continue     k*.**...
1Help    2Hex    3Text    4Dir    5FAT    6Partn  7        8Choose 9Undo    10QuitNU
```

4-26 The Root directory in HEX format (version 4.5AE). Non-printing characters have been changed to a ''*,'' while the actual HEX code has not.

```
====================== Hex Editor Help ======================

   Enter, Esc          Save (or discard) your editing changes
   Tab                 Switch between Hex (left) and ASCII (right) windows
   Backspace           Undo changes to the byte under the cursor
   Cursor keys         Move the cursor through the data
   PgDn, PgUp          Move to the next or previous page of data
   Home, End           Move to the first or last page in the item

                                   Advanced Edition only

   F1      Display this help screen      F4      Directory Editor
   F2      Hex Editor                    F5      FAT Editor
   F3      Text display                  F6      Partition Table Editor

   ─────────── FAT or Partition Table Editing (AE only) ───────────

   FAT                 Under Choose item, select the FAT area
                       pseudo-file from the root directory ( \ )

   Partition Table     Under Choose item, select the Absolute sector
                       Side 0, Cylinder 0, Sector 1

                       Press any key to continue...
```

4-27   The HEX editor helpscreen (version 4.5AE).

Now that NDD (Norton Disk Doctor) has been added to the Utility package, isn't NU (Norton Utility) unnecessary?

By no means. Many recovery operations can only be done using NU. A few special features require the power of NU to perform, such as hiding directories.

How many more changes can be made to NU before it is fully mature?

I wouldn't even want to hazard a guess. Let me put it to you this way: when you can no longer send a want list to Peter Norton of additions you'd like to see, the program may be nearing its maturity.

I've never seen a partition table.

The following illustration, Fig. 4-28, is the Partition Table, displayed by NU when it accessed my AT clone. It appears a bit different from an IBM because I'm running Compaq DOS. The help screen shown in Fig. 4-29 briefly explains what you are seeing.

I've added the help screens so that you can get a better feel for what can be done and also see just how dangerous it is to get into this area and play.

As long as you're showing off, how about a picture of a FAT?

Your wish is my command. The following illustration, Fig. 4-30, shows part of the first FAT from the C drive of my clone. Only part of the FAT is shown, and there is a second copy of the FAT in the sectors following it. Again, the help screen is provided in Fig. 4-31 so you can better understand how to do any editing necessary.

```
┌ Sector 0-1 ═════════════════════════════════════ Partition Table format ═┐
│ Sector 0 in Boot Area                                                     │
│                                                                           │
│                       Extended Partition Editor                           │
│                                                                           │
│┌──────┬────┬─────────────────────┬─────────────────────┬──────────┬─────────┐
││      │    │  Starting location  │  Ending location    │ Relative │Number of│
││System│Boot│Side Cylinder Sector │Side Cylinder Sector │ Sectors  │ Sectors │
│├──────┼────┼─────────────────────┼─────────────────────┼──────────┼─────────┤
││  ?   │Yes │ 32    366    33     │ 32    357    43     │1752637561│1914728037│
││  ?   │Yes │ 97    377    36     │ 13     10    36     │1936278541│1868701803│
││  ?   │Yes │ 11    102    32     │ 10    373    44     │1126458738│ 779251823│
││  ?   │Yes │ 67    333    15     │ 65    288    17     │ 859322673│2151102509│
│└──────┴────┴─────────────────────┴─────────────────────┴──────────┴─────────┘
│                                                                           │
│                                                                           │
│                                                                           │
│                       Press Enter to continue                             │
│1Help    2Hex    3Text   4Dir    5FAT     6Partn  7         8Choose 9Undo  10QuitNU
```

4-28 A Partition Table (version 4.5AE). Drive C is running Compaq DOS 3.31.

```
┌══════════════════════ Partition Table Editor Help ══════════════════════┐
│                                                                          │
│  Each line of the Table represents one of the four possible partitions   │
│  of a DOS hard disk.  The System entry can have three values:            │
│                                                                          │
│     ?            Indicates a non-DOS partition                           │
│     DOS-12       DOS partition with a 12-bit FAT (DOS 2.0 and above)      │
│     DOS-16       DOS partition with a 16-bit FAT (DOS 3.0 and above)      │
│                                                                          │
│  Careful, now!  Be wary of setting more than one DOS partition.          │
│                                                                          │
│  ─────────────────────────────── Keys ─────────────────────────────────  │
│  Enter, Esc           Save (or discard) your editing changes             │
│  Tab, Shift-Tab       Move to next or previous field                     │
│  Space                Cycle through System and Boot values               │
│  F9                   Undo changes to the entry under the cursor         │
│  Cursor keys          Move the cursor through the data                   │
│                                                                          │
│                                       Advanced Edition only              │
│  F1     Display this help screen      F4        Directory Editor         │
│  F2     Hex Editor                    F5        FAT Editor               │
│  F3     Text display                  F6        Partition Table Editor   │
│                                                                          │
│                    Press any key to continue...                          │
└──────────────────────────────────────────────────────────────────────────┘
```

4-29 The Partition Table helpscreen (version 4.5AE).

You aren't in quite as much danger here. NDD can repair most of the damage you can do, so long as you only play with one copy of the FAT. If you insist on messing up both copies, all could be lost.

Now that you've seen representations of both FATS, I suggest that you not mess with yours until you know what you are doing. NDD can correct many of the problems that you might have involving these areas, and NU can correct all of them so long as you key in the proper information. Do not make any changes to either of these areas just for the sheer joy of making changes.

```
    3        4        5        6        7        8        9       10       11       12       13    <EOF>
   15       16       17       18       19       20       21       22       23       24       25       26
   27       28    <EOF>    <EOF>    <EOF>    <EOF>    <EOF>    <EOF>    <EOF>    <EOF>    <EOF>    <EOF>
<EOF>    <EOF>       41    <EOF>    <EOF>    <EOF>    <EOF>    <EOF>       47       48       49       50
   51       52       53       54       55       56       57       58    <EOF>    <EOF>    <EOF>       62
   63       64    <EOF>    <EOF>       67       68    <EOF>       70       71       72       73       74
   75       76       77       78       79       80       81       82       83       84       85       86
   87       88    <EOF>    <EOF>    <EOF>    <EOF>    <EOF>    <EOF>    <EOF>    <EOF>       97       98
   99      100      101      102      103      104      105    <EOF>    <EOF>      108      109      110
<EOF>      112      113      114      115      116      117      118    <EOF>      120    <EOF>      122
  123      124      125      126      127      128      129      130      131      132      133      134
  135      136    <EOF>    <EOF>      139      140      141      142      143      144      145      146
  147      148      149      150      151      152      153    <EOF>      155      156      157      158
  159      160      161      162      163      164      165      166      167    <EOF>      169      170
  171      172      173      174      175      176      177      178      179      180      181      182
  183      184      185      186      187      188      189      190      191      192      193    <EOF>
  195      196      197      198      199      200      201      202      203      204      205      206
  207      208      209      210      211      212      213    <EOF>      215    <EOF>      217      218
  219      220      221      222      223      224      225      226      227      228      229      230

                        Press Enter to continue
1Help    2Hex    3Text    4Dir    5FAT    6Partn   7        8Choose 9Undo    10QuitNU
```

4-30   A FAT screen (version 4.5AE).

```
================= FAT Editor Help =================

   Enter, Esc        Save (or discard) your editing changes
   Tab, Shift-Tab    Move to next or previous field
   B                 Mark cluster with <BAD> value
   E                 Set cluster to <EOF> value
   F9                Undo changes to the entry under the cursor
   Cursor keys       Move the cursor through the data
   PgDn, PgUp        Move to the next or previous screen
   Home, End         Move to the first or last entry in the directory

   ------------------- Function Keys -------------------

                              Advanced Edition only

   F1    Display this help screen    F4    Directory Editor
   F2    Hex Editor                  F5    FAT Editor
   F3    Text display                F6    Partition Table Editor

                Press any key to continue...
```

4-31   The FAT helpscreen (version 4.5AE).

Have I repeated myself enough to make the point? Following very old Jewish tradition, let me say it one more time; do not mess around in the Partition Table or File Allocation Table areas unless you know exactly what you are doing. Enough said.

5
CHAPTER

Disk Monitor

Directory name   **DISKMON.EXE**
                                                       or
                                                       DM.EXE

Disk Monitor (DM) is a new Utility in version 5.0. It is a response to the apparently growing need for a better means of protecting systems from unnecessary problems. I cannot explain why it is so necessary to protect systems from outside destruction; such a thing shouldn't be happening. Still, like so many other things in today's world, even the churches have to lock their doors.

Command line usage

Format: DISKMON [switch] [switch] …

Switches
/STATUS   Tells DM to display its current status. This includes monitor on/off and drive light on/off.

/PROTECT+

> Turns DM on. The configuration will be the last one you selected. If you have not selected one, the default values are used.

/PROTECT−

> Turns DM off.

/LIGHT+ Starts displaying the small window in the upper right-hand corner of your screen when a hard disk is in use. It turns on and off just like a drive light on the CPU case, but it's smarter. It also displays the letter of the drive being accessed.

/LIGHT− Turns this feature off.

/PARK Moves all disk-drive heads to a safe location. Turn off the power immediately after the window appears. It is possible that the heads will be moved if the system remains under power for a length of time after this command is issued.

/UNINSTAL

> Removes the DM program from RAM. In order to use this switch, DM must be the last TSR program loaded. If it isn't, you must unload all the programs that came after it in order to unload DM.
>
> Be careful with your TSRs. They are not all well-behaved, and conflicts can arise. Install only those you need. Also, they all consume RAM space. When all is said and done, you will still require enough RAM to run the application programs that are the real purpose for your system.

Network considerations

DM works well with networks. It can protect local and network drives, but it cannot protect the System Area of the file server. Because most file servers have some type of self-protection for their System Area, this shouldn't leave too big a gap in your security.

The disk light feature of DM can be very useful to many users. With the CPU case in an out-of-the-way location, it can remove the doubt about which drive is being accessed and whether or not the last command is actually working.

The Disk Park feature of DM will only work for the drives of the PC on which it is running. This doesn't cause problems for the network unless the system remains connected too long after the command is issued.

Disk Monitor is a menu-driven Utility that opens with a selection screen. Figure 5-1 shows the options and the current status of the features. In this example, the features are both turned off. In order to change the status of the Protect feature, you have to select that option and move to the next screen.

Figure 5-2 shows the areas to be protected and what file types are offered. The available protection ranges from just the Systems Area to the entire disk.

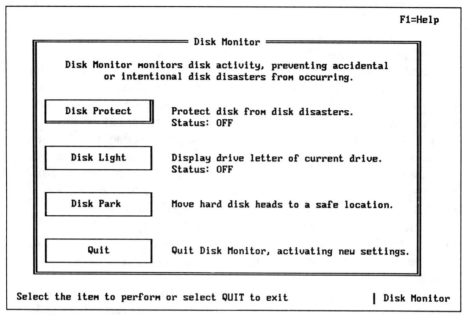

5-1 The Opening screen for Disk Monitor.

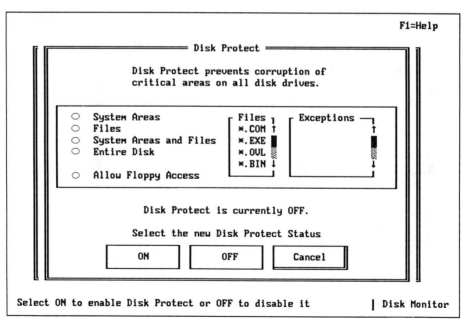

5-2 Protecting portions of the disk from unverified writes.

When selecting the files to be protected, you can either protect all of the files with a given extension, or you may exempt some by name. This flexibility may be a bit confusing at first, but with a little planning, you can protect without denying yourself access to your own data. If you protect everything, you will have to give yourself permission to write to the hard disk every time that you want to access your data.

The Allow Floppy Access option, when selected, means that you are free to format floppies without DM questioning every disk write.

Remember that your selections will apply to all drives; there is no option to change that. Thus, you may want to leave DM in the off state most of the time; having to press the RETURN key every time a portion of a program is loaded into memory or data is written back to the disk can be time consuming.

When the data is important enough to demand protection, then a little extra time and effort is worthwhile. One way to reduce the number of times you are asked for write permission is to turn DM off during selected operations. Using the /PROTECT− and /PROTECT+ switches in batch files to load programs is one way that you can retain protection without slowing down your work.

There are only two options for the Disk Light—on or off. Figure 5-3 illustrates the window that opens when you select this option. The window tells you the current status and also allows you to change it or exit without making any changes.

Stand-alone users may not think that they need to consider any type of protection scheme for their system. When they aren't there, the system is off; and when

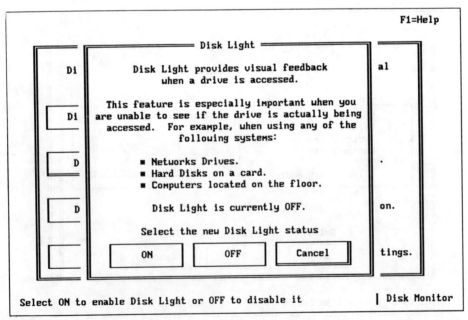

5-3 Toggling your disk light.

they are, they can control what is entered into it. For users without modems, this is almost true. For users who only obtain software in sealed packages from the developer, it is also almost true.

Many users don't fit into this model, though. Data exchanges via "sneaker" nets as well as electronic nets enter systems with increasing regularity. Under most circumstances, there isn't much need to worry about the integrity of the data. Only when the sender isn't sure about the integrity of the disk is there possible cause for concern.

One area that sometimes slips past many of the security checks in effect by users and employers is the disk itself. Picking up just any disk to write a file to so that it can be transferred to another system can be dangerous. To reduce the possibilities of problems from this source, use only diskettes that you are able to certify as "clean."

By clean, I mean that you have at least reformatted the disk before you write data to it and give it to another user. I use WipeDisk (and now, the WipeInfo Utility) to electronically erase everything from the disk first. Then I reformat it and place a clean label on it. I use these diskettes to send articles to magazines and manuscripts to publishers.

Working with clean disks reassures me to receive that only the information I want the editor or publisher is on the disk. Also, I'm sure that the disk is in good shape electronically. If there were any bad sectors, the reformat found them and marked them, reducing the possibility of your getting calls from irate individuals who were expecting your work and got only a mess.

There is nothing foolproof that can be done about what happens to diskettes, no matter how well protected, while they are in transit. Stiff mailers and large, bright-colored warning labels help. In spite of all of this, I have still received well-folded diskettes. Still, under most circumstances, the only real loss is the time waiting for a second shipment.

Electronic transfers of data do eliminate this problem, which is one of the many reasons that DM is so important. In order to accomplish electronic transfer, your system must be connected to another system. Most often, these systems will not be physically close. The gap is filled either by a direct-dialed telephone connection or by one of the public switching networks.

The other method of transfer is via a bulletin-board system (BBS). There are many local hobbyists who operate this type of service for free (or for a very small charge) for the users in their area. Many of the better local boards become known nationally, and users from all over call in to exchange information. The other type of BBS is the subscription service board. CompuServe and DELPHI are two examples of this type of BBS. They charge you for the time you are connected to them.

The various special interest areas of these services are not maintained by the staff of the service. Remote operators (or SYSOPs) are paid to perform this duty. Both the SYSOP and the service staff are very concerned with the data that comes and goes via their service. To this end, almost all of the programs you find on these services have been tested.

It would be nice if you could get a guarantee that every program is clean. I feel sure that it would be done if it were possible. Without getting into too much detail, there is a difference between a program that doesn't run on your system and one that can cause damage. Some users have issued false alarms because they were unable to run a program and cried "foul" before checking all of the details. All of the commercial services have an 800 (toll-free) Customer Service number. If you have a real problem, report it. With DM watching over your disks and data, you should be able to discover any problems before they do any real damage.

6
CHAPTER

DiskReet

Directory name   **DISKREET.EXE**
                                                        or
                                                        DR.EXE

DiskReet is a new Utility in version 5.0. It will encrypt and decrypt your files, encrypting them under a password and decrypting them only when you provide the correct password. In the event that you lose the password, the file information must be considered lost.

Still, any lock can be picked. If enough time, effort, and expertise are applied, you may be able to recover the contents of an encrypted file without access to the password. However, you must decide if this type of effort is justified. Under the majority of circumstances, the investment isn't warranted.

Command line usage

Format: DISKREET [switch] [switch] ...

The following switches are available from the command-line:

?   Displays a summary of the command-line switches available.

/ENCRYPT:*filename*
> Encrypts the specified file(s).

/DECRYPT:*filename*
> Decrypts the specified file(s).

/PASSWORD:*xxxxxxx*
> The password for encrypting or decrypting. Up to ten alphanumeric characters may be used.

/SHOW:*drive*
> Show NDisks (clears the Hidden attribute).

/HIDE:*drive*
> Hide NDisks (sets the Hidden attribute).

/CLOSE   Close all open NDisks.

/ON   Enables the DiskReet device driver.

/OFF   Disables the DiskReet device driver.

/SKIPUMB
> Prevents DiskReet from loading itself into an Upper Memory Block. Use this switch when memory management software is being used to load application programs into high-DOS memory. This will prevent conflicts.

Network considerations

NDisks cannot be created or accessed on a network drive. However, you can copy an NDisk to the network drive for storage purposes. Files may be encrypted and decrypted on a network.

Other considerations

The other Utilities (Disk Doctor, Disk Editor, UnErase, SysInfo, and WipeInfo) will work with NDisk but cannot decrypt it or the files it contains. Encrypted files are no different to the Utilities than clear-text files. NDisks will display as fixed file blocks when you run SpeeDisk.

Multiple-user computers may be as common as multi-user systems. In either case, there may be a need to keep some files confidential. Passwords or other types of limiting access may work in some environments. Where this very basic method is inadequate, another level of security is required. Encrypting is the most reasonable possibility at the present time. The DiskReet Utility is simple to use and contains two methods of encryption. The less secure proprietary method is faster than the more secure DES method; you should choose the more appropriate encoder.

Both methods use the password you supply in their operation, which is why it is so important to select the proper alphanumeric for a password and then remember it. Remember, combination may contain any number (up to 10) of both alphabetical and numerical characters. I recommend a total of 10 because it provides the best balance of speed and security for your file(s). Incidentally, spaces are not allowed in a password.

If you aren't going to encrypt many files, you may find it easier to do them individually. Figure 6-1 shows the opening panel, while Fig. 6-2 shows the File Selection panel. Each file or file group may be encrypted with an individual password, or you may use the same password for all encrypted files. Individual passwords for each file have the advantage of both not providing as many clues for decrypting while requiring the security of more passwords. An alternate to the one password for all files might be the NDisk.

An NDisk is another logical drive within one of your existing drives. Figure 6-3 illustrates an NDisk created within the C drive. Because it's an illustration drive and not one that is going to be used, it is small (19 kilobytes).

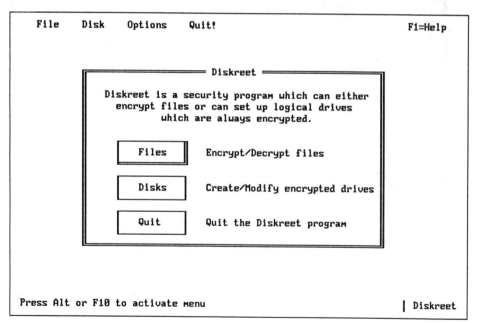

6-1 The Opening screen for DiskReet.

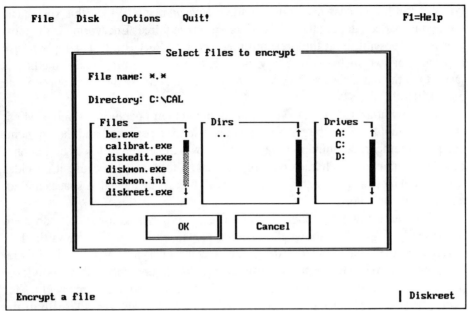

File   Disk   Options   Quit!   F1=Help

══════════════ Select files to encrypt ══════════════

File name: *.*

Directory: C:\CAL

┌─ Files ─────────┐   ┌─ Dirs ─────────┐   ┌─ Drives ─┐
│ be.exe   ↑ │   │ ..   ↑ │   │ A: ↑ │
│ calibrat.exe   │   │   │   │ C: │
│ diskedit.exe   │   │   │   │ D: │
│ diskmon.exe   │   │   │   │   │
│ diskmon.ini   │   │   │   │   │
│ diskreet.exe ↓ │   │   ↓ │   │   ↓ │
└─────────────────┘   └────────────────┘   └──────────┘

┌──────────────┐   ┌──────────────┐
│   OK   │   │   Cancel   │
└──────────────┘   └──────────────┘

Encrypt a file | Diskreet

6-2 Selecting files to encrypt.

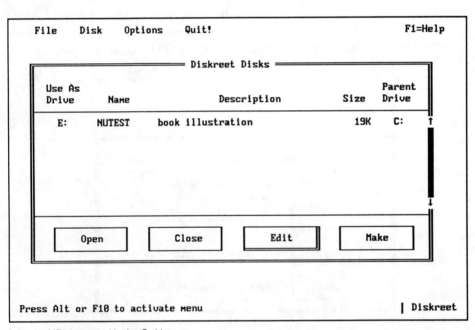

File   Disk   Options   Quit!   F1=Help

════════════════ Diskreet Disks ════════════════

Use As   Parent
Drive   Name   Description   Size Drive

  E: NUTEST   book illustration   19K   C: ↑

                                                    ↓

┌──────────┐   ┌──────────┐   ┌──────────┐   ┌──────────┐
│   Open   │   │ Close   │   │   Edit   │   │   Make   │
└──────────┘   └──────────┘   └──────────┘   └──────────┘

Press Alt or F10 to activate menu | Diskreet

6-3 An NDisk created in the C drive.

When you create an NDisk, you must set the various options you want. Figure 6-4, the Edit window, shows some of them. Advertising the fact that you have a secured information area in the system is almost like asking someone to try and break in. The fewer indications you can provide, the better. As a check on things, the audit info can provide an indication of possible problems; it displays the NDisk Creation date, the Password Change date, the Number of Unsuccessful Entry attempts, and the Number of Successful Entries.

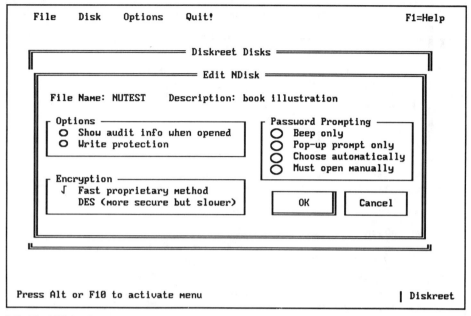

6-4 The NDisk edit screen.

After you have established the NDisk area, you have an option to have more than one drive letter for NDisks. In order to change the default value from 1 to the maximum of 5, you must know the password. Figure 6-5 illustrates the window that opens when you are making your first NDisk. Regardless of the number of NDisks in the system, only one may be open at any time; this helps to reduce the possibility of compromise.

The contents of your NDisks are secure from the usual peeking and prying, but they are still subject to the problems associated with data on hard disks. You should make backups of your NDisk files just like you should be making copies of your other data files. Copying encrypted files to a floppy diskette will not make it any easier for an unauthorized person to view or decrypt your files.

For those of you who have problems with unnecessary fingers roaming your keyboard, DiskReet provides a solution. As shown in Fig. 6-6, you can select to lock your keyboard when you leave your system on but unattended. Also notice that the screen is cleared. Clearing the screen may not be necessary in some cases, but it makes it obvious that you don't want anyone messing with your computer.

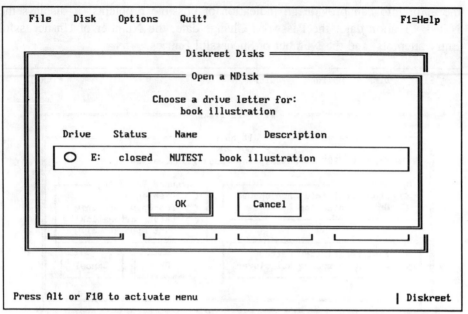

6-5 The NDisk Drive Letter screen.

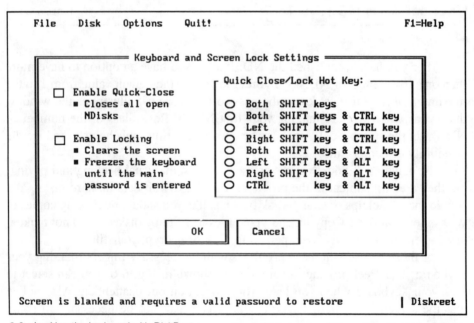

6-6 Locking the keyboard with DiskReet.

7
CHAPTER

Disk Tool

Directory name   **DISK TOOL.EXE**

The Disk Tool Utilities aren't really new; they were part of the Disk Doctor Utility in an earlier version. In version 5.0, they have improved functions and expanded menus, making it easier for you to use each tool.

Command line usage

    Format: DISKTOOL

There are no available parameters or switches that can be used with this Utility.

Network considerations

This Utility is compatible enough to be run on a PC connected to a network but is not designed to work on any remote disk(ette)(s).

When you run Disk Tool, you will see the panel shown in Fig. 7-1. Choosing the Continue option will take you to the Tool Selection panel (Fig. 7-2). The six utilities included on this screen are good, but they are not all of the tools you have available for recovery operations.

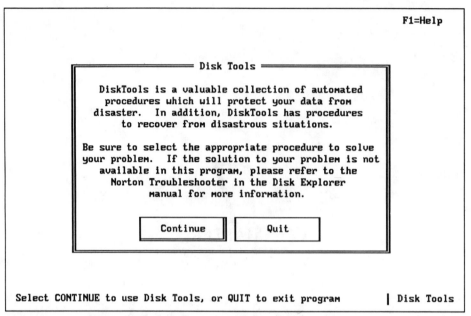

7-1 The Opening screen for Disk Tools.

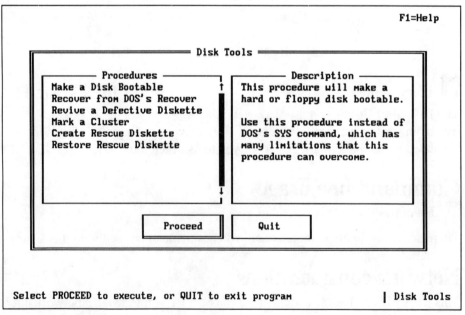

7-2 Selecting your tools.

Make a Disk Bootable is the solution to a diskette full of data which should be self-booting and isn't. If you try the DOS SYSTEM command, you will get the error message "no room for system files." This is a truth for DOS, though not an absolute one. This Utility will make room and transfer (copy) the necessary system files to your diskette.

It's no big secret how the Utility can make a disk bootable. Every disk(ette) has special areas that can hold only one type of data, some of these areas being the Boot Record area, the File Allocation Table, the System Files area, and the Directory area. When DOS writes information to a disk, then, it writes it to the proper area. When you use a disk(ette) that doesn't have system files on it, DOS will not use this area for additional information storage. Thus, Disk Tool can write the hidden files to the proper area without fear of overwriting any information already on the disk(ette).

Recover from DOS's Recover helps you retain all of the data on your backup diskettes that DOS doesn't seem to want to transfer back onto your hard disk. Again, the problems which cause DOS not to operate properly and are still solvable by Norton do not include physical or magnetic damage to the diskettes. A limited amount of file corruption can be replaced, but software still cannot perform miracles.

When you use the DOS BACKUP command, two files are written to each diskette. One is the control file, and the other is the data file. They are a *couple*, which means that neither works without the other and thus you cannot afford to lose either. DOS reads the control file and copies the data file. When it finds an error or anything else it is not expecting, it quits. When DOS does quit, it doesn't always leave the diskette files in the best condition. A relatively quick trip through the recovery ward can solve this problem. Remember that the filenames will be changed after this trip.

Revive a Defective Diskette can be a very useful Utility when you have diskettes that haven't been used in a long time, and it will still work on those that you have been using every day. This Utility refreshes the coding on the media. It doesn't remove or refresh the actual data, but it does restore the format information.

Diskettes that are used frequently will be continuously getting new data written on them. Unfortunately, the format information or addressing is not touched once the diskette has been formatted. This continual wiping by the drive's read/write heads can cause the coding to degrade. After a period of time, the coding may be too weak for the drive to even read. When this happens, you will no longer be able to access the information stored there.

Disks that are stored for long periods of time can suffer the same kind of coding degradation, which is why you should have proper storage conditions for your diskettes as well as regular rotation of backup diskettes. Remember, your information will be useless unless you can read it from the diskette. The stronger the data coding is, the better your chances of reading all of it correctly, a fact that holds true for format coding as well as information coding.

Mark a Cluster allows you to indicate that a cluster is bad or change a marked cluster to good. Marking a good cluster bad will do no harm. Disk Tool will move the information stored there to another good cluster and then mark the desired cluster. Taking the mark off a bad cluster could be disastrous, however. Without the mark on it, DOS will consider the cluster to be good and attempt to store information there. You could say that the information that goes into a bad cluster actually goes into a black hole or the "bit bucket." It goes in but it doesn't come out.

Create Rescue Diskette (see Fig. 7-3) is another of the "lifesaver" Utilities. It writes to a floppy the essential information for getting your system back in running order after a problem has been solved.

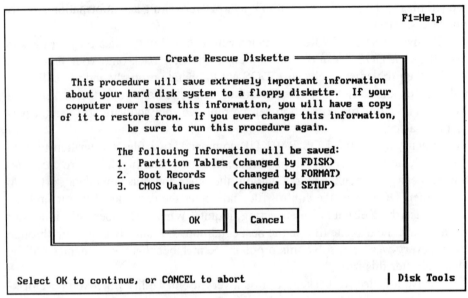

7-3 Creating a rescue diskette.

If you change the battery in an AT-class machine, the live memory that it has been powering dies. Thus, the information is no longer available to the system and you may have to go through a time-consuming reconfiguration sequence. If all of the needed information were on a diskette that could be run after the new battery is in place, however, the process would take only a few minutes.

Restore Rescue Diskette is the other part of this Utility. With it, you read the information on the diskette back into the system. Thus, in order to be most effective, you should make the rescue diskette just before shutting the system down for a battery change.

The assumption that you can control all of the conditions where a rescue diskette are useful is incorrect. I have used controlled conditions to illustrate the usefulness of the diskette. In order to obtain maximum recovery of information from a system crash, you may need to use every one of the helps available within the Norton Utilities.

The best time for a system problem to occur is immediately after you have made a complete backup. Since crashes never occur at the best possible time, however, it follows that system maintenance must be a continuing thing. Proper maintenance will reduce the number and magnitude of the problems to be solved before productive work can continue. Making rescue diskettes every time a backup is made takes very little time and saves hours of work if it is needed.

Learning how to make backups is at least as important as learning how to create the files that should be backed up. For whatever reason, many people feel that the information on their hard disk is as safe as that written in stone. Still, this has never been true, and even disk crashes fail to convince some. With the compression utilities available, including Norton BACKUP, it isn't a monumental task to make a backup copy of a hard disk. You don't even have to back up every file every time.

Application programs are already backed up on the distribution diskettes. The configuration and initialization files that they create when you customize them for your use should be backed up. If you have a sole-user system, however, these files are not likely to change as often as you make backups of other information. Also, not every data file is changed between backups.

Each user should be responsible for making a daily backup of the files that have been changed that day. At the end of the week, a backup of the important data and information files should be made and taken off-site. This removal ensures that the information is available for use on Monday morning, even if the hardware must be replaced. Once every quarter, a full backup should be made and stored off-site in a secure location. More often than this would even be better. Monthly backups of this nature would cut to one-third the amount of work required to restore the system. An annual backup can be compressed and stored off-site, so that if it becomes necessary to rebuild the history of a company or project, it can be done from accurate records. Your memories can be very selective when there has been a passage of time between the event and the requirement to recall details.

The monumental part comes in when you have no backup and must re-enter all of the data that was lost. Even worse is when you cannot find all of the information in order to re-enter it. Your creditors will be more than happy to provide information on how much you owe them, but verifying their figures without your records might prove difficult. Can you reasonably expect all of the people that owe you money to come forward and tell you exactly how much and when it is or was due? It would be nice if the world operated on an honor system, if a man's word was his bond and you could still seal a contract with a handshake.

I don't mean to say that honesty doesn't exist; I simply acknowledge that dishonesty does. The system of checks and balances is designed to keep people honest and reduce the losses when the worst happens. Failure to maintain accurate and current information on your areas of responsibility will result in costly consequences.

Regardless of the situation and the circumstances, each of us has responsibilities. There aren't conditions under which any thinking, mature adult can claim that they are totally without responsibility. It would be nice to not have a boss, not be responsible to someone who checks on what you are doing and how well you are doing it; but because this condition doesn't exist in this world, let's forget about the possibility. Assuming responsibility for yourself is a big step. Neither size, age, nor physical strength make it appear that you are a responsible person. Responsibility is a mental attitude that forces you to acknowledge that you are human and that you do make mistakes. It demands that you admit your mistakes. Responsibility also maintains that you don't take credit that belongs to other people.

Finger-pointing exercises will not recover lost data. Your ability to do your job depends upon your data, and your ability to retain your job may depend on how well you protect that data from loss. Accidents and errors will happen; but preventing them from being full-blown disasters requires assuming the responsibility to ensure that the system is maintained and backed up in a reasonable manner. An old adage asserts that "if you want the job done right, do it yourself." Your superiors will appreciate this concept, and your peers should respect it. If you are in a leadership position, then you will convince others better by example than you could ever hope to with words.

8
CHAPTER

FileFind

Directory name

FILEFIND.EXE
or
FF.EXE

FileFind in v5.0 is not the same FileFind (FF) Utility you remember from earlier editions. FF itself has been enhanced and combined with File Attributes (FA), FileDate (FD), FileSize (FS), and TextSearch (TS). This integrated package of Utilities does everything the others did as well as a few new things.

If you choose to use the short name for this new Utility, the INSTALL program will rename your existing FileFind Utility FL.EXE.

Command line usage

Format: FILEFIND [filespec] [search-text] [switches]

These are the command-line options available:

filespec   The name of the file to locate. The DOS wildcard characters * and ? may be used if the whole filename isn't known.

The search limits:

.   Search the current drive.

. \ *.*   Search the current directory only.

* : *.*   Search all drives.

search-text

This is the word(s) to be located within a filename which exists. Error handling on this is such that the Utility can cope with a "not found" result. The shorter and more unique the "search-text" is, the better your chance of finding that one certain location you really need to find. One of the problems that can occur in word processor files is that the processor could have placed either a carriage return or a page break between the words of your search string. If this happens, you will see a "not found."

Switches

/S   Include files in subdirectories.

/C   Search current directory.

/CS   Case-sensitive search.

Switch modifiers for the remaining switches:

[ ]   No modifier. Locate files with this attribute set.

−   Turn attribute off.

+   Turn attribute on.

/A   The archive attribute bit. Without modifier, locates files with attribute set on.

/R   The read-only attribute.

/HID   The Hidden attribute.

/SYS   The System attribute.

/CLEAR Clear all set attributes.

/D[*mm-dd-yy*]

Set file date to *mm-dd-yy*. If no new date is specified, the existing datestamp is deleted.

/T[*hh:mm:ss*]

Set file time to *hh:mm:ss*. If no date is specified, the existing timestamp is deleted.

/NOW   Set the time- and datestamps to the current system time and date.

/TARGET:*d*

Check drive *d:* to see if selected files will fit.

/O:*filename*

Save the list to *filename*.

/BATCH   Automatically exit FileFind.

Network considerations

FileFind will find files anywhere. It also has an Owner option that allows you to search network drives for files by owner in addition to the other search parameters you are able to set for a local search.

The Opening panel, shown here in Fig. 8-1, provides a starting place for your searches. Very little information is present at the beginning. Like all of the other menu variables in this new version, you fill in the blanks where the choices are not limited. Where the choices are limited, you can choose options from the listed items by pressing the SPACEBAR to fill in the open circles (or "bullets"). You can also de-select them by pressing the SPACEBAR a second time.

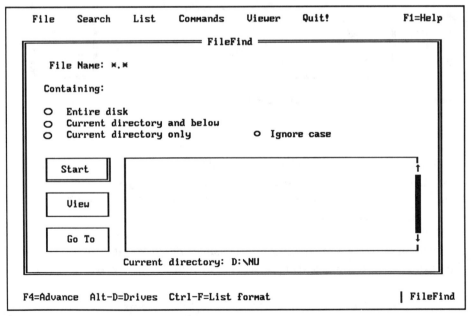

8-1 The Opening screen for FileFind.

Each of the words across the top of the screen is the tag for a pull-down menu. The number of options under the Quit tag are very limited—you can only exit the Utility.

The Advanced Search menu, seen in Fig. 8-2, provides a whole new set of parameters which can be used to more closely define the file you are attempting to locate. You don't have to use them if they aren't needed. Also, in some cases, using one reduces the need to use its mate. The Date pair is a good example; a date after last week would search until now, while a date before last week will search everything up until last week. Using both date parameters provides a very limited search range. This is good if you know the approximate datestamp of the file. The smaller the range, the faster the search.

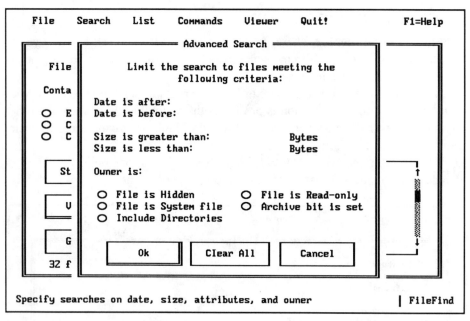

8-2   The Advanced Search options for FileFind.

You don't need to be anyplace in particular when you begin using FileFind. Once the program screen is displayed, you can move to any other location available. Figure 8-3 shows three subdirectories in this directory or two other drives that you may choose without entering a new directory name.

Remember that all of the Utilities are now mouse-compatible; jumping around to make quicker, bolder moves is possible. Better yet, this mouse compatibility extends to the new trackball versions of the mouse. To me, trackballs are the only way to go.

Changing the timestamp or datestamp on a file may not be one of your priority activities, but it is a very useful feature for those who exchange information between locations. Someone may take a few days and many hours to prepare the information; but, with a common time- and datestamp, the file group can easily be identified at either location. The information shown in Fig. 8-4 was current at the time the illustration was made and suggests (quite accurately) that I work late.

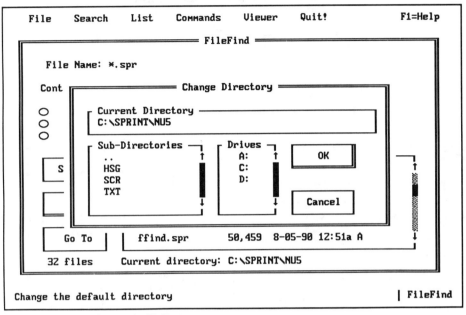

8-3 Changing the directory in FileFind.

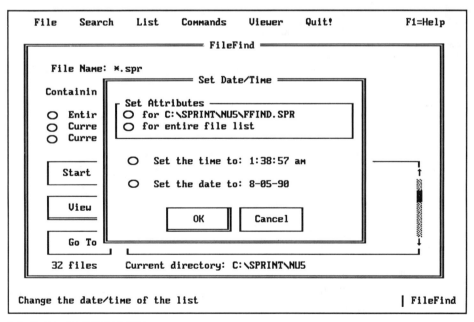

8-4 Setting the time and date.

The range of values allowed by either field is limited to valid times and dates. The Utility will not allow times over 24 hours nor dates which do not appear on our current calendar system.

The amount of information displayed and the order it takes are all set in the List Display window (see Fig. 8-5). The DOS standard-display format is Name, Size, and Date/Time. This format isn't an option here, which may or may not be a problem to some users. The displayed options should be more than adequate for the majority of uses. Knowing a file's set attributes shouldn't make any difference unless you are trying to change or delete it.

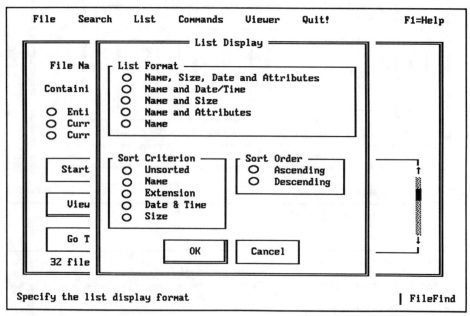

8-5 Formatting and sorting for listing.

Sorting the list is more important to me. Many of my files are date-sensitive. Being able to put newer files first or last makes my work easier. Ascending-order files begin with A or 1 and go up. Descending order is just the reverse.

How you retain a copy of the list of files you have generated is determined on the Print List Options panel (see Fig. 8-6). The options are a hardcopy or a media copy. Place solid balls in each of the open bullets that apply; the ARROW keys or the TAB key and SPACEBAR or the mouse clicks will toggle them. When you finish, you still have an option; you can retain your copy by tagging the OK box, or you can tag Cancel and forget the whole thing.

I continue to forget that not all disks are created equal. The A drive on my system will read and write both 360K and 1.2M floppies, while the B drive on another system I use will read and write 720K and 1.4M micro diskettes. I almost wore out my copy of FileSize (FS) from the last version of the Utilities trying to stay out of trouble with the DOS error message "Insufficient space" (see Fig. 8-7).

Running out of space before the end of a multi-file transfer is an avoidable problem. The list of files to be transferred is known, and the drive that holds the

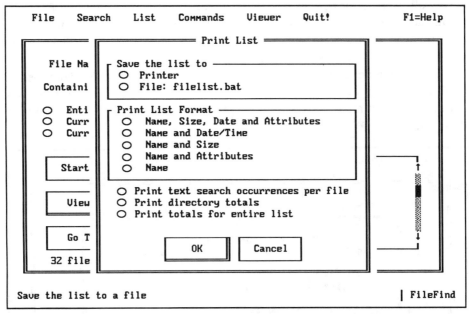

8-6 Formatting and sorting for printing.

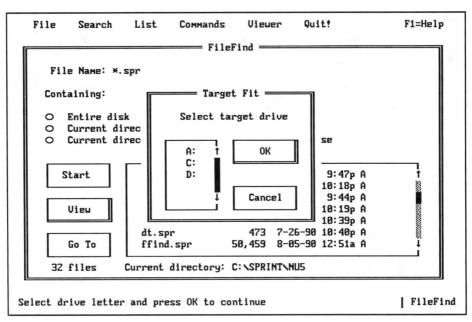

8-7 Reporting on FileFit.

disk(ette) where they are to go is also known. After you select the list, you select the target drive (Fig. 8-7 again).

FileFind will then determine just how much space your list of files currently occupies; how much space on the target disk(ette) is needed to hold the files; and, best of all, whether or not the list will fit on the target. For example, in Fig. 8-8, the list does not fit. I must admit that I set this example up; the list contains more bytes than the 360K diskette in the A drive can possibly hold, and the disk already contains a number of files.

This technique of forcing error messages has been used a number of times by book authors. If it weren't, you might never see an error message displayed. This doesn't reflect on my expertise as an operator but on the power and flexibility of these Utilities.

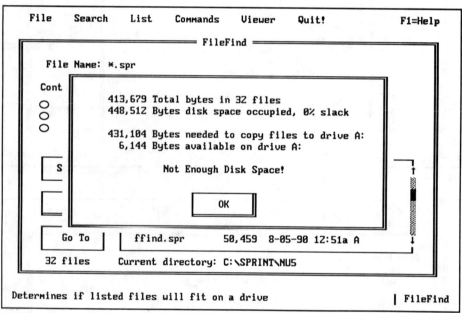

8-8   Preventing a fitting problem.

File Attributes version 4.0 & 4.5
Directory name   **FA.EXE**

Until you have FA.EXE or one of the later versions of MS-DOS, the attributes of the files on all of the disks you own are fixed. Under many normal conditions, this lack of control is not a problem. As shown later, however, these attributes or characteristics serve various purposes; being able to change them can be of benefit to most users. The FA program is an expansion of the functions found in the MS-DOS program ATTRIB.COM.

Format: Version 4.0 & 4.5

FA [d:] [path \ filename] [attribute switches] [switches] [> | > >]
[path \ filename|device]

The following command-line options are available:

path \ filename

> The drive, path, and filename specifications for the file to be changed. Using *.* will change all of the available files in the path.

> | > >   The DOS operators to redirect, or redirect and append, the output. There is no display when either operator is used.

/**R**   Read-only file which normally cannot be changed or deleted.

/**A**   Archive file. These files will be copied by an automatic backup program such as the DOS BACKUP program. This program also toggles this attribute off after the copy is made. DOS will turn it on again when a change is made to the file.

/**SYS**   Attribute of a hidden file that does not appear on the directory. It cannot be deleted by ordinary means. DOS uses two such files on disks that are self-booting.

/**HID**   Attribute of a Hidden file. These files are technically different from system files. They share the characteristics of not being visible on the directory and cannot be deleted by ordinary means.

These are the switches that control the functioning of the program:

+   Turns an attribute on.

−   Turns an attribute off.

/**S**   Instructs FA to include subdirectories in the specified path.

/**P**   Instructs FA to pause when the screen is full. Pressing any key will also pause the display. Pressing any key again will resume the scrolling display.

If one of the attributes listed above is included without the + or − switch, it becomes part of the file description. This means that the command

FA *.SYS /HID/R +

will add the read-only attribute to all system (.SYS) files that are also hidden files.

Figure 8-9 shows the directory of a sample disk using FA without making any changes.

```
A>FA B:*.*

FA-File Attributes, Advanced Edition, (C) 1988, Peter Norton

  B:\
     loader.sys      Archive Read-only Hidden System
     io.sys          Archive Read-only Hidden System
     msdos.sys       Archive Read-only Hidden System
     command.com     Archive Read-only
     cauzcomm.com    Archive
     cauzcomm.def    Archive
     emulate.com     Archive
     clock.com       Archive
     autoexec.bat    Archive

  9 files shown
  no files changed
```

To protect the .COM files from change or deletion, the read-only attribute is added as shown:

A > FA B:*.COM /R +

And the display looks like Fig. 8-10 below.

```
FA-File Attributes, Advanced Edition, (C) Copr 1988, Peter
Norton

  B:\
     command.com     Archive Read-only
     cauzcomm.com    Archive Read-only
     emulate.com     Archive Read-only
     clock.com       Archive Read-only

  4 files shown
  4 files changed
```

The full directory display now looks like Fig. 8-11 below.

```
FA-File Attributes, Version 3.10, (C) Copr 1984-86, Peter
Norton
  B:\
   Hidden System Read-only Archive  LOADER.SYS
   Hidden System Read-only Archive  IO.SYS
   Hidden System Read-only Archive  MSDOS.SYS
                 Read-only Archive  COMMAND.COM
                 Read-only Archive  CAUZCOMM.COM
                           Archive  CAUZCOMM.DEF
                 Read-only Archive  EMULATE.COM
                 Read-only Archive  CLOCK.COM
                           Archive  AUTOEXEC.BAT
```

The format change in the display for the new versions would be similar for this example also.

It would be possible to add the Hidden attribute to the COMMAND.COM, EMULATE.COM, and CLOCK.COM files so that they are not normally displayed when the DIRECTORY command is invoked but are still called by the AUTOEXEC.BAT file. Hiding these files would shorten the displayed directory.

FA without any parameters defaults to *.* and lists all of the files in the currently selected directory. Note that the NU program can display more information about the attributes of any file.

The Hidden and System attributes should not normally be removed. Expert users may be able to change these attributes without causing other problems. One exception might be during a housecleaning of a hard disk. By removing these attributes, all of the files will be listed to the printer or display. Then hidden data or copy-protected and extraneous files can be deleted by normal means.

Just prior to backing up a series of files, you could sort the backups by using the /A− and /A+ switches along with various location combinations. For example,

    FA *.* /A− /S

will toggle the Archive attribute off for all files in that path. The command

    FA *.DOC /A+ /S

will then toggle the Archive attribute on for the .DOC files in that path. After backing up those files, you could issue a command like

    FA *.DAT /A+ /S

to toggle the Archive attribute for the .DAT files. The Archive attribute was toggled off by the BACKUP program as it copied the .DOC files, which means that only the .DAT files will be copied on this pass. This sorted copying might provide a logical method for backing up a hard disk onto floppies.

The /CLEAR switch is equal to /A-/HID-/R-/SYS-. In essence, it removes all of the active attributes from the files specified or all of the files in the specified path.

Hiding files can be dangerous. Since they will no longer appear on the directory display, they could be forgotten.

Are there any limitations on which attributes can be set for which files?

Yes, the SYSTEM (/SYS) attribute should only be used with files that have an extension of .SYS. The read-only (/R) attribute should not be set (/R+) on any file that is subject to frequent changes.

An exception to this recommendation would be an AUTOEXEC.BAT file that you didn't want changed or deleted by another user. Read-only files cannot be deleted or destroyed using WipeFile unless confirmed. I've used this technique when setting up systems for new users; it prevents them from deleting everything, usually. If they learn enough to be able to change the read-only attribute, they should know better than to delete the file(s).

Do some programs hide files on purpose?

Yes, a number of copy-protection schemes use a signature file to verify that a legitimate copy of the program is being run. Don't worry about them unless you make changes in their attributes.

Are any of these Hidden files in danger if I use SpeeDisk (SD) or a similar defragmenter?

They are in no danger from SD, which recognizes that type of file and doesn't move it. They may be in danger from another program if it doesn't recognize the files and leaves them where it finds them.

I know that using the /H+ switch hides a file, is it possible to hide an entire subdirectory?

Yes, the process isn't quite as simple, but it's not really difficult. FA will not change the attributes of a subdirectory. To do that, you will have to use the Norton Utility (NU).

After making the subdirectory with either NCD or the DOS MD command, run NU and go to the Root directory. There you should see your new subdirectory. Use the TAB key to move the reverse video block over to the Hidden attribute column, and tap the SPACEBAR to turn the attribute on.

Do I have to do anything different to access a Hidden subdirectory?

About the only thing that is really different is that neither DOS nor NCD will display that subdirectory and its Hidden files. This means that you must remember at least the subdirectory name if you want to be able to get back into it.

Will the command FA /CLEAR change the subdirectory back to an unhidden one?

No, to unhide a subdirectory, you must use NU and reverse the attribute switch.

Does this mean that everything I can do with FA I can also do using NU?

Yes, with the big difference being that if you are only interested in changing file attributes, FA is much faster and easier to work with.

FileDate version 4.5
Directory name
FileDate is a new Utility in version 4.5. You can use it to set, change, or remove the timestamp and/or datestamp from any file(s) on any disk(s)/diskette(s) that are not write-protected.

FD.EXE

It has always been possible to change these items if you were willing to work at it; using NU and making entries directly to the time- and datestamp areas of the directory was perhaps one of the easier ways. Now, even I can do it without making too many mistakes.

Format: FD filespec [switches]

The following command-line switches are available:

/S   Include all of the subdirectories on the drive when searching for matches to filespec.

/P   Pause the display after each full screen of information. Press any key to continue.

Note: If this switch has not been included on the command line, you can still pause the display by pressing any key. A second key press will continue the display. Even if the /P switch has been included, the key press to pause toggle is still active.

/D*date*   Set the datestamp of the file(s) to *date*. The currently set date is cleared if no *date* is specified. The *date* should be in the format MMDDYY or the proper format for your country code.

Note: NO spaces between /D and date.

/T*time*   Set the timestamp of the file(s) to *time*. The currently set timestamp is cleared if no *time* is specified. The *time* should be in the format HH:MM:SS or the proper time format for your country code. Remember that DOS uses a 24-hour clock, so your afternoon/night time hours will be the hour +12 (i.e., 6PM is 18:00:00).

Note: No spaces between /T and time. If the /D and /T switches are not used, the new set time and date will be the current system time and date. Either way, this capability provides control of one more parameter. Now you know how the software developers are able to set the same date- and timestamp for a full disk of programs. For those of us who do not come under that heading, there are still useful applications. Sorting and backing up can be facilitated by using these parameters when there aren't any common filenames or extensions.

FD is also useful if you use the MAKE program which comes with many compilers. Consult your compiler manual for more information about the MAKE program.

Figure 8-12 shows our starting point.

8-12 A typical directory listing in DOS.

```
C:\>dir a:

Volume in drive A has no label
Directory of  A:\

TERM      LOG      4505     3-18-89    12:55a
TERM      SAV         0     1-05-89    11:13p
INSIDE    1         907    12-13-88    11:38p
DGTERM    ARC     15360     1-13-89    12:03a
FLUSHOT2  ARC      5120    12-10-88     5:36p
UNBLINK   COM      1920    12-20-88    12:35a
CLK26     COM       640    12-20-88    12:36a
ANN       MEN       709    12-24-88     1:58p
          8 File(s)     327680 bytes free
```

Using just one switch, either the time or the date can be changed. In Fig. 8-13, the /D switch with the date "1-1-89" was used. Figure 8-14 shows file dates that have been changed using the /T switch and a time of "12:34:56." Notice that DOS doesn't list the seconds and also rounds the minutes to reflect the closest time.

8-13 The same directory after FD with the /D switch active.

```
FD A:*.* /D1-1-89

TERM      LOG      4505     1-01-89    12:55a
TERM      SAV         0     1-01-89    11:13p
INSIDE    1         907     1-01-89    11:38p
DGTERM    ARC     15360     1-01-89    12:03a
FLUSHOT2  ARC      5120     1-01-89     5:36p
UNBLINK   COM      1920     1-01-89    12:35a
CLK26     COM       640     1-01-89    12:36a
ANN       MEN       709     1-01-89     1:58p
          8 File(s)     327680 bytes free
```

8-14 The same directory after FD with the /T switch active.

```
FD A:*.* /T12:34:56

TERM      LOG      4505     1-01-89    12:35p
TERM      SAV         0     1-01-89    12:35p
INSIDE    1         907     1-01-89    12:35p
DGTERM    ARC     15360     1-01-89    12:35p
FLUSHOT2  ARC      5120     1-01-89    12:35p
UNBLINK   COM      1920     1-01-89    12:35p
CLK26     COM       640     1-01-89    12:35p
ANN       MEN       709     1-01-89    12:35p
          8 File(s)     327680 bytes free
```

Figure 8-15 shows selective changing; the two files with the .ARC extension have had both their time- and datestamps changed. The time shown is the time when the changes were made.

```
FD A:*.ARC

TERM       LOG      4505     1-01-89    12:35p
TERM       SAV         0     1-01-89    12:35p
INSIDE     1         907     1-01-89    12:35p
DGTERM     ARC     15360     3-17-89     1:02a
FLUSHOT2   ARC      5120     3-17-89     1:02a
UNBLINK    COM      1920     1-01-89    12:35p
CLK26      COM       640     1-01-89    12:35p
ANN        MEN       709     1-01-89    12:35p
           8 File(s)     327680 bytes free
```

In Fig. 8-16, FD was run without any switches. The *.COM indicates which files are to be changed. As you can see, there are no dates or times shown for either of the .COM files in the example directory.

```
FD A:*.COM

TERM       LOG      4505     1-01-89    12:35p
TERM       SAV         0     1-01-89    12:35p
INSIDE     1         907     1-01-89    12:35p
DGTERM     ARC     15360     3-17-89     1:02a
FLUSHOT2   ARC      5120     3-17-89     1:02a
UNBLINK    COM      1920
CLK26      COM       640
ANN        MEN       709     1-01-89    12:35p
           8 File(s)     327680 bytes free
```

Is there any limit to the number of times I can change the time - and/or datestamps?

No.

Are there any limitations on what time and/or date I can set?

Yes. They must be valid DOS values. A time of "65:71:80" is as unacceptable as a date of "13-40-04." FileDate displays an error message whenever the format or the value of the date/time is incorrect.

What will happen if I do put a space between the switch and the value?

FileDate will display an error message saying "invalid parameter." It will not tell you whether you entered a wrong value or just added a space where it is unacceptable, however, which is one reason for placing the note under each of those switch descriptions. Maybe the error handling will be improved in the next version.

Will my changing these parameters influence the running of the programs or operation of my system?

Not under normal circumstances. If a program reads the time and/or datestamp expecting a specific value, there could be a problem when the value returned isn't the one expected.

Where can I learn more about the MAKE program?

Information on the Microsoft Program Maintenance Utility (MAKE) should be in the manual of any Microsoft language compiler which has a copy of MAKE on the disk(s). Microsoft's Macro Assembler is one such program.

FileFind version 4.0 & 4.5

Version 4.0 & 4.5 directory name   **FF.EXE**

FF locates a filename by searching through all of the directories on one or all disk drives. No filename or a partial filename may be specified. FF uses a default specification of *.* and will list all of the filenames present in the directories searched.

> **Format:**   FF [d:] [filename] [switches] [> | > >] [path \ filename|device]

The following command-line options are available:

d: Indicates the drive to be searched for the *filename*. Omitting the drive letter here will cause FF to search the default disk drive.

filename

          The *filename* to be located. Wildcard characters ? and * may be used with partial names or to replace extensions. Omitting the *filename* will cause FF to use the default of *.* and list all file-names.

These are the switches available from the command line:

/P   Tells FF to pause when the display screen is full. Pressing any key will also pause the display. Pressing a second key will resume the scrolling display.

/W   Tells FF to list the files in wide format and only show the filename. This format is 5 filenames wide and can display over 100 filenames at a time.

/A   Tells FF to search all of the disk drives installed in the system.

> | > >   Redirect or redirect and append the program output.

path/filename|device

          To a disk file or the system printer.

FF searches for all filenames matching the one specified. It will search every directory and subdirectory as well as all drives, if you set it to do so. All matches are shown along with the directory in which they are located. Hidden and System files are also displayed in FF listings. For those who store everything, FF also lists the size and time/datestamp of each filename that is matched, which means that all versions of a filename will be displayed.

You can control the extent of FF's search by either specifying a drive, setting the /A switch, or defaulting to the current drive. Pressing the CTRL/BREAK key combination or the ESC key will abort a FF search or listing at any time without danger.

Using the DOS output-redirection command allows the FF output to be sent to a disk file or the system printer. The usual method of invoking this feature would be

FF [d:] [filename] [switches] > [d:] [new filename|device]

or

FF [d:] [filename] [switches] > > [d:] [existing filename]

The second example will append this new FF report to the end of the report(s)/file(s) that are now in the existing filename.

Why would I ever want to find a Hidden or System file?

One reason might be to check a floppy to see if the files MSDOS.COM, or IBM-DOS.COM and IBMBIO.COM, or IOSYS.COM are on the disk. Using FF is as fast as using FA, and it reports more information.

Another reason might be to find other types of files that have been hidden. I hide some files using the /HID+ command of FA and only call them through batch (.BAT) files. For me, the shorter visible directory is easier to manage.

If FA will do the same thing, why have or use FF?

FA lists all of the files in the directory or all of the files that have an active switch while FF lists only the filename and directory. Thus, FF makes the display easier to read.

How can I find out where all of the .COM files are on my hard disk?

Just ask FF to list them all for you. Assuming that you have placed the Norton Utilities in a subdirectory called NU, the command from the Root directory would be

C:\:C:\NU\FF *.COM /W >FFCOM.LOG

This command runs the FileFind utility program and writes all of the .COM filenames found into a diskfile called FFCOM.LOG. Because there are no other specifications on the diskfile name, FFCOM.LOG will be written into the Root directory. The /W switch will format the file just like the /W display (five across and no size or datestamp information).

Why doesn't your C prompt look like C>?

I changed the prompt from C> to C:\ (directory name) so that I would always know where I was. This means that

    C:\ is the Root directory
    C:\EW is the EasyWriter directory
    C:\NU is the Norton Utilities directory, and
    C:\EW\BOOK is the subdirectory of EW where this text is stored.

Neat! Now how can I do the same thing?

Put the line

```
prompt = $p $G
```

in the AUTOEXEC.BAT file that runs when your system boots. This would be in the Root directory and is the same file containing the SA command line to change the default colors of the background and text on your color monitor.

    The space between the *p* and the *$* is optional. I like it because it moves the cursor a space away from the text of the prompt.

    Shown in Fig. 8-17 are the first few lines of two FF diskfiles. The first uses the default *.* and the second uses *.COM. Both also use the /W switch.

    This last truncated dump, shown in Fig. 8-18, is the end of a 10-page listing of all of the files that were on drive C at the time.

Can I also search for just the Hidden files?

Yes, as long as you know the filenames. The same is true of System and signature files.

Is there any possibility that I will damage anything with all of my searching?

No, FF will not damage anything. Only the usually occurring accidents, acts of God, and the local power company can be expected to cause damage.

Finding files is fine, but is there any way to get just the subdirectories to display?

Yes. The Norton Utilities can't do it for you, but the DOS command DIR *. works. I can't take credit for this one; I read it in **Directions** magazine a few months back. They received it from a user.

    Note: There is no star (*) after the period (.).

8-17 Typical FileFind screen displays, truncated to only a few lines.

```
C:\:C:\NU\FF /W

FF- File Find, Advanced Edition, (C) 1988, Peter Norton

C:\
    ibmbio.com      ibmdos.com      DOS             NU              R5K
    ARC             EW              PKX             PAS             BAS
    FASTBACK        GAME            DIAG            BACKIT          QDOS
    MACE            DBASE           MISC            AMU             auto.bat
    autotemp.bat    ansi.sys        fileinfo.fi     treeinfo.ncd    qd2.log
    config.sys      savscr.com      command.com     autoexec.bak    master.mdf
    utility.mdf     lang.mdf        game.mdf        dir.log         autoexec.bat

C:\QDOS

C:\:C\NU\FF *.COM /W

FF- File Find, Advanced Edition (C) 1988, Peter Norton

C:\
    ibmbio.com      ibmdos.com      savscr.com      command.com

C:\DOS
    assign.com      backup.com      chkdsk.com      comp.com        debug.com
    fdisk.com       format.com      keyb.com        edlin.com       mode.com
    command.com     restore.com     label.com       select.com      sys.com
    recover.com     graphics.com    diskcomp.com    diskcopy.com    print.com
    tree.com        more.com        graftabl.com

C:\ARC
    arce.com        autocust.com    automenu.com    sw.com

C:\EW

58 files found
```

8-18 The truncated default format of FF.

```
FF- File Find, Advanced Edition (C) 1988, Peter Norton

        zipcode.ndx        2,048 bytes    9:00 am   Thu Dec 26 85

C:\MISC
            .                  <DIR>.      8:12 pm   Mon Jul  6 87
            ..                 <DIR>       8:12 pm   Mon Jul  6 87
        wcx.arc            1,280 bytes    12:30 am   Sat Jun 13 87
        wcx.com              553 bytes     1:17 am   Tue Jun 10 86
        wcx.doc            1,029 bytes     6:40 am   Mon Jun  9 86
        msspad.com         1,641 bytes    12:05 am   Tue Jan  1 80
        msspad.doc         1,340 bytes    12:17 am   Tue Jan  1 80
        masspad.arc        1,920 bytes    12:28 am   Sat Jun 13 87

C:\AMU
            .                  <DIR>      11:19 pm   Fri Jul 10 87
            ..                 <DIR>      11:19 pm   Fri Jul 10 87
        automenu.com      17,214 bytes    12:10 am   Sat Jul 11 87
        autocust.com       9,311 bytes     4:01 am   Fri May 15 87
        automake.exe      78,956 bytes     4:01 am   Fri May 15 87
        dos.mdf            4,072 bytes     4:01 am   Fri May 15 87
        automenu.mdf       1,510 bytes    12:16 am   Sat Jul 11 87
        autotemp.bat         256 bytes    12:17 am   Sat Jul 11 87
        auto.bat             171 bytes    12:12 am   Sat Jul 11 87

559 files found
```

As long as I'm on the subject of users, I want to get on my soapbox for a few moments. Every developer, like every writer, tries to produce the best possible product. In some cases, like the Norton Utilities, it turns into the standard. In others that will remain unnamed, the product creates monumental problems for the user or purchaser. Your involvement will help both Norton Utilities and this book to improve. Your praise is nice, but your constructive comments and suggestions for improvements are even more valuable. You have praised Norton and me once by buying the fruits of our labors. Praising us again might cause us to become overconfident. I don't like to be criticized; but when I deserve it, I must accept it. Be clear, concise, and polite; and I will listen. I will have to assume that those at Norton will listen also.

I've included my on-line address in the Epilogue so that you can easily send me any comments you have. You might also check on DELPHI for someone from Peter Norton Technical Support. We want to get them into the mainstream too.

File Information version 4.0 & 4.5

Version 4.0 & 4.5 directory name   FI.EXE

The FI Utility permits the addition of descriptive comments to the DOS filename. These comments can be displayed by using the FI command rather than the DOS DIR command. Computers that are not fully IBM-compatible must use EMU-LATE.COM or a similar utility to run this program.

Format: FA [path \ filename] [comment] [switches]

The following command-line options are available:

path \ filename

>The specific file to which the comment is to be attached. The default is *.*, which will display all of the files in the root directory of the currently selected drive. Because this is the interactive mode, FI will display each filename in order. If no comment is to be added or edited, pressing RETURN will display the next filename.

comment

>The text of the comment to be attached to the filename selected.

These switches available are:

/C   Tells FI to list only those files that already have comments attached.

/D   Tells FI that the comment attached to [path \ filename] is to be deleted.

/E	Tells FI that a comment is to be edited or entered. [path \ filename] is required. Maximum comment length is 65 characters.
/L	Tells FI to display a long format, which means that the entire comment will be shown.
/N	Is used with computers that are not fully IBM-compatible. This is a case where the TIPC is fully compatible.
/P	Tells FI to pause when the screen is full.
/PACK	Is a sub-utility that compresses the data in the comment file.
/S	Tells FI to include the subdirectories of the selected drive and directory.

Figure 8-19 shows a partial dump using the FI /L command. Without the /L switch, the display would look like Fig. 8-20. The file size and datestamp information are not shown when the full comment is displayed. Using the FI command alone allows only the first 36 characters to be displayed. Not even this partial display of characters appears when the DOS DIR command is used.

Before entering any text, the comment line is blank (as seen in Fig. 8-21). Pressing RETURN writes the comment into the FILEINFO.FI file, which becomes part of the indicated directory. You could replace all use of the DOS DIR

8-19 FI with an active /L switch.

```
A>FI B:/L

FI-File Information, Advanced Edition, (C) Copr. 1988, Peter Norton

DIAG
BACKIT
QDOS
MACE
DBASE
MISC
AMU
auto      bat
autotemp  bat
ansi      sys
fileinfo  fi    the file holding all of these comments
treeinfo  ncd
qd2       log
config    sys
savscr    com   Saves a screen to a disk file
command   com
master    mdf
utility   mdf
lang      mdf
game      mdf
autoexec  bat
```

```
A>FI B:

FI-File Information, Advanced Edition, (C) Copr. 1988, Peter Norton

DIAG              <DIR>      1-01-80   12:01a
BACKIT            <DIR>      1-01-80   12:03a
QDOS              <DIR>      7-05-87    7:42p
MACE              <DIR>      1-01-80   12:08a
DBASE             <DIR>      7-06-87    7:49p
MISC              <DIR>      7-06-87    8:12p
AMU               <DIR>      7-10-87   11:19p
auto     bat         176     7-10-87   11:17p
autotemp bat         128     7-10-87   11:18p
ansi     sys       1,678     3-17-87   12:00p
fileinfo fi          753     6-27-87    8:43p   the file holding all of these commen
treeinfo ncd         203     7-10-87   11:19p
qd2      log       3,206     7-05-87    7:46p
config   sys          28     7-06-87    3:22p
savscr   com       2,048     7-06-87    8:56p   Saves a screen to a disk file
command  com      26,624     7-06-87    8:56p
master   mdf         508     7-10-87   11:46p
utility  mdf         579     7-10-87   11:54p
lang     mdf         392     7-10-87   11:57p
game     mdf         564     7-11-87   12:07a
autoexec bat          59     7-11-87    4:50p
```

```
A>FI B:treeinfo.ncd /E

FI-File Info, Advanced Edition, (C) Copr 1988, Peter Norton

┌─────────────────────────────────────────────────────────────────┐
│  Directory: B:\                                                   │
│  File name: treeinfo.ncd                                          │
│    Comment:                                                       │
│                            Press Esc to quit                      │
└─────────────────────────────────────────────────────────────────┘
```

command with the FI command. Doing this has certain advantages. Typing FI without any command-line options provides a continuous scroll of the files in the directory. To pause the scrolling, press any key except for ESC or F10. To continue scrolling after pausing, press any key. Pressing the RETURN key will scroll the screen one filename at a time. Pressing the SPACEBAR will scroll the screen one page of filenames at a time. Pressing any other key will return the display to the normal auto-scroll mode.

Being able to attach comments to DOS filenames can be very useful when faced with filenames as informative as some of the following:

EMW0700Q0.LOD
EMW0710RT.LOD
DK93001V3.COM
XBA6802M2.EXE

With descriptive commenting, these filenames no longer become just so many characters after the reasoning behind the cryptic notation has grown cold. Commenting can also prove very useful when files are compressed. The comment can clearly indicate the contents of the file when the filename doesn't.

Within the editing box in Fig. 8-20 (displayed in response to using the /E switch), the following WordStar compatible commands are available:

[CTRL-RIGHTARROW]	Cursor right one word
[CTRL-F]	Cursor right one word
[CTRL-LEFTARROW]	Cursor left one word
[CTRL-A]	Cursor left one word
[HOME]	Cursor to beginning of line
[RIGHTARROW]	Cursor right one character
[CTRL-D]	Cursor right one character
[LEFTARROW]	Cursor left one character
[CTRL-S]	Cursor left one character
[BACKSPACE]	Delete one character left
[DEL]	Delete character under cursor
[CTRL-T]	Delete word right
[CTRL-W]	Delete word left
[CTRL-Y]	Delete entire line
[ESC]	Abort
[F10]	Abort
[F1]	Display next filename

Note: There are two possibilities for most of the commands, which allows you to choose the more comfortable or familiar combination. The command FI [path \ filename] /D also will delete the existing comment for a filename.

When you are adding or editing comments for more than one file (the FI /E command), you should press the RETURN key to complete the activity on the indicated filename and clear the FI program. By pressing the F1 key, you can single-step through the entire directory, adding, editing, or deleting comments before clearing FI.

The FILEINFO.FI file will automatically compact itself at some point in time in order to restore data into contiguous sectors. Fragmenting files often occurs on disks where there are many writes or deletes. The /PACK switch does for the FILEINFO.FI what the DS utility program does for the entire disk.

Can you give me some examples of when you might use FI to tag comments to a filename?

Sure. I use electronic mail extensively with most of my messages being created off-line and then transferred to DELPHI via a protocol. To keep things simple, I usually just use a person's username as the filename. A number is included if there is more than one message to that individual. I use the date as the extension, which serves the dual roles of identification and providing a common factor for batch transfers (*.nnn). The four numbers are adequate to describe the day and the month. Comments describing each of these files saves time later when I try to determine if the message should be saved for days or months.

In addition, I've tried to remember why I wrote the answer I did after a message gets a few weeks old. It isn't always easy, especially if the message that prompted the reply is not filed close at hand.

Files that have been compressed using ARC or another compression utility can contain numerous files. FI lets me indicate the contents more efficiently than using the L or V commands. Even then, the L and V commands will only give the filenames. I find the descriptive comments much more useful.

Can I still use DIR and DIR/W after using FI?

Yes. FI creates FILEINFO.FI where the comment records are stored. When you use FI, you will not see that file. Using DIR or DIR/W will display it.

What are the practical limits for FI?

Each comment is limited to 65 characters, and each file is limited to one comment. Beyond that, only disk space can limit FI.

Does FILEINFO.FI retain the comments that I had on a file that was deleted?

Yes and no. Immediately after the filename is deleted, the comment is still on file. If the /PACK switch is used, the comment records of deleted files will be eliminated. FI will also perform a /PACK when it reaches a certain point. Packing eliminates unnecessary comment records and thereby improves response time.

If I delete a filename by mistake and recover it using QU, will FI still be able to display the comment I had for it?

Yes, as long as a /PACK has not been done by you or FI while the file was deleted.

FileSize version 4.0 & 4.5

Version 4.0 & 4.5 directory name   **FS.EXE**

FS displays the amount of disk space occupied by the files in a directory. FS also displays amount of slack (dead space) currently included in the file space. In addition, FS can look at a target disk and report the amount of space available and whether there is enough room for a copy of the named file. Redirection is available and useful when checking a hard disk with the default *.* parameter and the /S switch active.

Format: Version 4.x

FS [path \ filename] [d:] [switches] [> | > >] [path \ filename | device]

These are the command-line options available:

path \ filename

    The file(s) to be sized and their location. If no filename is specified, the default is *.*. If no path is specified, the default is the Root directory.

d:

    The target drive letter. When not specified, the currently selected drive is searched. This switch is used to check for open disk space before copying a file to the disk in this drive.

/P

    Tells FS to pause when the display screen is full. If you forget to include this option, pressing any key will pause the display. Pressing a second key will resume the scrolling display.

/S

    Tells FS to include all subdirectories in its search for filename.

/T

    Tells FS to display and report totals only. Individual file sizes will not be included. Using this switch together with redirection reduces the size of the report file significantly.

> | > >

    The DOS operators to redirect, or redirect and append, the program output. There is no display when either of these operators is used.

path \ filename|device

    To a disk file or the system printer.

The default search for FS is *.* and the currently selected drive. Thus, it will report on all of the files in the currently selected directory of the currently selected drive.

A printout of an FS report (version 3.x) would look something like Fig. 8-22.

8-22 A typical FS report in version 3.x.

```
FS-File Size, Version 3.10, (C) Copr 1984-86, Peter Norton

  A:\
        2,444 BEEP.COM
       15,957 COMMAND.COM
        7,724 DS.COM
        7,522 DT.COM
   - etc. -

      262,705 total bytes in 27 files in A:\
      276,480 bytes disk space occupied, 5% slack
```

In version 4.x, this same type of report would look similar to Fig. 8-23.

8-23 A typical FS report in version 4.x.

```
FS-File Size, Advanced Edition, (C) Copr 1988, Peter Norton

   A:\
     loader.sys        1,024 bytes
     ask.exe           1,270 bytes
     beep.exe          4,688 bytes
     ds.exe           25,474 bytes
   - etc. -

       269,548 total bytes in 25 files
       281,600 bytes disk space occupied, 4% slack

Drive usage
       362,496 bytes available on drive A:
        80,896 bytes unused on drive A:   22% unused
```

The change in this case may be the more noticeable. I find that the added three lines on drive usage are perhaps the most valuable addition.

The way disk space is managed means there will be some slack space on every disk. The total amount of slack must be minimal for efficient disk usage. The Utility program SD (SpeeDisk) is designed to make maximum use of the space available on any DOS disk, floppy or hard. Compression programs also exist that will reduce the size of files that are being placed on disk for storage purposes. Careful usage of both will ensure that your disks hold every last bit of information that can be packed on them.

Slack space is a function of the file size versus the space allocation scheme being used by DOS. These schemes vary with the version of DOS and the type of disk. Currently, allocations range from 1K clusters on a standard 360K floppy to 8K clusters on a DOS 2.x formatted hard disk. DOS 3.x, where available, can format hard disks using a 2K cluster; this can provide a dramatic slack space reduction on disks having many small files. Remember to always back up your hard disk before reformatting.

I just used SD to unfragment all of the files on my hard disk. When I run FS, it still shows one directory with over 30% slack. Is there something wrong?

I doubt it, if this directory constantly does this. Briefly, what you are seeing is a report of the blank spaces at the end of each file. Your problem usually indicates that there are many small files in your directory. My Root directory sometimes looks like that because I keep a number of .BAT files there. Most of them are less than 100 bytes, but still occupy a full cluster. On the C drive, they occupy 1024 bytes of space. The problem would be worse on the D drive, however, because there the cluster size is 2048 bytes.

Is there any way to reduce this slack space?

Reducing cluster size is the only way. However, cluster size is set by the FOR-MAT command. If you can find a version of FORMAT with a smaller cluster size, it is a worthwhile investment.

If the cluster were reduced to a sector (512 bytes), what would happen?

It would take longer to read the hard disk, and you could store less bytes on the disk. The reduction would be due to addressing problems, not the inability of the disk to hold them. Current DOS addressing techniques provide addresses for 32 megabytes of hard-disk storage. Larger disks are divided into different drives, which means that a single hard-disk assembly could actually be two, three, or even more drives, logically. Logically means that the computer looks for these different drives electrically, not physically.

Can you give me an example of how to check a disk for adequate space before trying to copy the file?

The illustrations shown provide the clearest way to explain how to do it and what to expect. The first one, Fig. 8-24, indicates that there is enough space on that disk for the file named DBASE.OVL. The second example, Fig. 8-25, claims there is not enough space.

8-24 FS indicating sufficient space.

```
C:\DBASE: c:\nu\fs dbase.ovl a:
FS-File Size, Advanced Edition, (C) Copr 1988, Peter Norton

  C:\DBASE
    dbase.ovl        272,384 bytes

      272,384 bytes disk space occupied, 0% slack

      272,384 bytes disk space needed to copy to A:
      287,744 bytes available on A:, enough disk space
 Drive usage
   21,309,440 bytes available on drive C:
   13,281,280 bytes unused on drive C:, 62% unused

C:\DBASE:
```

8-25 FS indicating insufficient space.

```
C:\DBASE: c:\nu\fs dbase.ovl a:
FS-File Size, Advanced Edition, (C) Copr 1988, Peter Norton

  C:\DBASE
    dbase.ovl        272,384 bytes

      272,384 bytes disk space occupied, 0% slack
```

```
    272,384 bytes disk space needed to copy to A:
     57,344 bytes available on A:, insufficient disk space

Drive usage
  21,309,440 bytes available on drive C:
  13,281,280 bytes unused on drive C:, 62% unused
```

Are there files with 0% slack?

One such file is used in the illustrations shown above.

Is there any type of file that cannot be checked by FS?

Every type of file that DOS can read or write to can be checked by FS. Remember that FS is one of the Utilities that can provide information on Hidden and System files. If you have any personal Hidden files or directories, you might want to take additional precautions to ensure that other users cannot discover them.

List Directory version 4.0 & 4.5

Version 4.0 & 4.5 directory name   LD.EXE

LD is designed to make it easier to display all of the directories and subdirectories that are present on a disk. It is especially useful when attempting to manage large hard-disk systems. A graphic capability has been added to version 4.0.

Format: Version 4.0 & 4.5
            LD [d:] [\ pathname] [switches] [> | > >] [device|filename]

d: Indicates the drive from which LD is to get the directory informa-
            tion. Figure 8-26 is a typical display.

8-26 LD output without any active switches.

```
C:\>ld
LD-List Directories, Advanced Edition 4.50, (C) Copr 1987-88, Peter Norton
  C:\ (root)
  C:\ARC
  C:\DH
  C:\EWT
  C:\EWT\ART
  C:\EWT\BK1
  C:\EWT\BK2
  C:\EWT\CHRIST
  C:\EWT\GVC
  C:\GAME
  C:\NU_REF
  C:\SPRINT
  C:\TEST
  C:\TEST\PT3
  C:\USA
  C:\ZIP

16 directories

C:\>
```

\ **pathname**

Selects a path within a disk to be listed. This new switch allows you to obtain partial listings.

/A List the directories of all drives. Figure 8-27 is a typical display.

/G Display the directory tree graphically. This switch is mutually exclusive with the /T switch. Figure 8-28 is a typical display.

8-27 LD output with an active /G switch.

```
C:\>ld/g
LD-List Directories, Advanced Edition 4.50, (C) Copr 1987-88, Peter Norton

C:\──┬─ARC
     ├─DH
     ├─EWT──────────┬─ART
     │              ├─BK1
     │              ├─BK2
     │              ├─CHRIST
     │              └─GVC
     ├─GAME
     ├─NU_REF
     ├─SPRINT
     ├─TEST───────────PT3
     ├─USA
     └─ZIP

16 directories

C:\>
```

8-28 LD output with an active /A switch.

```
C:\ ld/a
LD-List Directories, Advanced Edition 4.50, (C) Copr 1987-88, Peter Norton
Unable to read from drive A
  C:\ (root)
  C:\ARC
  C:\DH
  C:\EWT
  C:\EWT\ART
  C:\EWT\BK1
  C:\EWT\BK2
  C:\EWT\CHRIST
  C:\EWT\GVC
  C:\GAME
  C:\NU_REF
  C:\SPRINT
  C:\TEST
  C:\TEST\PT3
  C:\USA
  C:\ZIP
16 directories

  D:\ (root)
  D:\AUTOMENU
  D:\COMM
  D:\COMM\MR
```

```
  D:\COMM\PC
  D:\COMM\XT
  D:\DOS
  D:\EW
  D:\NU
  D:\WS.
10 directories

Total
26 directories
```

/N   Used with the /G switch when redirecting the output to a printer that does not support the IBM extended character set.

/P   Pause the display after each filled display screen. Pressing any key will also pause the display if this switch has not been included on the command line.

/T   Display the total number and total size of the files in each directory. This is in addition to the directory listing. Filenames are not displayed. This switch cannot be used when the /G (graphic) display switch is used. Figure 8-29 is a typical display.

8-29 LD output with active /A and /T switches.

```
c:\ld/a/t

LD-List Directories, Advanced Edition 4.50, (C) Copr 1987-88, Peter Norton

Unable to read from drive A

  C:\ (root)
        20 files         196,512 bytes
  C:\ARC
        33 files         554,734 bytes
  C:\DH
        61 files         987,539 bytes
  C:\EWT
         1 file           43,520 bytes
  C:\EWT\ART
         3 files         125,952 bytes
  C:\EWT\BK1
        42 files         720,197 bytes
  C:\EWT\BK2
        29 files         738,686 bytes
  C:\EWT\CHRIST
         3 files         384,000 bytes
  C:\EWT\GVC
        16 files         619,689 bytes
  C:\GAME
        39 files         723,757 bytes
  C:\NU_REF
         2 files         529,815 bytes
  C:\SPRINT
        52 files       2,020,200 bytes
```

```
  C:\TEST
       115 files      1,172,950 bytes
  C:\TEST\PT3
         8 files        239,774 bytes
  C:\USA
        48 files        603,994 bytes
  C:\ZIP
        11 files        182,439 bytes

16 directories      483 files      9,843,758 bytes

  D:\ (root)
         7 files         44,969 bytes
  D:\AUTOMENU
         8 files        112,606 bytes
  D:\COMM
         0 files
  D:\COMM\MR
        16 files        280,383 bytes
  D:\COMM\PC
        16 files        456,100 bytes
  D:\COMM\XT
        17 files        190,418 bytes
  D:\DOS
        54 files        695,975 bytes
  D:\EW
        53 files        980,201 bytes
  D:\NU
        34 files        950,715 bytes
  D:\WS
        16 files      2,418,792 bytes

10 directories      221 files      6,130,159 bytes

Total
   26 directories      704 files    15,973,917 bytes
```

/W   Display the directory listing in wide format. This switch is not operational in version 4.0 or 4.5.

\>   The DOS redirect operator used to send the output of LD to a printer or disk file. DOS will create the file if it does not exist and overwrite it if it does.

Note: There is no display visible with either of the redirection operators active.

\> \>   DOS redirection operator which appends the new information to an existing file. This operator is normally used only with disk files. DOS will create the file if it does not exist.

device|filename

Where the redirected output is to be sent. >PRN or >LPT1 will produce a hardcopy of the output of LD. > >A:DIR.LST will write the output of LD to the end of the file named DIR.LST in drive A. These selections are usually mutually exclusive, so you should select one or the other.

LD is not a duplicate of NCD (Norton Change Directory), but it is a complement. NCD's primary purpose is to provide you with an easy method of making, renaming, and deleting directories along with the capacity to move from directory to directory without having to key in complete pathnames for every move. LD provides you with the ability to see, on display or hardcopy, the directory structure you have created using NCD. It is not interactive and does not permit you to make changes in an existing structure.

Can you give me an example of when LD might be useful?

You might use it to introduce a database tutorial to newusers, providing them with an overview of how the software is constructed.

What if I don't have such an application?

Then you might want to keep a copy handy so that you can find the subdirectory where you hid those games you just bought. You might also save yourself the trouble of having to step through two or three levels of subdirectories to get to a seldom used program, such as the tax tables that you dread having to access annually.

LD doesn't appear to be the most valuable Utility in the package.

It may not be; but, like the rest of the Utilities, LD's true value can only be measured in the time it saves you when you find uses for it. Knowing the full pathname to a specific file from the Root directory saves time and effort. As your directory structure becomes more complex, you will find it easier to consult the chart produced by LD than to remember those pathnames.

TextSearch version 4.0 & 4.5
Version 4.0 & 4.5 directory name   **TS.EXE**

TS started out as a simple search routine that allowed the user to look for a string of characters consisting of letters, words, or punctuation. Its only option was the /N switch. For you old Norton users, TS used to be called SSAR. You must have the EMULATE.COM file to run that version of TS.

Format: TS (invokes the interactive or prompting mode)
TS [drive \ path \ filename] [search-text] [switches] (invokes the automatic mode)

drive \ path \ filename
Searches a specific filename. The wildcard characters ? and * may be used in the filename or extension.

search-text

> Specifies the text to be searched for. If the search is for a string of more than one word, it must be enclosed in quotes. TS is not case-sensitive; therefore, it does not require you to enter the search-text exactly as it should be found in the file(s). Thus, you may have a few more matches than anticipated.

/D   Searches the entire disk. The default search area is the data area containing existing files.

/E   Searches only the erased/available space of a disk.

/A   Automates the search by answering yes to the questions asked at the various prompts.

/EBCDIC

> Tells TS that the file(s) to be searched are EBCDIC code or main-frame file(s).

/LOG   Formats the output of TS for printing or writing to a disk file.

/N   Is used for systems that are not fully IBM-compatible and must use the ANSI.SYS driver file.

/WS   Tells TS not to search the ASCII characters between 128 and 255. The default is to search all characters, including the extended character set.

/S   Searches subdirectories.

/CS   Make the search case-sensitive.

/T   Sets the non-interactive or Total mode, which provides only a summary of the activities performed by TS.

/Cn   Start search at cluster n.

/EUR   Tells TS, version 3.1 and later, that European language characters could be present in the file(s) to be searched.

When TS matches the text specified in the parameter search-text, it highlights it. The method used is IBM-specific; if your system is not fully IBM-compatible, be sure to set the /N switch and install the driver file ANSI.SYS. Failure to follow these recommendations could cause your system to lock. No damage is done when this happens, but you must waste time starting over and doing everything right the second time.

Version 3.0 uses only the /N switch to allow TS to search the disks of systems that are not fully IBM-compatible. Many of the functions that are now options external to TS were selectable from within the earlier version.

TS is not limited to searching out the text in ASCII or word processor files. TS can also search for the cell label of a Lotus spreadsheet or the procedure name of a source code file.

The /WS switch is useful when searches are being conducted in WordStar or other files that use the eighth bit for special purposes. The IBM extended character set (ASCII 128 thru ASCII 255) all have the eighth-bit set.

Using the /EBCDIC switch enables the TS translation table to translate ASCII to EBCDIC and vice versa. Using this switch when searching ASCII files will not cause any problems, but not using it during searches of EBCDIC files will invalidate the search.

Even if it is not listed in the manual, the /EUR switch is still available in version 4.0 and the Advanced Edition. The /A and /T switches serve different purposes. /A makes a yes response for you as if it were an interactive session. The /T switch shows only the filename where matches were found, which means that the text surrounding the search-text is not shown. One useful combination might be /A/LOG, which allows you to print or file the search results for use at a later time.

Unless the /LOG switch is used, the output of TS is not suitable for printing or filing. You can see this very quickly on the screen as the output lines overwrite previously displayed lines. This same type of overwrite occurs at the printer or in a disk file.

When TS is being used in an attempt to recover data, the matching information can be (and should be) written to another drive. You can do this by including the drive letter as a part of the filename that TS is writing to. An example of this would be

A:SALFI   (within the 8-character limitation of a DOS filename)

Should you fill the disk currently in the specified drive, TS will pause and request that a different disk be placed in the drive.

You can also use TS to locate missing portions of a file that you are trying to UnErase.

TS completes its tasks faster when the search area is smaller. TS also works faster when searching for only a single word. Searching the whole disk (the /D switch) should not be necessary too often. If a search must be conducted outside the active file area, the /E switch will be more useful and faster than the /D switch.

Why would I want to search by cluster?

How about when you're looking for the next cluster of a fragmented text file during a recovery operation?

Does TS make changes in text files?

No. TS is not like a search-and-replace feature found in a word processor package. It is a search-and-report utility.

9
CHAPTER

Filefix

Directory name   **FILEFIX.EXE**

Filefix is a new Utility that helps you repair damaged database data files. It is
compatible with Lotus 1-2-3, Symphony, and dBASE file structures.

Command line usage

Format: FILEFIX [filename]

filename The name of the data file to be repaired. Filefix can determine the
type from the filename extension, so it doesn't bother to display
the first program screens.

Network considerations

Filefix will run on a networked system, but it cannot UnZap a file from a network, or a substituted or assigned disk. Remember that these Utilities are designed for operation on a single system by a single user. Still, they will not create problems for network operations.

There are only three database programs listed on the opening panel, shown in Fig. 9-1; but the Utility will repair the data files of any database program which uses the same format as one of these. Many of these repairs can be completed automatically by Filefix, but there will be times when human assistance is required.

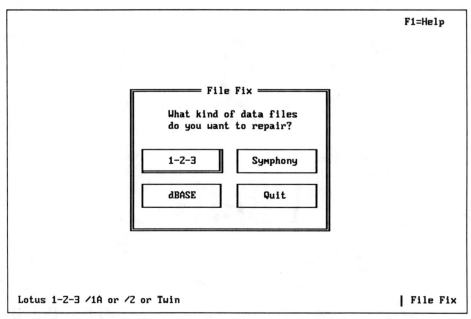

9-1 The Opening screen for FileFix.

When you select the database program from the Opening panel, the File Selection panel (pictured in Fig. 9-2) will already have the correct extension shown. The directory selected by Filefix will be the default directory. The TAB key will move the reverse video block into the other boxes so that you can change both directory and drive as necessary.

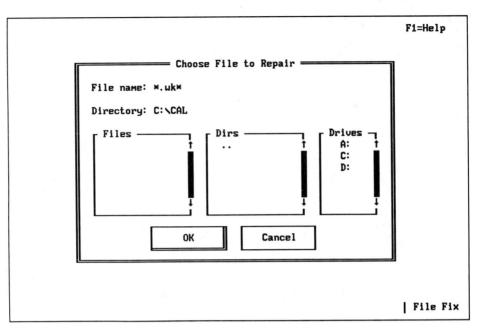

```
========================= Choose File to Repair =========================

   File name: *.uk*

   Directory: C:\CAL

   ┌─ Files ──────────┐   ┌─ Dirs ──────────┐   ┌─ Drives ─┐
   │                ↑ │   │ ..            ↑ │   │ A:    ↑ │
   │                █ │   │               █ │   │ C:    │ │
   │                │ │   │               │ │   │ D:    │ │
   │                │ │   │               │ │   │       │ │
   │                │ │   │               │ │   │       │ │
   │                │ │   │               │ │   │       │ │
   │                ↓ │   │               ↓ │   │       ↓ │
   └──────────────────┘   └─────────────────┘   └─────────┘

        ┌──────────────┐        ┌──────────────┐
        │     OK       │        │   Cancel     │
        └──────────────┘        └──────────────┘
```

9-2 Selecting files for fixing.

10
CHAPTER

FileSave

Directory name   **FILESAVE.EXE**

FileSave is a new Utility. It provides another layer of protection for your data. Until version 5.0, it was possible to recover a deleted file only as long as it wasn't overwritten by new data being entered. This Utility can prevent data from being overwritten.

Command line usage

Format: FILESAVE [switch]

The following switches are available from the command line:

/STATUS   Displays the current FileSave status.

/ON   Enables FileSave.

/OFF   Uninstalls FileSave.

/UNINSTALL
            Uninstalls FileSave. Same as /OFF.

Network considerations

Filesave works on network drives.

The purpose of FileSave is to provide you with extra time in which to recover deleted files. When DOS deletes a filename, it doesn't erase any of the information in the data storage portion of your hard disk. In fact, it really only changes the first character of the filename. Until new data is written to the disk, everything but the first character of the filename is just as you originally entered it.

The UnErase Utilities have always been able to recover all of the information for a file where only the first character of the filename has been changed. Partial recoveries have also been possible when some of the data sectors have been used by files entered after the deletion.

With FileSave, all of the data storage sectors of deleted files are protected from overwriting for a period of time. Figure 10-1 provides both a list of options and the status of those options.

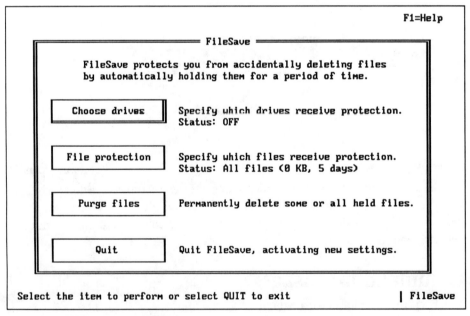

10-1   The Opening screen for FileSave.

FileSave will also list all of the drives currently active on your system in the drive window, shown here in Fig. 10-2. Depending on how you use your drives, it may not be necessary to protect all of them. My system is set up with programs on the D drive and data on the C drive. When I delete a program from the D drive, I can always recover it by copying it. I still have all of the distribution diskettes I receive when I obtain the software. The information on the C (data) drive will probably also be on the backup diskettes I've made.

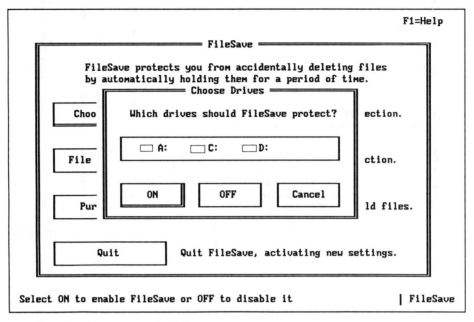

10-2 Choosing drives to protect in FileSave.

Accidents tend to happen when you are least prepared for them. If something were to happen between backups, I could be in real trouble without FileSave. Loss of data isn't something you want to have happen, but it is something you must expect. I've said it before, but I'll say it again. "proper prior planning prevents poor performance."

The types of files to be saved must be carefully considered. When FileSave retains them, the disk space isn't cleared for other uses. As you can see in Fig. 10-3, there are both time and space options available on the files to be retained. The day range is from 1 to 99, while the kilobyte range is from 1 to 9999. Incidentally, 9,999 kilobytes is only 1 kilobyte short of 10 megabytes, which means that you will either have to limit the number of kilobytes that FileSave retains or have a very large hard disk.

The three file options should provide enough flexibility to meet almost everybody's needs. Including archived files may not be necessary if you back up your data very regularly and frequently. FileSave can tell which files have been backed up by reading the archive bit of the file attributes. Any file that has been changed also has the archive bit set on. When files are backed up, that bit is turned off until the next change occurs. If no change occurs before the next scheduled backup, it may not be necessary to make another copy of this file.

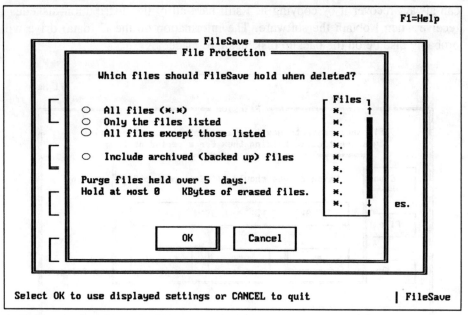

10-3 Choosing files to protect in FileSave.

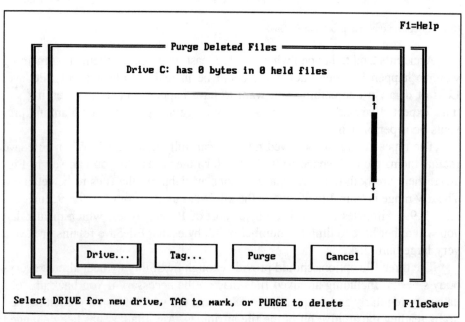

10-4 Purging deleted files in FileSave.

Figure 10-4 shows the Purge Deleted Files window. The current drive appears at the top of the screen, and a short description of how to use each of the boxes across the bottom of the screen may be found in the status line a bit lower. TAG is used when you want to PURGE a number of files as a single operation. If you just use PURGE, you will have to purge each file individually. By tagging or marking all of the files to be removed, the PURGE command resembles the DOS DEL command when a wildcard is used.

11
CHAPTER

Image

Directory name   **IMAGE.EXE**

IMAGE.EXE is the successor to FRECOVER.EXE. All of the version 5.0 Utilities recognize the FRECOVER.*xxx* files created by version 4.5. The version 5.0 Utilities that reference the FRECOVER.*xxx* files will rename them IMAGE.*xxx* files the first time one of those Utilities encounters the old filename.

Command line usage

Format: IMAGE [switches]

The following command-line switch is available:

/NOBACK   Do not create an IMAGE.BAK file.

Network considerations

Image is network-compatible, but it cannot protect a network drive.

There are both hidden and visible Image files. Their purpose is to hold the necessary information the recovery Utilities require to salvage your data after an error or failure of some kind.

Any "X" block you notice at the end of your hard disk that SpeeDisk ignores is the Image file. Its location is important and therefore it is marked as "unmovable," meaning that it is in a known location regardless of conditions. This section is also the data-storage portion of the disk and is not overwritten under most circumstances.

Don't worry about overwriting the Image file in the normal use of your hard disk. If the disk gets so full that your information approaches the Image file, DOS will report that there is insufficient disk space. All of the Image files are DOS-type files and visible if you know where to look for them. They aren't really very interesting to look at, though, and they are really very important, so don't mess with them.

12
CHAPTER

LinePrint

Version 4.0 & 4.5 directory name   LP.EXE

LinePrint is not in version 5.0. While I am saddened at its passing, I still have the copy from version 4.5 and plan to retain it in my NU subdirectory.

LP provides a simple means of printing text files. Although similar to the DOS PRINT or TYPE commands, LP offers formatting options that are not available with either of the others. However, LP is not a word processor.

Format: LP [d:] [\ path \ filename] [device] [switches]

d: The drive where the file is located.

\ path \ filename

The location and name of the file(s) which are to be used as the input for LP. More than one file may be specified by using the DOS wildcard characters.

device	The printer or drive \ path \ filename which is to receive the output of LP. If a filename is specified, wildcard characters must not be used.
/T*n*	The number of lines to allow for the top margin. The default value in version 4.0 is *3*.
/B*n*	The number of lines to allow for the bottom margin. The default value in version 4.0 is *5*.
/L*n*	The number of columns to allow for the left margin. The default value in version 4.0 is *5*.
/R*n*	The number of columns to allow for the right margin. The default value in version 4.0 is *5*.
/H*n*	The page length in lines. The default in version 4.0 is *66*.
/W*n*	The width of the page in columns. The default value in version 4.0 is *85*.
/S*n*	The line spacing to be used. The default value in version 4.0 is *1*.
/P*n*	The starting page number. The default value in version 4.0 is *1*.
/N	The line-numbering toggle. The default value in version 4.0 and later is off. Thus, you must include this switch when you want the line numbers printed.
/80	The page-width toggle. The default value in version 4.0 is *on*. This means that the /W switch and value are used only when the page width is any value other than 80, or the /132 switch is being used.
/132	The compressed-print toggle. Using this switch will preface the text to be printed with the IBM printer codes to enable the compressed-print mode in compatible printers.

/HEADER*n*

Sets the header to be printed on each page. Values are

0 = no headers.
1 = current time and date are printed.
2 = current time and date plus the file time and date.

The default value in version 4.0 is *1*.

/EBCDIC

Tells LP that the file to be printed is in EBCDIC code. LP will convert the coding to ASCII and print the "printable" characters. The default value of this toggle is *off*.

/EXT   This toggle tells LP to print the extended character set, assuming that the printer is compatible. This includes the European character set. The default setting in version 4.0 is *off*. This means that the eighth bit is stripped off by LP in the default mode.

/SET:drive \ path \ filename

Tells LP where to find the batch file with the switch settings to be used for the current task. You must develop the batch file. Also, there is no default value for this switch.

One useful task that LP can perform is the printing of READ.ME type files that are not received in ready-to-print form.

Using a text file such as TEST.TXT in Fig. 12-1, we can demonstrate some of the features available within LP. If the following command is entered

A > LP B:TEST.TST B:DEFAULT

Then Fig. 12-2 is the output.

12-1   The sample ASCII file examined in the next five figures.

```
This text is being used to display the various options available using the
NORTON UTILITIES program LP (LinePrint). The bulk of this text file is just
random key strokes to fill space. For those options where the length of this
file runs over a single page the balance of the file has been truncated. There
is nothing in the portions omitted that cannot be seen in the remainder.

This line is exactly 80 characters long - asdrqweradfgwerasdfhrtaefsdfgwegaerrx.

This line is 120 characters long - poiujhasdfnqwer;oizxxcvnesr;oixzx ;lwerbasdlkjasdfuhvlkjerbzx oiurtnasdfasdrsagezsvt.

This line is 132 characters long - l;knv weihoc qwer;kjuisdfmcawekjnzdscdoiretnasdfpoiuwertbasddpfoitrbnasdfpoitrkjsdeuiretblzsdfde.

This is a random paragraph. weroixf l;kjjeertv zd louiwe4trlkdfguiol sdf ;kesrt
asdlfkjn asdf;lkasdf asdlkugv aser;lkasdfvbnlasdf dhliu asd aeertkjuzd vdfl;ka
flk j ads;lk;vt asdfkjuert. nsdfiusdfv x lksdfg sdfg;lkasc sdfgl kjxfbnger tl;
sdfgkjlcv erlkjsdfgowertbsd sdfg lsdkfglkj dfbp apjtr asdf;kjdzcv. dasf;kjzvc
asdf ljasdf;jkat asdlkcvb drg sefoiijxcvb ers;osdfsg asr;lk ;c asdjkdfgnweaa
asd;j ;alertnzxfvuioetr sdfg;kjsd sdfg;kjlert dfg;serty sdf; asdlkjterpoiu cs
asd;lkfgoiuwert ertypoiuxfb sdtipou pewewrt wepoiucvb sdyfpo ser werpoisdfgsvs
aeropliev wertlku oieurtbe vytreopixc sstdpoiwer v fgdspoiuwert servpoiweryu
drgpoise c;oiertycvp[osdfg sertpoi sdywpoifgb sdpoisdfb wetpoiusdfcgv sertgps
sdf vpsrt sdfgpiu sgfhrtyyu seopidb w5nm sdfgp sertynshtp poimsdy sp rgyertsdg
ty;oxdf rtypoifgh ertpdfgnbnmrte wep dfghwr sdfgpoi dfty4erdfghb rtypdfghs rydf
si sfgh dfghl;kfty dftypwerty dfgh;pldfghdsfln pijn poiubn rtypm s d wetrypo
This is line 25. aeropi qpertioun asertoidsffg aertpoi dsa

cmmlert opiumsert ertldgfhh yuirety dfghjc ponsdvpioiet sefvprty xsdv oiwert
errt csdfgopity dfghbpotry sdfpoi pserty c pidstfg p pn wertyl; jert eyrtwe
adgbnopijretg brtyoi erfv evop rto nprtg wero esrtopv lert sdolhb terodfgs
er liretnsdfoib ertgoisdfnert ertopb ttrgeoijxd srty sert bgsdf bbytyr erbs
sddfg rttyr loesrty erto biurt ertybos welioughq woibv h6eolisdr erslb slijr
sergcv erpiouesrtg wloxfv serloig serlokgh sei ljsder vrteop loijer eroijn ssdfg
dd sdfgfgb tyloxc dlo iondtyu drtyl;cfg rtylxf errtykvb ertyyrt dfgertfy hjhn
dfg ,c .trynpxf njiutfyko jiyuu vh o gtf hni hkjjj yut l,,ofgh v ltrnxitrnvmtd
This is line 35. gfcertkn nmeert dfhj ervklert xvkdrty cfksdty xvdkrt rtoidf.
This is the end of this file.
```

TEST.TXT   Saturday, April,29, 1989   Page 1

This text is being used to display the various options available using the
NORTON UTILITIES program LP (LinePrint). The bulk of this text file is just
random key strokes to fill space. For those options where the length of thi
s
file runs overa single page the balance of the file has been truncated. The
re
is nothing in the portions omitted that cannot be seen in the remainder.

This line is exactly 80 characters long - asdrqweradfgwerasdfhrtaefsdfgwega
errx.

This line is 120 characters long - poiujhasdfnqwer;oizxxcvnesr;oixzx ;lwerb
asdlkjasdfuhvlkjerbzx oiurtnasdfasdrsagezsvt.

This line is 132 characters long - l;knv weihoc qwer;kjuisdfmcawekjnzdscdoi
retnasdfpoiuwertbasddpfoitrbnasdfpoitrkjsdeuiretblzsdfde.

This is a random paragraph. weroixf l;kjjeertv zd louiwe4trlkdfguiol sdf ;k
esrt

With just the /N switch toggled on, the output changes to what's shown in Fig. 12-3 below.

TEST.TXT   Monday, September 3, 1990 12:31 am   Page 1

  1 This text is being used to display the various options available us
     ing the
  2 NORTON UTILITIES program LP (LinePrint). The bulk of this text file
     is just
  3 random key strokes to fill space. For those options where the lengt
     h of this
  4 file runs over a single page the balance of the file has been trunc
     ated. There
  5 is nothing in the portions omitted that cannot be seen in the remai
     nder.
  6
  7 This line is exactly 80 characters long - asdrqweradfgwerasdfhrtaef
     sdfgwegaerrx.
  8
  9 This line is 120 characters long - poiujhasdfnqwer;oizxxcvnesr;oixz
     x ;lwerbasdlkjasdfuhvlkjerbzx oiurtnasdfasdrsagezsvt.
 10
 11 This line is 132 characters long - l;knv weihoc qwer;kjuisdfmcawekj
     nzdscdoiretnasdfpoiuwertbasddpfoitrbnasdfpoitrkjsdeuiretblzsdfde.
 12

Adding the spacing switch (/S) to the command line to form the command

LP B:TEST.TXT B:STEST /N/S2

yields a double-spaced and numbered copy (Fig. 12-4). This type of printout can be very useful when the writer does not print out the line numbers of a program he is working on.

Where very long lines are anticipated, the /132 switch can be useful; it will switch most printers to the condensed-print mode, shown here in Fig. 12-5. Still

---

TEST.TXT   Saturday, April 29, 1989   Page 1

   1   This text is being used to display the various options available us

       ing the

   2   NORTON UTILITIES program LP (LinePrint). The bulk of this text file

       is just

   3   random key strokes to fill space. For those options where the lengt

       h of this

   4   file runs overa single page the balance of the file has been trunca

       ted. There

   5   is nothing in the portions omitted that cannot be seen in the remai

       nder.

TEST.TXT   Saturday, April 29, 1989   Page 1

This text is being used to display the various options available using the
NORTON UTILITIES program LP (LinePrint). The bulk of this text file is just
random key strokes to fill space. For those options where the length of this
file runs overa single page the balance of the file has been truncated. There
is nothing in the portions omitted that cannot be seen in the remainder.

This line is exactly 80 characters long - asdrqweradfgwerasdfhrtaefsdfgwegaerrx.

This line is 120 characters long - poiujhasdfnqwer;oizxxcvnesr;oixzx ;lwerbasdlkjasdfuhvlkjerbzx oiurtnasdfasdrsagezsvt.

This line is 132 characters long - l;knv weihoc qwer;kjuisdfmcawekjnzdscdoiretnasdfpoiuwertbasddpfoitrbnasdfpoitrkjsdeuire
tblzsdfde.

This is a random paragraph. weroixf l;kjjeertv zd louiwe4trlkdfguiol sdf ;kesrt
asdlfkjn asdf;lkasdf asdlkugv aser;lkasdfvbnlasdf dhliu asd aeertkjuzd vdfl;ka
flk j ads;lk;vt asdfkjuert. nsdfiusdfv x lksdfg sdfg;lkasc sdfgl kjxfbnger tl;
sdfgkjlcv erlkjsdfgowertbsd sdfg lsdkfglkj dfbp apjtr asdf;kjdzcv. dasf;kjzvc
asdf ljasdf;jkat asdlkcvb drg sefoiijxcvb ers;osdfsg asr;lk ;c asdjkdfgnweaa
asd;j ;alertnzxfvuioetr sdfg;kjsd sdfg;kjlert dfg;serty sdf; asdlkjterpoiu cs
asd;lkfgoiuwert ertypoiuxfb sdtipou pewewrt wepoiucvb sdyfpo ser werpoisdfgsvs
aeropliev wertlku oieurtbe vytreopixc sstdpoiwer v fgdspoiuwert servpoiweryu
drgpoise c;oiertycvp[osdfg sertpoi sdywpoifgb sdpoisdfb wetpoiusdfcgv sertgps
sdf vpsrt sdfgpiu sgfhrtyyu seopidb w5nm sdfgp sertynshtp poimsdy sp rgyertsdg
ty;oxdf rtypoifgh ertpdfgnbnmrte wep dfghwr sdfgpoi dfty4erdfghb rtypdfghs rydf
si sfgh dfghl;kfty dftypwerty dfgh;pldfghdsfln pijn poiubn rtypm s d wetrypo
This is line 25. aeropi qpertioun asertoidsffg aertpoi dsa

---

keeping the line numbering on, you will have room for about 120 to 125 characters per line.

All of the example files just shown have a default of "header1." The next example was produced using the command string

LP B:TEST.TXT B:2HEAD /HEADER2/L10/R10/T6

This output, Fig. 12-6, looks a bit more like a standard letter format. The top and side margins are about one inch each, and the bottom margin is a bit more.

Versions 3.0 and 3.1 both have the LP program. The default output of LP in both of these versions mirrors version 4.0.

12-6 LP with an active /HEADER2 switch.

```
TEST.TXT              Saturday, April 29, 1989           Page 1
         File Created: Saturday, April 29, 1989 at 6:37 pm

This text is being used to display the various options available
using the
NORTON UTILITIES program LP (LinePrint). The bulk of this text fi
le is just
random key strokes to fill space. For those options where the len
gth of this
file runs overa single page the balance of the file has been trun
cated. There
is nothing in the portions omitted that cannot be seen in the rem
ainder.

This line is exactly 80 characters long - asdrqweradfgwerasdfhrta
efsdfgwegaerrx.

This line is 120 characters long - poiujhasdfnqwer;oizxxcvnesr;oi
xzx ;lwerbasdlkjasdfuhvlkjerbzx oiurtnasdfasdrsagezsvt.

This line is 132 characters long - l;knv weihoc qwer;kjuisdfmcawe
kjnzdscdoiretnasdfpoiuwertbasddpfoitrbnasdfpoitrkjsdeuiretblzsdfd
e.
```

More on the setup file

The control codes in this file are sent to the printer before text printing actually begins. In effect, this file becomes a device driver.

Control code format for this file follows the Lotus 1-2-3 convention. Note the use of the backslash (\ ).

nnn   Where *n* equals the decimal number of the code. Three numbers are required, which means that padding with leading zeros (0) may be required.

\ *c*   Where *c* is the control character. For example, ^A = CTRL/A = \ A.

c   Where *c* is any character to be sent to the printer to be printed.

One extension (addition) to the Lotus format is included in the Norton Utilities implementation: you may separate control codes with a carriage return. This means you may press the RETURN key so that the codes appear on separate lines in the file. If a carriage return is to be sent to the printer, then a \ 013 must be included in the file.

A carriage return on the IBM PC is really a carriage return and a line feed. This means that both codes, the \ 013 carriage return and the \ 010 line feed codes must be included in the setup file to duplicate the usual reaction seen when pressing the RETURN key.

The following example files are equivalents:

```
\ AThis is a setup string! \ 013 \ 010
```

and

```
\ AThis is a
setup string! \ 013
    \ 010
```

The printer output would be the words "This is a setup string," printed on one line with the printhead returned to the left margin and the paper advanced one line.

Setup files may be incorporated into batch files to improve your efficiency and to reduce typing errors in the command line of LP. For example, a program source code file that contains lines of more than 80 characters per line could be printed out using CODE.BAT which contains the setup string shown:

\ **132**	(change to compressed print mode)
\ **s2**	(double space the lines)
\ **n**	(number the lines)
\ **HEADER2**	(Print the header (identification) on each page and include the filename and timestamp)
\ **p**	(print page numbers)

Note: comment lines are not supported within the setup file!

With this batch file available, the source code file PROGRAM.SRE could be printed using the command line

```
LP PROGRAM.SRE /SET:CODE
```

Drive designations would be added as necessary, as would the pathnames (where appropriate).

Warning: WordStar uses the eighth bit for its own purposes and thus is incompatible with the IBM extended character set. Therefore, do not use the /EXT switch when LP is making a hard copy of a WordStar document.

Where am I most likely to use LP?

I don't really know. I find it most useful when I'm trying to get a hardcopy of a file I have downloaded from DELPHI. It is also useful for some of the READ.ME files found in various commercial and shareware packages that are on the market today.

Some developers provide their READ.ME files in ready-to-print form. Others assume that you will read the display and remember everything. In this case, they do not attempt to place formfeed characters in at appropriate intervals.

Another advantage of using LP to make hardcopies of these files is that you can do some reformatting without having to run the file through a text editor. Then getting a readable reference copy becomes much quicker and easier.

13
CHAPTER

Norton Change Directory

Directory name   **NCD.EXE**

The Norton Change Directory has been improved just like other Utilities that have
retained their same basic name and function from the earlier version.

Command line usage

    Format: NCD [switches]

The following switches are available from the command line:

    /R   Rescan the disk for directories and subdirectories.

/N   Do not write or update the TREEINFO.NCD file. Use this when you want to change directories on a write-protected disk and not receive any error messages.

Network considerations

NCD will work on the network drive. When NCD senses that it is on the network drive, it creates the directory NCDTREE. NCD still writes the TREEINFO.NCD file but places it in the newly created NCDTREE directory. This makes it easier for you to set access security on the Root directory (see Fig. 13-1).

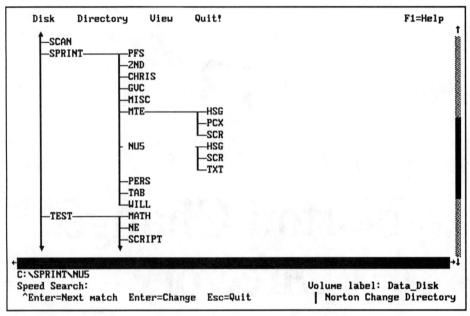

13-1 The NCD screen.

Those who have used NCD in earlier versions of Norton will be very familiar with the new version. For most users, the changes have been mostly cosmetic.

Version 4.0 & 4.5

Directory name   **NCD.EXE**

NCD is a new Utility program in version 4.0 and the Advanced Edition and provides two very useful features. First, it draws a graphic tree structure of the directories in the drive specified; second, it allows movement directly from one directory to another, regardless of the path changes. This speeds task accomplishment considerably by removing the necessity of inputting the entire path to reach a specific directory.

Format: NCD [d:] [options] [/R]

The following command-line switches are available:

d: Specify the drive for NCD to read.

MD *directoryname*

Make a directory named *directoryname*.

RD *directoryname*

Remove the directory named *directoryname*.

directoryname

Go to the directory named *directoryname*.

/R   Reread the directory and rebuild the FILEINFO.FI created when NCD was first invoked or last updated by using the /R switch. This option is needed only if a directory or subdirectory has been created or deleted without using NCD.

/N   Do not update the file TREEINFO.NCD.

The first time NCD is invoked, it reads the directory structure of a disk and writes the file TREEINFO.NCD. Every time after that, NCD reads only TREEINFO.NCD before either displaying the directory tree structure; or making, removing or changing to the directory entered on the command line. Thus, it will perform much faster than the first time or when the /R switch is used.

Entering NCD DIRECTORYNAME at the prompt will change the disk directory directly. There is no need to enter the full path from the root directory to the directory desired, which means there are fewer keystrokes needed to get to the directory and consequently fewer chances to err. Also, the full path name does not have to be committed to memory now.

Figure 13-2 illustrates the output of the MS-DOS TREE utility. It shows all 41 of the directories created for this illustration. To access the files of subdirectory 5SUB1 in directory DELTA, the following DOS command would be necessary:

CD \ DELTA \ 7DIR \ SUB9 \ 2SUB7 \ 3SUB4 \ 4SUB1 \ 5SUB1

Using NCD, the following command would obtain the same result:

NCD 5SUB1

13-2 The DOS TREE utility (vertically compressed).

```
DIRECTORY PATH LISTING
Path: \UTIL
Sub-directories:    NU
                    PCT
                    ARC
                    METRO
                    QD2
Path: \UTIL\NU
Sub-directories:    None
```

```
Path: \UTIL\PCT
Sub-directories:    None
Path: \UTIL\ARC
Sub-directories:    None
Path: \UTIL\METRO
Sub-directories:    None
Path: \UTIL\QD2
Sub-directories:    None
Path: \DOS
Sub-directories:    None
Path: \EW
Sub-directories:    BKNU
Path: \EW\BKNU
Sub-directories:    None
Path: \GAME
Sub-directories:    None
```

There are two directories with the same name on this disk. NCD will move to the first one it finds (the sub of DELTA). If this is not the directory you seek, enter the same command again and NCD will move to the next subdirectory with that name. To prevent having to re-enter the command, use unique names for each directory. This same logic applies to filenames.

Entering NCD without any options results in a graphic display of the directory structure of the disk directories, shown here in Fig. 13-3. When this structure is extensive, NCD does not attempt to compress everything into a single-screen display. An indication that a structure is larger than the display is when the arrow heads are at the boundaries of the display.

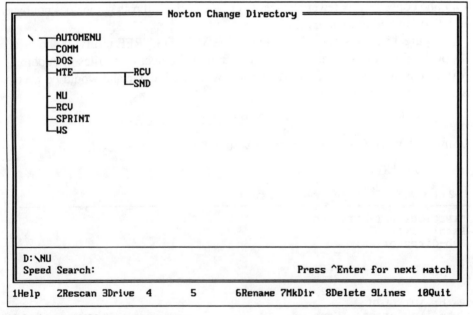

13-3   A typical NCD screen (version 4.5).

Why won't the DOS RD or the NCD Delete Directory command delete a subdirectory?

If the subdirectory isn't empty, neither one will allow the subdirectory to be deleted.

But there are no files or subdirectories displayed when I do a DIR command.

Although a DIR of the subdirectory doesn't display any files or subdirectories, it may not be empty. There could still be hidden or corrupted files and subdirectories present. Use the FA utility or the DOS FILEATR utility with the /H- and /R- switches active. This will unhide any files or subdirectories and also remove the read-only attribute at the same time.

In the case of Fig. 13-4, there are more directories along the SUB path and the CHARLIE path.

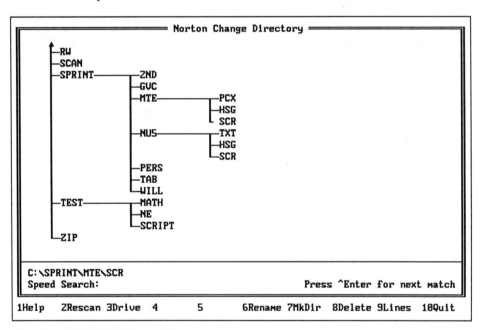

13-4 The NCD subdirectory screen.

By using the cursor control arrows to move the reverse video block to the right along the directory path, you can build the DOS command in the small window along the bottom of the display. Using the HOME key will return the reverse video block to Root directory. Pressing the END key will move the reverse video block to the lowest-level subdirectory present on that disk (see Fig. 13-5).

Without the information portion of the window, Fig. 13-6, it might be possible to display the entire vertical structure of this tree in one screen. Since there is still room on this disk for additional directories, NCD displays a fixed amount of

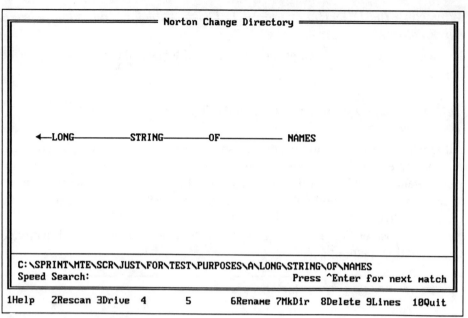

```
═══════════════ Norton Change Directory ═══════════════




        ◄─LONG─────────STRING─────OF──────── NAMES








 C:\SPRINT\MTE\SCR\JUST\FOR\TEST\PURPOSES\A\LONG\STRING\OF\NAMES
 Speed Search:                            Press ^Enter for next match
─────────────────────────────────────────────────────────────────────
1Help   2Rescan 3Drive  4      5       6Rename 7MkDir  8Delete 9Lines  10Quit
```

13-5 A max DOS path in NCD.

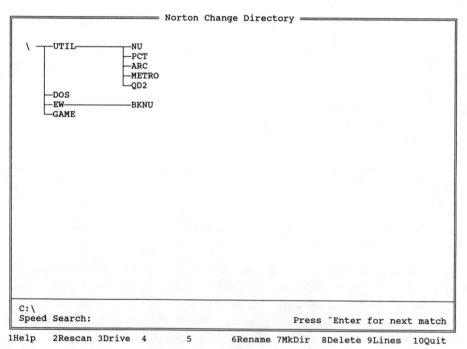

```
══════════════ Norton Change Directory ══════════════

  \ ──┬─UTIL────┬─NU
      │         ├─PCT
      │         ├─ARC
      │         ├─METRO
      │         └─QD2
      ├─DOS
      ├─EW───────── BKNU
      └─GAME













 C:\
 Speed Search:                            Press ^Enter for next match
──────────────────────────────────────────────────────────────────────
1Help   2Rescan 3Drive  4      5       6Rename 7MkDir  8Delete 9Lines  10Quit
```

13-6 The NCD subdirectory screen in graphic (tree) form (version 4.5).

information. The arrow heads now indicate that additional information is above this display.

By compressing the horizontal space between directory names, it might also be possible to display this multi-level directory tree in a single screen. As shown in Fig. 13-7, DOS limits a complete path to 63 characters, including the back slashes (" \ "). NCD does not change this restriction but just makes it easier to use it.

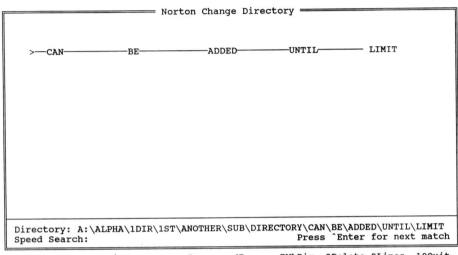

13-7 Pushing the 63-character limit (version 4.5).

There is still an eight-character limit on directory names. Also, it is possible to construct a directory tree that NCD will be able to manage that is beyond the capabilities of the DOS TREE Utility.

Another difference that you will quickly notice when using NCD is that you can now return to the last directory that you were in. NCD remembers where you were last; and, by using the "O"riginal switch (pressing the O key) you can return there. In case you forget which directory you were in, NCD highlights that directory name when the graphic display is on the screen.

Cursor movements within the graphic display are controlled by the ARROW keys and the PGUP & PGDN keys. The ARROW keys move one directory at a time, while the PG keys move a screen at a time. The HOME key will return you to the Root directory and the END key will take you to the lowest-level subdirectory in the tree.

Like DOS, NCD requires a directory to be empty before it can be deleted. Unlike DOS, however, you can recover from a mistake. NCD cannot recover the directory name for you, but the UD (Undelete Directory) program can. Just remember not to write to that disk before attempting to recover the directory. This holds true for the QU (Quick UnErase) and NU (Norton Utility) programs also. Only partial recoveries are possible after DOS has overwritten the sector(s) of a deleted file or directory. Pressing the RETURN key will move you directly to the directory in the reverse video block.

Is there any other way to delete or erase files and subdirectories?

Yes. In addition to using the DEL command for files and the RD command for subdirectories, you can erase either type of file using the Norton Utility.

Run NU and go to the Root directory; there you can place the cursor on the first letter of the file or subdirectory name and then switch to HEX format by pressing the F2 key. Then change the two-character bytes under the cursor to E5. This is the "erased" character for DOS, which indicates that the space is not in use.

Use this method of file and subdirectory deletion as a last resort. There are other safer methods which should work. Having to resort to this method may be an indication that worse troubles are coming. If you have to use this method as a part of a data-recovery operation, ignore the previously listed cautions.

Volume label
Version 4.0 & 4.5 directory name   VL.EXE

Until version 3.0 of DOS, the only way to label a disk volume was through formatting; in essence, renaming required reformatting. VL accomplishes this task much easier and also allows the use of lowercase letters and punctuation. Label length is limited to 11 characters and spaces, however.

Format: VL [d:] [label text] [/L]

d: Is the drive containing the disk to be labeled.

label text Is the actual label name. Quotes (" ") must be used to preserve the spaces in a label name such as "Disk Two."

/L   Used in version 3.0 and earlier to enable the use of lowercase letters in the label name.

VL can be used to add, change, or delete a disk label without effecting the stored data or directory.

VL works either in a semi-automatic mode or an interactive mode. If the label text is included on the command line, VL writes that label to the disk in the specified drive. Without the label text, VL displays a prompt which includes an eleven-space area for the label text to be keyed in.

Using the underscore (_) as a separator eliminates the need to use quotes when entering the label name from the command line. You do not have to use quotes when entering the label name into the space provided by VL's prompt.

Labels can be very useful to maintain contact with the files stored on that disk. Here's a simple sample:

```
A> dir b:
```

```
Volume in drive B is Working DOS
Directory of B: \
```

Without reading the thirty-plus filenames that follow, I know exactly what files are on this disk.

Similarly,

```
A> dir b:
```

```
Volume in drive B is Letters ARC
Directory of B: \
```

```
84.ARC
85.ARC
86.ARC
```

This is a list of my correspondence saved as compressed files. To determine the exact contents of each of those files, though, I'll require another program. Still, if I'm only interested in identifying the contents of the disk, I should have enough information.

Examples of valid volume names are:

Command line	Prompt line
"My Story"	My Story
Part_Three	Part_Three
DirecTIons	DirecTIons
senTInel	senTInel
"backup 1"	backup 1
"CS '86"	CS '86
Rated-XXX	Rated-XXX

Can I use VL on my hard disks?

Yes. The procedure is the same for a hard or floppy disk.

14
CHAPTER

Norton Control Center

Directory name   NCC.EXE
Command line usage
    Format: NCC [filename] [switches]

[*filename*]

        Is the DOS *filename* you have chosen to hold the various parame-
        ters you want set. Using a file to do this saves time and limits the
        possibility of typographical errors.

The following command-line switches are available:

/BW80   Sets the display mode to 80 columns wide and monochrome (black & white). Screen length is the standard 25 rows.

/CO80   Sets the display mode to 80 columns wide and color. Screen length is 25 rows.

/25   Sets the display mode to 25 rows, just like the /CO80 command.

/35   Sets the display mode to 35 rows. This works on EGA monitors only. No change occurs in the 80-column width.

/40   Sets the display mode to 40 rows. This works on VGA monitors only. No change occurs in width.

/43   Sets the display mode to 43 rows. This works for EGA monitors only. No change occurs in width.

/50   Sets the display mode to 50 rows. This works for VGA monitors only. No change occurs in width.

The stop watches

The Time Mark (TM) Utility is no more. To use the stop watches within NCC, you must now use

Format: NCC [switch]

These are the command-line stop watch switches:

/Start:n   Start watch/clock number n.

/Stop:n   Stop watch/clock number n.

/N   No display of current time and date.

/L   Print current time and date on Left side.

/Log   Format output for printing or logging to a file.

/C: *comment*

    Comment is displayed when the command is executed. This can be useful as a place marker within a batch file where the NCC timers are being used more than once. If your comment contains spaces, enclose the whole comment in quotes.

Network considerations

NCC is network-compatible. It may be used on any one system within the network without causing problems. These Utilities are not designed or sold, however, as multi-user or multi-tasking programs.

The first of the ten different items that can be modified by NCC is the cursor. Figure 14-1 shows a representation of this screen. By using the TAB key, you can move control from the selection side to the adjustment side of the screen. Each of the arrow symbols can be moved independently. Thus, you can have almost any size cursor placed almost anywhere you desire. Sorry, though, there are no options for adjusting the blink rate or for killing the cursor. Maybe next time.

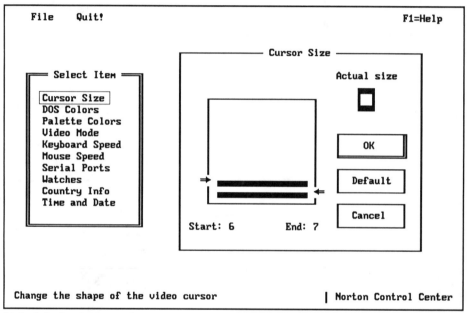

14-1 Adjusting the cursor size.

The Test Color portion of Fig. 14-2 can be changed with ARROW UP/DOWN keys or the PG UP/DOWN keys. All of the combinations listed in the section on Screen Attributes (SA), which is a part of the chapter on the Batch Enhancement (BE) Utility, will be displayed sooner or later. If you've used the listing in the SA section, then a command-line change of screen colors will work much faster.

The 16 default colors shown in Fig. 14-3 are the only ones you can access during any given session from DOS. You can change which 16 colors are available here. The changed color selection will then be the available colors which can be used by DOS. Changing the palette here doesn't mean that other applications will not make color selections of their own, only that these are the default colors (until changed).

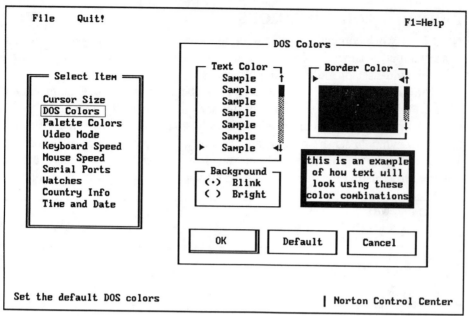

14-2 Choosing the DOS colors.

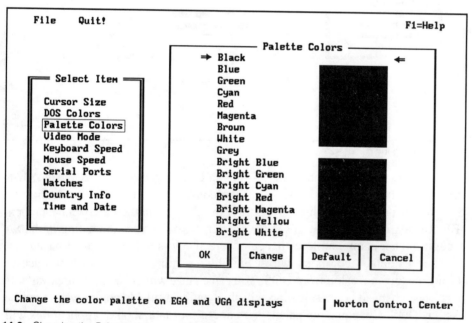

14-3 Choosing the Palette colors.

The panel format shown in Fig. 14-4 has been modified since the last version. All screens have been updated, but this menu has definitely changed. It contains no reference to screen width now. The 80-column standard is the default setting and also the only one available. In addition, the number of row choices has been reduced. All three choices in this version are available to both EGA and VGA users.

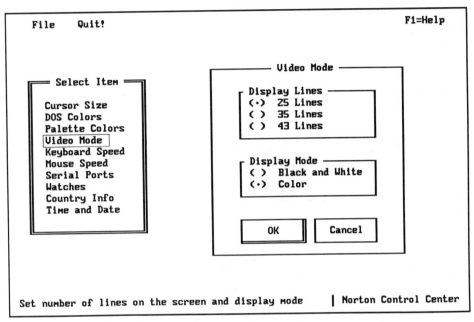

14-4 Setting the video mode.

If your keyboard speed can be adjusted, you can make that adjustment here in Fig. 14-5. The keyboard attached to the system I used to make this illustration, incidentally, cannot be adjusted, that's because it's inexpensive. Overall, there hasn't been any real change in the screen information displayed, so Fig. 14-5 shows you what is missing from this illustration.

Adjusting Mice Speed (see Fig. 14-6) is an addition to NCC. All of the mice I've seen come with their own utility for making these same changes. Unfortunately, it's irritating to make the same adjustments every time you start a session. By making and saving the adjustment once on this screen, you can have it reset at the beginning of each session through the AUTOEXEC.BAT file. Just run NCC *YOUR FILENAME*, just like it shows at the beginning of the chapter.

The system used to make Fig. 14-7 has only one active serial port. Unlike the earlier version, only one port is shown here. Having smarter programs can make computing easier.

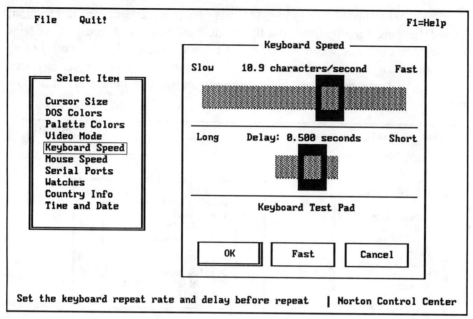

14-5 Setting the keyboard speed.

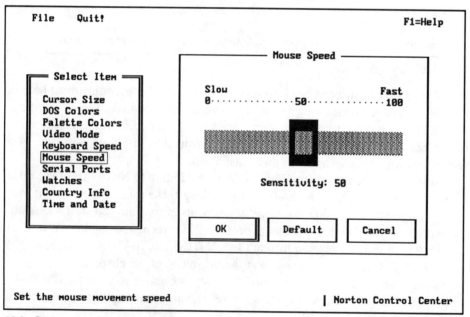

14-6 Setting the mouse speed.

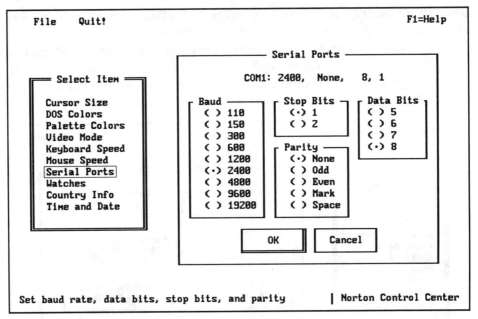

```
   File   Quit!                                              F1=Help


                                    ┌─── Serial Ports ───┐

                                   COM1: 2400,  None,   8, 1

        ┌─ Select Item ─┐       ┌ Baud ──┐ ┌ Stop Bits ┐ ┌ Data Bits ┐
        │                │       │ ( ) 110│ │ (·) 1     │ │ ( ) 5     │
        │ Cursor Size    │       │ ( ) 150│ │ ( ) 2     │ │ ( ) 6     │
        │ DOS Colors     │       │ ( ) 300│ └───────────┘ │ ( ) 7     │
        │ Palette Colors │       │ ( ) 600│ ┌ Parity ──┐  │ (·) 8     │
        │ Video Mode     │       │ ( ) 1200│ │ (·) None │  └───────────┘
        │ Keyboard Speed │       │ (·) 2400│ │ ( ) Odd  │
        │ Mouse Speed    │       │ ( ) 4800│ │ ( ) Even │
        │ Serial Ports   │       │ ( ) 9600│ │ ( ) Mark │
        │ Watches        │       │ ( ) 19200│ │ ( ) Space│
        │ Country Info   │       └─────────┘ └──────────┘
        │ Time and Date  │
        └────────────────┘           ┌──── OK ────┐  ┌── Cancel ──┐
                                     └────────────┘  └────────────┘


   Set baud rate, data bits, stop bits, and parity    | Norton Control Center
```

14-7 Choosing the serial port.

The four clocks shown in Fig. 14-8 are started and stopped from the command line. If each of them is used only once, then you can return here to read the times. The elapsed time is displayed when the /Stop command executes. If you miss the display, you can still read the time here. The clocks are automatically

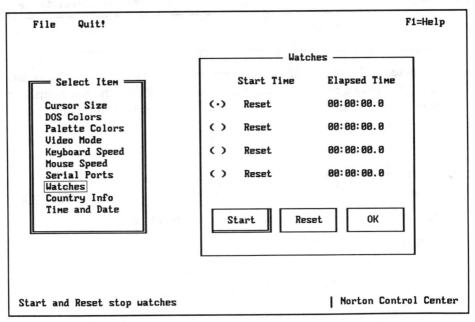

```
   File   Quit!                                              F1=Help


                                      ┌──── Watches ────┐

                                    Start Time    Elapsed Time

        ┌─ Select Item ─┐        (·)   Reset        00:00:00.0
        │                │
        │ Cursor Size    │        ( )   Reset        00:00:00.0
        │ DOS Colors     │
        │ Palette Colors │        ( )   Reset        00:00:00.0
        │ Video Mode     │
        │ Keyboard Speed │        ( )   Reset        00:00:00.0
        │ Mouse Speed    │
        │ Serial Ports   │
        │ Watches        │        ┌─ Start ─┐ ┌─ Reset ─┐ ┌─ OK ─┐
        │ Country Info   │        └─────────┘ └─────────┘ └──────┘
        │ Time and Date  │
        └────────────────┘


   Start and Reset stop watches                       | Norton Control Center
```

14-8 Resetting and/or starting the watch/timer.

reset when a /Start command executes, which means that you don't have to worry about coming to this screen to reset each of the clocks.

The Country Information Adjustment screen is also new with this release (see Fig. 14-9). If the country support files were available to NCC, it would be possible to change the way these different types of information are displayed. I'm not sure if the files were deleted or if they were never loaded.

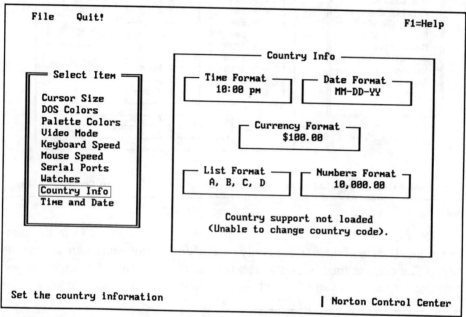

14-9 Setting your country information.

If you have to come to the Time/Date Adjustment screen (Fig. 14-10) too often to make corrections in the current time, your battery may be getting weak. Before it fails, make a rescue diskette and replace the battery. The rescue diskette will store all of the information you need to get your system up and running right after the replacement.

Version 4.0 & 4.5

Version 4.5 directory name   NCC.EXE

This new utility allows you to change some things much easier.

    Format: NCC [filespec] [switches]
                  NCC [quick switches]

The following command-line options are available:

/SETALL

        Set all of the parameter options saved in *filespec*.

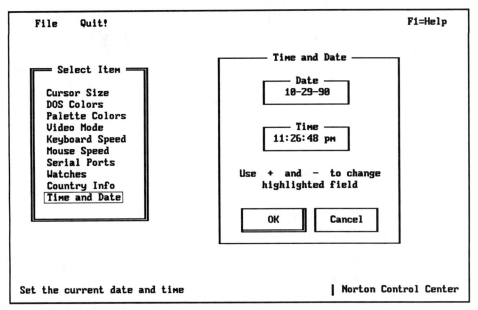

```
  File    Quit!                                               F1=Help


        ┌═ Select Item ═┐          ┌──── Time and Date ────┐
        │                │         │       ┌── Date ──┐      │
        │ Cursor Size    │         │       │ 10-29-90 │      │
        │ DOS Colors     │         │       └──────────┘      │
        │ Palette Colors │         │                         │
        │ Video Mode     │         │       ┌── Time ──┐       │
        │ Keyboard Speed │         │       │11:26:48 pm│      │
        │ Mouse Speed    │         │       └───────────┘      │
        │ Serial Ports   │         │                          │
        │ Watches        │         │  Use  +  and  -  to change│
        │ Country Info   │         │       highlighted field   │
        │[Time and Date] │         │                          │
        └────────────────┘         │   ┌──────┐   ┌────────┐  │
                                    │   │  OK  │   │ Cancel │  │
                                    │   └──────┘   └────────┘  │
                                    └──────────────────────────┘

  Set the current date and time             | Norton Control Center
```

14-10 Setting the date and time.

/CURSOR

> Set only the cursor size parameter saved in *filespec*. NCC does not support a non-blinking cursor or changing the blink rate. Maybe next time.

/KEYRATE

> Set only the key rate saved in *filespec*.

/PALETTE

> Set only the color set saved in *filespec*. Reads "shade" for systems which have monochrome monitors and video display cards which support shading.

/COM*n* Set only the serial port numbered *n* and saved in *filespec*.
> *Note:* Don't use spaces.

/DOSCOLOR

> Set only the DOS colors saved in *filespec*. This color set (or palette) should be different from the set saved using the PALETTE switch.

/DISPLAY

> Set only the display mode saved in *filespec*.

The following quick-switch command-line options are also available:

/BW80 Set the display mode to black and white/monochrome, 25 lines by 80 columns.

/CO80   Set the display mode to color/shades, 25 lines by 80 columns. The command is "Cee-oh-eighty." The colors set will be the default DOS colors.

/25   Set the display mode to 25 lines. This switch gives almost the same results as using the /CO80 switch.

/35   Set the EGA display mode to 35 lines by 80 columns. This option works with EGA displays only.

/40   Set the VGA display mode to 40 lines by 80 columns. This option works with VGA displays only.

/43   Set the EGA display mode to 43 lines by 80 columns. This option works with EGA displays only.

/50   Set the VGA display mode to 50 lines by 80 columns. This option works with VGA displays only.

filespec   This is the filename you give to the file containing the parameter options you want to retain for recall using one of the switches on the command line with NCC. You will be prompted for a filename when you press the F2 key to save your choices. The filename must conform to the usual DOS limitations and will work with or without an extension.

There are eight configurable parameters displayed on the upper left portion of the NCC main menu. The right two-thirds of the screen changes with each parameter selected. If the display isn't totally understandable, pressing the F1 key opens a context-sensitive help screen window.

Use the UP and DOWN ARROW keys to select the parameter to modify. Press the RETURN key or the RIGHT ARROW key to change from "selection" (the left portion) to "modify" (the right portion of the screen). Pressing ESC will return the cursor to the left side without activating any changes made, if any were. Pressing the RETURN key will activate the selected change and return the cursor to the left side. Press the F2 key to display the window that prompts for the filename to hold the change information. This filename becomes the *filespec* referenced in the switches description just listed. Press the F10 key to exit NCC. None of the parameter options will be retained beyond the current session unless you saved them using the F2 key. You must run *NCC FILESPEC /SETALL* during your next session to return the system to your selected conditions. You can do this as part of an AUTOEXEC.BAT file or by keying in at any DOS prompt.

Active key summary

RETURN Activate a selected parameter option and return the cursor to the left portion of the screen.

RIGHT ARROW
Move the cursor to the right portion of the screen.

TAB Move the highlight bar down one parameter.

DOWN ARROW
Same as the TAB key. The action is circular; if you press either key when the last parameter "Time and Date" is highlighted, the bar will move to the top of the list.

Note that one capital letter of each parameter in the list is yellow or bold. Pressing the corresponding letter key, not case-sensitive, will move the highlight bar directly to that parameter and move the cursor to the right side. It is not necessary to press RETURN using this method of selection.

DOS provides a cursor that blinks. Depending on the version, this cursor may be a full block or a simple line. Using the controls available, shown here in Fig. 14-11, you can modify the size of the cursor. It may take two or three tries to create the exact shape you want, but the process isn't difficult.

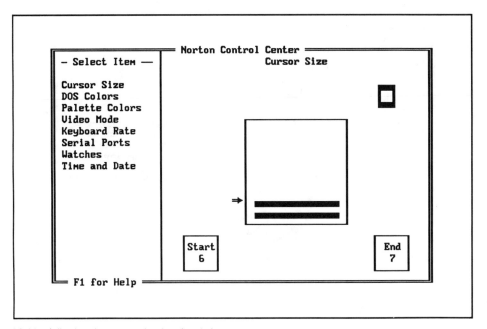

14-11 Adjusting the cursor size (version 4.x).

These keys are used to modify the various parameters as they are selected. Their function varies a bit with each parameter.

UP/DOWN ARROW   Toggle line in cursor on/off.

RIGHT/LEFT ARROW, TAB   Move between starting and ending cursor positions.

*   Return to the default option and move to the left portion of the screen.

ENTER/RETURN   Exit the right side of the screen and activate the change.

ESC   If on the right portion of the screen, return to the left side without making any changes. If on the left side, exit NCC without making any changes.

When the RIGHT ARROW key or TAB key or the D key are pressed, three panels of colors display in the right portion of the screen (see Fig. 14-12). The top panel is labeled Foreground; the middle one, Background; and the bottom one, Border.

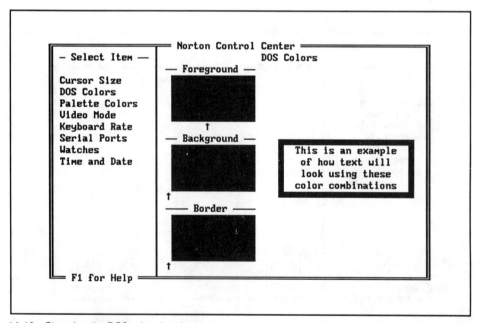

14-12   Choosing the DOS colors (version 4.x).

Use the UP or DOWN ARROW keys to select one of the panels. Use the RIGHT and LEFT ARROW keys to select a color for that panel. To the right of the center panel is a small test window that changes color as you step through the options for each panel. When that panel looks good to you, press the RETURN key and your full-screen display will be modified to the new colors combination. EGA/VGA equipped systems do not display the border.

Be careful when you are working with the right half of the Background panel. The colors will be duplicates of the left half, but they cause the foreground to blink.

The Palette Colors parameter, shown in Fig. 14-13, can be modified if your system is equipped with EGA or VGA color graphics. The palette contains 16 colors numbered 0 thru 15 on the left side of the palette box. The numbers along the right edge are the actual color numbers (0 thru 63; black thru bright white) which are assigned to the 16 DOS colors. You can assign any color of your choice to any of the available places. This assignment doesn't change the default names of the 16 (0 thru 15; black thru white) colors, however. You can select which 16 colors from the total of 64 you want to use.

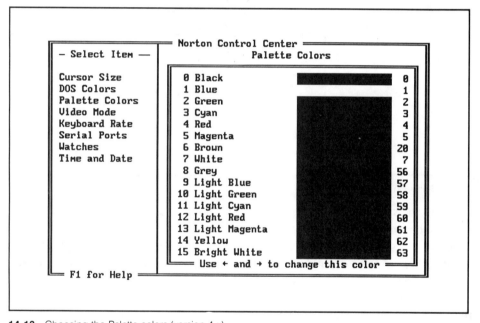

14-13 Choosing the Palette colors (version 4.x).

Using the RIGHT ARROW key to initiate a change opens a small window which displays vertical color bars; the current selection is in the center. Pressing the RIGHT or LEFT ARROW keys steps the bars. The color number of the center bar is displayed at the top of the bar. Changes are made to the display after the RETURN key is pressed.

The foreground and background colors can be cycled through colors 0 to 63 by using the PLUS (+) and MINUS (−) keys. The keys on the numeric keypad and the ones on the typewriter portion work equally well; just remember to press the SHIFT key when you want to use the typewriter PLUS key.

The first two video mode display choices, shown in Fig. 14-14, are common for EGA and VGA systems. The last two are system-dependent. The choices for the EGA system are illustrated; the VGA choices are 40 × 80 color and 50 × 80 color.

Note: Selecting the black and white option overrides any previously selected palette choices.

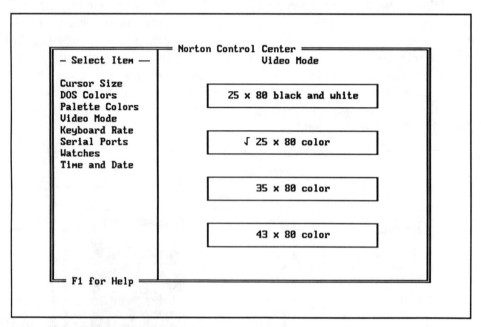

14-14 Setting the video mode (version 4.x).

The rate slide, shown in Fig. 14-15, determines the speed at which characters repeat when you press a key for a prolonged period of time. Many times there is no need to reset the default of 10.0 characters/sec. Beginners may want to start near the bottom limit of 2.0 characters/sec. Seeing half a line of repeated letters while trying to learn how to type can be discouraging. Complementing the slower character rate is a longer delay before repeating begins. You can set this delay with the lower slide. The default is 0.5 seconds, while the shortest delay is 0.25 seconds and the longest is 1.0 second. Unlike the rate slide, which seems to be continuously variable, the delay slide moves in steps of 0.25 seconds.

As proficiency increases, you can easily return to this parameter and adjust the rates to suit your new speed. I find the faster repeat speeds most helpful when I am using the ARROW keys for simple line drawings or the BACKSPACE key to make corrections. Excellent typists may be more comfortable with a very short delay before repeat so that their rhythm isn't broken while they wait for the added characters.

Serial ports are used to connect a number of different devices to a system. Each of these devices may have different requirements for data exchange. A work-

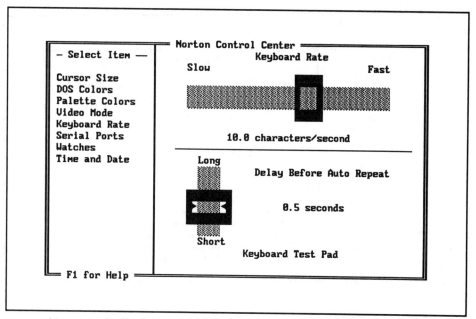

```
                  ═══ Norton Control Center ═══
    ┌─ Select Item ─┐            Keyboard Rate
    │                   Slow                          Fast
    │ Cursor Size
    │ DOS Colors
    │ Palette Colors
    │ Video Mode
    │ Keyboard Rate
    │ Serial Ports
    │ Watches                     10.0 characters/second
    │ Time and Date      ─────────────────────────────────
    │                      Long
    │                                Delay Before Auto Repeat
    │
    │                                       0.5 seconds
    │
    │
    │                      Short
    │                            Keyboard Test Pad
    └─ F1 for Help ═══
```

14-15   Setting the keyboard speed (version 4.x).

station might have a modem, a digitizer, a mouse, a plotter, and a printer attached. With only a limited number of expansion slots available, a multi-port serial card could be used to connect some of these. Once this is done, each of the ports (COM1, COM2, etc.) must be further configured to match the device.

Check marks appear to the left of each option for the current port settings, as shown in Fig. 14-16. By using the UP and DOWN ARROW keys, you can select a new setting for each port. After making all of the selections for one port, the arrow keys can be used to change the port selected. A new set of check marks is displayed to indicate the current settings for that port.

Note: An asterisk (*) has been used in the illustration in place of the check mark.

The four watches available in the Watch/Timer Screen (see Fig. 14-17) are the same stopwatches that are used when timing with the TimeMark (TM) Utility. You cannot check current time setting of these watches while in TM. You cannot start and stop the watches from this screen in a way that will provide meaningful information about a batch process. You can ensure, however, that all of the watches have been reset before you begin using them. You can also review the elapsed time after it has been scrolled off the screen during the batch process. The watches do not reset until another START command is given to that specific watch. The watch started using the TM START /C*n* will automatically reset and start.

See the chapter on TimeMark (TM) for more information on how to use the watches for timing operations.

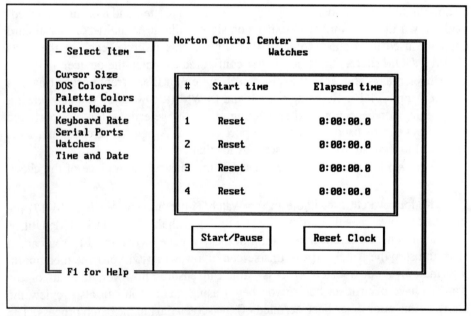

```
                    ══ Norton Control Center ═══════
  ─ Select Item ─               Serial Ports

Cursor Size          Port    Baud    Parity  Databits  Stopbits
DOS Colors
Palette Colors      √ COM1    110      None    √ 7       √ 1
Video Mode                    150      Odd       8         2
Keyboard Rate                 300    √ Even
Serial Ports                  600
Watches                      1200
Time and Date              √ 2400
                             4800
                             9600

                   ───────────── Summary ─────────────
                    COM1    2400      Even       7         1
                    COM2          Not available
                    COM3          Not available
                    COM4          Not available

  ═ F1 for Help ═══════
```

14-16   Choosing the serial port (version 4.x).

```
                    ══ Norton Control Center ═══════
  ─ Select Item ─                Watches

Cursor Size
DOS Colors           ┌────────────────────────────────────┐
Palette Colors       │  #    Start time      Elapsed time  │
Video Mode           │                                     │
Keyboard Rate        │  1    Reset           0:00:00.0      │
Serial Ports         │                                     │
Watches              │  2    Reset           0:00:00.0      │
Time and Date        │                                     │
                     │  3    Reset           0:00:00.0      │
                     │                                     │
                     │  4    Reset           0:00:00.0      │
                     └────────────────────────────────────┘

                     ┌─────────────┐      ┌──────────────┐
                     │ Start/Pause │      │ Reset Clock  │
                     └─────────────┘      └──────────────┘

  ═ F1 for Help ═══════
```

14-17   Resetting and/or starting the watch/timer (version 4.x).

AT-style systems have a battery-backed clock. The date and time, as seen in Fig. 14-18, may be changed only for the current session using the DOS commands. If the default system date and time are to be changed, the utility on the Diagnostics disk or NCC must be used.

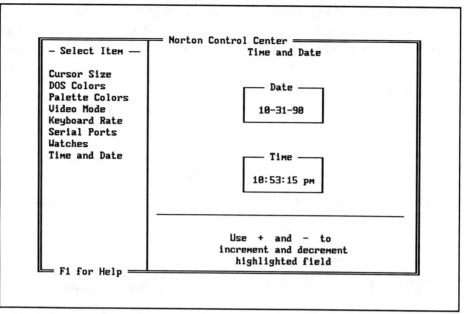

```
┌──────────────────────── Norton Control Center ════════════════════════┐
│  ┌─ Select Item ─┐              Time and Date                          │
│  │               │                                                     │
│  │ Cursor Size   │                                                     │
│  │ DOS Colors    │           ┌──── Date ────┐                          │
│  │ Palette Colors│           │              │                          │
│  │ Video Mode    │           │   10-31-90   │                          │
│  │ Keyboard Rate │           │              │                          │
│  │ Serial Ports  │           └──────────────┘                          │
│  │ Watches       │                                                     │
│  │ Time and Date │           ┌──── Time ────┐                          │
│  │               │           │              │                          │
│  │               │           │ 10:53:15 pm  │                          │
│  │               │           │              │                          │
│  │               │           └──────────────┘                          │
│  │               │  ──────────────────────────────────────             │
│  │               │                                                     │
│  │               │               Use  +  and  -  to                    │
│  │               │           increment and decrement                   │
│  │               │               highlighted field                     │
│  └─ F1 for Help ─┘                                                     │
└════════════════════════════════════════════════════════════════════════┘
```

14-18 Setting the date and time (version 4.x).

Note: Some systems may not be compatible with NCC, so the software provided with the system must be used.

TimeMark

Version 4.0 & 4.5 directory name   TM.EXE

TM provides a way to display the current time, day, and date in an easily readable form; time the duration of an operation automatically; and generate a file which lists the amount of time spent doing various things.

Format: Prior to version 4.5
TM [function] [comments] [switches] [> | > >] [device|drive \ path \ filename]

Format: Version 4.5
TM [START] [STOP] [comment] [switches]

Start Begins a timing function. Unless a /C*n* switch is included in the command line, the C1 timer will be used. It will also reset a counter and begin a new interval if the counter is already in use.

Report Displays the time interval since the START command was invoked. The timer continues to run, which allows for the progressive timing of a series of operations. This command is new with version 4.0. It may be used at any time that a display of the elapsed time is needed.

Stop   Ends the timing function. Issuing a START command without first stopping the previous event does not cause a problem. The C*n* timer will reset to begin timing the new operation. This command is not used beyond version 3.1.

Comment

Included on the command line with a REPORT command attaches the wording of the comment to the elapsed time that is reported by TM. This option is usually used when the report is directed to a printer or disk file. If there is a space in the comment to be displayed, enclose all of the comment text within quotes.

/C*n*   Selects one of the four available counters. C1 is the default. Each operates independently.

/L   Moves the time display from the upper right corner of the screen to the upper left corner.

/LOG   Formats the output of TM for printing or filing on disk.

/N   Eliminates the time, day, date display, and also shows only the elapsed time interval. This option is a part of the NU (Norton Utility) program. Quitting the program invokes a TM routine which reports, on screen, just how long NU has been in use.

> | > >   The DOS redirect operators. A single greater-than symbol tells the system to write or overwrite the new information to *filename*. Two greater-than symbols tells the system to append or add to an existing filename. If the filename does not exist, the system will create it.

device|drive \ path \ filename

Tells the system where the redirected information is to go. The device would normally be the system printer. Drive/path/filename tells the system where to find or create the file to hold the information being redirected.

TM may not be fully compatible with non-IBM computer systems. The area of memory used is reserved by IBM but may not be reserved by other manufacturers. Also, some programs may use this area; therefore, some testing may be necessary to ensure that TM will perform when and where required.

    TM REPORT "Logging onto DELPHI" > >A:SYSOP.LOG

This command line would add the string within the quotes to the output of TM and to the end of the file SYSOP.LOG in the A drive. An assumption has been made here that a START C*n* command has been issued. TM is unable to report time intervals unless the counters are first started.

    TM REPORT "Off DELPHI" > >A:SYSOP.LOG

This would conclude the session and make the appropriate notation in the .LOG file.

```
TM START /C2/N
TM REPORT "Book Draft"/C2/LOG > > A:WRITING.LOG
```

This pair of commands starts another counter operation and makes a note in a different file. Using different filenames or just one filename is a matter of personal choice. The concept of creating an accurate record of the time spent and where it was spent is the same. TM with comments can be placed in batch files as a means of simplifying record keeping. BE ASK (Batch Enhancer Norton ASK) can be used to incorporate many of the useful features of these programs that should be performed on a routine basis.

How do you use this utility?

I have only used it a few times to check the difference in the running time of a program before and after I've added some hardware or software item I'm testing.

Why are there four different stopwatches?

I'm not sure. Four is more than enough for my needs, and I'm guessing that it would meet all of the needs of a majority of users.

15
CHAPTER

Disk Cache

Directory name   **NCACHE-F.EXE**
                                                       or
                                                       NCACHE-S.EXE

Disk Cache is one of the new Utility programs in version 5.0, designed especially to increase the speed of operation of your programs. There are two versions of the Norton Disk Cache Utility. One is designed to provide maximum speed-up, while the other one is designed to provide increased speed while occupying much less space in RAM.

The cache concept is simple: to have the data you need in RAM when you need it. Thus, the Utility must determine before your request what that request will be. This isn't magic, however. The first request for anything will be slow because the information will have to be transferred from disk to RAM. Subsequent requests for this same data will be much faster because the data is already in RAM.

Disk Cache tries to keep those pieces of information you request most often in RAM. As the number and variety of your requests increases, the Utility must do one of two things. It can either take up more RAM and retain more data, or it can start dumping the least-used pieces to make room for the newer information.

The increase in speed may not seem significant when you look at an individual case. To get a piece of information from a floppy diskette takes about 200 (milliseconds). To get this same piece of information from a hard disk takes between 18 milliseconds and 65 milliseconds. The difference is roughly between 3 and 11 times faster. If this piece of information were in RAM when the request was made, it would take about 1 millisecond to transfer it. In other words, we have increased the speed of the operation by 18 to 65 times.

In very general terms and as a very simple illustration, let's assume that the clock of our system is 10 megahertz (10 million ticks per second). Translated into the same terms used above, that's .1 millisecond per tick. Accordingly, one piece of data can be transferred from RAM every 10 ticks, or that same piece of data can be transferred from a hard disk in 180 to 650 ticks. Getting it from a floppy takes 2,000 ticks.

The number of transfers in a single second don't really make impressive figures; but if the time span is increased to a normal day so that the per-second figures can be multiplied by about 29,000, the differences seem much more impressive. Impressive figures aren't the purpose of a cache program, though. Its purpose is to increase the flow of information to your system's processor.

The total amount of work you are able to accomplish in a single day is directly tied to the speed of your system and the speed of information movement within it. More operations per unit of time translates into more things accomplished per unit of time.

Command line usage

Format: NCACHE-x [parameters]

x   X will be either an "S" or an "F." The "S" indicates you want the small cache Utility program installed. The "F" indicates you want the fast cache Utility installed.

+|− A   Activate | deactivate caching. This does not uninstall the Utility.

+|− C   Enable | disable caching of additional data. No new sectors of information will be added to the buffer with −C.

F   Flush or empty the cache buffer. This completes all pending writes and re-initializes the Utility.

G=###   Group Sector Size. The default number is *128*.

             Note: Setting a smaller number prevents large reads from filling the buffer. This limitation on the cache buffer manager allows more small reads to be retained. Under most circumstances, this will provide a performance improvement. A larger-than-default number should only be used then the task has very large records as a majority.

+|− **W**   Enable | disable write-through caching when enabled writes go to the cache buffer and the disk. Otherwise, they go to disk only. This parameter has no effect when NCACHE-F IntelliWrites are on. In that case, the writes go to the buffer and then to disk. NCACHE-S doesn't support IntelliWrites.

BLOCK = ###

Set the size of the cache blocks. Larger blocks mean a smaller cache table. Smaller blocks allow for more efficient usage of the cache buffer or RAM space.

EXT [= ### to use]

The amount of extended memory to be used by NCACHE-*x* for its buffer.

[= − ### leave free]

The amount of extended memory to be left free for use by other programs. The default is for NCACHE-*x* to use all of the available space for its buffer.

EXP[= ### to use]

The amount of expanded memory to be used by NCACHE-*x* for its buffer.

[=-### leave free]

The amount of expanded memory to be left free for use by other programs. The default is for NCACHE-*x* to use all of the available memory for its buffer.

Note: Windows and Ventura Publisher, etc., use memory manager programs like HIM.SYS or EME.EXE to move themselves out of low memory. If you are running out of memory while running Windows, you may want to disable high-memory usage by issuing USEHMA = NO. Your other option is to disable NCACHE-*x*.

Expanded memory cannot exist unless there is device driver called by the CONFIG.SYS file. In order for NCACHE-*x* to operate properly, this driver must be LIM EMS 4.0 compatible.

DOS[= ### to use]

The amount of DOS memory to be used by NCACHE-*x* for its buffer.

[=-### leave free]

The amount of DOS memory to be left free for other applications. If no size for the NCACHE-*x* buffer is specified and no other memory is available, NCACHE-*x* sets a buffer size of 128KB (kilobytes). The default is for NCACHE-*x* to use as little DOS memory as possible.

Note: This parameter should not be used if your system has any other memory available. DOS memory is the RAM needed by the application programs you want to run. If you include the parameter without a size specification, the buffer size is fixed. If you do not include the parameter, NCACHE-*x* will use a dynamic buffering technique that will occupy the minimum amount of DOS RAM.

INI = path \ filename

Specifies where NCACHE-*x* should look to find the initialization file. This is the file where you have made your default parameter choices.

RESET   Reset the cache statistics for the status screen.

STATUS Display the status screen.

Note: If NCACHE-*x* is not installed when this command is issued, it will install itself and take all of the extended or expanded memory available.

UNINSTALL

Removes the TRS portion of NCACHE-*x*.

Note: This command is not effective unless NCACHE-*x* is the last TSR program installed. You will have to use the −A option to disable NCACHE-*x* when you cannot UNINSTALL it.

If NCACHE-*x* has been installed from the CONFIG.SYS file, it cannot be UNINSTALLed. The Norton Install program places the NCACHE-*x* Utility in the CONFIG.SYS file for maximum compatibility.

If NCACHE-*x* has been installed as the last line of the AUTOEXEC.BAT file or from the command line, UNINSTALL will remove it.

USEHIDOS [=YES|NO]

Minimizes usage of conventional, low DOS memory if high memory is present. High memory is provided by advanced memory managers such as QEMM and 386-to-the-Max. This will default to no if neither EMS nor XMS High Memory Area is present. Using this setting allows NCACHE-F to use as little of 12 kilobytes of conventional DOS RAM.

USEHMA [YES|NO]

Use XMS High Memory Area to help reduce the use of DOS RAM. This is only available with extended memory managers like HIMEM.SYS or EME.EXE. The default is yes, loading the cache management memory high if possible.

NCACHE-F specific

DELAY=*ss.hh*

Delay writes. Units are seconds and hundredths. Databases and similar write intensive applications can often benefit signifi-cantly from write-delays. The default is write-delay *off*.

Warning: Be sure that write buffer has been cleared before pulling a floppy out of the drive. Turning the lever or opening the drive door are as damaging to the data transfer as physically removing the diskette. Shutting down the system too soon also can destroy the buffered data.

QUICK [ON|OFF]

When enabled, (on) while IntelliWrites is ON, this returns the DOS prompt *before* writing is completed. When disabled (off), display of the DOS prompt is delayed until after all writes are completed. The warning shown above applies here too.

+|− I

Enable or disable IntelliWrites. When enabled, it buffers any writes and returns control to the application while still writing to disk.

R=[D]##

Read-ahead [disabled]. Allowable values are from 0 to 15. Tells NCACHE-F how many sectors to read ahead. R=0 or R=D0 disables read-ahead. R=## enables always read-ahead. R=D## enables read-ahead for sequential reads only. For maximum efficiency, set R=0 for fragmented files/disks and R=D## (dynamic) for packed, unfragmented files/disks.

+|− S

Enable | disable SmartReads. SmartRead allows reading before writing. In essence, data reads have a higher priority than data writes. Normally there are many more reads than writes in an application.

Network considerations

NCACHE-x is network compatible in that it will operate normally on a PC con-nected to a network. It doesn't cache any of the reads or writes that are made to a network disk.

Configuration considerations

BUFFERS   The line in your CONFIG.SYS file which reads BUF-FERS=xx should be set to a value between 3 and 10. This will maximize the capabilities of NCACHE-x. The actual best value will be determined by the %Hits shown on the status screen. Start with 5 buffers and adjust until the hits percentage is max.

FASTOPEN   Remove FASTOPEN from your AUTOEXEC.BAT file if it is present. FASTOPEN buffers the FAT and directory structure. NCACHE-x does the same thing in a more efficient manner and has fewer conflicts with application programs.

When you make the decision to use NCACHE-x, place it in the first line of your CONFIG.SYS file. This will reduce the number of possible conflicts. The limitation of this arrangement is that you cannot uninstall NCACHE-x. It also means that it will be loaded every time you start your system.

When you install NCACHE-S, you will see the panel illustrated in Fig. 15-1, which shows you how NCACHE-S is installed. In this case, caching is enabled (+ in the A column) for all of the drives that the Utility has determined are active in the system. Also, the cache buffer for each drive can accept additional data (+ in the C column). The +W indicates that write-through caching is also enabled.

All of the available memory is equally divided (384K /3 = 128K) between the three drives. This illustration was made when the cache was being installed, so the hit ratio and % hits are both zero. These figures will change as you use the system and NCACHE-S is able to work.

Note the differences between Fig. 15-1 and Fig. 15-2. The operational parameters are the same, but there are some differences. Almost 80% of the available memory is in use. The number of hits on drive C is greater, but the percentage of cached information hits is better for drive D. This illustration was made on my system, so I know what is on each of those drives; the C drive is a data drive, while drive D is programs only. In essence, I used a program on drive D that was accessing data from a number of different places on drive C.

Had I waited longer to make the illustration, the percentage of hits on drive would have been even higher while there might not have been a great change in the drive C percentage. The actual numbers and percentages are going to vary from user to user. Each of us has our own way of using a computer, and these differences will be reflected in the cache statistics. The other parameter that will make a difference in these statistics is where you keep your programs and where you store your data. If both are on the same disk, then the other disk may remain idle.

```
                        ═══ Norton Cache ═══
┌───────────────────────┬───────────────────────┬───────────────────────┐
│      DOS Memory       │    Extended Memory    │    Expanded Memory    │
│ NCACHE-S:        4 K   │ Cache:         384 K  │                       │
│ Cache Manag:     1 K   │                       │                       │
│ Available:     497 K   │ Available:       0 K  │ Available:       0 K  │
├───────────────────────┴───────────────────────┴───────────────────────┤
│ Cache Allocated:     0.0K of 384.0K  [00.0%]. Now Using:    0.0K [00.0%]│
├────────────────────────────────────────────────────────────────────────┤
│                            Cache Options                                 │
│    DOS=0K              EXT=384K            EXP=0K            BLOCK=8K      │
├────────────────────────────────────────────────────────────────────────┤
│        Drive Options                         Drive Statistics            │
│         A   C   W   G                    Cache Hit Ratio      %Hits       │
│ Drive A: +   +   +   128                     0/0            [00.0%]       │
│ Drive C: +   +   +   128                     0/0            [00.0%]       │
│ Drive D: +   +   +   128                     0/0            [00.0%]       │
└────────────────────────────────────────────────────────────────────────┘
```

15-1 The Small Cache screen.

```
                        ═══ Norton Cache ═══
┌───────────────────────┬───────────────────────┬───────────────────────┐
│      DOS Memory       │    Extended Memory    │    Expanded Memory    │
│ NCACHE-F:        9 K   │ Cache:         384 K  │                       │
│ Cache Manag:    35 K   │                       │                       │
│ Available:     456 K   │ Available:       0 K  │ Available:       0 K  │
├───────────────────────┴───────────────────────┴───────────────────────┤
│ Cache Allocated:   306.5K of 384.0K [79.9%]. Now Using: 306.5K  [79.9%] │
├────────────────────────────────────────────────────────────────────────┤
│                            Cache Options                                 │
│  DOS=0K    EXT=384K    EXP=0K        BLOCK=512   DELAY=0.0   QUICK=OFF    │
├────────────────────────────────────────────────────────────────────────┤
│        Drive Options                         Drive Statistics            │
│         A   C   I   W   S   R   G         Cache Hit Ratio      %Hits      │
│ Drive A: +   +   +   +   +   D8  128          0/0            [00.0%]      │
│ Drive C: +   +   +   +   +   D8  128         57/562         [10.1%]       │
│ Drive D: +   +   +   +   +   D8  128         18/42          [42.8%]       │
└────────────────────────────────────────────────────────────────────────┘
```

15-2 The Fast Cache screen.

16
CHAPTER

Disk Doctor

Directory name **NDD.EXE**

When you INSTALL this new version of the Norton Utilities, your old copy of NDD will be overwritten unless you request that INSTALL make a backup copy. If you want to keep both copies of Disk Doctor active for a time, leave the old copy with the name NDD.EXE and rename the new copy DDII.EXE. The new version is much more powerful and easier to use because of its menu interface. It has also been upgraded to work with most of the newer hardware and software changes that have been introduced since the last version was released.

Command line usage

Format: NDD [d:] [switches]

d: The drive to be tested.

The switch options available are:

/quick   Tests the Partition Table, Boot Record, Root directory, and looks for lost clusters. It doesn't do a surface test.

/complete

Performs all of the /quick tests plus does a surface test.

/r:*filename*

Generates a report file that is written to *filename*. Normally used with /quick or /complete.

/ra:*filename*

Generates a report that it appends to *filename*. Normally used with the /quick or /complete switches.

Limitation

NDD will not work on hard disks with more than 1,024 cylinders at this time.

Compatibility

NDD is compatible with most partitioning schemes including DOS 3.31, 4.0, Disk Manager, and SpeedStar.

Network considerations

NDD will run on a network, but it will not test network drives.

Disk Doctor II

Disk Test (DT) from earlier versions has been incorporated into this version of Norton Disk Doctor (NDD) known as NDD II. It is a diagnosis and repair Utility. DD II's area of expertise is the Partition Table, the DOS Boot Record, the File Allocation Tables, and also the directory and file structure. Additionally, it looks for lost and/or cross-linked chains, tests for physical defects on the disk surface, and marks and reports any defects found.

Running DD II with the /quick switch active from your AUTOEXEC.BAT file doesn't take a lot of time and is an excellent way to practice safe computing.

The Opening panel shown in Fig. 16-1 indicates some of the changes that have taken place, the most noticeable of these being the Undo Changes option. All of the version 5.0 Utilities that make changes that could alter your ability to access your hard disk create an undo file. NDD II allows you to reverse the things that have been done and be no worse off than you were at the beginning of the editing session. While this may not sound like a good deal, consider it in the light of one of the changes denying you access to the hard disk. Then, having access, even with problems, becomes a better situation.

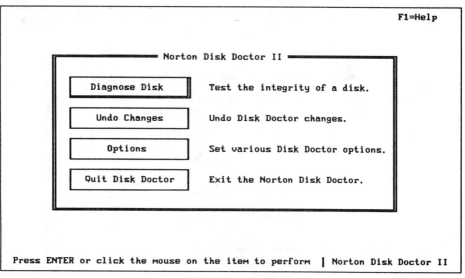

```
                          Norton Disk Doctor II

      ┌──────────────────┐
      │  Diagnose Disk  ▌│        Test the integrity of a disk.
      └──────────────────┘

      ┌──────────────────┐
      │  Undo Changes    │        Undo Disk Doctor changes.
      └──────────────────┘

      ┌──────────────────┐
      │    Options       │        Set various Disk Doctor options.
      └──────────────────┘

      ┌──────────────────┐
      │ Quit Disk Doctor │        Exit the Norton Disk Doctor.
      └──────────────────┘
```

Press ENTER or click the mouse on the item to perform | Norton Disk Doctor II

16-1   The Opening screen for Disk Doctor II.

Disk Doctor II will work in the batch mode just like most of the other Utilities. You must first set some options, however. The three boxes shown in Fig. 16-2 present you with these options.

```
                          Disk Doctor Options

      ┌──────────────────┐
      │  Surface Test   ▌│        Set default Surface Test settings.
      └──────────────────┘

      ┌──────────────────┐
      │ Custom Message   │        Set Custom Message.
      └──────────────────┘

      ┌──────────────────┐
      │  Tests to Skip   │        Select tests to skip.
      └──────────────────┘
   ┌─────────────────────────────────────────────────────────┐
   │ ┌──────────────┐   ┌──────────────┐   ┌──────────────┐   │
   │ │ Save Settings│   │      OK      │   │    Cancel    │   │
   │ └──────────────┘   └──────────────┘   └──────────────┘   │
   └─────────────────────────────────────────────────────────┘
```

Select the option to change | Norton Disk Doctor II

16-2   Choosing the Disk Doctor options.

The way DDII runs its test is partially determined on the panel shown in Fig. 16-3. Testing by files is usually quicker than testing by disk. In the file test, only those clusters that contain current file data are tested. In the disk test mode, the entire disk is tested. The same holds true of the test types. A daily test is quicker than the weekly test. The auto weekly test is a combination of the daily and

```
                                                              F1=Help


                      Surface Test Options
                Select the default settings for the Surface Test

     ┌ Test ──────────────────┐  ┌ Passes ─────────────────┐
     │   ☐   Disk Test        │  │   ☐   Repetitions 1     │
     │   ☐   File Test        │  │   ☐   Continuous        │
     └────────────────────────┘  └─────────────────────────┘

     ┌ Test Type ─────────────┐  ┌ Repair Setting ─────────┐
     │   ☐   Daily            │  │   ☐   Don't Repair      │
     │   ☐   Weekly           │  │   ☐   Prompt before Repairing │
     │   ☐   Auto Weekly      │  │   ☐   Repair Automatically │
     └────────────────────────┘  └─────────────────────────┘


              ┌─────────────┐    ┌─────────────┐
              │     OK      │    │   Cancel    │
              └─────────────┘    └─────────────┘


   Select OK to accept changes or CANCEL to ignore them  │ Norton Disk Doctor II
```

16-3 Selecting defaults for Surface Testing.

weekly test and is run only on Friday (this day is a default value for DDII). Any of the computers that can run these Utilities and has a battery-backed clock will trigger the auto weekly default.

How many repetitions of the surface test are necessary to ensure that all of the defects have been found? One pass on the whole disk of the auto weekly test should find all of them. Please note the word *should*. Some defects can escape detection on a single pass. The limit for a counted number of passes is 999. If you feel that more passes are necessary, then select the Continuous option. This will allow DDII to run for an unlimited period, such as overnight, while testing. Press the ESC key to abort the testing at any time.

If you are going to be using DDII in a batch file or letting it run for an extended period, the Automatic Repair option is the only choice. Not repairing will provide you with an indication of the trouble and a recommendation on how to correct the problem. When the first problem is detected, the program will pause and await instructions or at least an input from you. The same is true of the prompt before repair option.

The Custom Message option can be used any way you feel appropriate, but it is most useful for users who have a resource person immediately available. In many business settings, this option can be used to have the user call the in-house expert or the company support section. In addition to the text of the message itself, there are some eye-catching changes that can be employed. Figure 16-4 indicates that the text attribute is currently set on normal. Pressing the F2 key will cycle the other options, which are Reverse, Bold, and Underline.

```
┌─────────────────── Set Custom Message ───────────────────┐
│      Type the message you wish to display if an error      │
│       is encountered while testing System Areas            │
│                                                            │
│   ☐  Prompt with Custom Message                            │
│  ┌──────────────────────────────┐  Press F2 to             │
│  │                              │  change text             │
│  │                              │  attribute.              │
│  │                              │                          │
│  │                              │  Current attribute       │
│  │                              │  is Normal.              │
│  │                              │                          │
│  │                              │  Press Tab to move        │
│  │                              │  between controls.        │
│  │                              │                          │
│  │                              │  ┌──────────┐            │
│  │                              │  │    OK    │            │
│  └──────────────────────────────┘  └──────────┘            │
└────────────────────────────────────────────────────────────┘
```

Select OK to accept changes or ESC to ignore them │ Norton Disk Doctor II

16-4 Composing your own warning message.

The descriptive sentences after each of the options shown in Fig. 16-5 indicate when you should skip that test. Under normal circumstances, none of these tests should be omitted.

The panel shown in Fig. 16-6 appears only if you have not designated a drive on the command line. All of the drives that DDII has been able to detect will be listed. The SPACEBAR or the UP/DOWN ARROW keys can be used to move the

```
┌═══════════════════════ Tests to Skip ═══════════════════════┐
│    This option allows you to skip specific tests, so that NDD │
│  can still be run on computers which are not 100% compatible. │
│                                                               │
│  ☐  Skip Partition Tests    Select if your drive system uses  │
│                             non-standard partition software.  │
│                                                               │
│  ☐  Skip CMOS Tests         Select if your computer uses a    │
│                             non-standard CMOS format.         │
│                                                               │
│  ☐  Skip Surface Tests      Select if you wish to ALWAYS skip │
│                             Surface Tests.                    │
│                                                               │
│  ☐  Only 1 Hard Disk        Select if your computer erroneously│
│                             reports more than 1 hard disk.    │
│                                                               │
│          ┌──────────┐    ┌──────────┐                        │
│          │    OK    │    │  Cancel  │                        │
│          └──────────┘    └──────────┘                        │
└───────────────────────────────────────────────────────────────┘
```

Select OK to accept changes or CANCEL to ignore them │ Norton Disk Doctor II

16-5 Deciding to skip tests.

reverse video bar over the desired drive. Use the TAB key to change from the selection box to the Diagnose box. The TAB key will cycle through each of the boxes in a circular fashion.

While DDII is running its tests, you will see a display very similar to the ones provided by SD and Calibrate. Figure 16-7 shows this screen; the current status of the test, the type of testing, and the estimated time to complete testing are all listed.

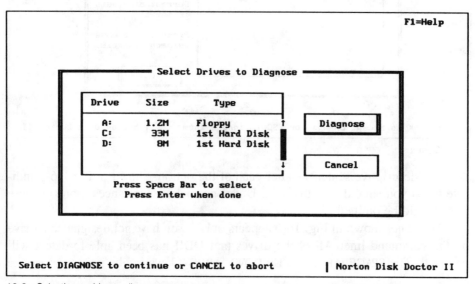

16-6 Selecting a drive to diagnose.

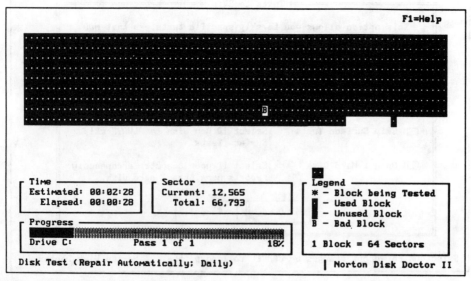

16-7 The Test Display screen.

When the testing and any repairs are complete, the panel pictured in Fig. 16-8 will display. If there were no problems detected, there may be no need to have a report generated. If this was the first-ever test of the drive, you might wish to save a copy of the report as a part of your baseline documentation.

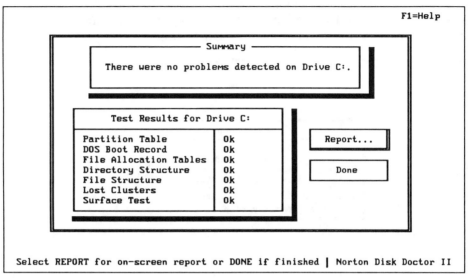

16-8 Desirable test results.

Collecting reports of repairs made may be a waste of time for some users. For others, or those responsible for the maintenance of a number of PCs, reports might serve as a good resource to determine when a drive began to develop problems. These reports might also indicate a need for additional operator training.

Norton Disk Doctor

Version 4.5 directory name   NDD.EXE

NDD is a new Utility with version 4.5; it detects and corrects to the best of its ability any physical and logical errors on both hard and floppy disks.

Format: NDD [d:] [/Quick|/Complete]

d: The drive to be doctored.

/Quick   Omit the test for bad sectors.

/Complete
             Run all tests (the default mode).

/R:_filename_
             Send the report to _filename_.

/AR:_filename_
             Append the report to _filename_.

If neither drive nor switch is entered on the command line, NDD will begin an interactive session and display a screen that prompts you to select one of three options. The mode will be /Complete and the drive will be the default drive. The Complete mode encompasses over 100 tests.

The Main menu shown in Fig. 16-9 lets you choose which part of NDD you wish to use. Diagnose Disk analyzes and repairs any disk, and Common Solutions primarily repairs disks already known to be defective.

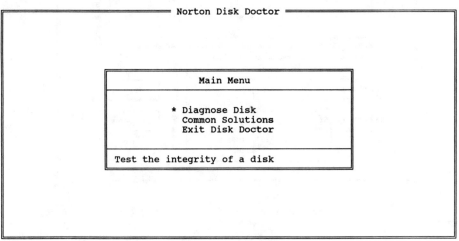

```
═══════════════ Norton Disk Doctor ═══════════════

              ┌──────────────────────────────┐
              │          Main Menu           │
              ├──────────────────────────────┤
              │     * Diagnose Disk          │
              │       Common Solutions       │
              │       Exit Disk Doctor       │
              ├──────────────────────────────┤
              │ Test the integrity of a disk │
              └──────────────────────────────┘
```

16-9   The Opening screen for Disk Doctor (version 4.5).

Let's examine Diagnose Disk first. Hopefully you will not have to visit the other option too often. The reverse video bar highlights the first logical hard drive when the panel pictured in Fig. 16-10 displays. Pressing the RETURN key will select the highlighted drive and begin the analysis and repair session. If you press

```
═══════════════ Norton Disk Doctor ═══════════════

            ┌──────────────────────────────────┐
            │    Select Drives to Diagnose     │
            ├──────────────────────────────────┤
            │  Drive    Size       Type        │
            ├──────────────────────────────────┤
            │    A:     1.2M     Floppy        │
            │  * C:      33M     1st Hard Disk │
            │    D:       8M     1st Hard Disk │
            ├──────────────────────────────────┤
            │  Press Space Bar to select       │
            │    Press Enter when done         │
            │     Press Esc to cancel          │
            └──────────────────────────────────┘
```

16-10   Selecting a drive to diagnose (version 4.5).

the SPACEBAR, a check mark will appear next to the "C" and the bar will drop to the next possibie selection. You have the option of pressing the RETURN key or the SPACEBAR. Pressing RETURN will begin the session. Pressing the SPACEBAR will select the second drive. Pressing RETURN now will begin the session on the first drive and not end until all selected drives have been analyzed and repaired, if necessary.

To deselect a drive, place the reverse video bar over that drive and press the SPACEBAR again. The SPACEBAR acts as a toggle for selecting and deselecting drives. The quickest way to start an NDD session in this mode is to press the letter key corresponding to the drive you want analyzed. Be sure to have the floppy disk ready if your selection is "A." You will also have to tell NDD what type of disk you are placing in the A drive to be analyzed. See Fig. 16-18 for the available options. The options will always be appropriate for the installed hardware; accordingly, a system with a 3.5″ drive installed will have different options from a system with a 5.25″ drive installed.

NDD begins by analyzing the drive/disk, as shown in Fig. 16-11. Whenever it detects an error or a condition that it cannot cope with, a window with a red background opens in the center of the screen and an error message is displayed. These messages are concise but won't require translations.

```
═══════════════════ Norton Disk Doctor ═══════════════════


          ┌─────────────────────────────────────────┐
          │             Analyzing Drive C:          │
          │                                          │
          │   Would you like to test ALL of Drive C: │
          │           for Defective Sectors?         │
          │                                          │
          │              * Yes    No                 │
          └─────────────────────────────────────────┘


    ══════════════════════          ══════════════════════
      Logical Characteristics         Physical Characteristics
    ──────────────────────────────┬─────────────────────────────

         Drive Letter:  C:        │    Drive Number:   80h
                Size:   33M        │          Heads:    6
      Media Descriptor:  F8h       │      Cylinders:    655
      Large Partition:  Yes        │ Sectors Per Track: 17
             FAT Type:  16-bit     │   Starting Head:   1
        Total Sectors:  66,793     │ Starting Cylinder: 0
        Total Clusters: 16,657     │  Starting Sector:  1
      Bytes Per Sector: 512        │     Ending Head:   5
    Sectors Per Cluster: 4         │  Ending Cylinder:  654
       Number of FATs:  2          │    Ending Sector:  17
```

16-11 The Disk Analysis screen (version 4.5).

The reverse video bar moves down the list of areas to be analyzed as NDD progresses through the tests. Remember that most of the 100 tests that NDD performs are done now. You might consider reading through the information being displayed on the lower portion of the screen while NDD is busy.

Both the logical and physical characteristics of the drive being analyzed are displayed. As the different drives are analyzed, this information is updated to reflect the physical and logical characteristics of that drive. Don't interrupt an NDD run to get copies of this information; all of it will be on the report that NDD produces at the end of its analyzation. Keep at least the latest copy of the report for every logical drive you have installed.

During the analysis of the directory structure, NDD will search the drive for lost chains (Fig. 16-12) and sectors. Both of these are usually portions of deleted files that appear as orphans. No directory entries exist for them, and their FAT (File Allocation Table) information isn't correct. If NDD finds any of either, another window with a red background will open from the center of the display advising you of the fact and ask if you want NDD to correct the problem. "Yes" is the default answer; just press RETURN to put NDD back to work. The converted orphans will become files in the root directory of that drive. You will easily recognize them by their distinctive filename and extension (xxxx._DD).

```
╔══════════════════ Norton Disk Doctor ══════════════════╗
║                                                         ║
║          ┌────────────────────────────────────┐        ║
║          │        Analyzing Drive C:          │        ║
║          ├────────────────────────────────────┤        ║
║          │ √ Analyzing DOS Boot Record         │        ║
║          │ √ Analyzing File Allocation Tables  │        ║
║          │ * Analyzing Directory Structure     │        ║
║          └────────────────────────────────────┘        ║
║                                                         ║
╟─────────────────────────────┬───────────────────────────╢
║   Logical Characteristics   │   Physical Characteristics ║
║                             │                            ║
║         Drive Lett  ┌───────────────────────┐  umber: 80h║
║                 Si  │ Searching for Lost Chains │ Heads: 6 ║
║     Media Descript  │                       │  nders: 655║
║     Large Partiti   │         7,571         │  Track: 17 ║
║            FAT Ty   └───────────────────────┘   Head: 1  ║
║         Total Secto                            inder: 0   ║
║      Total Clusters: 16,657      Starting Sector: 1       ║
║     Bytes Per Sector: 512          Ending Head: 5         ║
║  Sectors Per Cluster: 4        Ending Cylinder: 654       ║
║      Number of FATs: 2          Ending Sector: 17         ║
╚═════════════════════════════════════════════════════════╝
```

16-12 Analyzing and searching drive C (version 4.5).

Figure 16-13 pictures a typical report generated by version 4.5 Advanced Edition.

16-13 A Disk Doctor report file (version 4.5).

```
                    Norton Disk Doctor
                   Advanced Edition 4.50
               Sunday, December 25, 1988 3:56 pm
               **************************
               *   Report for Drive C:   *
               **************************
                     DISK TOTALS
          ----------------------------------------
            34,113,536 bytes Total Disk Space
             5,535,744 bytes in 278 User Files
                26,624 bytes in 12 Directories
                65,536 bytes in 5 Hidden Files
            28,485,632 bytes Available on the Disk
                 LOGICAL DISK INFORMATION
          ----------------------------------------
              Media Descriptor:   F8h
              Large Partition:    Yes
```

```
                   FAT Type:  16-bit
              Total Sectors:  66,793
             Total Clusters:  16,657
           Bytes Per Sector:  512
         Sectors Per Cluster:  4
          Bytes Per Cluster:  2,048
             Number of FATs:  2
         First Sector of FAT:  1
     Number of Sectors Per FAT:  66
     First Sector of Root Dir:  133
   Number of Sectors in Root Dir:  32
   Maximum Root Dir File Entries:  512
      First Sector of Data Area:  165
              PHYSICAL DISK INFORMATION
-------------------------------------------
               Drive Number:  80h
                      Heads:  6
                  Cylinders:  655
          Sectors Per Track:  17
              Starting Head:  1
          Starting Cylinder:  0
            Starting Sector:  1
                Ending Head:  5
            Ending Cylinder:  654
              Ending Sector:  17
                SYSTEM AREA STATUS
-------------------------------------------
          No Errors in the System Area
              FILE STRUCTURE STATUS
-------------------------------------------
        No Errors in the File Structure
                DISK TEST STATUS
-------------------------------------------
              Disk Test not performed
```

The Common Solutions menu may get more use than you expect. The first
and third selections as seen in Fig. 16-14 can be quite useful.

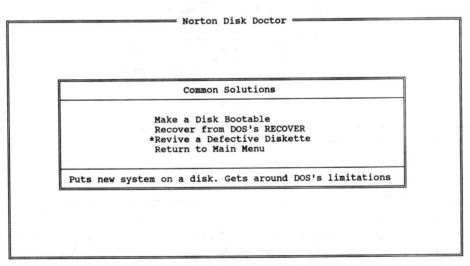

16-14 Finding a simple and common solution (version 4.5).

After selecting the Revive option (Fig. 16-15), the next screen shown is the Drive Selection screen. The system in use for this illustration was an AT clone with only one diskette drive. NDD recognized this fact and provided only one choice, as Fig. 16-16 suggests.

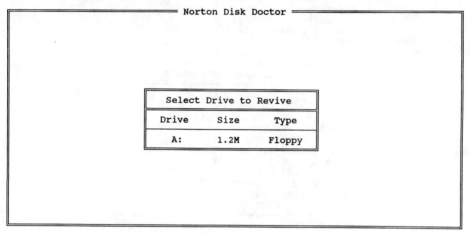

16-15 Reviving a defective diskette (version 4.5).

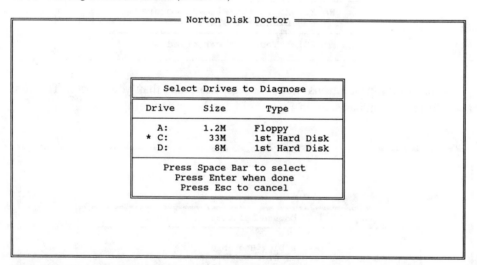

16-16 Selecting a drive to diagnose.

Before NDD will allow you to continue, it provides a reminder screen (Fig. 16-17). If the diskette is already in the drive, just press the RETURN key. If it isn't, place it in the drive, close the door, turn the lever, and then press the RETURN key.

You must provide the capacity to NDD before it begins testing (Fig. 16-18). If you don't and the diskette has an error, NDD might begin making the wrong type of corrections. Note that even though the illustration shows an AT clone with a nominal 1.2 floppy drive, diskettes of other capacities can be tested and repaired.

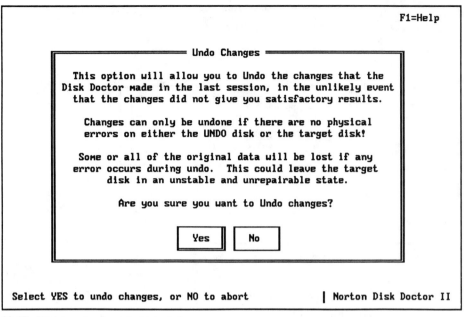

16-17 Undoing changes—last minute insurance.

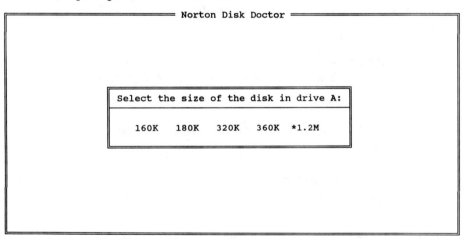

16-18 Selecting the diskette capacity (version 4.5).

When the test or correction procedure will take a period of time, NDD (and the rest of the Utilities) provide a screen or window that displays the current status of the situation (Fig. 16-19).

DiskTest

Version 4.0 & 4.5 directory name   DT.EXE

DT tests a disk for damage and also can repair some types of damage. Unmarked bad sectors on the disk are shown and, at your option, marked as unusable.

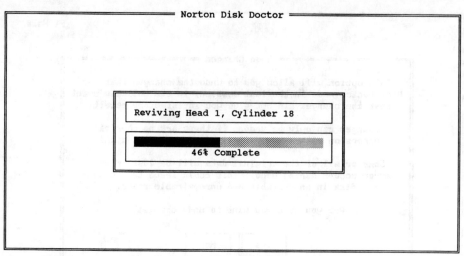

```
                 Norton Disk Doctor

       ┌─────────────────────────────────────┐
       │     Reviving Head 1, Cylinder 18     │
       │  ┌───────────────────────────────┐   │
       │  │███████████▒▒▒▒▒▒▒▒▒▒▒▒▒▒▒▒▒▒▒▒│   │
       │  │          46% Complete          │   │
       │  └───────────────────────────────┘   │
       └─────────────────────────────────────┘
```

16-19 The Dynamic Progress reporting screen (version 4.5).

Format: DT [d:] [path \ filename] [switches] [> | > >] [d: \ path \ file-
name|device]

The following command-line options are available:

d: Tells DT which drive contains the disk under test.

path \ filename
   Tells DT which file or file type (i.e., *.COM) is under test.

/F   Test each file on the selected disk.

/D   Test the entire disk, boot, FAT, directory, and data areas.

/B   Test everything. This combines both of the tests listed above.

/LOG   Adapts the program's running output into a form that is sent to the
   printer or a disk file. Only the final results are displayed, printed,
   or filed.

/Cn   Mark Cluster *n* as bad. This command is repeated as necessary.

/Cn-   Mark Cluster *n* as good. This command is repeated as necessary.

/M   Move data in questionable clusters to a safe location and mark the
   questionable clusters as bad.

/S   Test files in subdirectories. This switch is only used when the
   [location] parameter is used.

> | > >   The DOS operators to redirect or redirect and append the output.
   There is no display when either of these operators is used.

path \ filename|device

To a disk file or the printer. Figure 16-20 represents the screen during a DT session using the B(oth) option but not the [/LOG] option.

16-20 DT with the B option on and the /LOG option off.

```
A>dt

DT-Disk Test, Advanced Edition, (C) Copr 1989, Peter Norton

Select DISK test, FILE test, or BOTH
Press D, F. or B ... B
During the scan of the disk, you may press
BREAK (Control-C) to interrupt Disk Test

Test reading the entire disk A:, system area and data area
   The system area consists of boot, FAT, and directory
      No errors reading the system area

   The data area consists of clusters numbered 2 - 355
      No errors reading data area

Test reading all files
   Directory A:
      No errors reading files
```

The difference in the representation using the /LOG option is that the count-down during cluster reading and the display of the filenames during file reads is not shown. This permits orderly printing or filing of the results.

If DT finds errors in the system area of a disk, you can expect serious problems almost immediately. The best course of action is to carefully copy all of the data onto another disk and discard the old disk. Reformatting the disk may correct the problem. Using WipeDisk before attempting to reformat may also eliminate the possible cause of the problem. If the problem persists after using WipeDisk and reformatting, discarding the disk is the only safe solution.

Sectors within a disk marked as bad are reported as "no danger" by DT. DOS will mark and not use bad sectors during format. While this can reduce the capacity of the disk, it does not mean that the disk is unsafe to use.

A problem is reported with danger now when DT finds an unmarked, unreadable portion of the disk within a file. There may have been data written to that portion of the disk and now it may not be recoverable. Using the NU program will recover as much of the data as possible.

The warning "danger to come" is reported when DT finds a bad, unmarked sector in an area of the disk where files are not currently being stored. DT will request permission to mark the sector(s) so that DOS will not attempt to write data into these areas. This is the extent of the repair that DT can perform.

The types of checking done by DOS's CHKDSK and DT are different. CHKDSK checks the logical order of space allocation on a disk. DT checks the ability of the disk to permit error-free reads and writes in the various areas of the disk. Using CHKDSK D:*.* /F directs that program to attempt to correct any errors found in the directory or file structures. This is an interactive process.

Before panicking, clean the heads of your floppy drive when DT reports errors. Cleaning your heads should also be a routine part of your computer maintenance program. On a hard disk, regular discovery of unmarked bad sectors is an indication that the hard disk is in need of repair or replacement.

When there are differences in the error reports provided by the disk-read and file-read portions of DT, you should copy all transferable data onto another disk as soon as possible. Using CHKDSK may increase the amount of data that can be recovered. The disk may be reusable after it has been wipe'd and reformatted. Be sure to check it before writing data to it again.

When DOS reports a read error while trying to copy a file from a suspected bad disk, tell DOS to Ignore the error and continue; this will allow the maximum data transfer. Use the NU program to try and rebuild the data that was lost. DT cannot correct the errors that may be caused by trying to read and transfer the data that is in a sector which DT deems bad.

The two practices that seem to be the hardest to internalize are proper floppy care/routine and frequent backups. By internalizing, I mean that the habit of doing both of these things becomes so strong that they are done without consciously thinking about performing the activities.

Floppies need to be in their sleeves as well as in some type of protective case when they are not in the machine. A desk full of sleeved and unsleeved floppies is an almost irresistible invitation to disaster.

Murphy's laws are valid. Making a backup of your hard disk is the only way to be sure that the contents won't be lost during the next thunderstorm or by some other accident involving family or friends.

I know that there are files on the disk, but DOS will not read them. Is there anything I can do?

You have a number of options. If you run a disk that refuses to display its directory to the DOS DIR command, any number of possible problems exist. If it is really worth the effort, run NDD first to determine the extent of the problem. I just "happened" to have a disk with a problem available. As you can see from the results in Fig. 16-21, this disk appears to have a problem with its directory. Like you, I know there are files on this disk. In order to verify that knowledge, I ran the NU program and took a look at the things it was able to find.

Our claims are proven! There are files on our disk (see Fig. 16-22), collected here in a rather odd and perhaps interesting list. It would seem that a closer look at some of the items is justified.

While the Root directory listings shown in Fig. 16-23 are not really all that revealing, we now know more about what was on this disk. It appears that it started out as a bootable disk that immediately ran a program (I've made a number of these containing public-domain games for my sons). The balance of the disk appears to be some experimenting that I was doing with the NCD program. Because none of the information is current or needed, I should probably just recycle the disk. Were the data worth recovering, I would return to the main menu of NU and start collecting sectors into programs or text files.

16-21 The DT interactive mode (version 4.5). Note the message after the phrase "directory area."

```
C:\NU: dt a:
DT-Disk Test, Advanced Edition, (C) Copr 1989, Peter Norton

Select DISK test, FILE test, or BOTH
Press D, F, or B ... B

During the scan of the disk, you may press
BREAK (Control-C) to interrupt Disk Test

Test reading the entire disk A:, system area and data area
   The system area consists of boot, FAT, and directory
      directory area ERROR IN READING

   The data area consists of clusters numbered 2 - 355
      No errors reading data area

Test reading files
   Directory A:\ Error reading directory
      No files found
```

```
Menu 1.1.3
                      Select file or sub-directory

             Boot area              loader.sys
             FAT area               msdos.sys
           * Root dir *             read.me
             00000000               sol.arc
             11111111               sol.exe
             88888888               term.sav
             A                      test.2
             CCCCCCCC               test.s
             autoexec.bat           treeinfo.ncd
             command.com
             init.s11
             init.s12
             init.s13
             io.sys

                   23 entries to choose from
                   Speed search:
```

Item type	Drive	Directory name	File name
Directory	A:	\	Root dir

16-22 The NU directory screen (version 4.5). Compare this listing with the other examples.

```
┌ Root dir ══════════════════════════════════ Directory format ═┐
│  Sector 5 in root directory                    Offset 0, hex 00 │
│                                                   Attributes    │
│Filename Ext     Size     Date      Time    Cluster  Arc R/O Sys Hid Dir Vol │
╞═══════════ ══     ════    ════      ════    ═══════  ═══ ═══ ═══ ═══ ═══ ═══╡
│LOADER   SYS      1024   12/10/84  11:00 am      2    Arc R/O Sys Hid        │
│IO       SYS     12037    7/15/86   6:30 pm    299    Arc R/O Sys Hid        │
│MSDOS    SYS     17012   12/10/84  11:00 am    311    Arc R/O Sys Hid        │
│COMMAND  COM     15957   12/10/84  11:00 am    328    Arc                    │
│AUTOEXEC BAT        6     4/21/87   9:32 am    344    Arc                    │
│SOL      EXE     90240    8/05/86  12:13 am     67    Arc                    │
│INIT     SL1     27607    4/03/86   3:57 pm    156    Arc                    │
│INIT     SL2     27607    4/03/86   3:57 pm    183    Arc                    │
│INIT     SL3     27607    4/03/86   3:57 pm    210    Arc                    │
│11111111                 4/02/87   3:14 pm      3                        Dir │
│TREEINFO NCD      4211    4/03/87  12:57 pm      8    Arc                    │
│88888888                 4/02/87   3:18 pm     11                        Dir │
│00000000                 4/02/87   3:18 pm     13                        Dir │
│CCCCCCCC                 4/02/87   3:19 pm     16                        Dir │
│A                        4/02/87   3:21 pm     20                        Dir │
│READ     ME       3569    7/23/86   8:25 pm    237    Arc                    │
╞═══════════ ══     ════    ════      ════    ═══════  ═══ ═══ ═══ ═══ ═══ ═══╡
│                    Press Enter to continue                      │
│1Help    2Hex    3Text   4Dir    5FAT    6Partn  7       8       9Undo    10QuitNU│
```

16-23 The Root directory of the same disk (it doesn't look promising).

17
CHAPTER

Norton

Directory name   **NORTON.EXE**
Command line usage
Format: NORTON [switches]

The following switches are for display modification only and are available from the command line:

/G0   Disables the mouse graphic (i.e., the arrowhead) along with the check boxes and *radio buttons* (open circles with a bullet in the center). Works with EGA and VGA displays only.

/G1   Disables the mouse graphic only. For both of these options, the mouse symbol becomes a non-blinking cursorlike box. The check boxes and the radio buttons remain in their standard graphic form. Works with EGA and VGA displays only.

/BW	Forces the use of the black and white color set. For monochrome monitors, although you could still run this mode on your non-monochrome monitor to see what it looks like.
/LCD	Forces the use of the LCD color set. For laptop displays in particular, but it also runs on a non-laptop display.

/NOZOOM
Disables the dialog box zooms.

Network considerations

Norton works on a network-connected PC. Like all of the other Utilities, it is not designed to be run by more than one user. There are a few special considerations if individualization of the Norton Utility program set is being done in a network environment.

The initialization file for the Norton Utility programs has only a single filename: NU.INI. This name would cause a problem if you tried to customize your copy of the Utilities in a multi-user environment. Multiple copies of a single filename causes trouble. The various versions of the .INI files for each user of the Utilities can be renamed. Use the DOS RENAME command after you have made all of the changes you desire. You must wait until after making the changes because the Utilities write these changes to a fixed filename. However, they are capable of finding the .INI file with a changed filename. Do NOT change the extension (.INI) under any circumstance.

The Opening panel of version 5.0, shown in Fig. 17-1, is very similar to the previous version. The changes in this version make it easier to find the Utilities by functioning grouping. If you're used to an alphabetical listing like I am, you might have to use it a few times to get into the swing of this new arrangement. If you must have it the other way, check out the Configure pull-down menu, shown in Fig. 17-2.

Tagging the section title tells you a little about the Utilities. As you tag each of the Utility titles, the right-side box displays a short help file on that Utility, which is the way it has always been.

Menu expansion and modification

Version 5.0 allows you to customize the Norton program menu. You can use it to access all of your applications, eliminating the need for any other menu-type programs that you currently use as an interface. If you do, this program will remain TSR and will still reduce the amount of available DOS RAM for your applications. You will have to decide which of your menu programs takes the least space.

The last three selections on the Configure pull-down menu offer menus that let you reorganize the Norton menu items.

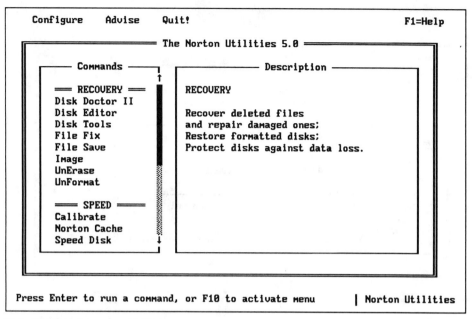

17-1 The Opening screen for Norton.

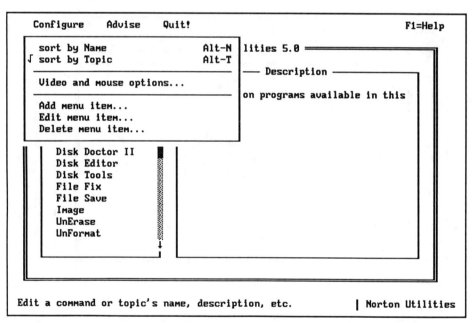

17-2 Configuring the Norton utility.

If you keep the Utilities sorted into groups, you will have the option of naming your own group(s). Once you enter the group names, you will then have to place them. Figure 17-3 illustrates the edit window with the other group name in position to be relocated. If you use groups, then you might want your group first,

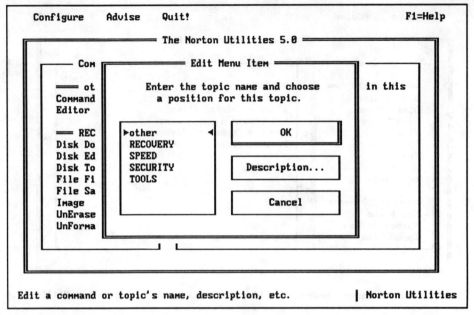

17-3 Editing menu items.

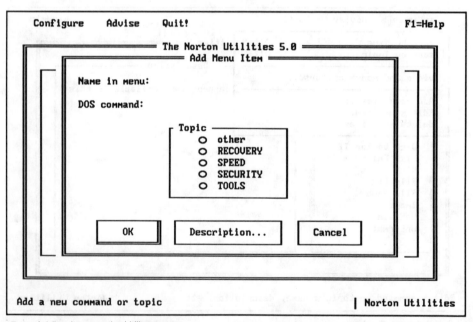

17-4 Adding items to the Utility menus.

especially when you are using the Norton Program for your interface menu. The programs I've added to the menu are the Norton Commander and the Norton Editor.

If you don't use the grouping feature, your additions to the menu will appear in alphabetical order with the rest of the entries. This organization is easier for searching, but I find it more difficult for an interface. Switching between the two possibilities isn't hard, as they are the first two selections on the Configure menu. You can either use the mouse or press F9 and then use the DOWN ARROW key to move the reverse video bar.

It is possible for you to add items (i.e., programs) into the groups established for the Utilities. After selecting the topic group (see Fig. 17-4), enter the menu name for the program. On the DOS command line, enter the necessary drive: \ path \ program.name to run the program. When you tag the description block, you will be given space to make appropriate comments about the addition. These comments will display in the right-hand box when you tag your menu name. You will have all of the space in the box that opens to provide information and hints on program operation.

Keep your comments short and to the point. Another user will need to know how to get your addition running, not why you added it or even that you are the one that added it.

Norton Integrator version 4.5
Version 4.0 & 4.5 directory name   NI.EXE

NI is a new addition to the Norton Utilities. It is a convenience program, which means that it is not one of those for which you might be willing to give up dessert for a week just to own. It does accomplish two useful functions, however. First, it uses a menu display that gives both the two-letter abbreviation for the program and the full name of all 27 Utilities (this takes up the left-hand one-third of the screen). Second, NI lists a short helpfile in the balance of the screen about the selected Utility. The information provided on the screen is not as complete as the manual provided with the Utilities, however, which also means that the screen is much less informative than this book.

If you know which Utility you are looking for, the Speed Search feature is available by pressing the TAB key. This is also a new feature with version 4.x and the Advanced Edition. Rather than using the ARROW keys to move the reverse video block to your selection, press the TAB key and then enter the first and second letter of the Utility you want to run. If the first letter is unique, as it is for BEEP, Unremove, Directory, and Volume Label, only the first letter is necessary.

Format: NI

NI is useful for both the frequent and the infrequent user. It provides a reminder of the available switches along with the complete listing of the Utility program names.

Both the HOME and END keys are active for quickly moving to either end of the program listing.

On the Opening panel (see Fig. 17-5), the cursor is located after the Utility name. This allows you to enter the rest of the parameters (path name, etc.) needed

```
╔══════════════════ The Norton Integrator ═══════════════════╗
║ BE   Batch Enhancer                                          ║
║ DI   Disk Information    Batch Enhancer     BE command [parameters] ║
║ DS   Directory Sort                   or  BE filespec        ║
║ DT   Disk Test                                               ║
║ FA   File Attributes        Enhance Batch files with sound (BEEP), ║
║ FD   File Date/Time         color (SA), keyboard input (ASK), screen ║
║ FF   File Find              addressing (ROWCOL), character output ║
║ FI   File Info              (PRINTCHAR, BOX, WINDOW), and other ║
║ FR   Format Recover         attributes (CLS and DELAY).      ║
║ FS   File Size                                               ║
║ LD   List Directories    Available Commands                  ║
║ LP   Line Print             ASK        BEEP        BOX        ║
║ NCC  Control Center         CLS        DELAY       PRINTCHAR  ║
║ NCD  Norton CD              ROWCOL     SA          WINDOW     ║
║ NDD  Disk Doctor                                             ║
║ NU   Norton Utility      BE menufile                         ║
║ QU   Quick UnErase          Execute multiple BE commands from the ║
║ SD   Speed Disk             file, 'menufile'.                 ║
║ SF   Safe Format                                             ║
║ SI   System Information  BE ASK ?                            ║
║              more...        Get help on using the ASK command. ║
║                                                              ║
║  BE                                                          ║
║══════════════════════════════════════════ Press F1 for Help ║
╚══════════════════════════════════════════════════════════════╝
```

17-5 The Opening screen for the Norton Integrator.

to run the selected file. Pressing the RETURN key will execute the command.

To edit the command you have entered, the following WordStar-compatible commands may be used:

CTRL-F	Cursor right one word
CTRL-RIGHT-ARROW	Cursor right one word
CTRL-A	Cursor left one word
CTRL-LEFT-ARROW	Cursor left one word
CTRL-HOME	Cursor to the beginning of the line
CTRL-END	Cursor to the end of the line
RIGHT-ARROW	Cursor right one character
CTRL-D	Cursor right one character
LEFT-ARROW	Cursor left one character
CTRL-S	Cursor left one character
BACKSPACE	Delete the character to the left
DEL	Delete the character under the cursor
CTRL-G	Delete the character under the cursor
CTRL-T	Delete the word to the right
CTRL-W	Delete the word to the left
CTRL-Y	Delete parameters
TAB	Delete the entire line and enter the Speed Search feature

Of the above, only the TAB key will delete the Utility filename. Use CTRL-HOME or CTRL-END to move the command-line cursor.

NI also has a circular buffer. This buffer keeps a listing of the commands that have been previously used and can be displayed for reuse. Press CTRL-E to move backward or CTRL-X to move forward.

NI calls DOS to run the various programs; therefore, the rules for using DOS (pathnames, filenames, etc.) must be observed when entering information on the command line.

The NI selection screen is redisplayed after running each Utility. To exit NI, press the ESC key. This feature permits you to perform all of the tasks necessary to complete work on a disk or project.

NI is one program that allows you to access all of the Norton Utilities from within an ASK menu.

Why put a half-screen of helpfile into NI?

I'm not sure why Peter did it because I didn't ask. I do thank him for it because it saves me time. Like many users, I know I read the instructions only when all else fails; the helpfiles in NI make referring to the book less necessary (Fig. 17-6).

```
┌──────────────────────── The Norton Integrator ════════════════════════┐
│ F                                                                       │
│ F   ┌───────────────────────────────────────────────────────────────┐  │
│ F   │                    The Norton Integrator                       │  │
│ L   │                    Advanced Edition 4.50                        │  │
│ L   │              Copyright (C), Peter Norton 1987-1988             │  │
│ N   │              Designed and Written by Brad Kingsbury             │  │
│ N   ├───────────────────────────────────────────────────────────────┤  │
│ N   │ You can execute any of the Norton Utilities from within NI.    │  │
│ N   │ Move the highlight to the command, type any arguments, and     │  │
│ Q   │ press Enter.                                                    │  │
│ S   │                                                                 │  │
│ S   │ Tab          Erase command line and enter Speed Search mode    │  │
│ S   │ Enter        Run the program on the command line               │  │
│ T   │ Space        Leave Speed Search                                 │  │
│ T   │ ▲ or ▼       Move to previous or next command                  │  │
│ U   │ Letters      Type arguments on the command line                │  │
│ V   │ Esc, F10     Quit NI                                            │  │
│ W   │                                                                 │  │
│ W   │ Speed Search Typing letters moves the highlight to the first   │  │
│ Q   │              program that matches the letters typed so far.    │  │
│     └───────────────────────────────────────────────────────────────┘  │
│ NDD                                                                      │
│                                                    Press F1 for Help ═══│
└─────────────────────────────────────────────────────────────────────────┘
```

17-6 The NI menu with an overlaid helpfile.

When would it seem more logical to use the ARROW keys to move the cursor, rather than use the speed search feature?

In a very large directory, you could use speed search to move the cursor to a block of similarly named files and then use the cursor keys to select the individual file.

Is there any difference in the way these Utilities run on a hard disk versus a floppy?

The only difference I've noticed is the speed. The hard disk access at 65 ms is quicker than floppy disk access. You also have a lot less disk swapping when using the hard disk.

Is there any way to set up a disk so that NI is always the first Utility run?

Yes. On a floppy, a .BAT file can be added to your working copy of the Norton Utilities to run NI first every time. This will not give you access to all of the Utilities because both NU and QU are on a separate disk. On a hard disk, the same technique will give you access to all of the programs.

18
CHAPTER

SafeFormat

Directory name

Command line usage

Format: SFORMAT [switches]
SF [switches]

The following command-line switches are available:

/A   Automatic mode. This is how you can use SF in batch files.

/S   Copy the system files to the disk(ette). These files are necessary if the disk(ette) is to be a bootable disk(ette).

/B   Leave space for the system files. This will permit you to place the system files on the disk(ette) at a later date if they are needed.

/V:label	Place a volume label on the disk(ette).
/1	Format a single-sided diskette.
/4	Format a 360K diskette in a 1.2M drive.
/8	Format 8 sectors per track.
/N:*n*	Number of sectors per track (8, 9, 15, or 18).
/T:*n*	Number of tracks (40 or 80).
/size	The size (capacity) of the diskette in kilobytes (such as /720 to format a 720 kilobyte diskette).
/Q	Quick format.
/D	DOS format. This is the same as the DOS FORMAT command.

Network considerations

SFormat works on the local drives of a network-connected PC.

In part, what you see on the Opening panel (see Fig. 18-1) when you run SFormat (SF) depends on how you have configured the Utility. You can exclude your hard disk(s) from this Utilities operations.

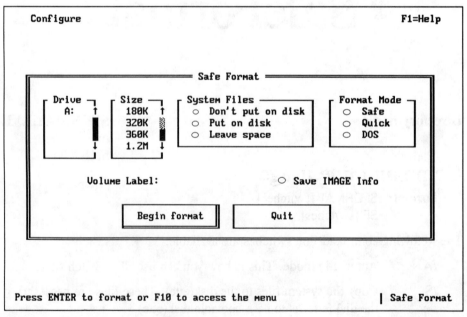

18-1 The Opening screen for SafeFormat.

Using the Hard Disk window (Fig. 18-2) from the Configure pull-down menu will preclude your hard disk being formatted. With this option set, you are also safe if a user tries to format from the command line.

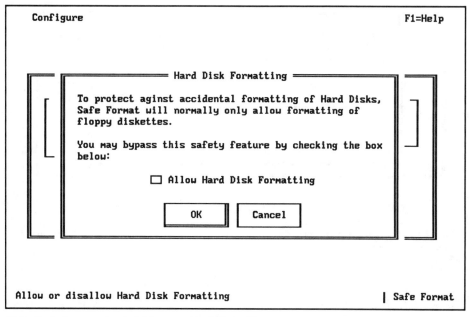

18-2 Protecting your hard disk from accidental formatting.

Any attempt to format should call SFormat. In this way, the safeguards built into the Utility will protect your information.

SFormat will detect the type(s) of floppy drive(s) active in your system (see Fig. 18-3 at the top of the next page). The left-hand box will list it/them, while the right-hand box displays the available options. The Auto Detect selection is the most flexible, allowing SFormat to check the diskette in the drive to determine its capacity. If you choose any of the other possibilities, you will be limiting your formatting capability to that type of diskette.

In some cases, this might be a desirable option, as it would prevent another user from using your system to format unapproved diskettes. The default for this selection series is Auto Detect.

SafeFormat version 4.0 & 4.5
Version 4.5 directory name   SF.EXE
SafeFormat is new with version 4.5 and a valuable addition. The DOS FORMAT command writes zeros into the file allocation tables (FATs) and the directory areas. It is possible to recover the information still in the data or files area of a

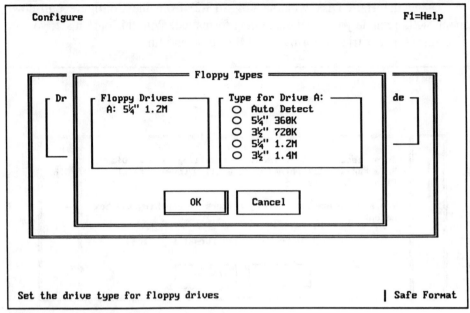

```
  Configure                                                F1=Help


                    ╔═══════════ Floppy Types ═══════════╗
         ┌ Dr      ┌ Floppy Drives ──┐  ┌ Type for Drive A: ──┐    de ┐
                      A: 5¼" 1.2M         ○  Auto Detect
                                          ○  5¼" 360K
                                          ○  3½" 720K
                                          ○  5¼" 1.2M
                                          ○  3½" 1.4M
         └                                                          ┘


                          ┌────────┐    ┌──────────┐
                          │   OK   │    │  Cancel  │
                          └────────┘    └──────────┘


  Set the drive type for floppy drives              | Safe Format
```

18-3 Detecting the active floppies in your system.

disk after such a formatting. The procedure is slow and subject to incomplete recovery, though. Using SafeFormat (SF) provides a means of complete data recovery if and only if the recovery procedures are used before any new information is written to this disk.

If complete information removal is the purpose for formatting the disk, use WipeDisk before reformatting.

Format: SF [drive:] [switches]
FORMAT [drive:] [switches]

Note: Use FORMAT only if you answered yes to having the INSTALL program substitute SF for the FORMAT.COM program of DOS. To verify that this has been done, check your DOS directory. FORMAT.COM should have been renamed XXFORMAT .COM.

The following command line options are available:

/A   This option, Automatic, can be used within a batch process (such as a backup) or similar type operation to allow you to use unformatted (new) disks or reuse disks which contain obsolete files. Having to abort a batch process for lack of disks can be one of the more frustrating experiences for any user. The default is to Safe-Format the diskette to the default of the drive.

/S	This option, System, formats the disk and then copies the system files. SF must have a PATH to the DOS directory of your hard disk, or a floppy swap must be made to complete the copying operation.

/B	This option, Blank, leaves the system files area blank so that they may be copied onto the disk at a later time. Blank isn't quite the right term to use when describing the condition of the system files area. The correct number of sectors will be left unused so that the system files can be added. System files require a fixed location on any disk. You can find out more about files and their location requirements in chapter 26. One possible reason for using this option might be to SafeFormat diskettes that are to be used on another system. The various versions of DOS as well as the vendor (IBM, MS, Compaq, etc.) have minor differences. These may not cause problems for application programs, but they do not mix well.

/V:*labeltext*

Using Volume Label writes the volume label *labeltext* to the disk before completing the formatting process.

Note: No spaces between any of the characters. Spaces will cause the option to run improperly.

/1	The number one (1). Using this option causes SF to format only one side of the diskette. Adding a write-enable notch to single-sided diskette as a way to use the second side is not recommended. The horror stories are far worse than the slight expense of purchasing additional disks.
/4	Format a 360K floppy disk using a 1.2M drive.
/8	Format 8 sectors per track. Using this option, you can format a 160K or 320K diskette. Add the /1 switch when formatting single-sided (160K) diskettes.
/N:*n*	Format *n* sectors per track. Eight (8) sectors for 160K/320K, nine (9) sectors for 180K/360K, fifteen (15) sectors for 1.2M and nineteen (19) sectors for 1.44M.

Note: No spaces between the characters. |
| /T:*n* | Format *n* tracks per side. Forty (40) tracks for 160K/320K and 180K/360K or eighty (80) tracks for 1.2M or 1.44M diskettes.

Note: No spaces between characters. |
| /SIZE | The Size or capacity of the diskette. This option provides an easy way to get the proper combination of switches (sides, sectors, and |

tracks) to yield the size selected. Remember that the size selected must be allowable by both the diskette and the drive.

/Q Use Quick format. This option just replaces the system area of the diskette. It will also remove a large directory tree from a hard disk. Because so little is actually changed, the Quick format is very fast.

/D Use DOS format. This option yields the same result as using the FORMAT.COM program of DOS.

/C Use Complete format. This option is an enhanced SafeFormat option. In addition to Safe Formatting, Complete reformats bad sectors to increase disk reliability. This option cannot be used on a hard disk.

Like all of the other Utilities, SafeFormat is menu-driven. The amount of information displayed in the upper left portion of the Configuration Options portion of the screen will reflect the options selected by adding switches to the command line when calling SF. The default configuration is "no drive specified," "no size specified," "no system files," "no volume label," and SafeFormat. This is one of the ways that the Utilities prevent accidental formatting.

The center portion of the left side of the display (Fig. 18-4) is the list of modifiable configuration parameters. Note that one capital letter of each option is yellow or bold. Pressing this letter (not case-sensitive) opens a window in the center of the screen that lists the allowable options for that parameter. Pressing the ESC key or the Q key will abort the Utility and return you to the DOS prompt or shell menu.

Watch the lower left corner area as you change parameters. The short help message changes with each selection. The entire right portion of the screen is a

```
================= Safe Format =================
|         Configuration Options     |  ░░░░░░░░░░░░░░░░░░░░░░░░░░░░░░░░░  |
|                                   |         0% Complete                |
|       Drive:                      |                                    |
|        Size:                      |                                    |
|  System Type:  No System files    |       No Format in progress        |
| Volume Label:  (no volume label)  |                                    |
|  Format Mode:  Safe Format        |                                    |
|                                   |                              istics|
|        Begin Fo ┌────────────────────────────────┐                     |
|        Drive    │ Select the Drive to Format     │                     |
|        Size     │                                │                     |
|        System T │      A:    C:    D:            │                     |
|        Volume L │                                │                     |
|        Format M └────────────────────────────────┘         in progress |
|        Quit                                                             |
|                                                                         |
| Begin formatting the disk.                                              |
|                                                                         |
| Safe Format will save the previous                                     |
| System Area in case of accidental                                      |
| formatting (except DOS Format mode).                                    |
```

18-4 Selecting a drive to format.

feedback display and starts at the top with a bar-type graph that changes to yellow or bold as an indication of the percentage completed. The same information is displayed numerically immediately below the graph. The next portion displays the head and cylinder being formatted at that moment (this portion is the most accurate display during formatting).

The statistics portion of the display (Fig. 18-5) provides the balance of the information on what is happening. The estimated time appears to be correct for each type of operation. Some error will be evident if a diskette swap is necessary to copy the system files. The elapsed time display doesn't run like your common digital clock. The display is updated each time the percentage-completed graph and numbers are changed. Watch the bad-sectors count in the center portion. If this count increases too regularly, there may be a mismatch in the parameters selected versus the diskette being formatted. The bottom Space statistics are totals that display when the formatting process selected is complete.

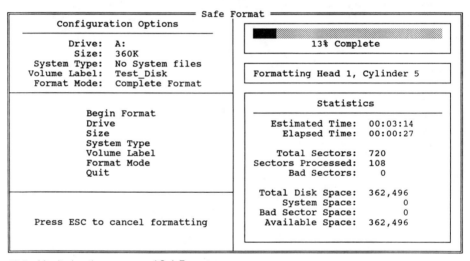

18-5 Monitoring the progress of SafeFormat.

I still don't understand why you would format diskettes for another system.

If one system has a hard disk and the other one doesn't, it's easier to do all of the formatting with the hard-disk system. I have a dual floppy almost compatible and an AT clone. The AT is faster and easier to use for many operations.

Are there any other reasons diskettes from another system might be used?

Bringing all of the disks, regardless of compatible system, up to version 4.5 compatibility makes any recovery operation easier. Remember that QU and NDD use some of the information written by SF to speed up recovery. This also enhances the probability that all of the data can be recovered.

19
CHAPTER

SpeeDisk

Version 5.0 directory name	SPEEDISK.EXE or SD.EXE

There have been significant changes to SpeeDisk (SD) since it was last seen in version 4.5. Perhaps the first one to be noticed is the name change. Prior to version 5.0, it has been listed as SD.EXE. In this version, it is called SPEEDISK.EXE. Like most of the other Utilities in version 5.0, it is menu-driven. The increase in interactive screens provides you with more control over how the program works with your system. In addition to the interactive mode, there is also the automatic mode that allows you to use SD within a batch file.

Before you do try to use SD in the batch mode, be sure to change the switches. The version 5.0 switches differ and are shown on the next page, followed by information on v4.0 and v4.5. SD was introduced in version 4.0, so all of the information on all of the different versions is presented here.

The warning shown below about SD physically moving files around on your hard disk still applies. The automatic update of the Format Recovery file is still present in version 5.0, but the filename is now IMAGE.

Command line format

Format: SD [d:] [switch] [switch] [switch] …

Switches:

/B   reBoot after optimization

/C   optimize Complete disk

/D   optimize Directories only

/Q   Quick compress. This unfragments only the free space on the disk. In other words, it fills in all of the gaps between your existing files without changing the existing fragmentation of those files.

/SD [−]   Sort by Date. Using the minus [−] sorts newest to oldest.

/SE [−]   Sort by Extension. Using the minus [−] sorts in descending alphabetical order (A to Z).

/SN [−]   Sort by Name. Using the minus [−] sorts in descending alphabetical order (A to Z).

/SS [−]   Sort by Size. Using the minus [−] sorts in largest to smallest order.

/U   Unfragment files only.

/V   Turn on Verify After Write. If your default configuration already has Verify turned on, there is no way to turn it off from the command line. For this reason, it might be best to leave it off and just turn it on from the command line when necessary.

Network considerations

Unfortunately, SD is not for use on network drives. It will work on the drives within the PCs attached to the network. There has not been any significant improvement in this Utility for network users and managers, but there should be an improvement in the condition of the individual drives within the network.

The Opening panel, Fig. 19-1, has most of the same information displayed. The Drive Selection window still interrogates your system to determine the active drives to display. More space is allowed for this function in the window because we, as users, are adding more logical and physical drives to our systems. Notice that the selection allows for only a single drive to be optimized, which ensures that each drive is optimized specifically as your needs dictate.

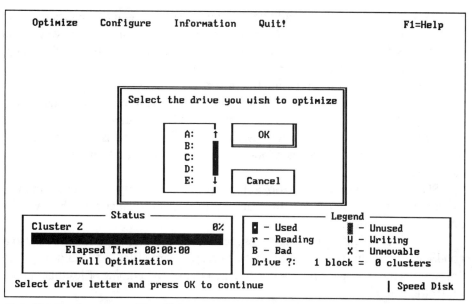

19-1 The Opening screen of SpeeDisk.

After you select a drive, SD will analyze it. When the analysis is complete, the program makes a recommendation. In Fig. 19-2, drive E is not fragmented, so no optimization is recommended.

In version 5.0, the Utilities such as SD have been designed to reduce the amount of work you are required to do. One of the benefits of this is seen in

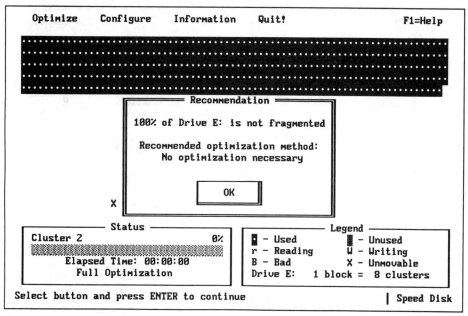

19-2 The Optimization Recommendation window.

Fig. 19-2. If a drive doesn't really need to be optimized, then SD makes that recommendation. You are not required to accept this recommendation, however, but just to consider it. Some of the weighing factors toward accepting SD's recommendations will be covered a little later.

The types of optimization available in version 5.0 are the same as in previous version with the addition of the FileSort option. This feature replaces the Directory Sort (DS) Utility in the earlier versions. I find DS useful and have not deleted it from the subdirectory that holds my Norton Utility programs. Be careful with the DS and SD program names. They perform much different functions. A typo can cause confusion.

SD recommends that you do a full optimization only once each month. Depending on how you use the other features of this Utility, that could be an accurate recommendation.

In addition to unfragmenting free space before copying large files, it is also a good idea to run this portion of SD before creating large files. I found it useful to unfragment the free space routinely while generating the graphics files that are the illustrations in this book.

To select the various options displayed in the window shown in Fig. 19-3, you should press the SPACEBAR to toggle the check marks on or off. Checked options are active options. Use the ARROW keys, TAB key, or a mouse to move the reverse video block to the little box you want to change. Clicking the mouse with the arrow in the OK box will set the options checked and move you on.

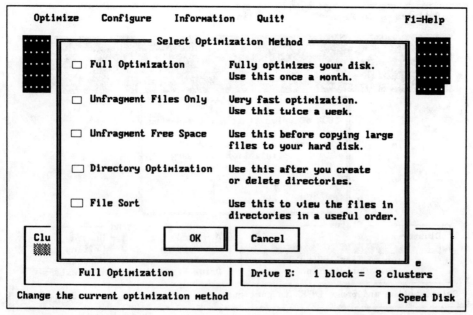

19-3 Selecting optimization.

The way you configure SD during the interactive phase will determine how it operates when you run it in the batch mode. It is possible to override some of these parameters with the switches used when SD is invoked in the batch mode. Some of the switches, such as Verify, do not have a reverse toggle, which can slow down its operation.

The options shown in Fig. 19-4 don't quite match the new ones in name. They are basically the same in function, however. The fifth choice in the new version isn't available in any earlier version, or at least not in SD.

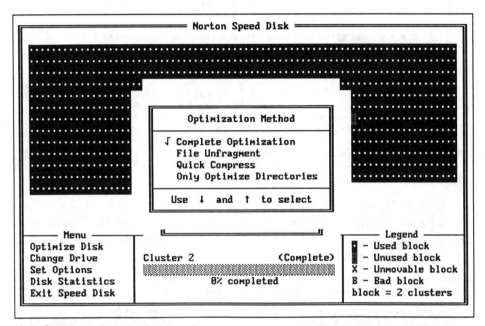

19-4 Selecting optimization (version 4.5).

There are two methods of verification available in version 5.0. One, the Read After Write option, is a proprietary Norton routine. Because it reads after each write, it will cause SD to slow down to about quarter-speed. The DOS Verify option runs much faster because it only verifies that the CHECKSUM of both copies of the information remains the same. The last option in Fig. 19-5 is Clear Unused Space. This is a modified WipeFile routine.

When SD completes its work, there are portions of files at various places in the available space of the hard disk. These sections are not lost in that they are not part of active files or orphan parts of deleted files. Under most circumstances, they will cause no problem as your new files overwrite these sectors, clusters, and blocks.

If your data is very sensitive or requires special protection because of regulations, you should keep the Clear Unused Space option on. This will cause SD to slow down in its operation. However, you can be sure that the only place your information can be found is in your active files.

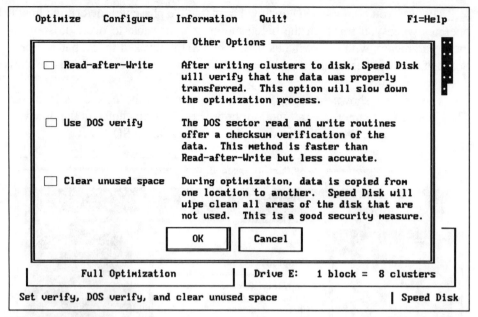

19-5 Selecting other options.

Each of the words along the top of the display in Fig. 19-6 can be tagged so that a pull-down menu becomes visible. I chose to pull down the "Walk Map" option, which has many interesting uses. Some of them are described later and a few of them are left for you to discover.

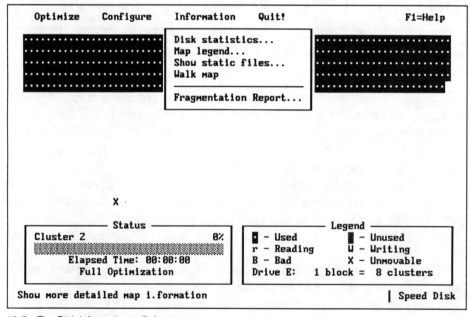

19-6 The Disk Information pull-down menu.

As you can read in Fig. 19-7, Walk Map allows you to select any block represented in the underlying map and discover its contents. You would have discovered very quickly that it takes only one bad sector of 512 bytes to make a bad cluster of 1K or 2K bytes. This shows up as a bad block, anywhere from 2 to 14 clusters.

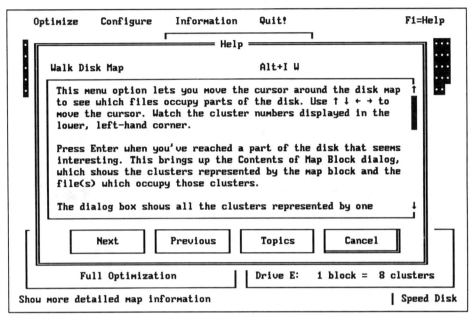

Optimize   Configure   Information   Quit!   F1=Help

Help

Walk Disk Map   Alt+I W

This menu option lets you move the cursor around the disk map to see which files occupy parts of the disk. Use ↑ ↓ ← → to move the cursor. Watch the cluster numbers displayed in the lower, left-hand corner.

Press Enter when you've reached a part of the disk that seems interesting. This brings up the Contents of Map Block dialog, which shows the clusters represented by the map block and the file(s) which occupy those clusters.

The dialog box shows all the clusters represented by one

Next   Previous   Topics   Cancel

Full Optimization   Drive E: 1 block = 8 clusters

Show more detailed map information | Speed Disk

19-7 The Walk Disc Map helpscreen.

Don't get upset too quickly. Remember that these Utilities do not do the reading and writing when you are in an application program. The map you see when you are in this Utility is only a representation of the hard-disk contents. DOS will continue to use the space around the bad sector. There will be some additional lost space in that DOS writes to clusters, not sectors; each bad sector will actually cause a cluster to be marked bad. Depending on the format of the hard disk, an additional 512 to 1,536 bytes of the disk space will remain empty for every bad sector.

Yes, you can change the marking of bad sectors with another Utility. And no, it is not recommended that you change markings. DOS or Norton has discovered a reason for marking the sector(s). Unless you are absolutely sure you know that the sector is safe to use, don't change it.

A number of symbols have been added to SD in version 5.0. Figure 19-8 displays all of them. Most of the letter symbols move as SD does its work. The letters "X" and "B" remain static and are also displayed differently. They are the symbols for unmovable files and bad sectors. The balance of the letters will move in what can best be described as organized confusion. Only one at a time will be

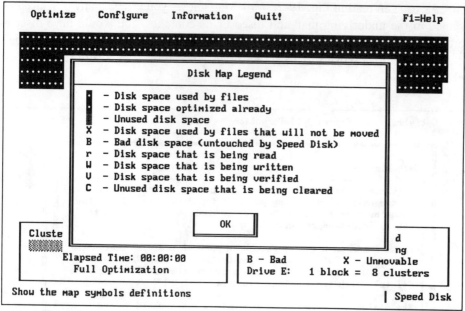

```
   Optimize    Configure    Information    Quit!              F1=Help
.........................................................
.........................................................
.........................................................
.........................................................
.........................................................
                  ┌──────────────────────────────────────┐
.........         │           Disk Map Legend             │
.........         │                                       │
.........         │  ▪  - Disk space used by files         │
.........         │  ▌  - Disk space optimized already     │
                  │  █  - Unused disk space                │
                  │  X  - Disk space used by files that will not be moved │
                  │  B  - Bad disk space (untouched by Speed Disk)        │
                  │  r  - Disk space that is being read     │
                  │  W  - Disk space that is being written  │
                  │  V  - Disk space that is being verified │
                  │  C  - Unused disk space that is being cleared │
                  │                                       │
                  │          ┌──────────────┐             │
                  │          │      OK      │             │
  ┌──────         │          └──────────────┘             │        d
  │Cluste         └──────────────────────────────────────┘        ng
  │▒▒▒▒▒
  ├───────────────────────────────────┬─────────────────────────────
  │   Elapsed Time: 00:00:00           │  B - Bad        X - Unmovable
  │   Full Optimization                │  Drive E:   1 block =  8 clusters
  └────────────────────────────────────┴─────────────────────────────
Show the map symbols definitions                        │ Speed Disk
```

19-8 The Disc Map Legend (version 5.0).

visible, and the "V" and "C" letters will not display at all unless you have Verify and/or Clear Unused Space turned on.

There aren't too many differences between the Disk Statistics window shown in Fig. 19-9 and the one shown in Fig. 19-10. The information provided and the

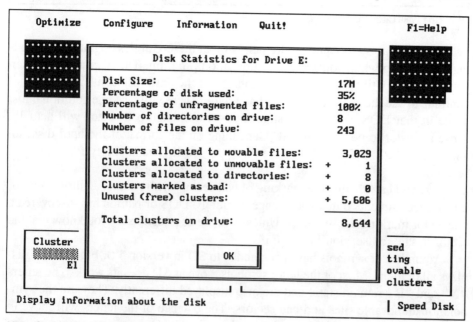

```
   Optimize    Configure    Information    Quit!              F1=Help
..........                                          ..........
..........          ┌────────────────────────────────────┐  ..........
..........          │     Disk Statistics for Drive E:     │  ..........
..........          │                                      │  ..........
                    │  Disk Size:                    17M    │
                    │  Percentage of disk used:      35%    │
                    │  Percentage of unfragmented files:  100%  │
                    │  Number of directories on drive:    8 │
                    │  Number of files on drive:          243 │
                    │                                      │
                    │  Clusters allocated to movable files:    3,029 │
                    │  Clusters allocated to unmovable files: +    1 │
                    │  Clusters allocated to directories:     +    8 │
                    │  Clusters marked as bad:                +    0 │
                    │  Unused (free) clusters:                + 5,606 │
                    │                                      ────────  │
                    │  Total clusters on drive:                8,644 │
  ┌──────           │                                      │
  │Cluster          │          ┌──────────────┐            │     sed
  │▒▒▒▒▒▒           │          │      OK      │            │     ting
  │        E1       │          └──────────────┘            │     ovable
                    └────────────────────────────────────┘     clusters
  └──────────────────────────────────┘ └─────────────────────────────
Display information about the disk                       │ Speed Disk
```

19-9 Statistics of your disk.

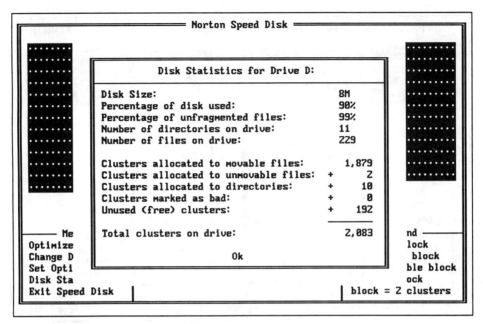

```
═══════════════════════ Norton Speed Disk ═══════════════════════

        ┌──────────────────────────────────────────────┐
        │         Disk Statistics for Drive D:         │
        │                                              │
        │  Disk Size:                           8M     │
        │  Percentage of disk used:             90%    │
        │  Percentage of unfragmented files:    99%    │
        │  Number of directories on drive:      11     │
        │  Number of files on drive:            229    │
        │                                              │
        │  Clusters allocated to movable files:   1,879│
        │  Clusters allocated to unmovable files: +   2│
        │  Clusters allocated to directories:     +  10│
        │  Clusters marked as bad:                 +   0│
        │  Unused (free) clusters:                 + 192│
        │                                              │
──── Me │  Total clusters on drive:             2,083  │  nd ────
Optimize│                                              │  lock
Change D│                   Ok                         │   block
Set Opti└──────────────────────────────────────────────┘  ble block
Disk Sta                                                   ock
Exit Speed Disk │                              │ block = 2 clusters
```

19-10 Statistics of your disk (version 4.5).

format in which it is provided is very similar. About the most noticeable change is the "OK" at the bottom of the window. Where it was in a small reverse video block before, it now has an outlined block to keep it safe. You cannot make changes in this window, and no choices are offered. You either leave the window on display, or press a key to remove it.

The ability to set a priority on the placement of various files may not be useful to some users. I find that it takes SD less time to do its work when I keep the files that should not be changing at the top of the directory listing. This forces all of the data files to be written after the application files and also means that when I make data changes, the files will be fragmenting each other and not disturbing my program files.

Both Figs. 19-11 and 19-12 display much the same information and provide the same service. The editing capability included in version 5.0 will make it easier to adjust this window to changing conditions. I don't expect to use this feature often. Once the file priority is set by extension, you shouldn't have to change it again. When an exceptional circumstance comes up making a change necessary, then the added time it will take for SD to get everything back in order is worth the wait.

Fragmenting program or application files with data files should not cause any problems. The only thing it will do is slow down the operation of the program because of the way information is read from the disk and placed in system memory.

Fragmentation will really cause problems only when the file fragments get lost. Again, this shouldn't happen. Of course, your hard disk shouldn't go bad

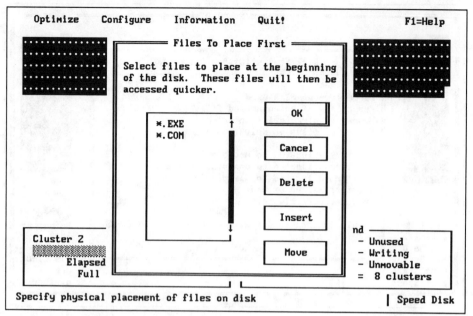

19-11 Placing files for easier access (version 5.0).

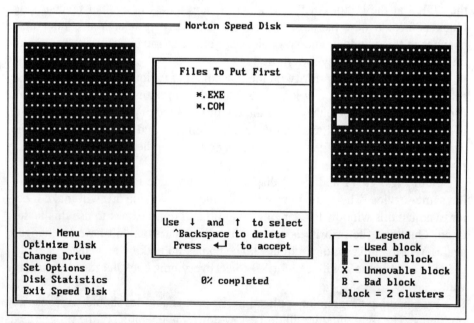

19-12 Placing files for easier access (version 4.5).

either. Remember that a hard-disk death is a "when," not an "if," situation. I mention this again because I want to remind you (and myself) to back up our disks.

Reordering directories shouldn't be undertaken any oftener than the re-ordering of files. The directories are kept in a designated area so that their movement doesn't change anything in the file storage area. There is still a direct link between the files and the directory or subdirectory they are stored in. Changing things around will change the way DOS and the Utilities read the directories and their associated files. Relocation of files and directories for the sake of movement should be avoided (see Fig. 19-13).

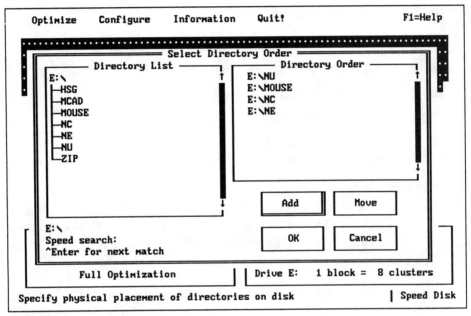

19-13 Re-ordering your directories on the disk.

SpeeDisk version 4.0 & 4.5

Version 4.0 & 4.5 directory name

SD.EXE

SD is found only in the Advanced Editions but does a number of very useful tasks. It reduces to a minimum the wasted space on a disk; it eliminates all file fragments; and it provides a visual indication of what it is doing. Redirection may be used when the Report option (which provides a hard copy of the results) is used.

Warning: SD physically moves file(s) and sector(s) as it operates. Thus, the memory resident programs may not be able to locate the program file when SD has done its work; and if the system is interrupted during the operation of the SD program, information may be lost.

SD may not be compatible with all of the copy protection schemes in use on your disk(s), especially hard disks. Before running SD the first time, back up the entire hard disk. After verification of compatibility, you should not have to perform this step. Remember to run FR (format recover) after running SD. Version 4.5 has an improvement in that it automatically updates your FR files after it completes re-organization of your hard disk.

Format: SD [d:] [switches]
              SD [filespec] [switches]

d: The drive designation.

Switches

/A   Automatic operation—no prompts

/C   Complete optimization

/D   Directory optimization

/P   Pause the display after each screenful. Pressing any key will also pause the display. A second keypress will restart the scrolling.

/REPORT or **/R**
       Generates a report and does not make any changes to the files on the disk. This report may be redirected using the DOS redirection operators > or > > with d: \ path \ filename.

/V   Turn Verify on

filespec   The filename or subdirectoryname to be optimized by SD.

/S   Instructs SD to include all Subdirectories when rearranging the files.

/T   Show Totals only. This switch is used with the /R switch when a hardcopy report is desired.

/U   Unfragment files optimization

SD improves disk usage and reduces access times by relocating the fragmented sectors of a file into a contiguous sector chain. SD also reduces read/write head motion during disk accessing. In addition, SD places all directories before all files at the beginning of the disk.

A typical session with SD would start with the Opening screen after SD was entered at the DOS prompt (see Fig. 19-14).

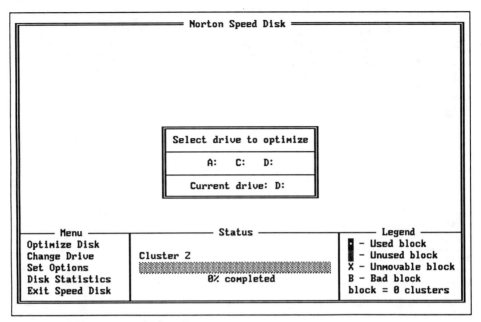

```
════════ Norton Speed Disk ════════




                    ┌─────────────────────────┐
                    │ Select drive to optimize │
                    │                          │
                    │     A:   C:   D:         │
                    │                          │
                    │   Current drive: D:      │
                    └─────────────────────────┘



── Menu ──        ───────── Status ─────────        ── Legend ──
Optimize Disk                                       ▌ - Used block
Change Drive      Cluster 2                         ▌ - Unused block
Set Options       ▓▓▓▓▓▓▓▓▓▓▓▓▓▓▓▓▓▓▓▓▓▓▓▓▓▓▓       X - Unmovable block
Disk Statistics           0% completed              B - Bad block
Exit Speed Disk                                     block = 0 clusters
```

19-14 The Opening screen for SpeeDisk (version 4.x).

Note the organization of this screen. The cursor sits on the drive letter and blinks for version 4.0. With version 4.5, there is a reverse video block that indicates the letter of the default drive. The options are to press RETURN, ESC, or a letter key. You may also use the ARROW keys to reposition the cursor and then press the RETURN key. This allows you to run SD on the disk indicated, exit SD altogether, or change the drive selection and then run SD.

After reading all of the information on the disk, SD begins re-arranging it into contiguous sectors of directories and then files. One thing it will not do is move hidden or system files, which prevents problems with some programs that install "keys" in certain locations and then must be able to locate them again at the same place. In Fig. 19-15, there is a problem. SD doesn't repair damage, so the message recommends that NDD (Norton Disk Doctor) be run. Unless the problem is very unusual, NDD should be able to repair the damage and let you run SD.

Good operating practices will reduce to a minimum the number of times you see an error message while attempting to run any program.

There are times when you just cannot wait for SD to complete its work. If you press the ESC key while SD is working, you will see a flashing "One Moment Please" message where you usually see the "Reading," "Writing," and "Sorting" indicators in the status area at the bottom center of the screen. Don't do anything more until you get the prompt to exit as shown in Fig. 19-16.

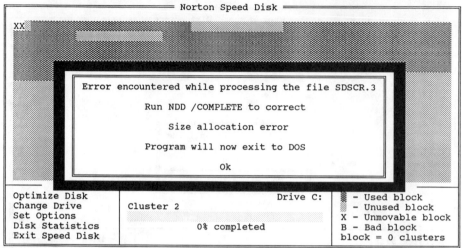

19-15 A typical error window (version 4.5).

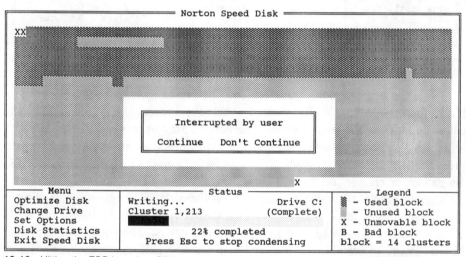

19-16 Hitting the ESC key when SD is running.

Continued use of a disk with marked bad sectors is not immediately dangerous to data storage. Still, it could indicate a defect in manufacture, or it could indicate that the disk is getting worn. Because the sectors are marked, DOS will not
attempt to write anything to them. I prefer to use these disks for archival purposes
to reduce the possibility of data loss.

A hard disk with a bad sector is normal. There are very few hard disks manu-
factured with 100% perfect media on all surfaces of all platters. So long as the
number of bad sectors doesn't increase and there are no other indications of problems, the disk should be safe to use.

When setting the various options available, you should balance the speed you want with the efficiency you need. How you organize each of the selections shown in Fig. 19-17 will determine how efficient your system operates after SD runs.

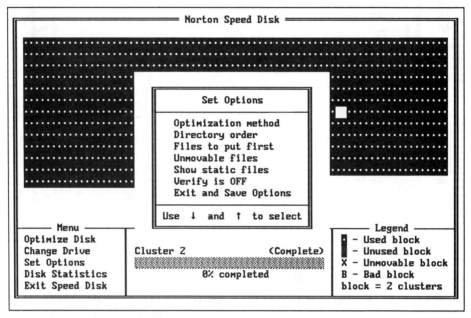

19-17 Setting SD options (version 4.5AE).

Where absolute data reliability is necessary, the extra time Verify takes is well spent. When you can take a few minutes extra each morning to do a complete optimization, the balance of the day's applications programs should run better. Also, because the FRECOVER files have been updated, the potential for loss is less.

As you can see in Fig. 19-18, I haven't changed the directory order. This logical disk is a programs disk, so it doesn't get much data written to it. Also, because I use these programs about equally, their order doesn't make much difference.

Under other circumstances, it might be worthwhile to change the order so that the most used programs are at the top of the list. This would place them at the head of the search path and therefore reduce the time to find and read them.

Why is it that some of the illustrations have more drives shown than others?

In developing the illustrations for this book and some of the previous editions, I have had access to other systems. When it helps to clarify a point or improve an illustration, I try to use the one from the system with the more interesting picture.

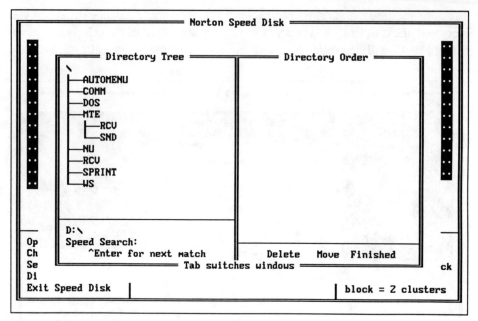

```
═══════════════ Norton Speed Disk ═══════════════
  ··                                              ··
  ··  ╒═══════ Directory Tree ═══════╕ ╒══════ Directory Order ══════╕
  ··  │  ╲                           │ │                            │
  ··  │   ┝━AUTOMENU                 │ │                            │
  ··  │   ┝━COMM                     │ │                            │
  ··  │   ┝━DOS                      │ │                            │
  ··  │   ┝━MTE                      │ │                            │
  ··  │      ┝━RCU                   │ │                            │
  ··  │      ┗━SND                   │ │                            │
  ··  │   ┝━NU                       │ │                            │
  ··  │   ┝━RCU                      │ │                            │
  ··  │   ┝━SPRINT                   │ │                            │
  ··  │   ┗━WS                       │ │                            │
      │                             │ │                            │
      │  D:╲                        │ │                            │
  Op  │ Speed Search:               │ │                            │
  Ch  │     ^Enter for next match   │ │   Delete   Move  Finished  │
  Se  ╘═══════════ Tab switches windows ═══════════╛            ck
  Di
  Exit Speed Disk  │              │            │  block = 2 clusters │
```

19-18 Re-ordering your directories (version 4.5AE).

Can I abort SD at any time without danger?

SD can be aborted using CTRL-C safely. Aborting by any other means can cause problems. When you do, SD will complete whatever operations it must to ensure that you can safely start another program or operation.

Pressing the ESC key also works. In fact, this way of aborting SD is recommended by the note at the bottom of the screen. A dialog box opens in the middle of your screen to confirm that you really want to abort the running of SD. If you choose not to terminate SD, it will continue to operate normally. If you do terminate it, SD will provide a safe exit. If you look carefully at Fig. 19-19, you will note that the last complete line of in-use blocks and the partial line below it have gaps. SD was interrupted or aborted before it had finished its work of defragmentation.

Will SD respond immediately after I press the CTRL-C key combination?

Yes and no. SD will finish whatever operations are necessary to leave your disk-(ette) fully operational at the time SD aborts. This means that it will have completed some operations and not others, although no operation will be left incomplete.

What types of problems can be caused by improper exits?

SD relocates files on the disk. If the file is relocated and the new location is not written to the FAT (file allocation table), it will be impossible for DOS to find. Or, if SD is aborted during a write, it may not write the entire file back to the disk.

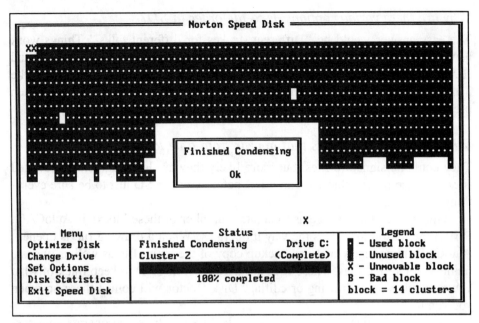

```
═══════════════════ Norton Speed Disk ═══════════════════
XX··············································································
··········································································
··········································································
·····································           ···························
··········································································
····                                   █                         ········
·········                                                         ········
····                                                              ········
······       ·                          ┌──────────────────┐     ········
···········                             │                  │     ········
··········                              │ Finished Condensing  ·········
··········                              │                  │     ····
·····                                   │       Ok         │     ····
····  █                                 │                  │     ····
···                                     └──────────────────┘     ····
··········                                                       ····
··   ·      ·        ·       ·                       ·····        ·····
                                                    X
─── Menu ───────────── Status ──────────────── Legend ───
Optimize Disk      Finished Condensing    Drive C:    █ - Used block
Change Drive       Cluster 2             (Complete)   █ - Unused block
Set Options        ▐██████████████████████████▌       X - Unmovable block
Disk Statistics            100% completed             B - Bad block
Exit Speed Disk                                       block = 14 clusters
```

19-19   Safely exiting SD.

Will SD work if there are problems with any of the files?

No. SD will report problems and then abort its operation.

After running SD, is there any data left in the sectors or clusters that are now empty?

Yes and no. SD operates much like WipeFile or WipeDisk in that respect. However, until version 5.0, it had no provisions for going back over the empty space and overwriting any data that might still remain. This is where WipeDisk with the /E switch is sometimes used.

How large a disk can SD manipulate?

How large a disk do you have? SD and DOS have the same limits. It will seem to work slower on larger disks because the blocks will represent more clusters. Also, the multiple partitions of a single physical disk will appear to be lettered logical disks to SD.

Why would I want to use SD on just one file?

If you use a word processor or spreadsheet program that builds very big datafiles, you could have only one file for a whole week's work. This is the case with my word processor; this whole book is broken down by chapter in a single file. I run SD at regular intervals to keep things moving.

Why are there various options as to file order in SD?

The easy answer would be "Different strokes for different folks." Things work better when fragmenting is kept at a minimum, thus keeping all of the .COM and .EXE files in a subdirectory ahead of the datafiles. This way, when you add to the datafiles, they won't have to jump over those files that will retain their size when present.

What are the "X" blocks that appear from time to time?

They could be signature files, but more likely they are lost fragments of deleted files. I'd recommend that you run NDD before you run SD just to be sure everything is in order.

One application that seems to create a number of these blocks is AutoCAD. Part of the reason for this is the way it operates. When a drawing file is opened, AutoCAD immediately makes a backup copy of the entire file as well as opens a number of internal files. These files are used by AutoCAD to keep track of what you do while you're drawing or editing. Disk Doctor will collect these up when you run it.

If you are getting a number of these blocks every time you operate your system, there's a good chance that there is another problem.

Directory Sort version 4.0 & 4.5

Directory name   **DS.EXE**

DS sorts the files in directories and subdirectories by one or a combination of parameters. For reverse order sorting, use the minus sign ($-$) immediately after the parameter or switch. When using the minus sign and/or more than one sort parameter, do not use any spaces or punctuation between characters.

Note: This Utility is retained when you upgrade from version 4.5 to version 5.0.

Format: DS [sort keys] [directory name] [/S] (for automatic sort)

When DS is doing its thing automatically, there really isn't much to see. The words shown in Fig. 19-20 appear from left to right until all of the sorting is done.

19-20 An automatic sort using DS with Name, Extension, and Size switches active.

C: \ : c: \ nu \ ds nes a:
DS-Directory Sort, Advanced Edition, (C) Copr 1988, Peter Norton

  A: \ . . . reading, sorting, writing, done.

---

or

        DS [directory name] (for a full-screen interactive sort)

Working in the interactive mode, Fig. 19-21, is just that: you control where the files go. The automatic options are still available along the right side of the screen; but if you had wanted to use them, you probably wouldn't be in interactive mode.

```
╔═══════════════════════ Directory Sort ═══════════════════════╗
║              ┌─────────────── A:\ ───────────────┐             ║
║   Name       │ Size    │  Date    │  Time        │ Sort by        Order ║
║ aids    txt  │ 55,102  │ Jul  5 87│ 9:39 pm      │               ║
║ arc     doc  │ 57,214  │ Jan 12 87│ 5:06 pm      │               ║
║ arc     exe  │ 32,184  │ Apr 22 87│ 3:08 pm      │               ║
║ arc     txt  │  2,109  │ Apr 22 87│ 4:28 pm      │               ║
║ arc521  com  │ 58,368  │ Jun 27 87│ 1:47 am      │               ║
║ arce    com  │  5,710  │ Dec 31 86│ 1:54 pm      │               ║
║ art          │  2,328  │ Jun 20 87│ 6:16 pm      │               ║
║ ca      for  │  1,643  │ Aug  7 87│ 4:32 pm      │ ──────────────║
║ changes 521  │  1,939  │ May 14 87│ 8:39 am      │               ║
║ ed      for  │  1,632  │ Aug  7 87│ 4:07 pm      │     Name      ║
║ host         │  5,504  │ Jun 16 87│ 10:56 pm     │     Extension ║
║ packman arc  │ 11,136  │ Jul 10 87│ 12:29 pm     │     Date      ║
║ peposcrn asm │  5,284  │ Jun 18 87│ 10:24 pm     │     Time      ║
║ submit  fil  │  3,034  │ Jul  5 87│ 6:47 pm      │     Size      ║
║ sug     for  │  1,891  │ Jan  1 80│ 12:23 am     │               ║
║ term    log  │    592  │ Jul 14 87│ 11:38 pm     │ Clear sort order ║
║ term    sav  │      0  │ Jul  8 87│ 6:00 pm      │ Move sort entry ║
║                                                                 ║
║       Space bar selects files for moving                        ║
║                                                                 ║
║  Re-sort      Move file(s)      Change sort order   Write changes to disk ║
║ Line=15    Col=1       C:SPRINT\NU5\SCR\SCREEN.DS    Insert  WW=60  Indent ║
╚═════════════════════════════════════════════════════════════════╝
```

19-21 An interactive sort using DS with the same directory used in Fig. 19-20.

The sort keys are:

D   Sorts files by their date from oldest to newest.

E   Sorts files by their extension from none to $0-9$ to $A-Z$.

N   Sorts files by their name from A to Z.

S   Sorts files by their size from smallest to largest.

T   Sorts files by their timestamp from 00:01AM to 23:59PM.

$(-)$ Reverses the sort order indicated above.

Note: Unlike some of the other programs, DS does not use the slash (/) as a separator between the switches. It also does not require any other punctuation or spaces between the switches. Only the next switch uses the "/."

[/S]   Includes all subdirectories in the sort process. This switch is only active (available) during automatic sorts.

DS must not be used when other files in the directory(ies) may be used by other programs. This means that DS must be the only program running on a multi-user or multi-tasking system.

Because DS changes the file order in the directory(ies), you should not attempt to abort it by using the CTRL-BREAK key combination or by turning the power off. Only in version 4.0 or the Advanced Edition is it possible to abort the program using the CTRL-BREAK key combination.

DS will move hidden and system filenames during either type of sort session. Both are displayed during the interactive session.

Version 4.5 and the Advanced Edition also have an interactive mode that allows the totally arbitrary ordering of files within a directory.

DS will place all subdirectories before the files in the directory. DS will not move any hidden or system files data, as to prevent causing problems with copy-protected software.

Entering DS without any parameters or switches will begin an interactive sort session in the default directory.

D   Set date as a sort parameter.

DOWN ARROW or **PAGE DN**
               Move the reverse video block down the list of files.

ENTER   Fix the file in its new location.

ESC   Return a moved file to its original location, or leave DS and return to the DOS prompt.

F10   Exit DS and return to the DOS prompt.

RIGHT ARROW
               Shift the reverse video block from the filename listing section to the sort order section.

M   Indicates that the file highlighted by the reverse video block is to be moved.

R   Re-sorts the directory based on the changed parameter switches.

TAB   Acts as a toggle to move the reverse video block between the two areas.

UP ARROW or **PAGE UP**
               Moves the reverse video block up the filename listing.

Is there any really good reason to sort a directory?

For me, yes. I don't always remember filenames; but by putting the program (.EXE or .COM) files at the beginning, I can let them scroll off the screen while the files I've created (.DAT, .TXT, or .SPT) are at the end of the listing—still visible when the prompt returns.

Can't I use the /W switch with the DIR command and see just as much?

Almost. The /W will display the filenames and extensions five to a line. Not displayed are the file size, time, and datestamp information. It's a matter of choice and/or need. Different versions of a filename might also appear as duplicate entries.

Can you prove that DS will not cause me problems with the signature files of the copy-protected software on my hard disk?

Yes and no. While DS will relocate the filenames in the directory, it does not move the data portions of the files. Essentially, the address (cylinder, side and cluster/sector) of that file remains unchanged, which should prevent problems. I've used NU to look at the Root directory of a floppy disk before and after a DS N sort (seen in Figs. 19-22 and 19-23 respectively). Note that the starting cluster number for each file is unchanged.

```
 Root dir ═══════════════════════════════════════  Directory format
 Sector 5 in root directory                           Offset 0, hex 00
                                                          Attributes
|Filename Ext      Size      Date      Time     Cluster  Arc R/O Sys Hid Dir Vol|

|LOADER   SYS      1024    12/10/84   11:00 am      2    Arc R/O Sys Hid
|INSTR    KZI       676     2/19/87   12:37 am      3    Arc
|SMSG               604     2/21/87    8:04 pm      4    Arc
|TERM     SAV               3/14/87   12:01 am
|TELE     SAV      4854     3/13/87   11:39 pm      5    Arc
|FRIED    SAV      7449     3/14/87   12:34 pm     10    Arc
|PROWARE  ARC     88960     3/14/87    1:35 am     18    Arc
|SYSOPMAS          34304     4/01/87   12:00 am    105    Arc
|SYSOP    HAN     32278     3/30/87    9:19 pm    139    Arc
|CURSOR   COM     21524     3/09/87   12:00 am    171    Arc
|DATER    COM     21353     3/09/87   12:00 am    193    Arc
|MENU     COM     32302     3/09/87   12:00 am    214    Arc
|CURSOR   PAS     40960     3/09/87   12:00 am    246    Arc
|DATER    PAS     23552     3/09/87   12:00 am    286    Arc
|σPL      ARC     32768     3/31/87    7:03 pm    309    Arc
|σSPL     ARC               3/31/87    7:08 pm           Arc

        Filenames beginning with 'σ' indicate erased entries
                    Press Enter to continue
|Line=49     Col=1         C:SPRINT\NU5\SCR\SCREEN.DS     Insert     WW=60   Indent
```

19-22 The unsorted Root directory shown by NU.

I noticed you have a filename displayed with no size. How did you do that?

I didn't do it. The communications software I use on that computer opens a default filename of TERM.SAV on my data capture disk as a part of its startup procedure. That way, it is immediately ready to begin a capture when the proper key is pressed.

```
 Sector 5 in root directory                               Offset 0, hex 00
                                                            Attributes
Filename Ext     Size      Date       Time     Cluster  Arc R/O Sys Hid Dir Vol
     .
LOADER   SYS      1024   12/10/84   11:00 am       2    Arc R/O Sys Hid
CURSOR   COM     21524    3/09/87   12:00 am     171    Arc
CURSOR   PAS     40960    3/09/87   12:00 am     246    Arc
DATER    COM     21353    3/09/87   12:00 am     193    Arc
DATER    PAS     23552    3/09/87   12:00 am     286    Arc
DDS      SCR      2051    7/17/87   10:24 am     309    Arc
FRIED    SAV      7449    3/14/87   12:34 pm      10    Arc
INSTR    KZI       676    2/19/87   12:37 am       3    Arc
MENU     COM     32302    3/09/87   12:00 am     214    Arc
PROWARE  ARC     88960    3/14/87    1:35 pm      18    Arc
SMSG              604     2/21/87    8:04 pm       4    Arc
SYSOP    HAN     32278    3/30/87    9:19 pm     139    Arc
SYSOPMAS         34304    4/01/87   12:00 am     105    Arc
TELE     SAV      4854    3/13/87   11:39 pm       5    Arc
TERM     SAV              3/14/87   12:01 am            Arc
σSPL     ARC              3/31/87    7:08 pm            Arc
     .
         Filenames beginning with 'σ' indicate erased entries
                    Press Enter to continue
1Help    2Hex    3Text   4Dir    5FAT    6Partn  7        8        9Undo  10QuitNU
Line=102    Col=1           C:SPRINT\NUS\SCR\SCREEN.DS        Insert    WW=60  Indent
```

19-23 The sorted Root directory shown by NU.

Will the starting cluster numbers remain unchanged if I copy the sorted files onto another disk or into another directory?

They will if you use the DISKCOPY Utility program. Using the DOS COPY command will transfer the filenames and data areas in sorted order. Then the starting cluster number will change and the fragmented files will be reconnected.

Isn't this almost the same as using the SD (SpeeDisk) Utility?

No. SD does not change the starting cluster number to suit the directory sort order. COPY is the only way to reorder the data storage area. SD will relocate files in the data storage area, but it will not always place them in directory listing order. The exception to SD moving files is the signature file.

Isn't this a duplication of the abilities of the DOS Utilities?

I don't think so. I much prefer to use SD on the hard disk as part of my routine maintenance. Using DS and then copying the files to a floppy or another portion of the hard disk seems very time-consuming. I do sort and COPY files prior to sending a floppy disk to someone because I think that it looks more professional. It also ensures that I use a newly wiped disk, which means that there will not be any other data present.

I can do the same sorts of things with another program I have, why do I need the Norton Utilities?

I'm sure that there are a number of utility programs that can do the same things that DS does. I'm not sure that you can get an entire package of utility programs that will duplicate all of the Norton Utilities in any combination of other utility programs. If you have an unlimited software budget, you might find almost everything.

20
CHAPTER

System Information

Directory name

SYSINFO.EXE
or
SI.EXE

SysInfo has been revised and expanded to the point of almost being a new program. There are no special command-line switches to be remembered; everything is menu-driven. Just enter SI at the prompt, and the program unfolds a menu at a time. The following are the switches that are available for use when running SysInfo.

Command line usage

Format: SYSINFO /[AUTO:n|DEMO|TSR|N|SUMMARY]

/AUTO:*n*   Cycles SysInfo through its screens with an *n* second delay between each screen.

/DEMO   Places SysInfo in the demonstration mode.

/TSR   Displays the identifiable resident programs.

/N   Causes SysInfo to bypass the live memory probe.

/SUMMARY
SysInfo prints a shortened report. The information provided is
the same as that provided by version 4.5.

Network considerations

SysInfo will report on user and network information if it is attached to a network.
At this time, SysInfo is compatible with the Novell network only.

The basics of what your system is and what's attached to the CPU are spelled
out in the Opening panel, (Fig. 20-1). If there are any differences between what is
displayed and what you know is there, you'd better check your setup. If you press
the RETURN key, SI moves onto the next screen.

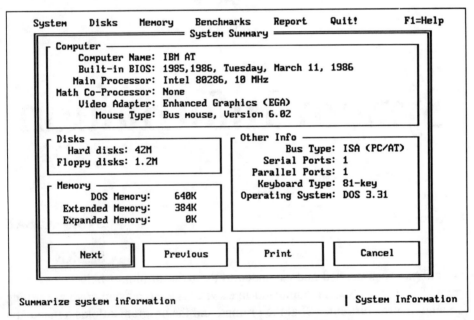

20-1 The Opening screen for SysInfo.

If you don't need to check everything, the keywords across the top of the
screen will let you jump to the section you need. Before jumping around, though,
let's look at each screen and the provided information.

The Video Summary panel, Fig. 20-2, details the type of video driver card
installed, the monitor type, and the mode of operation. The mode can be changed
using the DOS commands, or you can call on the Norton Control Center Utility.

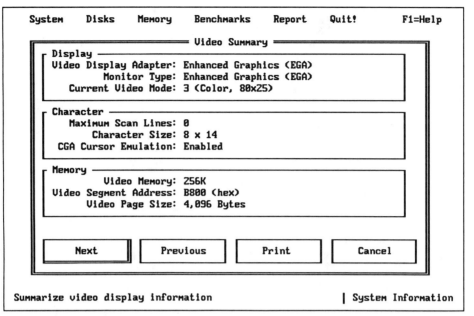

```
════════════════════════ Video Summary ════════════════════════
┌─ Display ──────────────────────────────────────────────────────┐
│  Video Display Adapter: Enhanced Graphics (EGA)                 │
│            Monitor Type: Enhanced Graphics (EGA)                │
│      Current Video Mode: 3 (Color, 80x25)                       │
└─────────────────────────────────────────────────────────────────┘
┌─ Character ────────────────────────────────────────────────────┐
│     Maximum Scan Lines: 0                                       │
│          Character Size: 8 x 14                                 │
│   CGA Cursor Emulation: Enabled                                 │
└─────────────────────────────────────────────────────────────────┘
┌─ Memory ───────────────────────────────────────────────────────┐
│          Video Memory: 256K                                     │
│  Video Segment Address: B800 (hex)                              │
│       Video Page Size: 4,096 Bytes                              │
└─────────────────────────────────────────────────────────────────┘

┌──────────┐ ┌──────────────┐ ┌──────────┐ ┌──────────┐
│   Next   │ │   Previous   │ │  Print   │ │  Cancel  │
└──────────┘ └──────────────┘ └──────────┘ └──────────┘
```

Summarize video display information | System Information

20-2 The Video summary screen.

Character Size displays the number of pixels wide by the number of pixels high used to produce a standard alphanumeric character. This is fixed by the information permanently recorded on the ROM chip in your system. The actual shape of the different characters may vary from system to system. I know that the character display of my TIPC is significantly different from the display of my AT clone.

The amount of video memory present is a variable. Video cards designed for use with programs like AutoCAD may have more memory on the card, while monochrome adapter cards may have less or none at all. The starting address for the video memory is standard, with few exceptions. I cannot say that there aren't any exceptions, though, because I haven't been able to check every possible combination of system and video card.

Page Size is a function of the video card. Four thousand bytes isn't much, but it appears to be adequate for my needs. There may come a time when I will have to change the video card, but the only possibility I'm aware of right now is going to an AutoCAD-intensive situation. Along with the card change, I will also have to add a math coprocessor chip as well as a number of other pieces of hardware.

The Hardware Interrupt list shown in Fig. 20-3 isn't complete, as the elevator bar on the right edge of the display window indicates. There are a total of 15 hardware interrupts, and each of them is listed when you print out the System Information report. Otherwise, you can use the UP and DOWN ARROW keys or the PAGE UP and PAGE DOWN keys to view all of the interrupts and the owners.

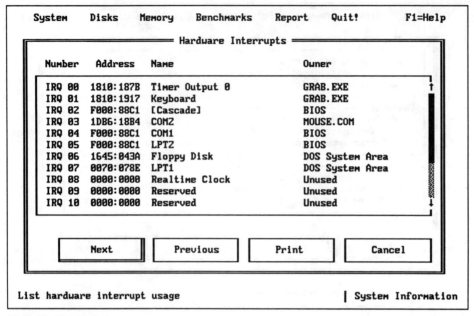

| System | Disks | Memory | Benchmarks | Report | Quit! | F1=Help |

═══════════════ Hardware Interrupts ═══════════════

Number	Address	Name	Owner
IRQ 00	1810:187B	Timer Output 0	GRAB.EXE
IRQ 01	1810:1917	Keyboard	GRAB.EXE
IRQ 02	F000:88C1	[Cascade]	BIOS
IRQ 03	1DB6:18B4	COM2	MOUSE.COM
IRQ 04	F000:88C1	COM1	BIOS
IRQ 05	F000:88C1	LPT2	BIOS
IRQ 06	1645:043A	Floppy Disk	DOS System Area
IRQ 07	0070:078E	LPT1	DOS System Area
IRQ 08	0000:0000	Realtime Clock	Unused
IRQ 09	0000:0000	Reserved	Unused
IRQ 10	0000:0000	Reserved	Unused

| Next | Previous | Print | Cancel |

List hardware interrupt usage | System Information

20-3 The Hardware Interrupts screen.

Don't let the "Unknown owner" under the Owner column scare you. This just means that the Utility didn't look far enough to find the name of the program(s). The reason for this omission is program overhead; it would take time and code to determine each program owner by name. The interesting one is the COM2 owner: according to SysInfo, it is MOUSE.COM. I'm not really sure why, because the mouse card is a bus card and should not be using the serial port address for access.

There are just a few more software interrupts available. Notice that the elevator bar shown in Fig. 20-4 is much smaller now. In essence, there are more lines in this display than there were in Fig. 20-3. The total number of software interrupts available to my system is 145. Most of them are not being used, and some of them are reserved. You will notice too that some of the interrupts share the same address, which is true throughout.

The CMOS value panel, Fig. 20-5, gets deeper into the system. Disks, memory, and CMOS all finally reveal their secrets. Until now, all of this information could be found, but only if you knew how to extract it.

After making changes to your system, this should be one of the first screens you check; if an error has been made, you're likely to find it here. The Configured Equipment comment in the CMOS Status block should still read "Correct." If it doesn't, you should recheck everything that you have changed. It would also be wise to check the things you didn't change.

The Disk Summary screen is another window with an elevator bar, this time for disk drives. Figure 20-6 lists all of the 26 possible drives, A through Z. Where

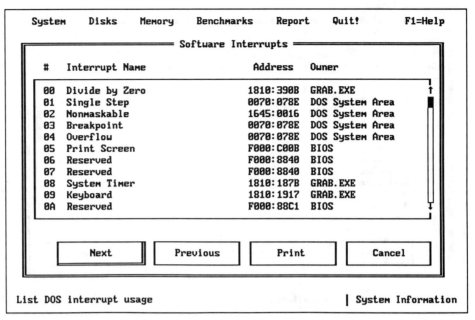

#	Interrupt Name	Address	Owner
00	Divide by Zero	1810:390B	GRAB.EXE
01	Single Step	0070:078E	DOS System Area
02	Nonmaskable	1645:0016	DOS System Area
03	Breakpoint	0070:078E	DOS System Area
04	Overflow	0070:078E	DOS System Area
05	Print Screen	F000:C00B	BIOS
06	Reserved	F000:8840	BIOS
07	Reserved	F000:8840	BIOS
08	System Timer	1810:187B	GRAB.EXE
09	Keyboard	1810:1917	GRAB.EXE
0A	Reserved	F000:88C1	BIOS

20-4 The Software Interrupts screen.

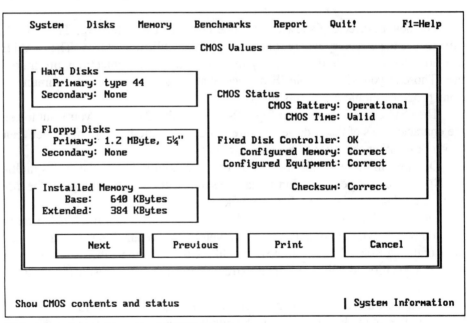

20-5 Information on your system's CMOS values.

a drive is attached and configured, it will be listed. My drive B isn't. It is still possible to get a B: \ > prompt, but the physical A drive will be used. Notice that both the C and D drives are called "Hard Disk 1." Essentially, one physical drive is partitioned into the two logical drives present.

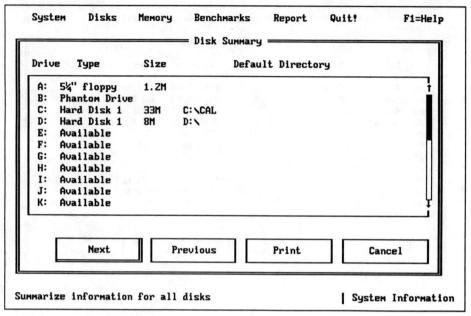

Disk Summary

Drive	Type	Size	Default Directory
A:	5¼" floppy	1.2M	
B:	Phantom Drive		
C:	Hard Disk 1	33M	C:\CAL
D:	Hard Disk 1	8M	D:\
E:	Available		
F:	Available		
G:	Available		
H:	Available		
I:	Available		
J:	Available		
K:	Available		

Next   Previous   Print   Cancel

Summarize information for all disks | System Information

20-6 Summary of all your disks.

The default directory shown is the one last used by each drive. The \CAL directory is the directory where this version of the Utilities is stored. The \MTE directory on drive D is the directory that holds the communications program I use. Those of you who have an IBM or compatible and need a good communications program should check this one out.

The characteristics shown in Fig. 20-7 are for the C drive. If you want to see the characteristics of the A drive, be sure to put a diskette in it. To move between drives, use either the ARROW keys or a mouse click.

Don't try to make the numbers add. The sides multiplied by the tracks multiplied by the sectors per track don't total the same as the sectors occupied; the difference is 14 sectors. A hard disk has to keep a little space for itself.

Figure 20-8 shows a safe place to look at your Partition Table. This screen lets you see everything while not allowing you to change anything. In earlier editions of the Utilities, the only time you could see the Partition Table was when you were in a position to edit it. Without extreme care, this could result in unwanted changes.

If you must make numbers agree, check here. The number of sides multiplied by the number of tracks multiplied by the number of sectors multiplied by 512 (the number of bytes per sector) will total 42,771,456. Referring back to Fig. 20-1 confirms that this is in fact a 42 megabyte hard drive.

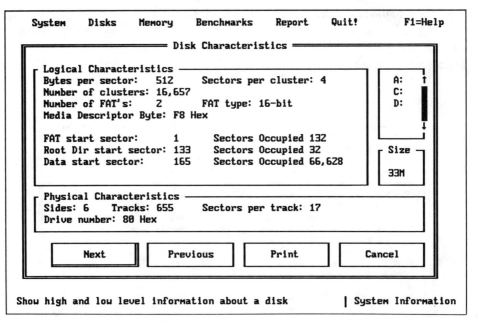

20-7 The characteristics of your disk.

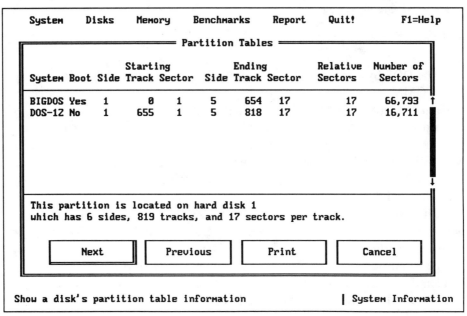

20-8 Partition Table information.

Who are the residents in RAM? A quick look at the Memory Summary panel (see Fig. 20-9) will reveal all. Those "Unknown owner" programs are usually easy to find if you look in the right spot. Here isn't that spot; but if you look ahead, you will see that more information is forthcoming.

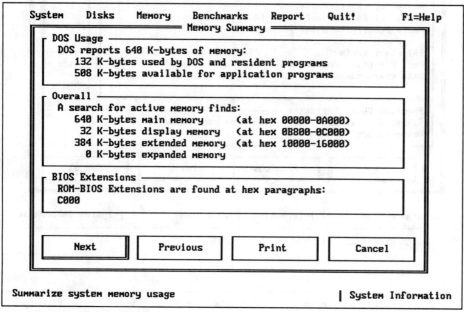

```
 System    Disks    Memory    Benchmarks    Report    Quit!        F1=Help
                        ═══════ Memory Summary ═══════
  ┌─ DOS Usage ──────────────────────────────────────────────────────────┐
  │   DOS reports 640 K-bytes of memory:                                   │
  │       132 K-bytes used by DOS and resident programs                    │
  │       508 K-bytes available for application programs                   │
  │                                                                        │
  ├─ Overall ──────────────────────────────────────────────────────────── │
  │   A search for active memory finds:                                    │
  │       640 K-bytes main memory     (at hex 00000-0A000)                 │
  │        32 K-bytes display memory  (at hex 0B800-0C000)                 │
  │       384 K-bytes extended memory (at hex 10000-16000)                 │
  │         0 K-bytes expanded memory                                      │
  │                                                                        │
  ├─ BIOS Extensions ───────────────────────────────────────────────────  │
  │   ROM-BIOS Extensions are found at hex paragraphs:                     │
  │   C000                                                                 │
  │                                                                        │
  │  ┌──────────┐  ┌──────────┐  ┌──────────┐  ┌──────────┐                │
  │  │   Next   │  │ Previous │  │  Print   │  │  Cancel  │                │
  │  └──────────┘  └──────────┘  └──────────┘  └──────────┘                │
  └────────────────────────────────────────────────────────────────────── ┘
  Summarize system memory usage              | System Information
```

20-9   The Memory summary screen.

The DOS System Area contains all of the internal parts of the operating system. COMMAND.COM is also memory-resident. These are the minimum basics to get this microcomputer up and running. Figure 20-10 also lists two other resident programs. GRAB.EXE is the resident part of a program package used to capture and edit the various screens used as illustrations throughout this book. MOUSE.COM is the mouse program and is used to allow me to operate a Logitech TrackMan in place of a mouse. In addition to being a stationary device on a very cluttered desk, the TrackMan is easy to operate.

The information shown in Fig. 20-11 is useful. When trying to solve a number of problems, it helps to know what programs or utilities are Terminate and Stay Resident (TSR) and where they are. The "Out of Memory" error message will be eliminated if enough DOS RAM remains free. TSR program conflicts may be identifiable from this listing too. In addition, the listing indicates the order in which the TSR's will have to be uninstalled. They must be eliminated in a Last-In, First-Out (LIFO) order.

Comparing processors is always a game of "who has the faster computer." Just knowing the Central Processor Unit (CPU) speed, however, isn't the whole story. Notice the relative speed of the "This Computer" entry versus the "Com-

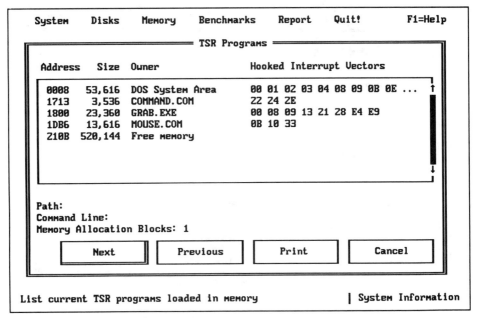

20-10   TSR program information.

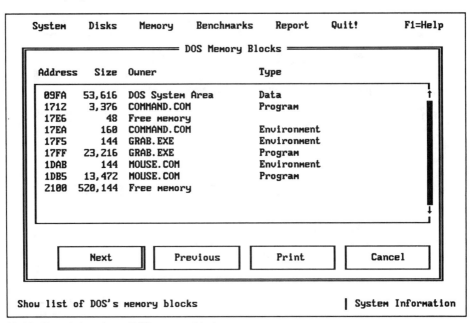

20-11   Description of your DOS memory blocks.

paq 386/33MHz" entry in Fig. 20-12. The Compaq is over six times faster than my unit.

Now look at Fig. 20-13, where hard-disk speed is checked. Here the difference is only about 2 to 1 in favor of the Compaq. So what does it mean when one

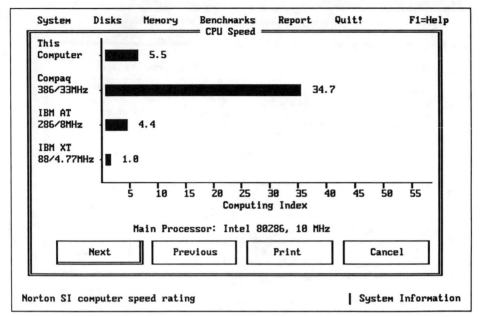

CPU Speed

This Computer ── 5.5

Compaq 386/33MHz ── 34.7

IBM AT 286/8MHz ── 4.4

IBM XT 88/4.77MHz ── 1.0

5 10 15 20 25 30 35 40 45 50 55
Computing Index

Main Processor: Intel 80286, 10 MHz

| Next | Previous | Print | Cancel |

Norton SI computer speed rating | System Information

20-12 Determining your CPU speed.

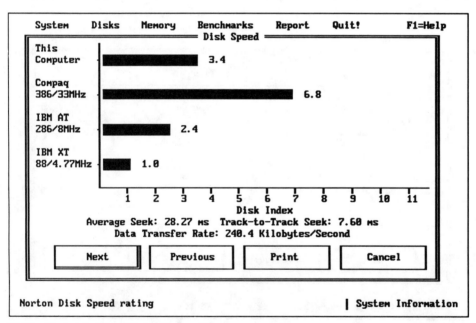

Disk Speed

This Computer ── 3.4

Compaq 386/33MHz ── 6.8

IBM AT 286/8MHz ── 2.4

IBM XT 88/4.77MHz ── 1.0

1 2 3 4 5 6 7 8 9 10 11
Disk Index

Average Seek: 28.27 ms   Track-to-Track Seek: 7.60 ms
Data Transfer Rate: 240.4 Kilobytes/Second

| Next | Previous | Print | Cancel |

Norton Disk Speed rating | System Information

20-13 Discovering your disk speed.

system has a processor that is running at about 16% of the speed of another and has a hard disk that is only half as fast?

The Performance Index panel, Fig. 20-14, provides the answer. These figures are not to be taken as an absolute difference but are only a relative indication of

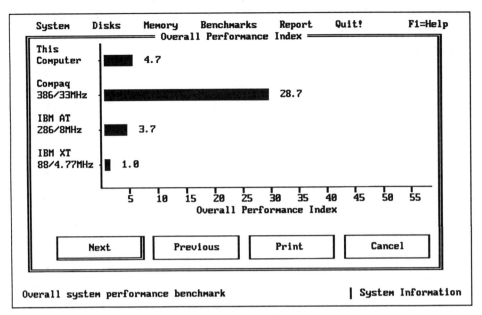

20-14 Finding your overall Performance Index.

the performance of typical systems. How fast or slow an actual application will run may be different. This does not mean that any program will run faster on a slower system than it does on the fastest but only that the speed difference may be more or less than indicated in these bar charts.

Recording the contents of your CONFIG.SYS file will help in troubleshooting problems at a later date. The less usual entries in Fig. 20-15 are a print spooler (spool32.sys) with a set size of 96 kilobytes and a Logitech ScanMan (C:\HHSCAND.SYS ....). If you combine this with the information shown in the AUTOEXEC.BAT file (Fig. 20-16), you can predict what normal operations should be as well as determine where potential problems may be hiding.

Last but not least is the screen where you select which of the 21 parts of the SysInfo Report you want printed (Fig. 20-17). The boxes across the bottom of this screen are a bit different than those common to the previous screens. With each of the others, you could elect to have a printed copy of just that portion of the system information. You could also move forward or back within the Utility to see other information. Here you are allowed only two options in addition to Cancel. If you select the Printer option, you will get just a hard copy of the report. If you select the File option, you will have a media copy which can be printed.

Unless your system is part of a network and you have network responsibilities, you may not need the SysInfo Utility on a frequent basis. After a system is set up and ready to run, a printed copy of the SysInfo should be kept as a baseline reference. Then when a problem occurs, the first report and the latest report can be compared for differences. The areas of difference are good candidates for being problem areas.

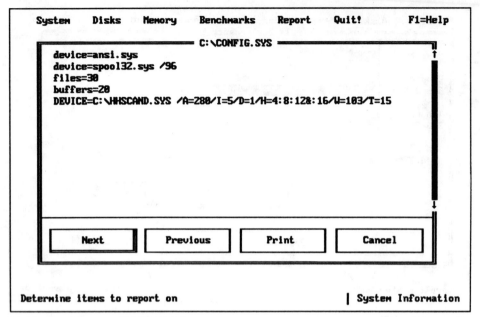

20-15 Examining your CONFIG.SYS file.

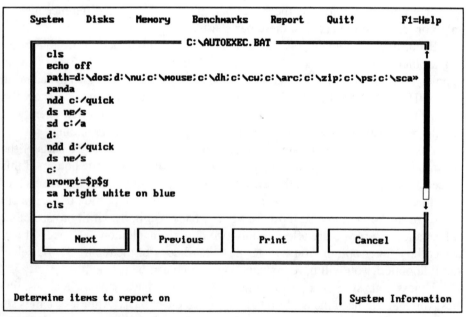

20-16 Examining your AUTOEXEC.BAT file.

```
        System    Disks    Memory    Benchmarks    Report    Quit!        F1=Help
                          ══════════ Report Options ══════════
        ┌ System ──────────────────┐   ┌ Memory ─────────────────────┐
        │   ☐   System summary      │   │   ☐   Memory usage summary   │
        │   ☐   Video summary       │   │   ☐   DOS memory block allocation│
        │   ☐   Hardware interrupts │   │   ☐   Installed TSR programs │
        │   ☐   Software interrupts │   │   ☐   Device Driver List     │
        │   ☐   Network information │   └──────────────────────────────┘
        │   ☐   CMOS status         │
        └───────────────────────────┘   ┌ Benchmarks ─────────────────┐
                                         │   ☐   CPU speed              │
        ┌ Disk ─────────────────────┐   │   ☐   Hard disk speed        │
        │   ☐   Disk summary         │   │   ☐   Performance Index      │
        │   ☐   Disk characteristics │   │   ☐   Network Performance    │
        │   ☐   Partition tables     │   └──────────────────────────────┘
        └────────────────────────────┘

        ┌ User Text ──────────────────────────────────────────────────┐
        │   ☐   Report header          ☐   Config.Sys file            │
        │   ☐   Notes at end of report ☐   Autoexec.Bat file          │
        └──────────────────────────────────────────────────────────────┘

              ┌──────────────┐   ┌──────────────┐   ┌──────────────┐
              │   Printer    │   │    File      │   │   Cancel     │
              └──────────────┘   └──────────────┘   └──────────────┘

        Determine items to report on                 │ System Information
```

20-17 Setting report options.

A typical SysInfo report

The report in Fig. 20-18 is typical of what your printer will deliver when you select all of the SI Utility option. By selecting the "Notes at the End of Report" options, you can add your own comments to the report's end. "Report Header" provides you with space to include your own report information.

20-18 A typical SysInfo report.

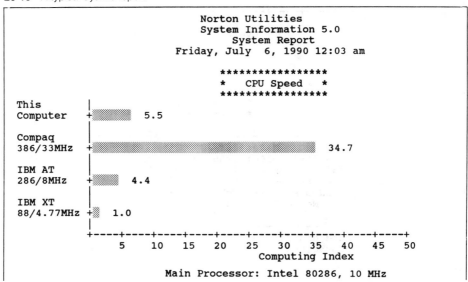

```
                          Norton Utilities
                        System Information 5.0
                           System Report
                     Friday, July  6, 1990 12:03 am

                         ******************
                         *   CPU Speed    *
                         ******************
        This        |
        Computer    +▒▒▒▒▒▒   5.5
                    |
        Compaq      |
        386/33MHz   +▒▒▒▒▒▒▒▒▒▒▒▒▒▒▒▒▒▒▒▒▒▒▒▒▒▒▒   34.7
                    |
        IBM AT      |
        286/8MHz    +▒▒▒▒   4.4
                    |
        IBM XT      |
        88/4.77MHz  +▒   1.0
                    |
                    +----+----+----+----+----+----+----+----+----+----+
                       5   10   15   20   25   30   35   40   45   50
                                    Computing Index
                      Main Processor: Intel 80286, 10 MHz
```

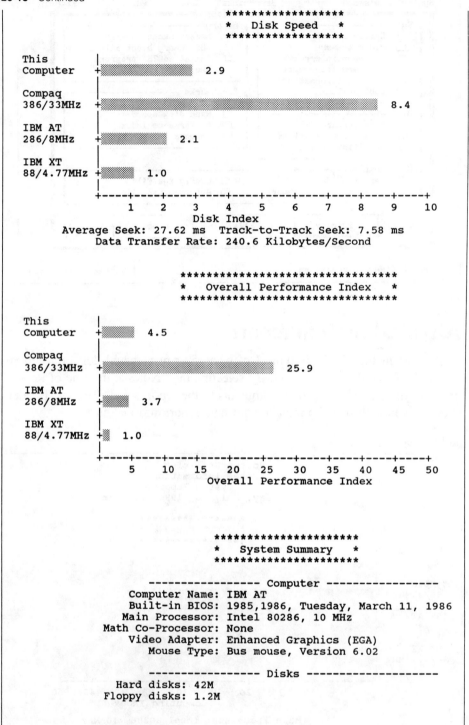

```
                    *******************
                    *   Disk Speed    *
                    *******************

This         |
Computer     +▓▓▓▓▓▓▓▓▓▓▓▓▓   2.9
             |
Compaq       |
386/33MHz    +▓▓▓▓▓▓▓▓▓▓▓▓▓▓▓▓▓▓▓▓▓▓▓▓▓▓▓▓▓▓▓▓▓▓▓▓▓▓▓   8.4
             |
IBM AT       |
286/8MHz     +▓▓▓▓▓▓▓▓▓   2.1
             |
IBM XT       |
88/4.77MHz   +▓▓▓▓▓   1.0
             |
             +----+----+----+----+----+----+----+----+----+----+
             1    2    3    4    5    6    7    8    9    10
                              Disk Index
        Average Seek: 27.62 ms   Track-to-Track Seek: 7.58 ms
             Data Transfer Rate: 240.6 Kilobytes/Second


                 *********************************
                 *   Overall Performance Index   *
                 *********************************

This         |
Computer     +▓▓▓▓▓▓   4.5
             |
Compaq       |
386/33MHz    +▓▓▓▓▓▓▓▓▓▓▓▓▓▓▓▓▓▓▓▓▓▓▓▓▓▓▓▓▓▓▓▓▓   25.9
             |
IBM AT       |
286/8MHz     +▓▓▓▓   3.7
             |
IBM XT       |
88/4.77MHz   +▓   1.0
             |
             +----+----+----+----+----+----+----+----+----+----+
             5    10   15   20   25   30   35   40   45   50
                         Overall Performance Index


                    *********************
                    *  System Summary   *
                    *********************

          ----------------- Computer -----------------
          Computer Name: IBM AT
          Built-in BIOS: 1985,1986, Tuesday, March 11, 1986
         Main Processor: Intel 80286, 10 MHz
       Math Co-Processor: None
          Video Adapter: Enhanced Graphics (EGA)
             Mouse Type: Bus mouse, Version 6.02

          ----------------- Disks --------------------
             Hard disks: 42M
           Floppy disks: 1.2M
```

```
----------------- Memory ------------------
        DOS Memory:    640K
   Extended Memory:    384K
   Expanded Memory:      0K

--------------- Other Info -----------------
          Bus Type: ISA (PC/AT)
      Serial Ports: 1
    Parallel Ports: 1
     Keyboard Type: 101-key
  Operating System: DOS 3.31


              ********************
              *  Video Summary  *
              ********************

----------------- Display ------------------
  Video Display Adapter: Enhanced Graphics (EGA)
           Monitor Type: Enhanced Graphics (EGA)
     Current Video Mode: 3 (Color, 80x25)

---------------- Character -----------------
   Maximum Scan Lines: 0
        Character Size: 8 x 14
   CGA Cursor Emulation: Enabled

----------------- Memory ------------------
```

17	Printer	0AF9:03E3	DOS System Area
18	Resident BASIC	F000:97A3	BIOS
19	Bootstrap Loader	0070:1A7C	DOS System Area
1A	Real-Time Clock Services	F000:E221	BIOS
1B	Keyboard Break	09FB:010A	DOS System Area
1C	User Timer Tick	F000:9803	BIOS
1D	Video Parameters	F000:98C0	BIOS
1E	Diskette Parameters	0000:0522	DOS System Area
1F	Video Graphics Characters	C000:42D0	BIOS
20	Program Terminate	0293:143F	DOS System Area
21	General DOS functions	1810:1993	GRAB.EXE
22	Terminate Address	1713:012F	COMMAND.COM
23	Ctrl-Break Handler Address	211B:1EDC	Free memory
24	Critical Error Handler	1713:0556	COMMAND.COM
25	Absolute Disk Read	0070:1994	DOS System Area
26	Absolute Disk Write	0070:19B9	DOS System Area
27	Terminate and Stay Resident	0293:652F	DOS System Area
28	DOS Idle	1810:19D3	GRAB.EXE
29	DOS Internal - FAST PUTCHAR	09FB:02EB	DOS System Area
2A	Reserved for DOS	0293:1445	DOS System Area
2B	Reserved for DOS	0293:1445	DOS System Area
2C	Reserved for DOS	0293:1445	DOS System Area
2D	Reserved for DOS	0293:1445	DOS System Area
2E	DOS - Execute Command	1713:0281	COMMAND.COM
2F	Multiplex (process interface)	0070:195D	DOS System Area
30	Reserved for DOS	9314:46EA	
31	Reserved for DOS	0293:1402	DOS System Area
32	Reserved for DOS	0293:1445	DOS System Area
33	Microsoft Mouse Driver	211B:2240	Free memory
34	Reserved for DOS	0293:1445	DOS System Area
35	Reserved for DOS	0293:1445	DOS System Area

36	Reserved for DOS	0293:1445	DOS System Area
37	Reserved for DOS	0293:1445	DOS System Area
38	Reserved for DOS	0293:1445	DOS System Area
39	Reserved for DOS	0293:1445	DOS System Area
3A	Reserved for DOS	0293:1445	DOS System Area
3B	Reserved for DOS	0293:1445	DOS System Area
3C	Reserved for DOS	0293:1445	DOS System Area
3D	Reserved for DOS	0293:1445	DOS System Area
3E	Reserved for DOS	0293:1445	DOS System Area
3F	Overlay Manager	0293:1445	DOS System Area
40	Diskette BIOS Revector	F000:A5F8	BIOS
41	Fixed Disk Parameters	F000:E6B1	BIOS
42	Relocated Video Handler	F000:F065	BIOS
43	Reserved	C000:3ED0	BIOS
44	Novell Netware API	F000:8840	BIOS
45	Reserved	F000:8840	BIOS
46	Fixed Disk Parameters	F000:E401	BIOS
47	Reserved	F000:8840	BIOS
48	Reserved	F000:8840	BIOS
49	Reserved	F000:8840	BIOS
4A	User Alarm	F000:8840	BIOS
4B	Reserved	F000:8840	BIOS
4C	Reserved	F000:8840	BIOS
4D	Reserved	F000:8840	BIOS
4E	Reserved	F000:8840	BIOS
4F	Reserved	F000:8840	BIOS
50	Reserved	F000:8840	BIOS
51	Reserved	F000:8840	BIOS
52	Reserved	F000:8840	BIOS
53	Reserved	F000:8840	BIOS
54	Reserved	F000:8840	BIOS
55	Reserved	F000:8840	BIOS
56	Reserved	F000:8840	BIOS
57	Reserved	F000:8840	BIOS
58	Reserved	F000:8840	BIOS
59	Reserved	F000:8840	BIOS
5A	Reserved	F000:8840	BIOS
5B	Reserved	F000:8840	BIOS
5C	Reserved	F000:8840	BIOS
5D	Reserved	F000:8840	BIOS
5E	Reserved	F000:8840	BIOS
5F	Reserved	F000:8840	BIOS
60	Reserved for User Programs	0069:0069	DOS System Area
61	Reserved for User Programs	0000:0000	Unused
62	Reserved for User Programs	0000:0000	Unused
63	Reserved for User Programs	0000:0000	Unused
64	Reserved for User Programs	0000:0000	Unused
65	Reserved for User Programs	0000:0000	Unused
66	Reserved for User Programs	0000:0000	Unused
67	Expanded Memory (LIM)	F000:8840	BIOS
68	Reserved	F000:8840	BIOS
69	Reserved	F000:8840	BIOS
6A	Reserved	F000:8840	BIOS
6B	Reserved	F000:8840	BIOS
6C	Reserved	F000:8840	BIOS
6D	Reserved	F000:8840	BIOS
6E	Reserved	F000:8840	BIOS
6F	Reserved	F000:8840	BIOS
70	Real-Time Clock	1645:01A4	DOS System Area
71	Reserved	F000:9712	BIOS
72	Reserved	1645:04C2	DOS System Area
73	Reserved	1645:054A	DOS System Area
74	Reserved	1645:05D2	DOS System Area

```
75   Redirect to NMI Interrupt            F000:8891   BIOS
76   Reserved                             1645:065A   DOS System Area
77   Reserved                             1645:06E2   DOS System Area
78   Reserved                             0000:0000   Unused
79   Reserved                             0000:0000   Unused
7A   Novell Netware (API)                 0000:0000   Unused
7B   Reserved                             0000:0000   Unused
7C   Reserved                             0000:0000   Unused
7D   Reserved                             0069:0069   DOS System Area
7E   Reserved                             0000:0000   Unused
7F   Reserved                             0000:0000   Unused
80   Reserved for BASIC                   0000:0000   Unused
81   Reserved for BASIC                   0000:0000   Unused
82   Reserved for BASIC                   0000:0000   Unused
83   Reserved for BASIC                   0000:0000   Unused
84   Reserved for BASIC                   0000:0000   Unused
85   Reserved for BASIC                   0000:0000   Unused
86   Reserved for BASIC interpreter       0000:0000   Unused
87   Reserved for BASIC interpreter       0000:0000   Unused
88   Reserved for BASIC interpreter       0000:0000   Unused
89   Reserved for BASIC interpreter       0000:0000   Unused
8A   Reserved for BASIC interpreter       0000:0000   Unused
8B   Reserved for BASIC interpreter       0000:0000   Unused
8C   Reserved for BASIC interpreter       0000:0000   Unused
8D   Reserved for BASIC interpreter       0000:0000   Unused
8E   Reserved for BASIC interpreter       0000:0000   Unused
8F   Reserved for BASIC interpreter       0000:0000   Unused
90   Reserved for BASIC interpreter       0000:0000   Unused
91   Reserved for BASIC interpreter       0000:0000   Unused
92   Reserved for BASIC interpreter       0000:0000   Unused
93   Reserved for BASIC interpreter       0000:0000   Unused
94   Reserved for BASIC interpreter       0000:0000   Unused
95   Reserved for BASIC interpreter       0000:0000   Unused
96   Reserved for BASIC interpreter       0000:0000   Unused
97   Reserved for BASIC interpreter       0000:0000   Unused
98   Reserved for BASIC interpreter       0000:0000   Unused
99   Reserved for BASIC interpreter       0000:0000   Unused
9A   Reserved for BASIC interpreter       0000:0000   Unused
9B   Reserved for BASIC interpreter       0000:0000   Unused
9C   Reserved for BASIC interpreter       0000:0000   Unused
9D   Reserved for BASIC interpreter       0000:0000   Unused
9E   Reserved for BASIC interpreter       0000:0000   Unused
9F   Reserved for BASIC interpreter       0000:0000   Unused
A0   Reserved for BASIC interpreter       0000:0000   Unused
A1   Reserved for BASIC interpreter       0000:0000   Unused
A2   Reserved for BASIC interpreter       0000:0000   Unused
A3   Reserved for BASIC interpreter       0000:0000   Unused
A4   Reserved for BASIC interpreter       0000:0000   Unused
A5   Reserved for BASIC interpreter       0000:0000   Unused
A6   Reserved for BASIC interpreter       0000:0000   Unused
A7   Reserved for BASIC interpreter       0000:0000   Unused
A8   Reserved for BASIC interpreter       0000:0000   Unused
A9   Reserved for BASIC interpreter       0000:0000   Unused
AA   Reserved for BASIC interpreter       0000:0000   Unused
AB   Reserved for BASIC interpreter       0000:0000   Unused
AC   Reserved for BASIC interpreter       0000:0000   Unused
AD   Reserved for BASIC interpreter       0000:0000   Unused
AE   Reserved for BASIC interpreter       0000:0000   Unused
AF   Reserved for BASIC interpreter       0000:0000   Unused
B0   Reserved for BASIC interpreter       0000:0000   Unused
B1   Reserved for BASIC interpreter       0000:0000   Unused
B2   Reserved for BASIC interpreter       0000:0000   Unused
B3   Reserved for BASIC interpreter       0000:0000   Unused
B4   Reserved for BASIC interpreter       0000:0000   Unused
B5   Reserved for BASIC interpreter       0000:0000   Unused
```

B6	Reserved for BASIC interpreter	0000:0000	Unused
B7	Reserved for BASIC interpreter	0000:0000	Unused
B8	Reserved for BASIC interpreter	0000:0000	Unused
B9	Reserved for BASIC interpreter	0000:0000	Unused
BA	Reserved for BASIC interpreter	0000:0000	Unused
BB	Reserved for BASIC interpreter	0000:0000	Unused
BC	Reserved for BASIC interpreter	0000:0000	Unused
BD	Reserved for BASIC interpreter	0000:0000	Unused
BE	Reserved for BASIC interpreter	0000:0000	Unused
BF	Reserved for BASIC interpreter	0000:0000	Unused
C0	Reserved for BASIC interpreter	0000:0000	Unused
C1	Reserved for BASIC interpreter	0000:0000	Unused
C2	Reserved for BASIC interpreter	0000:0000	Unused
C3	Reserved for BASIC interpreter	0000:0000	Unused
C4	Reserved for BASIC interpreter	0000:0000	Unused
C5	Reserved for BASIC interpreter	0000:0000	Unused
C6	Reserved for BASIC interpreter	0000:0000	Unused
C7	Reserved for BASIC interpreter	0000:0000	Unused
C8	Reserved for BASIC interpreter	0000:0000	Unused
C9	Reserved for BASIC interpreter	0000:0000	Unused
CA	Reserved for BASIC interpreter	0000:0000	Unused
CB	Reserved for BASIC interpreter	0000:0000	Unused
CC	Reserved for BASIC interpreter	0000:0000	Unused
CD	Reserved for BASIC interpreter	0000:0000	Unused
CE	Reserved for BASIC interpreter	0000:0000	Unused
CF	Reserved for BASIC interpreter	0000:0000	Unused
D0	Reserved for BASIC interpreter	0000:0000	Unused
D1	Reserved for BASIC interpreter	0000:0000	Unused
D2	Reserved for BASIC interpreter	0000:0000	Unused
D3	Reserved for BASIC interpreter	0000:0000	Unused
D4	Reserved for BASIC interpreter	0000:0000	Unused
D5	Reserved for BASIC interpreter	0000:0000	Unused
D6	Reserved for BASIC interpreter	0000:0000	Unused
D7	Reserved for BASIC interpreter	0000:0000	Unused
D8	Reserved for BASIC interpreter	0000:0000	Unused
D9	Reserved for BASIC interpreter	0000:0000	Unused
DA	Reserved for BASIC interpreter	0000:0000	Unused
DB	Reserved for BASIC interpreter	0000:0000	Unused
DC	Reserved for BASIC interpreter	0000:0000	Unused
DD	Reserved for BASIC interpreter	0000:0000	Unused
DE	Reserved for BASIC interpreter	0000:0000	Unused
DF	Reserved for BASIC interpreter	0000:0000	Unused
E0	Reserved for BASIC interpreter	0000:0000	Unused
E1	Reserved for BASIC interpreter	0000:0000	Unused
E2	Reserved for BASIC interpreter	0000:0000	Unused
E3	Reserved for BASIC interpreter	0000:0000	Unused
E4	Reserved for BASIC interpreter	190D:1FE0	GRAB.EXE
E5	Reserved for BASIC interpreter	0003:0103	DOS System Area
E6	Reserved for BASIC interpreter	0000:0607	DOS System Area
E7	Reserved for BASIC interpreter	0460:0000	DOS System Area
E8	Reserved for BASIC interpreter	0103:0000	DOS System Area
E9	Reserved for BASIC interpreter	18CD:0F1D	GRAB.EXE
EA	Reserved for BASIC interpreter	00CA:0101	DOS System Area
EB	Reserved for BASIC interpreter	0101:AB20	DOS System Area
EC	Reserved for BASIC interpreter	AB20:00CE	BIOS
ED	Reserved for BASIC interpreter	0286:F000	DOS System Area
EE	Reserved for BASIC interpreter	0101:0001	DOS System Area
EF	Reserved for BASIC interpreter	0000:0F00	DOS System Area
F0	Reserved for BASIC interpreter	0000:0000	Unused
F1	Reserved for User Programs	00FE:00FE	DOS System Area
F2	Reserved for User Programs	001C:0F00	DOS System Area
F3	Reserved for User Programs	0F00:007C	DOS System Area
F4	Reserved for User Programs	0F1D:020D	DOS System Area

```
F5   Reserved for User Programs      C000:29AB   BIOS
F6   Reserved for User Programs      0E0D:0246   DOS System Area
F7   Reserved for User Programs      0001:7DFE   DOS System Area
F8   Reserved for User Programs      9700:0080
F9   Reserved for User Programs      0080:007C   DOS System Area
FA   Reserved for User Programs      0F1D:0E0D   DOS System Area
FB   Reserved for User Programs      F000:8CC5   BIOS
FC   Reserved for User Programs      96FE:0296
FD   Reserved for User Programs      0001:0000   DOS System Area
FE   Reserved for User Programs      961A:96F9
FF   Reserved for User Programs      0286:F000   DOS System Area
```

```
            *******************
            *   CMOS Values   *
            *******************
```

```
          --------------- Hard Disks ---------------
      Primary: type 44
    Secondary: None
```

```
          --------------- Floppy Disks --------------
      Primary: 1.2M, 5 1/4"
    Secondary: None
```

```
          -------------- Installed Memory ------------
        Base:    640 KBytes
    Extended:    384 KBytes
```

```
          ----------------- CMOS Status --------------
              CMOS Battery: Operational
                 CMOS Time: Valid

    Fixed Disk Controller: OK
         Configured Memory: Correct
      Configured Equipment: Correct

                  Checksum: Correct
```

```
           **********************
           *   Memory Summary   *
           **********************
```

```
          ---------------- DOS Usage ----------------
    DOS reports 640 K-bytes of memory:
        132 K-bytes used by DOS and resident programs
        508 K-bytes available for application programs
```

```
          ---------------- Overall ----------------
    A search for active memory finds:
        640 K-bytes main memory      (at hex 00000-0A000)
         32 K-bytes display memory   (at hex 0B800-0C000)
        384 K-bytes extended memory  (at hex 10000-16000)
          0 K-bytes expanded memory
```

```
          ------------- BIOS Extensions -------------
    ROM-BIOS Extensions are found at hex paragraphs:
    C000
```

```
                          **************************
                          *   DOS Memory Blocks    *
                          **************************

         09FA     53,616   DOS System Area        Data
         1712      3,376   COMMAND.COM            Program
         17E6         48   Free memory
         17EA        160   COMMAND.COM            Environment
         17F5        144   GRAB.EXE               Environment
         17FF     23,216   GRAB.EXE               Program
         1DAB        144   MOUSE.COM              Environment
         1DB5     13,472   MOUSE.COM              Program
         2100        144   Free memory
         210A    156,448   Free memory
         473D    363,552   Free memory


                          ********************
                          *   TSR Programs   *
                          ********************

Address   Size   Owner                  Hooked Interrupt Vectors
-------------------------------------------------------------------------
 0008     53,616  DOS System Area       00 01 02 03 04 08 09 0B 0E ...
 1713      3,536  COMMAND.COM           22 24 2E
 1800     23,360  GRAB.EXE              08 09 13 21 28 E4 E9
 1DB6     13,616  MOUSE.COM             0B 10
 210B    520,144  Free memory


                          ***********************
                          *   Device Drivers    *
                          ***********************

         Address     Name     Description
-------------------------------------------------------------------------
         0293:0048   NUL      NUL device
         0AFA:0002   LPT1     First Parallel Printer
         0AF9:0000   PRN      First Parallel Printer
         0A5F:0000   HH$SCAN  Unrecognized Device
         09FB:0000   CON      Console keyboard/screen
         0086:000E   CON      Console keyboard/screen
         0088:0000   AUX      First Serial Port
         0089:0002   PRN      First Parallel Printer
         008A:0004   CLOCK$   System Clock Interface
         008B:0006   A: - D:  DOS Supported Drives
         008C:000A   COM1     First Serial Port
         008D:000C   LPT1     First Parallel Printer
         008E:000E   LPT2     Second Parallel Printer
         0090:0000   LPT3     Third Parallel Printer
         0091:0002   COM2     Second Serial Port
         0092:0004   COM3     Third Serial Port
         0093:0006   COM4     Fourth Serial Port


                          ********************
                          *   Disk Summary   *
                          ********************

    Drive   Type        Size        Default Directory
-------------------------------------------------------------------------
      A:   1.2M, 5 1/4"  1.2M
      B:   Phantom Drive
```

```
C:  Hard Disk 1      33M      \CAL
D:  Hard Disk 1       8M      \SPRINT
E:  Available
F:  Available
G:  Available
H:  Available
I:  Available
J:  Available
K:  Available
L:  Available
M:  Available
N:  Available
O:  Available
P:  Available
Q:  Available
R:  Available
S:  Available
T:  Available
U:  Available
V:  Available
W:  Available
X:  Available
Y:  Available
Z:  Available
```

```
          ****************************
          *   Disk Characteristics   *
          ****************************

          ---------------- Drive A: ----------------
                      No disk in drive
                   No physical information


          ---------------- Drive C: ----------------
                   LOGICAL CHARACTERISTICS

        Bytes per sector: 512
      Sectors per cluster: 4
       Number of clusters: 16,657
          Number of FAT's: 2
                 FAT type: 16-bit
    Media Descriptor Byte: F8 Hex
          FAT start sector: 1        Sectors Occupied 132
      Root Dir start sector: 133     Sectors Occupied 32
         Data start sector: 165      Sectors Occupied 66,632

                   PHYSICAL CHARACTERISTICS

                    Sides: 6
                   Tracks: 655
        Sectors per track: 17
             Drive number: 80 Hex


          ---------------- Drive D: ----------------
                   LOGICAL CHARACTERISTICS

        Bytes per sector: 512
      Sectors per cluster: 8
       Number of clusters: 2,083
          Number of FAT's: 2
                 FAT type: 12-bit
    Media Descriptor Byte: F8 Hex
          FAT start sector: 1        Sectors Occupied 14
```

```
        Root Dir start sector: 15      Sectors Occupied 32
            Data start sector: 47      Sectors Occupied 16,672

                        PHYSICAL CHARACTERISTICS

                              Sides: 6
                             Tracks: 164
                   Sectors per track: 17
                       Drive number: 80 Hex



                    *************************
                    *    Partition Tables    *
                    *************************

                    Starting            Ending         Relative  Number of
      System Boot Side Track Sector  Side Track Sector  Sectors    Sectors
      BIGDOS Yes   1      0    1       5    654   17        17      66,793
      DOS-12 No    1     655   1       5    818   17        17      16,711



                    ************************************
                    *   AUTOEXEC.BAT file from drive C:   *
                    ************************************

cls
echo off
path=d:\dos;d:\nu;c:\mouse;c:\dh;c:\cw;c:\arc;c:\zip;c:\ps;
c:\scan;c:\sprint;c:\panda
FR /SAVE
c:\cal\ndd c:/quick
ds ne/s
c:\cal\speedisk c:/c
d:
c:\cal\ndd d:/quick
ds ne/s
c:
prompt=$p$g
sa bright white on blue
cls
echo on


                    ************************************
                    *   CONFIG.SYS file from drive C:   *
                    ************************************

device=ansi.sys
files=30
buffers=20
DEVICE=C:\HHSCAND.SYS /A=280/I=5/D=1/H=4:8:12:16&/W=103/T=30
device=spool32.sys /96
```

System Information version 4.0 & 4.5

Version 4.0 & 4.5 directory name   SI.EXE

SI provides information about your system as a displayed, printed, or filed report.
Version 4.0 & 4.5 (Standard or Advanced Edition) provide this indicator relative
to the IBM/XT.

Format:

Version 4.0 SI [d:] [switches] [>|>>] [\path\filename |device]

Switches

/N   Tells SI not to perform an active memory test. This test will cause some not fully compatible computers to hang, requiring that they be rebooted.

/LOG   Tells SI to format the report in a manner suitable for printing or redirecting to a disk file. This is similar to the /T switch used in another utility.

>|>>   DOS operators to redirect, or redirect and append, the program output.

\path\filename|device

The location for the new file or file to be overwritten, or the file to be appended, or the device to receive the program output.

The Disk Index (DI) is only calculated for hard disks. The System Index (SI) requires the DI for an input; therefore, if there is no hard disk in the system, or the installed hard disk is not specified, only the Processor Index (PI) is calculated.

The information reported by SI for a not fully compatible system may not be as complete as a fully compatible one. The information report looks similar to the one in Fig. 20-19. The IBM/XT is a baseline (1.0) for this index.

Because the /N switch was used, the second (live) memory test was not performed. The live memory test actually goes out and tests the amount of main

20-19 The SI report for a TIPC.

```
A>SI /N

SI-System Information Advanced Edition, (C) Copr 1988, Peter
Norton

          Computer Name:  TI Professional
       Operating System:  DOS 2.11
         Main Processor:  Intel 8088          Serial Ports: 2
           Co-Processor:  None              Parallel Ports: 1
  Video Display Adapter:  Monochrome
     Current Video Mode:  Text, 80 x 25 Monochrome
  Available Disk Drives:  6, A: - F:

DOS reports 512 K-bytes of memory:
   168 K-bytes used by DOS and resident programs
   344 K-bytes available for application programs

Processor Index (PI), relative to IBM/XT:  1.1
    Disk Index (DI), relative to IBM/XT:  Not computed

   System Index (SI), relative to IBM/XT:  Not computed
```

memory, memory used by screen display adapters, and expanded and extended memory. ROM-BIOS extensions are also checked, which are the ROMs that are on some add-on boards. SI will report these under the heading of ROM-BIOS extensions.

Notice the differences between Fig. 20-20, and Fig. 20-19. For the AT report, the performance index (PI) has been computed and the active memory probe was enabled.

20-20 The SI report for an AT.

```
SI-System Information, Advanced Edition 4.50, (C) Copr 1987-88, Peter Norton

           Computer Name: IBM AT
        Operating System: DOS 3.31
       Built-in BIOS dated: Tuesday, March 11, 1986
          Main Processor: Intel 80286          Serial Ports: 1
            Co-Processor: None              Parallel Ports: 1
   Video Display Adapter: Enhanced Graphics (EGA), 256 K-bytes
       Current Video Mode: Text, 25 x 80 Black and White
   Available Disk Drives: 4, A: - D:

DOS reports 640 K-bytes of memory:
     70 K-bytes used by DOS and resident programs
    570 K-bytes available for application programs

   Computing Index (CI), relative to IBM/XT: 9.8
        Disk Index (DI), relative to IBM/XT: 2.7

Performance Index (PI), relative to IBM/XT: 7.4
```

The next report, Fig. 20-21, shows some of the many differences in the operation of an 8088 processor at 8MHz and an 80286 at the same speed. Some of them are hardware-related, and some are software-related.

Will SI report any increases that a program like Lightning might be responsible for?

Yes. If you run SI before installing one of these programs and then again after installation, SI will report the speed increase.

How is the System Index (SI) calculated?

It appears to be the mean of the sum of the Processor Index (PI) and the Disk Index (DI).

One example shows a TI professional computer report. Will SI report just the PI or can it access the hard disk and calculate the System Index (SI)?

The TI disk controller is not compatible and does not allow SI to access the TI hard disk. Essentially, only the Processor Index will be calculated.

```
SI-System Information, Advanced Edition, (C) Copr. 1987, Peter Norton

        Copyright Notice:  (C) 1984,1985,1986 PHOENIX TECHNOLOGIES LTD
        Operating System:  DOS 3.30
     Built-in BIOS dated:  Thursday, May 29, 1986
          Main Processor:  NEC V20              Serial Ports:  1
            Co-Processor:  None              Parallel Ports:  1
   Video Display Adapter:  Enhanced Graphics, 256 K-bytes
      Current Video Mode:  Text, 80 x 25 Black and White
   Available Disk Drives:  3, A: - C:

DOS reports 640 K-bytes of memory:
    57 K-bytes used by DOS and resident programs
   583 K-bytes available for application programs
A search for active memory finds:
   640 K-bytes main memory     (at hex 0000-A000)
    32 K-bytes display memory  (at hex B800-C000)
ROM-BIOS Extensions are found at hex paragraphs: C000 C800

   Computing Index (CI), relative to IBM/XT: Testing..3.1
       Disk Index (DI), relative to IBM/XT: Testing..1.4

Performance Index (PI), relative to IBM/XT: 2.5
```

Are there any really useful purposes to be served by SI, other than proving that my computer is faster than your computer?

The difference in the System Index figures will give you an indication of the difference in time that the system will require to process the same program. In other words, if Lightning changed the SI from 2.5 to 10, a decrease in running time of 50% to 75% might not be an unreasonable expectation. Remember that the SI figure is balanced between processor speed and disk-access speed. Lightning is a cache program that increases disk-access speed but does nothing for the processor speed.

You will have to use your own experience and judgment on the value to be placed in the figures and the changes that various software, firmware, and hardware enhancements actually make in the system operation for you.

Can I expect two systems with the same SI to perform equally?

Only if everything else is equal. CPU chips, available RAM, BIOS, and even the version of DOS can be responsible for differences in the total running and processing time.

Do I have to run all of the tests to see the results of any one of them?

No. As you can see in the next series of illustrations, you can select any one portion of SysInfo and get that information without having to wade through the part(s) that come before or after it.

Each of these selections (Figs. 20-22 through 20-26) are accessed either by tagging the keyword with a mouse click or by pressing the F9 function key and then using the ARROW keys to get to the desired selection.

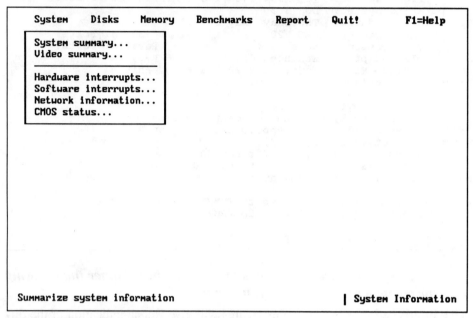

20-22 The System Summary pull-down window.

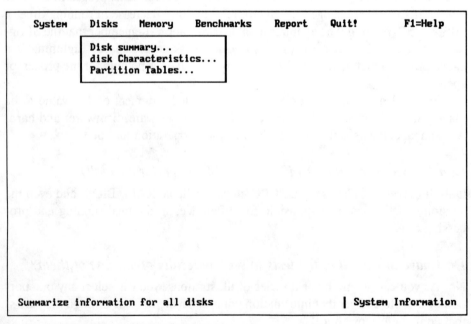

20-23 The Disk Summary pull-down window.

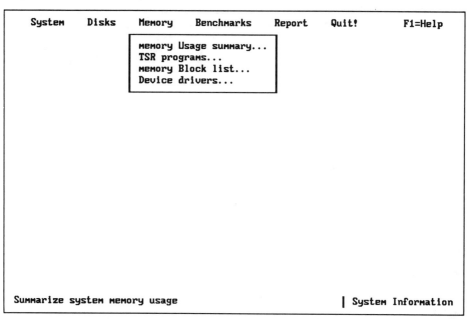

20-24 The Memory Summary pull-down window.

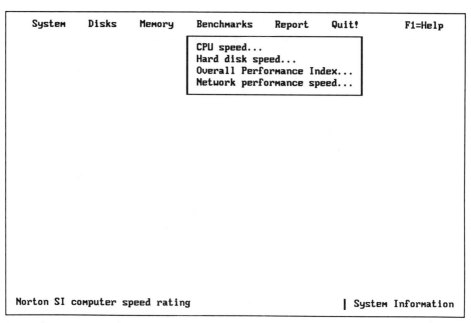

20-25 The Benchmark Summary pull-down window.

```
                                    view CONFIG.SYS...
                                    view AUTOEXEC.BAT...
                                    ─────────────────────
                                    Print report...
```

Determine items to report on | System Information

20-26 The Report Summary pull-down window.

Disk Information version 4.0 & 4.5
Directory name   DI.EXE

DI is new in version 4.5 and gives the most complete set of technical statistics yet available with the Norton Utilities.

>   **Format:**   DI [d:] [> | > > d: \ path \ filename|LPT1|PRN]

The options are:

> **d:**   The drive designation of the disk to be specced. If the drive is a floppy, you will be prompted to insert a diskette.

> **> or > >**   The DOS redirection commands. > is used to redirect the output to a filename or device. If the filename exists, it will be overwritten. > > is used to redirect and append. If no file exists, DOS will create one. If the filename exists, the output will be added to the end of the file.

> **LPT1|PRN** The system printer.

The information provided by this Utility is:

> **System ID**   The operating system under which the disk/diskette was formatted. IBM PNCI indicates that the disk/diskette was formatted using the Safe Format (SF) Utility.

Media Descriptor

The hexadecimal value that indicates what type of media is in the drive. The more common descriptor values are

F0   A 1.4M, 3.5in diskette

F8   A hard disk

F9   A 1.2M 5.25in or

      A 720K 3.5in diskette

FD   A 360K 5.25in diskette

FE   A 160K 5.25in diskette

FF   A 320K 5.25in diskette

Drive number

0 = Drive A

1 = Drive B

2 = Drive C

3 = Drive D

4 = Drive E

etc., to the maximum number of supported logical drives.

Bytes per sector

Usually 512.

Sectors per cluster

This value will vary from 1 up depending upon the media type and the operating system version.

Number of FATs

There should be 2 File Allocation Tables for all media types and all versions of DOS. It may be 1 or 2 for a RAM drive depending upon the driver software.

Root Directory Entries

The total number of files and subdirectories which may be written to the Root directory. The value will vary with the media type and the operating system version.

Sectors per FAT

This value will vary with the media type.

Number of clusters

The number of clusters is determined by the media type and/or DOS partition size. It is useful for determining the number of sectors in the FAT. A 12-bit entry is used for disks/partitions of 4,085 clusters or less. A 16-bit entry is used on all larger disks/partitions.

Number of sectors
> This is the total number of sectors on the disk/partition. It should be equal to the number of sectors per cluster multiplied by the number of clusters.

Offset to FAT
> The sector number where the first File Allocation Table begins.

Offset to Directory
> The sector number where the Root Directory begins.

Offset to data
> The number of the first data storage sector.

Sectors per track
> This value varies with the media type.
>
> 8 = 160K 5.25in or
>   320K 5.25in diskette
>
> 9 = 180K 5.25in or
>   360K 5.25in diskette
>
> 15 = 1.2M 5.25in diskette
>
> 17 = most hard disks
>
> 18 = 1.4M 3.5in diskette
>
> 25 and up describes large hard disks

Sides   The number of logical sides. 1 or 2 for diskettes, and up to 16 for hard disks.

Hidden sectors
> The sector number where the DOS partition begins. The first sector is designated 0.

The best possible way to describe the information displayed is to illustrate it. In the following figures (Figs. 20-27, 20-28, and 20-29), a "safe" formatted disk-(ette) can be recognized from the PNCI on the system id line.

Where else is this information available?

Most of this information is also displayed by the Norton Disk Doctor (NDD) and in the Norton Utility (NU).

When might I have a need to use this information?

You will need this during a data/disaster recovery procedure when stored information must be retrieved sector by sector.

```
C:\>di c:
DI-Disk Information, Advanced Edition 4.50, (C) Copr 1987-88, Peter Norton

   Information from DOS        Drive C:        Information from the boot record
---------------------------------------------------------------------------------
                              system id        'IBM  3.3'
                              media descriptor (hex)       F8
              2               drive number
            512               bytes per sector             512
              4               sectors per cluster            4
              2               number of FATs                 2
            512               root directory entries       512
             66               sectors per FAT               66
         16,657               number of clusters
                              number of sectors         66,793
              1               offset to FAT                  1
            133               offset to directory
            165               offset to data
                              sectors per track             17
                              sides                          6
                              hidden sectors                17
```

```
C:\>di a:
DI-Disk Information, Advanced Edition 4.50, (C) Copr 1987-88, Peter Norton

   Information from DOS        Drive A:        Information from the boot record
---------------------------------------------------------------------------------
                              system id        'IBM PNCI'
                              media descriptor (hex)       FD
              0               drive number
            512               bytes per sector             512
              2               sectors per cluster            2
              2               number of FATs                 2
            112               root directory entries       112
              2               sectors per FAT                2
            354               number of clusters
                              number of sectors            720
              1               offset to FAT                  1
              5               offset to directory
             12               offset to data
                              sectors per track              9
                              sides                          2
                              hidden sectors                 0
```

```
                 Figure DI-2
          A Safe Formatted 360K diskette
             Norton Disk Information
```

```
C:\>di a:
DI-Disk Information, Advanced Edition 4.50, (C) Copr 1987-88, Peter Norton

   Information from DOS          Drive A:        Information from the boot record
--------------------------------------------------------------------------------
                             system id                'IBM PNCI'
                             media descriptor (hex)         F9
            0                drive number
          512                bytes per sector              512
            1                sectors per cluster             1
            2                number of FATs                  2
          224                root directory entries        224
            7                sectors per FAT                 7
        2,371                number of clusters
                             number of sectors           2,400
            1                offset to FAT                   1
           15                offset to directory
           29                offset to data
                             sectors per track              15
                             sides                           2
                             hidden sectors                  0

                           Figure DI-3
                  A Safe Formatted 1.2M diskette
                     Norton Disk Information
```

Can I get a printout of this information with any other program?

Yes and no. The NDD report will print out all of the information it normally displays, which includes all of the test results and any repairs that were made. Using the DOS redirect operators (> or > >) will provide the most concise format for this information. A "frame-grabber" or "screen-saver" program would be another way to capture the information for printing or saving to a disk file. The only problem I've found with this method of getting hardcopies is that it usually crashes the program, and then I have to run the program again.

21

CHAPTER

UnErase

Directory name **UNERASE.EXE**

UnErase (UE) in version 5.0 is the combination of QuickUnerase (QU) and
UnErase (UE) from version 4.5 with improvements and the addition of menu-
driven enhancements.

Command line usage

Format: unerase [filename]

There are no command-line switches available.

Network considerations

UnErase may be used in combination with FileSave to unerase over a network.

When UE begins, it displays the directories of the current drive or the files of
the current subdirectory (Fig. 21-1).

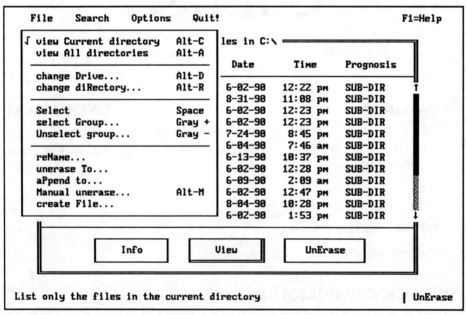

```
   File     Search    Options    Quit!                              F1=Help
           ╔══════════════ Erased files in C:\ ═══════════════╗
           ║    Name          Size      Date      Time     Prognosis      ║
           ║                                                               ║
           ║   ARC             DIR     6-02-90   12:22 pm   SUB-DIR    ↑   ║
           ║   CHESS           DIR     8-31-90   11:08 pm   SUB-DIR        ║
           ║   CW              DIR     6-02-90   12:23 pm   SUB-DIR        ║
           ║   DH              DIR     6-02-90   12:23 pm   SUB-DIR        ║
           ║   FP              DIR     7-24-90    8:45 pm   SUB-DIR        ║
           ║   HSG             DIR     6-04-90    7:46 am   SUB-DIR        ║
           ║   LHARC           DIR     6-13-90   10:37 pm   SUB-DIR        ║
           ║   MOUSE           DIR     6-02-90   12:28 pm   SUB-DIR        ║
           ║   MTEZ            DIR     6-09-90    2:09 am   SUB-DIR        ║
           ║   NC              DIR     6-02-90   12:47 pm   SUB-DIR        ║
           ║   PANDA           DIR     8-04-90   10:28 pm   SUB-DIR        ║
           ║   PS              DIR     6-02-90    1:53 pm   SUB-DIR    ↓   ║
           ║                                                               ║
           ║      ┌─────────┐    ┌─────────┐    ┌──────────┐              ║
           ║      │  Info   │    │  View   │    │ UnErase  │              ║
           ║      └─────────┘    └─────────┘    └──────────┘              ║
           ╚═══════════════════════════════════════════════════╝
   Select files to UnErase                              | UnErase
```

21-1 The Opening screen for UnErase.

To change the display, use the F9 key or a mouse click to display the File pull-down menu (Fig. 21-2).

```
   File     Search    Options    Quit!                              F1=Help
  ╔═══════════════════════════════════╗
  ║ √ view Current directory   Alt-C  ║ les in C:\ ═══════════
  ║   view All directories     Alt-A  ║
  ║                                    ║   Date      Time     Prognosis
  ║   change Drive...          Alt-D  ║
  ║   change diRectory...      Alt-R  ║  6-02-90   12:22 pm   SUB-DIR    ↑
  ║                                    ║  8-31-90   11:08 pm   SUB-DIR
  ║   Select                   Space  ║  6-02-90   12:23 pm   SUB-DIR
  ║   select Group...          Gray + ║  6-02-90   12:23 pm   SUB-DIR
  ║   Unselect group...        Gray - ║  7-24-90    8:45 pm   SUB-DIR
  ║                                    ║  6-04-90    7:46 am   SUB-DIR
  ║   reName...                       ║  6-13-90   10:37 pm   SUB-DIR
  ║   unerase To...                   ║  6-02-90   12:28 pm   SUB-DIR
  ║   aPpend to...                    ║  6-09-90    2:09 am   SUB-DIR
  ║   Manual unerase...        Alt-M  ║  6-02-90   12:47 pm   SUB-DIR
  ║   create File...                  ║  8-04-90   10:28 pm   SUB-DIR
  ╚═══════════════════════════════════╝  6-02-90    1:53 pm   SUB-DIR    ↓
           ┌─────────┐    ┌─────────┐    ┌──────────┐
           │  Info   │    │  View   │    │ UnErase  │
           └─────────┘    └─────────┘    └──────────┘

   List only the files in the current directory         | UnErase
```

21-2 Choosing file options for UnErase.

Depending on the prognosis of the file you need to recover (discovered on the panel in Fig. 21-3), you may be able to let UE do it automatically or be required to go into the manual recovery mode.

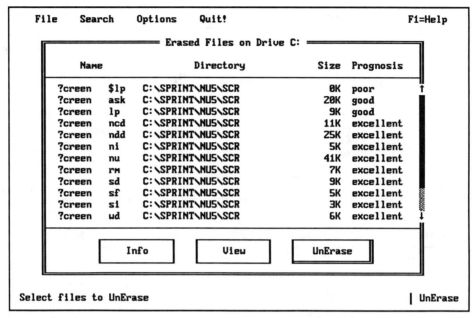

File   Search   Options   Quit!   F1=Help

```
================ Erased Files on Drive C: ================

        Name                  Directory          Size  Prognosis

      ?creen   $lp    C:\SPRINT\NU5\SCR            0K   poor           ↑
      ?creen   ask    C:\SPRINT\NU5\SCR           20K   good
      ?creen   lp     C:\SPRINT\NU5\SCR            9K   good
      ?creen   ncd    C:\SPRINT\NU5\SCR           11K   excellent
      ?creen   ndd    C:\SPRINT\NU5\SCR           25K   excellent
      ?creen   ni     C:\SPRINT\NU5\SCR            5K   excellent
      ?creen   nu     C:\SPRINT\NU5\SCR           41K   excellent
      ?creen   rm     C:\SPRINT\NU5\SCR            7K   excellent
      ?creen   sd     C:\SPRINT\NU5\SCR            9K   excellent
      ?creen   sf     C:\SPRINT\NU5\SCR            5K   excellent
      ?creen   si     C:\SPRINT\NU5\SCR            3K   excellent
      ?creen   ud     C:\SPRINT\NU5\SCR            6K   excellent       ↓

            Info              View              UnErase

Select files to UnErase                                      | UnErase
```

21-3 Viewing a list of erased files.

If manual recovery is necessary, the panel shown in Fig. 21-4 will give you a starting point. Notice that the cluster is the smallest unit of storage space that you can recover. The size of the cluster will depend on the disk(ette) you are working with. Expect to be able to recover text files much more quickly than other types of files.

Selecting the Info box on the Opening screen will display the window shown in Fig. 21-5. It should provide you with enough additional information about the file you have selected to determine if you can do an automatic recovery or if a manual UnErase is necessary.

To help you find the missing pieces of a file to be unerased, this Utility now has a search capability. Tagging one of the selections in the menu shown in Fig. 21-6 will open a window where you can enter what you want to find.

How you see the files that have been erased but may still be recoverable is determined by the Display option pictured in Fig. 21-7. Note that you can also view the files that have not been erased. For large hard disks or where a specific type of file is being sought, the sort-by-extension should produce a smaller listing.

If accidental erasures appear to be a problem, you might want to ensure that the FileSave Utility is active. The loss of disk space may be easier to justify than

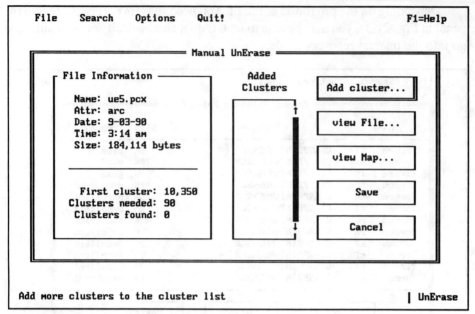

21-4 Manual UnErasing.

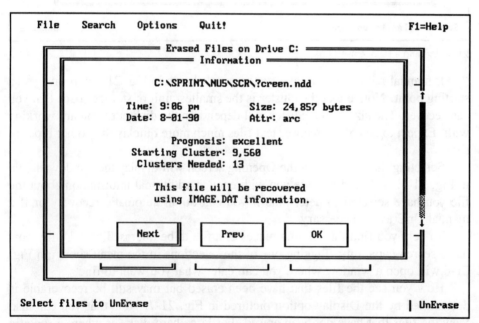

21-5 Information on erased files.

the time necessary to recover and rebuild the lost files. Accidental erasures may also be an indication of a need for operator training.

Application programs that create massive backup files should be monitored when FileSave is active. Recovery will be easier when the files are complete but

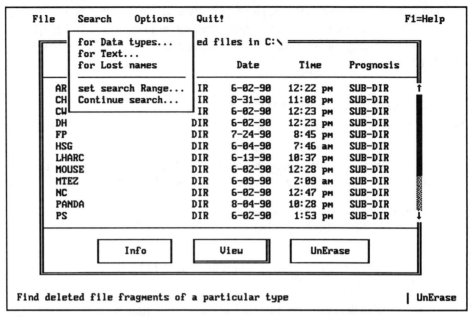

21-6 Options for search.

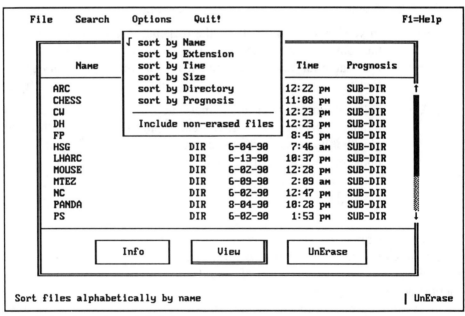

21-7 Options for sorting and displaying.

the loss of disk space may not be acceptable. This is just one case where a well-defined and enforced backup program will ensure that the files protected by File-Save can be purged in a timely manner without causing unnecessary lost time for recovery operations.

Do I follow my own good advice? Not always. Do I suffer because of it? Always. Am I learning from experience? I would like to think so. Hopefully you will do better at keeping your backups current and paying attention to the details of safe computing.

Quick UnErase version 4.0 & 4.5

Version 4.0 & 4.5 directory name   **QU.EXE**

QU is a streamlined version of the UnErase feature, which is the heart of the NU program. While it does not contain all of the NU features, QU has an automatic mode that permits goof-proof recoveries of many newly deleted files.

Format: QU [d:] [\ path \ filename]
             QU [filespec]
             QU /A

d: The drive designation where the file is to be found.

\ path \ filename

            The location on that drive where the file is to be found. QU defaults to *.* If no filename is specified. The wildcard characters * and ? may be used in the specification.

filespec In version 4.5, this replaces the [d:] [path \ filename] portion of the command line. The same rules of use apply. In all cases, the QU search for deleted files remains within the subdirectory specified.

[/A]   Tells QU to go about its attempt automatically. No user input is required. QU locates the file(s) and supplies a first letter that will give the file a unique filename. Later, using the DOS rename routine, you can convert that name to the proper name for the file(s) recovered.

If you use QU in the interactive mode, you will be asked to supply a first letter for each filename that QU is able to recover. Shown in Fig. 21-8 is a representative screen captured from an interactive QU session.

Again with version 4.0 and the Advanced Edition, the format changes somewhat. Without duplicating too much of the information, here in Fig. 21-9 is an example of the new display.

QU works on both hard and floppy disks but will work faster on smaller directories, such as those on a floppy disk. QU will only recover complete files; NU must be used if an attempt is to be made on a partial file.

If the attempt to recover a file with QU is not successful, delete the attempt and try again with NU. In Fig. 21-10 is a typical screen representation for an automatic QU session.

21-8 An interactive QU session. The lines marked with ''*''s are normally overwritten on the screen but are shown here for your convenience.

```
A>QU

QU-Quick UnErase. Version 3.10. (C) Copr 1984-86. Peter
Norton

    There are 2 erased files in this directory
    1 of them may possibly be Quick-UnErased

    Erased files lose the first character of their names
    After selecting each file to Quick-UnErase, you will be
    asked to supply the missing character

    ?L.COM           4,536 bytes   3:10 pm  Fri Nov  1 85
*Do you wish to Quick-UnErase this file (Y/N) ? y
*What is the first character of ?L.COM ? v
*The filename 'VL.COM' will be used for the new
Quick-UnErased file

    ?EAD.ME.BAT      1,060 bytes   3:10 pm  Fri Nov  1 85
It is not possible to Quick-UnErase this file
Its data space is being used by another file
Press and key to continue
```

21-9 An interactive QU session (version 4.x and AE). Lines marked with ''*''s are normally overwritten.

```
A>qu b:*.com

QU-Quick UnErase, Advanced Edition, (C) Copr 1988, Peter
Norton

Directory of B:\
    Erased file specification: *.COM
    Number of erased files: 8
    Number that can be Quick-UnErased: 8

    Erased files lose the first character of their names.
    After selecting each file to Quick-UnErase, you will be
    asked to supply the missing character

    ?ndersb.com         10 bytes   7:41 pm  Tue Sep 25 84

Quick-UnErase this file (Y/N) ? Y

* Enter the first character of the filename: U
* 'undersb.com' Quick-UnErased
    ?clock.com         512 bytes   6:43 pm  Mon Jan  5 87

Quick- . . . .
```

Notice that QU is file-oriented. Its speed and value are best seen when trying to recover a file that has just been (accidentally) deleted. CHKDSK/F, DT, and NU provide other means of recovering the data accidentally deleted or damaged. The capabilities of the Norton Utility programs DT and NU each have their own

```
A>qu /a

QU-Quick-UnErase, Version 3.10, (C) Copr 1984-86, Peter
Norton

    There are 3 erased files in this directory
    2 of them may possibly be Quick-UnErased

    Erased files lose the first character of their names
    Quick-UnErase will automatically replace them

    ?D.COM            10,400 bytes   3:10 pm  Fri Nov  1 85
The filename 'AD.COM' will be used for the new
Quick-UnErased file
    ?L.COM             4,536 bytes   3:10 pm  Fri Nov  1 85
The filename 'AL.COM' will be used for the new
Quick-UnErased file
    ?EADME.BAT         1,060 bytes   3:10 pm  Fri Nov  1 85
It is not possible to Quick-UnErase this file
Its data space is being used by another program
```

section later in this book. Some use of the DOS utility CHKDSK program is covered in the section on DT.

By using the FA (File Attributes) Utility program to make especially valuable files read-only, some additional safety can be included.

What does it mean when QU reports that a file is cross-linked?

Cross-linking means that two or more files are claiming that the same sector is a valid data location. This happens when new files are written to disks which contain deleted files. It can also occur if an existing file is modified on a disk with other deleted files on it.

To avoid cross-linking, do your file recovery before attempting to add to or modify the files on that disk.

Is there any way to prevent cross-linked files?

Yes. WipeFile can be used to delete a file, which ensures that all of the information about the deleted file is erased. WipeFile also prevents QU and NU from recovering any of the data. The other way to avoid cross-linking is to do all your file recovery first. Then, use WIPEDISK /E to clear all of the free data storage space.

Is there any way to use QU in more than one subdirectory?

QU may be used in every subdirectory, but only one at a time. If your question was "Can I use QU/A /S and automatically Quick UnErase all of the deleted files in all of the subdirectories?", the answer is no.

Unremove Directory version 4.0 & 4.5
Version 4.0 & 4.5 directory name   UD.EXE

UD is for directories what QU is for files.

Format: UD [d:] [\ pathname]

d: Specifies the drive where the directory is stored.

\ pathname

Specifies the name of the parent directory of the subdirectory to be unremoved. UD defaults to the current directory when none is specified. UD attempts to recover all of the identifiable directories that have been deleted in the path.

In addition to unremoving the directory name, UD will attempt to recover all of the files that were in that directory.

UD does not have the /A switch like the TS program or an automatic mode like QU; it operates interactively. Thus, it will evaluate the undelete possibilities and prompt for a new first letter if recovery is possible.

After recovering the directory name, UD then attempts to recover the contents—the deleted files that were a part of that directory.

To delete a directory name, all of the files in that directory must be deleted first. Once the directory name is deleted, QU cannot UnErase those files.

You can stop UD's search for additional files to UnErase at any time by answering no to the question "Search for more?" when it is displayed.

The capabilities of the NU program are superior to those available in UD, which means that you can use NU to attempt recovery operations which are beyond UD. This is similar to the use of NU after a failure using QU.

Good housekeeping techniques are also helpful. You can keep a current listing of the files in your directories. You can also make regular backup copies of stored data. Making important files read-only using the FA program will also reduce the possible accidental erasure of needed files. This indirectly protects the directory too because the directory cannot be deleted while it contains active files.

22

CHAPTER

UnFormat

Directory name
Command line usage

Format: UNFORMAT [d:]

d: The drive to be unformatted.

There are no command-line switches available for this Utility.

Network considerations

UnFormat can run in a network environment, but it will not unformat a network drive.

When you start trying to unformat a disk(ette), UnFormat needs to know if you have an IMAGE file on the disk(ette). As indicated by Fig. 22-1, the default answer is "yes."

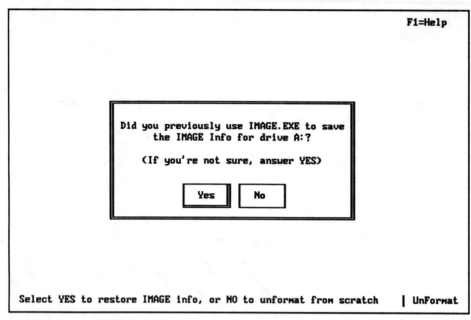

Did you previously use IMAGE.EXE to save
the IMAGE Info for drive A:?

(If you're not sure, answer YES)

Yes   No

Select YES to restore IMAGE info, or NO to unformat from scratch | UnFormat

22-1 Preparing to UnFormat.

Just in case you have the wrong information entered, UF gives you one last chance to change your mind. Figure 22-2 displays immediately after you press the RETURN key on the Selection screen. If you have any questions at all about what you are attempting to do, answer "no" and recheck everything before going any farther.

While UnFormatting is in progress, the Status Window (see Fig. 22-3) will keep you informed. The diskette used to make this illustration was not very full. Note too that each of the blocks displayed is only three clusters. This will give you some indication of the amount of time it will take UnFormat to complete its task.

Not having the IMAGE file to work from will make disk(ette) recover more difficult. If you have been using the FRECOVER Utility from version 4.5, your disk(ette)s will have a FRECOVER file on them. UnFormat can use this file to assist in recovery operations.

SafeFormat and SpeeDisk both write IMAGE files. SpeeDisk will also update an existing IMAGE file when it is present. In essence, if there is an IMAGE file, recovery will be much easier. Also, you might want to run the IMAGE Utility on your disk(ette)s when you start a session, especially if there is any possibility of a problem occurring during the session.

Safe computing may sound like just another buzz-word, but it's not. Safe computing is a mindset that hopes for the best while preparing for the worst. The amount of space and time required to keep a current IMAGE file on any disk(ette) is much less than the time and effort that will be required to recover the information lost on an unprepared disk(ette). Never go computing without protection.

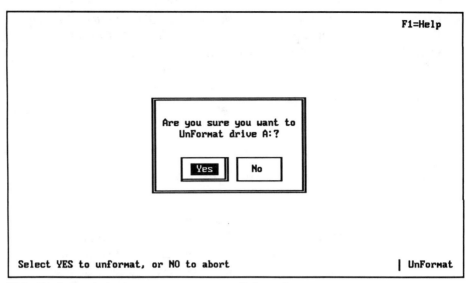

22-2 The Safety window: are you sure you want to UnFormat?

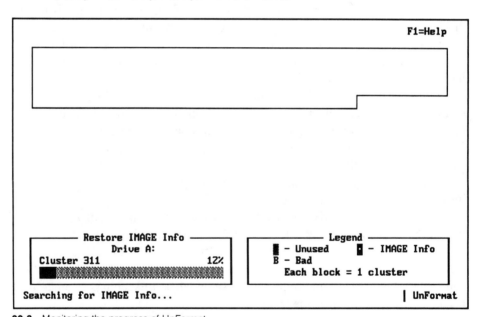

22-3 Monitoring the progress of UnFormat.

Format Recovery version 4.0 & 4.5
Directory name   **FR.EXE**

Format Recovery will undo the apparent damage done by the accidental reformatting of most hard disks, allowing for the recovery of the information that was on the hard disk. Exceptions are Compaq DOS 3.1 and AT&T DOS 2.11, which overwrite the disk during formatting. Version 3.2 DOS for the Compaq and AT&T systems correct this problem. The recovery file FRECOVER.DAT must also have been prepared before attempting to do this recovery operation.

Compaq DOS 3.31 has been tested and is no longer destructive.

Format: FR [d:] [switches]

d: Is the hard disk to be recovered.

The following command-line switches are available:

/SAVE   Prepares the file FRECOVER.DAT to be used in the recovery attempt.

blank   When FR is called without any switch being specified, it will look first for the FRECOVER.DAT file and then attempt to recover the format and information on the hard disk drive specified. No drive specification will default to the currently selected drive.

Losing all of the information stored on one of today's multi-megabyte hard disks can be very traumatic. Rationalizations can be made for defective equipment, power failures, and many other incidents that can cause hard disk failures. Entering a FORMAT command or having a "trojan horse" program reformat the hard disk for you cannot be justified.

Including the FR [d:] /SAVE command in an AUTOEXEC.BAT file will ensure that the hard disk recovery information is available and current. The ability of FR to recover information from a hard disk that has had nothing done to it since the FORMAT command was issued is totally dependent on the information in the FRECOVER.DAT file.

FR is not designed to replace the systematic backup of hard-disk files. It is instead much like the UnErase Utility available for file recovery—a last chance.

If it hasn't been clearly stated before, FR works only on hard disks—and only within the limits stated. It would also be very prudent to keep the FRECOVER-.DAT file on a floppy, not on a hard disk subject to a possible FORMAT command error. In spite of all of the advances being made in hardware and software, nothing can replace the security and importance of regular housekeeping. The hardware needs maintenance as does the software.

Warning for Advanced Edition Users: It is possible to destroy all access to your hard disk if the Partition Table is not readable by DOS. FR is designed to recover your information only after the disk has been reformatted, not after the Partition Table has been modified. FR may not be able to operate in that case.

Only expert users should attempt to make changes to the Directory, File Allocation Table (FAT), and Partition Table. The capability to make changes in these areas is present in the NU (Norton Utility) program contained in the Advanced Edition.

If a hard disk has been so extensively modified that the expert, using the new maintenance mode of the Advanced Edition NU program, is unable to re-establish contact between it and DOS, only the manufacturer will be able to reformat the hard disk. I have repeated this warning in the section on using the Partition Table editor.

Where should I keep my latest copy of FRECOVER.DAT?

FRECOVER.DAT will be written to a data portion of the hard disk and should not be lost during an accidental reformatting. If you want, make a backup copy on a floppy that also has FRECOVER.EXE on it.

Notice in Fig. 22-4 that there is a file called REC.EXE on the floppy. This is actually FR.EXE renamed. I've made use of the FR filename in the .BAT batch file. The single command line of REC C:/S is sufficient to have the program build a new FRECOVER.DAT file on the hard disk. Then, using the copy command, you can transfer it to the floppy.

22-4 The directory of a recovery floppy.

```
C:\: dir a:

 Volume in drive A is frecover
 Directory of  A:\

IBMBIO    COM    22100    3-18-87    12:00p
IBMDOS    COM    30159    3-17-87    12:00p
COMMAND   COM    25307    3-17-87    12:00p
REC       EXE    12500    5-15-87     4:00p
FRECOVER  DAT    61440    7-15-87     1:31p
FR        BAT       11    1-01-80    12:17a
         6 File(s)    207872 bytes free
```

Does that mean that I have to remember to get that disk out to update the .DAT file?

It does, unless you put a bit of code into an ASK file. If the menu selection says (B)ackup, the action code could be

A:FR C:/SAVE (or /S will also work)

If the disk isn't there, an error message will display. This same line could be the action code for the (Q)uit selection used just before shutting down the system.

Can I recover the data on a reformatted disk without a FRECOVER.DAT file?

An expert working under ideal conditions might be able to salvage a significant portion. NU in the maintenance (/M) mode may be able to recover data sector by sector. Text files are relatively easy to read; it's the compiled code files that cause the most problem.

Is there any way to prevent "trojan horse" programs from reformatting my hard disk?

Yes. There are a couple of things that you can do. You can rename the FORMAT-
.COM program to something else. I mentioned this in the section on the ASK
Utility program. You can also screen all of the programs you receive from a bulletin board or a questionable source with a program that reads the ASCII strings in
the new file. There are a number of these little utilities in the Public Domain.

The sick minds that develop "trojan horses" also desire recognition and usually get it by leaving some type of a message letting you know that they have just
destroyed your many hours of hard work. These messages are usually in the form
of ASCII strings that can be read by one of the Public Domain Utilities. Most of
the subscription services, like DELPHI and BIX, and many of the more active
local BBS systems will have some type of "checker" program available.

Why does FRECOVER work on a hard disk and not on a floppy?

When DOS formats a floppy disk, it overwrites the entire diskette. When a hard
disk is formatted, only the administrative (FAT and Root directory) areas are
overwritten, leaving the data areas untouched. Additionally, DOS uses a portion
of the data to store subdirectories, which means that they should still be intact if
you have not run FDISK or written anything to the hard disk since it was formatted. Users who have Compaq DOS 3.1 or AT&T DOS 2.11 are an exception.
These versions have a destructive format routine, which means all areas of the
hard disk are overwritten. The best utility to use for floppy disks is SF (SafeFormat). This Utility will help you recover data that might otherwise be lost from a
floppy. SF is new with version 4.5, so you should update your copy before the
need becomes critical.

23
CHAPTER

WipeInfo

Directory name

WipeInfo is new with version 5.0. The basic Utilities, WipeDisk and WipeFile, have been available since version 3.0. With this version, they are combined and improved. WipeInfo is menu-driven and contains a number of safeguards so that you don't cause permanent loss of needed data.

Command line usage

Format: WIPEINFO [d:] [disk switches] [common switches]
WIPEINFO [filename] [file switches] [common switches]

Disk switches

/E   Specifies that only the erased and unused space is to be wiped. Using this switch ensures that no current or active data is wiped.

File switches

/N   The non-wipe mode. This deletes files just like DOS and doesn't wipe any portion of the disk or file.

/K   Wipe the slack space only, which is the space at the end of a sector that is not being used by the file currently stored there. This ensures that any data remaining from a former resident will never be attached to the current file.

/S   Include subdirectories. Wipes or deletes (if the /N switch is active) all of the subdirectories of the specified disk also.

Common switches

/Gn   Invokes the government wiping rules. The n is the specifier for the number of times the pattern of 1s and 0s is to be written to every sector. The default value of n is 3.

/Rn   Sets repeat wiping. Similar to the government scheme, except that the value is normally 0 and the number of times, n, defaults to 1.

/Vn   Specifies the value to use in overwriting. The value n can be any number between 0d and 255d. The "d" indicates decimal. The default value, unless the /G switch is active, is 0d. The default value for the /G switch is 246d or F6h.

            The character, HEX, and binary translations of these values can be found in any good ASCII conversion table.

When values are not specified with active switches, the program default values are used.

Network considerations

WipeInfo should only be used on your local system drive while connected to a network. Along with the possibility of creating problems for other users' data, it also can take from several minutes to several hours to perform a wipe. The actual time will depend on the parameters set and the size of the disk being wiped.

The Opening panel for this Utility, shown in Fig. 23-1, displays the choices available. How you go through the various screens will depend upon whether or not you have used the Utility before and whether or not changes are required.

After adding the filename, there are a number of other choices to be made, listed in Fig. 23-2. This screen is really the updated version of the WipeFile Utility of earlier versions. The wiping method portion of this screen is just a different way of presenting the information that can be entered from the command line. In some cases, it may be easier and faster to use the command line to wipe a file. The menu system makes it easier to wipe a quantity of files. The older versions of this Utility had only a limited batch capability for wiping.

```
╔═══════════════════════ WipeInfo ═══════════════════════╗
║                                                          ║
║        WipeInfo protects confidential data by            ║
║        overwriting files or other drive areas            ║
║                                                          ║
║             What do you want to wipe?                    ║
║                                                          ║
║         ┌──────────────┐   ┌──────────────┐              ║
║         │    Files     │   │   Drives     │              ║
║         └──────────────┘   └──────────────┘              ║
║                                                          ║
║         ┌──────────────┐   ┌──────────────┐              ║
║         │  Configure   │   │    Quit      │              ║
║         └──────────────┘   └──────────────┘              ║
║                                                          ║
╚══════════════════════════════════════════════════════════╝
```

Select appropriate button and press ENTER | WipeInfo

23-1 The Opening screen for WipeInfo.

```
╔══════════════════════ Wipe Files ══════════════════════╗
║  ┌─ File Name ────────────────────────────────────────┐ ║
║  │                                                      │ ║
║  │                                                      │ ║
║  │  ☐ Include subdirs      ☐ Hidden files               │ ║
║  │  ☐ Confirm each file    ☐ Read Only files            │ ║
║  └──────────────────────────────────────────────────────┘ ║
║  ┌─ Wiping Method ────────────────────────────────────┐ ║
║  │  ☐ Wipe files                                        │ ║
║  │  ☐ Delete files only, don't wipe                     │ ║
║  │  ☐ Wipe unused file slack only                       │ ║
║  └──────────────────────────────────────────────────────┘ ║
║                                                          ║
║         ┌──────────────┐   ┌──────────────┐              ║
║         │    Wipe      │   │   Cancel     │              ║
║         └──────────────┘   └──────────────┘              ║
╚══════════════════════════════════════════════════════════╝
```

Select WIPE to begin wipe of selected drives | WipeInfo

23-2 Selecting files and options for wiping.

Figure 23-3 shows the updated version of the WipeDisk Utility. After selecting a drive, the available switches are given as choices in the lower box. Wipe can be aborted. Because it starts wiping at the far end of the data storage portion of the disk, you could possibly recover important data if necessary. The data in the wiped portions of the disk will never be recovered, however; the overwriting done by the Wipe Utility ensures this.

The default values for WipeInfo are shown here in Fig. 23-4. You can change and save them, in which case they become the new defaults; or you can change them for the current session only. When you select the Fast Wipe option, you will

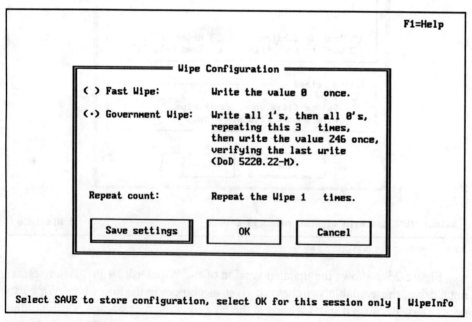

23-3 Selecting a drive for wiping.

23-4 Configuring WipeInfo.

also be able to change the value to be written during the wipe process. The same is true when the Government Wipe option is selected.

If you change the Repeat Count, the value to be written will come from the Fast Wipe option. This combination doesn't change the values written with repeated wipings, nor does it verify that the proper value has been written on the last pass. Because of this, it is faster but may not be quite as secure. Repeat Count should be more than adequate unless you are required by regulations to use the Government Wipe scheme.

WipeDisk version 4.0 & 4.5

Version 4.0 & 4.5 directory name **WIPEDISK.EXE**

WipeDisk overwrites all portions of a disk with a value. On early versions, that value was fixed as a zero (0d, 0h, 0000b). Starting with version 3.1, the user is given control of the value to be written, the number of writes, and other parameters.

This has been done to ensure that a disk can be cleared of any sensitive data prior to releasing it. It also helps to wipe a disk prior to recycling it, especially if development work is going to be stored on that disk. Sorting through current data and old data at the sector level can be confusing as well as frustrating and very time-consuming.

Format:	WIPEDISK [d:] [switches] [>|>>] [device|drive \ path \ filename]
d:	The letter of the drive containing the disk to be wiped.
/E	Instructs WipeDisk to overwrite only those areas of the disk that do not contain active files. This is a way to clear "trash" off a disk that is being passed on to another user and is also a bit of insurance against the problem of cross-linked files when doing a hard-disk reorganization. See the question & answer at the end of this section for an example of how a problem and its solution may be discovered.
/G	Wipes the disk in accordance with the appropriate government specifications.
/LOG	Formats the program output for redirection to either the printer or a disk file.
/R*n*	Sets the number of repetitions (times) that the wiping process will be performed. The default is one time. When the /G switch is set, there are three separate wipes (by specification), and this switch is inactive.

/**Vn**   Sets the value of the character used as the overwrite during the wiping process. The default value is zero. Any value between 0 and 255 may be specified. This switch may be used with the /G switch.

> | > >   The DOS redirection operators. " > " redirects the program to a device or file. " > > " redirects and appends the program output to an existing filename.

WipeDisk does not have a two-letter abbreviation, which should prevent its being used in error. You must also confirm that you want to run WipeDisk by answering yes to the prompt (which defaults to no). Pressing the RETURN key without first pressing the Y key will abort the program without doing anything to the disk. You can also abort WipeDisk while it is running. Pressing the key combination CTRL-BREAK will stop WipeDisk from proceeding. Data will be lost in those portions of the disk that have been wiped by the process. WipeDisk begins at the end of the data storage area and works toward the Directory, FAT, and System areas, so it is possible to save some information when a disk has been partially wiped.

WipeDisk overwrites all areas of a disk—System Area, FAT, Directory, and Data Storage. After wiping, disks must be reformatted before they can be reused. The exception is when you set the /E switch.

The /G switch writes three different values during three separate passes. On the first pass, all binary ones (15d, Fh, 1111b) are written; the second time, zeros (0d, 0h, 0000b); and the third time, a value of F6h (246d, 11111110b) is first written and then read. The write/read procedure is done in every sector of the disk, which ensures that all pre-existing data has been removed. The /Vn switch may be used to change the value used in the two passes, but the third value is fixed.

Invoking WipeDisk with the /E switch active overwrites only those areas of the disk which do not currently hold active file, Directory, or FAT data. Thus, only the information you wish to share is on the disk when you give it to another user. Using SD (SpeeDisk) before WipeDisk /E will ensure that there are no fragmented files and no recoverable "extra" data on the unused portion of the disk.

None of the Norton Utilities are copy-protected. This means that you can rename any of the programs. Renaming might be another way of preventing problems. Including WipeDisk and WipeFile in batch files with or without renaming the programs is also a possibility. Using a cryptic filename for WipeFile, WipeDisk, and the batch file(s) might provide another level of security from abuse. Putting the /E switch in the batch file with WipeDisk will prevent the loss of all data on a disk.

The level of protection provided for WipeDisk should equal the protection provided for the FORMAT command. Either one has the potential to create a problem. FR (Format Recover) can provide help in the event of an accidental reformat of a hard disk. There is no recovery from a properly executed WipeDisk.

Is there any way to prevent cross-linking?

Yes. Cross-linking can only occur when there is data in a cluster that is not over-written by the new data being placed in that cluster. By using WipeDisk with the /E switch active, all of the inactive space on the disk can be cleared of any remaining data.

I got the following display while running WIPEDISK C:/E. What does it mean?

It appears that WipeDisk, Fig. 23-5, has had a problem with those two clusters while FORMAT did not. Rather than chance data loss, I would mark those clusters. Then DOS will recognize them as bad and never again attempt to write data to them. The /C cluster-number switch of the DT utility is designed to do this type of task.

As shown in Fig. 23-6, the clusters are marked by number. You can use either DT or WIPEDISK /E to search your disk for bad or questionable clusters.

The screen in Fig. 23-7 checks to verify that DT did, in fact, mark the clusters bad. These B markings should also be displayed on the disk map that is a part of the SD Utility. The only way to remove the B's now is to use DT with the /C cluster-number-switch active.

23-5 WipeDisk with an active /E switch. Note the two bad sectors.

```
C:\: c:\util\nu\wipedisk c:/e
WD-Wipe Disk, Advanced Edition, (C) Copr 1988, Peter Norton

Action:        Wipe the Erased data space
Drive:         C:
Wipe count:    1
Wipe value:    0

DANGER! This will wipe-out the erased data space on the entire disk.
Proceed (Y/N) ? [y]

During this operation, you may press
BREAK (Control-C) to interrupt Wipe Disk

Wiping the Erased data space
8,041st cluster: error in writing
8,015th cluster: error in writing
Done
```

```
Menu 3.1                 Map of space usage for the entire disk

                         83% of disk space is free

                       Proportional Map of Disk Space
              . ...                   ................................... B
   represents ............................... ...........         represents
   space                                                          bad
   in use                                                         sectors



                                      BB


      Each position represents 21 clusters, 1/496th of the total disk space

                         Press any key to continue...

   Item type  │ Drive │ Directory name                  │     File name
   Directory  │  C:   │ \                                │     Root dir
```

23-6 A Map Disk screen verifying the location of the two bad sectors. The "B"'s will blink and will also appear red if you are using a color monitor.

23-7 Using DT to mark the reported sectors bad.

```
C:\: c:\util\nu\dt /c8041
DT-Disk Test, Advanced Edition, (C) Copr 1988, Peter Norton

Manually marking clusters as Bad
   Cluster 8,041 marked as Bad.


C:\: c:\util\nu\dt /c8015
DT-Disk Test, Advanced Edition, (C) Copr 1988, Peter Norton

Manually marking clusters as Bad
   Cluster 8,015 marked as Bad.
```

WipeFile version 4.0 & 4.5

Version 4.0 & 4.5 directory name   **WIPEFILE.EXE**

WipeFile is used to overwrite file data areas to prevent everyone from reading what was there. This feature can be used to ensure that data areas are clean before writing new information to the disk or to prevent out-of-date information from being viewed by others. From one file to an entire disk of files may be wiped. Operator confirmation of the parameters is required before WipeFile will run. When more than one filename is specified (i.e., *.COM), WipeFile will also prompt for a yes/no response to confirm the overwriting of each file prior to actually performing the overwrite.

Format: WIPEFILE [drive\path] [filename] SPACE [switches] [>|>]
             [device|drive\path\filename]

drive \ path

Tells WipeFile where to find the file to be overwritten.

filename Tells WipeFile which file to overwrite. The DOS global characters * and ? may be used in the *filename* specification. WipeFile does not have a default mode.

SPACE A space is required as a delimiter between the filename and the first switch.

Switches

/D An option in version 3.0 that was later incorporated into WipeFile that deletes the directory listing of the file that has been wiped.

/G*n* An option first seen in version 3.1 that overwrites files to conform to government specifications such as DoD 5220.22-M. When this switch is used, the selected file(s) are wiped a total of *n* times. The first wipe writes binary 1's; the second writes binary 0's; and the third writes HEX value F6. After the last write, WipeFile verifies the write by reading the last value written. First available in version 3.1. In version 4.5, the default value of *n* is 3.

/LOG Formats the output of WipeFile for redirection to a printer or disk file. First available in version 3.1.

/N This is the non-wiping mode. In this mode, WipeFile performs the same as the DOS DEL command. WipeFile requests confirmation after each file, however, but DOS does not. When the *.* parameter is used, DOS will ask for only one confirmation before deleting all of the files in the selected directory. WipeFile will require a "yes" response before every file, unless a "no" answer was returned at the "pause/confirm" prompt.

/NOD In version 3.1 wipes the files but retains the directory listings.

/P Forces a pause and operator input before acting on each file specified.

/R*n* Repeats the overwriting procedure *n* times.

/S Includes subdirectories in the procedure.

/V*n* Permits versions 3.1 and later to accept a decimal value between 0 and 255 as the overwrite value. It will replace the 0 value during a normal overwrite and the HEX value F6 when the /G switch is toggled on. In version 4.5, the default value is F6h (246d).

WipeFile must have some type of filename parameter before it will run.

Using WipeFile on disks to be recycled can save many headaches. Neither the DOS DELETE nor the FORMAT command removes the information from the file data areas. Until they are overwritten by new information or by WipeFile or WipeDisk, you can use a program like NU (Norton Utility) to recover the information.

WipeFile will overwrite hidden, system, or read-only files only when the /P switch is on. This forces the operator to say yes when asked if WipeFile is to overwrite this type of file. If the FA (File Attributes) program is used first to remove these attributes, WipeFile will operate normally.

For those who do not trust WipeFile to overwrite their data areas adequately, the /R(epetitions) switch with its *n* operator can specify just how many times WipeFile should overwrite the file(s).

This is also true of the /V(alue) switch with its *n* operator. Normally, WipeFile uses a binary zero (0) to overwrite. An operator can specify any decimal value in the range 0 to 255 as the overwrite value. The /V switch can be used with the /G switch while the /R switch cannot.

This is also true of the other mutually exclusive switches. For example, when using the /N (on-wiping) switch, it would be improper to specify the /Vn and/or / Rn switches.

Because WipeFile eliminates all possibility of data recovery, it is very unforgiving. It insists on the proper operator input before it attempts to run, which slows down the process of deleting files. Being forced to consider each file is one way to reduce the number of files that are wiped prematurely.

Figure 23-8 uses a full filename, while Fig. 23-9 uses the wildcard character "*".

23-8 WipeFile using a full filename.

```
A>wipefile b:arc51.com

WF-Wipe Files, Advanced Edition, (C) Copr 1988, Peter Norton

Action:        Wipe the file
Filename:      ARC51.COM
Wipe count:    1
Wipe value:    0

Directory: B:\
    arc51.com     Wiped clear. Deleted
```

23-9 WipeFile using a wildcard character.

```
A>wipefile b:*.*

WF-Wipe Files, Advanced Edition, (C) Copr 1988, Peter Norton

Action:        Wipe the files
Filenames:     *.*
Wipe count:    1
Wipe value:    0
```

```
Do you wish confirmation for each file [Y/N] ? N

Directory: B:\
    loader.sys    Read-only file; wiping not allowed.
                  Use /P option or FA program.

    always        Wiped clear. Deleted.
    consult       Wiped clear. Deleted.
    dates         Wiped clear. Deleted.
    for           Wiped clear. Deleted.
    appoint       Wiped clear. Deleted.
    ments         Wiped clear. Deleted.
    gofer         Wiped clear. Deleted.
    broke         Wiped clear. Deleted.
```

And Fig. 23-10 is an example of being in a hurry.

Figure 23-11 lets you see what WipeFile reports before doing its thing when the /G switch is used.

Using a combination of switches produces a display similar to the one in Fig. 23-12.

23-10 WipeFile done incorrectly.

```
A>wipefile b:

WF-Wipe Files, Advanced Edition, (C) Copr 1988, Peter Norton

Must specify files to wipe
```

23-11 WipeFile used with an active /G switch.

```
A>wipefile b:*.rbs /g

WF-Wipe Files, Advanced Edition, (C) Copr 1988, Peter Norton

Action:        Wipe the files using government specs.
Filenames:     *.RBS
Wipe count:    1

    Wipe File will write 1's, then write 0's, and finally
write the hex value 'F6'. Wipe File will then verify the
last write operation.

Do you wish confirmation for each file [Y/N] ?
```

23-12 WipeFile used with a combination of active switches. The ''*'' line normally overwrites the displayed line on the screen. If the /LOG switch had been active, only the ''*'' line would have been written.

```
A>wipefile b:*.asm /v255/r2

WF-Wipe Files, Advanced Edition, (C) Copr 1988, Peter Norton
```

```
Action:        Wipe the files
Filenames:     *.ASM
Wipe count:    2
Wipe value:    255

Do you wish confirmation for each file [Y/N] ? N

Directory: B:\
    1part.asm    Wiped clear 1 times.
   *1part.asm    Wiped clear 2 times. Deleted.
    2part.asm    Wiped clear 1 times.
   *2part.asm    Wiped clear 2 times. Deleted.
```

Is security the only reason to use one of these Wipe Utilities?

Security is the driving force for having the Utilities, but there are other valid reasons for using these Utilities.

Writing new data over old has been known to cause problems. One of the problems that I have seen is that a new file will "pick up" a character or more from the old file, which tends to make a mess of the new file.

Another problem is the possibility of getting files cross-linked. When two files think they share the same data sector, neither file can be used until the conflict is resolved.

24
CHAPTER

READ ME

Directory name READ.ME

A READ.ME file is added to the distribution disk(s) when a change has been made that is not reflected in the accompanying documentation. Once you have a hardcopy of this file, you don't have to copy it onto the working copy disk(s).

The people at Peter Norton Computing continue to work on the current version while developing new utility programs. The information contained in the READ.ME file will vary over the life of the version.

Format: TYPE [d:] read.me
PRINT [d:] read.me

d: Enter the letter of the drive that contains the READ.ME file, if it isn't the default drive.

Peter Norton Computing is a responsible and responsive software development company. Their mailing address is clearly printed in the booklet that accompanies the Utilities. If you should find a problem, contact them and get it resolved.

Based on my experience with Peter Norton Computing, I would also expect them to be responsive to suggestions about improvements and additions to the collection of programs known as the Norton Utilities. Just remember that it takes time and a fair amount of paperwork to get a new idea incorporated into anything.

When it becomes necessary to send out corrections, the READ.ME file is very often the only documentation that you will receive. In the gray area below is the READ.ME file from the update disk that was sent to the very early purchasers of version 4.5. Those of you who purchased your copy of the Norton Utilities version 4.5 after February 1989 should have received the corrected Utilities programs on the disks in the package. So far as I know, only the Utilities with a file datestamp of January 1989 need to be corrected. Contact Peter Norton Computing, Inc. if you have any problems or questions.

LATE ADDITIONS TO THE NORTON UTILITIES VERSION 4.5AE

We've added a few new commands to the Batch Enhancer program, included new switches in SpeeDisk, and made minor adjustments to the Norton Disk Doctor.

Batch Enhancer (BE)

We have added two additional subcommands to the Batch Enhancer program: CLS and DELAY.

CLS
Purpose: To clear the screen and reposition the cursor at the home position.
Format: BE CLS

DELAY
Purpose: To provide a user-defined delay period before execution of the next command.
Format: BE DELAY *ticks* (where *ticks* is the amount of time—in units of 1/18 second—to delay).

SpeeDisk

The following switches are not documented in the manual:

/A   Automatic mode; do not prompt
/V   Turn write-verify on

In addition, you may simply specify /R to activate the /REPORT switch listed in the manual.

Norton Disk Doctor

NDD is designed to automatically diagnose and fix a wide variety of technical problems that can plague disks. It requires no technical knowledge or expertise to run, however, allowing you to easily make disk repairs that could previously be done only by a true disk "wizard."

Some of the problems it can detect and/or correct include

- a physically bad Master Partition Table.
- an invalid or destroyed Master Partition Table.
- a destroyed Partition Table Program.
- destroyed Partition Table Signatures.
- an incorrectly set CMOS drive type.
- DOS-specific Partition methods (for example, trying to use a disk with Extended Partitions under a version of DOS previous to DOS 3.30.
- DOS 4.0's peculiar quirk of enforcing the OEM signature on Hard Disks to be "IBM," else giving the error message, "Invalid Media Type."
- physically bad Extended Partition Tables.
- invalid or destroyed Extended Partition Tables.
- an invalid bootable Partition.
- a physically bad Boot Record.
- an invalid or destroyed Boot Record program.
- an invalid or destroyed BIOS Parameter Block Table.
- a bad Boot Record signature.
- a physically bad File Allocation Table.
- an invalid Media Identifier in the File Allocation Tables.
- corrupted File Allocation Tables.
- cross-linked files, file allocation errors, bad clusters in the file chains, and other disk structure problems. NDD will even piece the parts together, so you won't have to swim through a list of FILExxxx.CHK files (as is the case with CHKDSK).
- physical problems with reading directories and/or files.

This is just a small number of the many things NDD can detect and correct for you. To use NDD, you will not need to know anything about disks. NDD will diagnose all problems for you and correct them if you wish. NDD also can optionally generate a report summarizing its test results. To get the best use out of NDD, you should install it in your AUTOEXEC.BAT file to analyze your disk at startup time. To have NDD do just a QUICK analysis of your C drive, put the following line in your AUTOEXEC.BAT:

NDD C: /QUICK

The following switches are missing from the manual for NDD (Norton Disk Doctor):

/R:*file*   Send a Report to *file*
/RA:*file*   Append a Report to *file*

Also note that after a disk has been tested, NDD will ask you if you wish to generate a report. If an error has been corrected, then you should have NDD generate a report.

Between the time that the version 5.0 software manual manuscript was sent off to the printer and the time that the software actually shipped, changes were made in the Utilities. Shown below is the READ.ME file for version 5.0.

WELCOME TO THE NORTON UTILITIES VERSION 5.0

This file contains information which doesn't appear in the manual. If you would like to print it, type COPY READ.ME PRN: at the DOS prompt.

General information

Many of the programs that were originally separate in Norton Utilities version 4.5 have been combined in version 5.0. Most of the previous program names have also been changed. The table below lists these changes.

Utility Name	4.5 Filename	5.0 Filename
Batch Enhancer	BE	BE
Directory Sort	DS	SpeeDisk
Disk Information	DI	SysInfo
Disk Test	DT	NDD
File Attributes	FA	FileFind
File Date/Time	FD	FileFind
File Find	FF	FileFind
File Information	FI	FileFind
Format Recover	FR	UnFormat
File Size	FS	FileFind
List Directory	LD	FileFind
Line Print	LP	doesn't exist
Norton Control Center	NCC	NCC
Norton Change Directory	NCD	NCD
Norton Disk Doctor	NDD	NDD, DiskTool
Norton Integrator	NI	Norton
Norton Utilities	NU	DiskEdit, UnErase, DiskTool

Utility Name	4.5 Filename	5.0 Filename
Quick UnErase	QU	UnErase
Speed Disk	SD	SpeeDisk
Safe Format	SF	SFormat
System Information	SI	SysInfo
Time Mark	TM	NCC
Text Search	TS	FileFind
UnRemove Directory	UD	UnErase
Volume Label	VL	NCD
Wipe File	WipeFile	WipeInfo
Wipe Disk	WipeDisk	WipeInfo

If the INSTALL program determines that Norton Utilities version 4.5 is already installed on the user's hard disk, it offers the option of overwriting the old version or saving the files to a backup directory. Regardless of the option chosen, the following 4.5 programs are always retained in the main NORTON directory:

Directory Sort (DS.EXE)
File Attributes (FA.EXE)
FileDate/Time (FD.EXE)
FileFind (FF.EXE renamed to FL.EXE)
FileSize (FS.EXE)
LinePrint (LP.EXE)

These programs are preserved because command-line users may find it easier to continue using them rather than their replacements in the 5.0 package. Users may also have batch files that rely on these 4.5 commands. The old FF.EXE is renamed to FL.EXE so that it doesn't conflict with the new FileFind.

Regardless of whether the old Utilities are installed, the user has the option of renaming certain programs to two-character names:

DISKEDIT.EXE can be renamed DE.EXE
SYSINFO.EXE can be renamed SI.EXE
SFORMAT.EXE can be renamed SF.EXE
SPEEDISK.EXE can be renamed SD.EXE
FILEFIND.EXE can be renamed FF.EXE

This will primarily benefit long-time Norton users who like abbreviations.

Additional program information

Calibrate

The following switches are not mentioned in the manual:

/BLANK   Turns the screen blanker on while performing Pattern Testing.
/NOCOPY   Don't make a duplicate copy of the track currently being tested.

DiskReet

DiskReet switches Switches are available to turn DiskReet off and on. The /OFF switch may be used from a batch file prior to executing a program that generates unwanted NDisk accesses (requests for a password).

For example, to load a disk-caching program like PCKWIK from Multisoft, you should include this command in the batch file (.BAT) prior to invoking the caching program. The syntax could look as follows:

```
C: \ NORTON \ DISKREET /OFF
C: \ PCKWCK \ SUPERPCK
C: \ NORTON \ DISKREET/ON
```

Note: The DISKREET /ON switch re-enables DiskReet. DiskReet with any other switch will also automatically re-enable DiskReet.

This technique can also be used if you are connected to a network and are using network utilities to locate network drives.

For example, MAP is a command which is used on NOVELL networks to locate network drives. Unfortunately, it also results in requests for DiskReet disk passwords. To disable password prompting, create a batch file similar to the following:

```
C: \ NORTON \ DISKREET /OFF
MAP
C: \ NORTON \ DISKREET /ON
```

XMS 2.0 support DiskReet fully complies with the Lotus, Intel, Microsoft, AST Extended Memory Specification (LIM XMS 2.0).

Some systems have available RAM in the address range above 640K and below the High Memory Area (HMA). This memory is referred to as Upper Memory Blocks (UMB). If the installed system supports this feature, DiskReet will take advantage of it. If DiskReet uses an UMB, under 1K of low memory will be used by DiskReet.

If you use a memory manager (e.g., QEMM or 386-MAX) to load programs into high DOS memory, you may wish to force DiskReet to avoid using UMB's by adding the /SKIPUMB switch. For example,

```
DEVICE = C: \ NORTON \ DISKREET.SYS /SKIPUMB
```

Use of the XMS High Memory Area When DiskReet uses the HMA, only 12K bytes of LOW memory are used. DiskReet will automatically use the HMA if it is available during initialization. To make this memory area available, you must include an XMS driver in the CONFIG.SYS file before the DISKREET.SYS line. The file HIMEM.SYS (available free from Microsoft) can be used.

If you intend to use Microsoft WINDOWS, DiskReet must not use the HMA. Add the /NOHMA switch to the DISKREET.SYS line. For example,

```
DEVICE = C: \ NORTON \ DISKREET.SYS /NOHMA
```

DiskReet will then leave the HMA free for Windows use. This switch can also be used to make more memory available for Desqview (using XDV).

To force DiskReet to always load into low memory, use both the /NOHMA and /SKIPUMB switches, and don't load the PCSHADOW.SYS driver. For example,

```
DEVICE = C:\NORTON\DISKREET.SYS /NOHMA /SKIPUMB
```

If you have network problems or are experiencing loss of characters during serial communications while using the HMA, you should add the /A200N switch to the DISKREET.SYS line in the CONFIG.SYS file.

```
DEVICE = C:\NORTON\DISKREET.SYS /A200N
```

This switch will eliminate the overhead incurred from enabling/disabling the A20 line. Note that this may cause other problems on some computers.

Support for COMPAQ 386 reserved memory   If you install DiskReet on a COMPAQ 386, DiskReet will use less than 900 bytes of low memory. A file PCSHADOW.SYS has been included on the distribution disks which serves this memory for DiskReet. If you use the installation program, CONFIG.SYS will be automatically updated. To enable use of this memory by DiskReet, the first line in your CONFIG.SYS should reference this new file.

```
DEVICE = C:\NORTON\PCSHADOW.SYS
```

Remember, it must be the first line in your CONFIG.SYS file. Note that if you are using Compaq's CEMM driver, the memory you save in DiskReet may be offset by the additional low memory used by the CEMM driver.

RAM drives   NDISKs can be created on RAM drives providing that the sector size is set to 512 bytes (the default is usually 256 bytes).

DiskReet's use of sounds   When using the audible prompt method to open an NDisk, you will hear different tunes. Because DiskReet cannot display its audit screen, a special tune that sounds similar to a European police car siren has been pre-selected to indicate that a prior access was attempted but failed. If you hear this sound, you should open NDisk manually (using DISKREET.EXE) in order to examine the audit information that contains a total count of failed accesses.

Install

During the install, the program will prompt the user as to whether or not the install program should rename DOS's FORMAT.COM to XXFORMAT.COM. If this step is completed and the user has DOS 4.xx, this will cause problems with the execution of DOS 4.xx BACKUP.COM. (DOS 4.xx looks for the presence of the file FORMAT.COM during its execution.) If this problem occurs, simply rename XXFORMAT.COM back to FORMAT.COM when using DOS 4.xx BACKUP.COM.

The Install program will prompt you as to whether or not you wish to install PCSHADOW. PCSHADOW is a reserved memory block manager for use with COMPAQ 386 class machines ONLY. If you have a COMPAQ 386 class machine and are using a memory manager (CEMM, QEMM or 386-MAX) you should *not* install PCSHADOW.

Custom tailoring of statements in AUTOEXEC.BAT and CONFIG.SYS files   The Install program can place several of the Utilities programs into your AUTOEXEC.BAT and/or CONFIG.SYS files if you wish. Many of the defaults for these programs may not be exactly what you want. If you want to fine-tune the statements that the Install program has added to your AUTOEXEC.BAT or CONFIG.SYS, you will need to manually edit the file yourself. You can use a text editor to do this. Please consult the documentation for the command line parameters you can use to tailor these programs.

Optimizing the scan at Install startup   You can lessen the time that it takes for the Install program to scan for previously installed files by making sure that

- you put all your Norton Utilities files into one directory.
- the "NU" environment variable is set. The Install program can do this for you. You'll need to set the NU variable to the directory that contains your Norton Utilities files.

Passwords   Please be aware that only one unique password can be set for ALL of the Norton Utilities files that are able to be password protected. For example, you are not able to set one password for NDD and another for UnFormat.

Archive file extraction errors   Several of the Norton Utilities programs are compressed into archive files. If you encounter an error during the extraction of the programs from the archive file, first try uncompressing them manually. Just launch the archive file with the destination drive and path name where you wish to install the Norton Utilities

Format: < Source Disk:Archive File Name > < Target Disk: \ Directory >

Example: A:NU5_ARC1.EXE C: \ NORTON

If you still encounter an error, here are the error codes and solutions:

Error Code   **Description**

1   Failed CRC. The archive file is defective.
    Solution: Contact Customer Service and request new disks.

2 & 3   Zipfile error. The archive file is corrupted.

Error Code	Description
	Solution: Contact Customer Service and request new disks.
4 – 8	Not enough memory. There wasn't enough available to launch the extraction program. *Solution:* Remove any memory resident programs (TSR's) and restart the install program.
9	File not found. The Install program couldn't find a particular archive file on the distribution disks. *Solution:* Contact Customer Service and request new disks.
10	Bad parameters. The parameters that the Install program sent to the archive file were incorrect. *Solution:* Contact Customer Service and request new disks.
11	No files to extract were found. *Solution:* Contact Customer Service and request new disks.
50	Disk is full. Norton Utilities 5.0 Full Install requires 2.5 megabytes. *Solution:* Choose another drive to install the Utilities on or create space on the drive by deleting files.
51	Unexpected EOF in the archive file. The archive file is corrupted. *Solution:* Contact Customer Service and request new disks.

Norton Cache

NCACHE only works on "normally connected" floppies. If a floppy drive requires a special interface board and/or a driver loaded in CONFIG.SYS, NCACHE probably won't be able to cache it. Most external drives are not supported by NCACHE.

NCACHE does contain special code to support Bernoulli Boxes, including the external models. Other removable hard disk are not supported.

Both the small and fast versions of Norton Cache will refuse to cache a floppy drive that does not have "Change Line" support. This is a hardware feature on the drive that tells the computer when a diskette has been removed. 360K drives often do not have a change line and thus cannot be cached. Most other drives (1.2M, 1.44M, etc.) will work fine.

NCACHE will automatically determine which drives can be cached. If a drive cannot be cached, NCACHE will either print "Cannot detect media change for this drive" or simply omit the drive from its status display.

For 8088 or 80286 based machines In order to use Expanded Memory (EMS) with NCACHE, you must have an Expanded Memory Manager that implements version 4 of the EMS specification (sometimes called the "LIM" specification). You must also have true EMS hardware and cannot use a software emulator like Above Disc.

If you have an older memory manager, check with your memory board manufacturer to see if an upgrade is available. In most cases, all you'll need is new memory manager software; no hardware changes will be required.

NCACHE will normally ignore EMS memory if you don't have the correct memory manager. If you run NCACHE with no parameters, it will simply skip over EMS and try to use extended or conventional memory instead. If you provide an explicit EXP = parameter, you will receive an error message and NCACHE will not install itself.

For users of Xerox Ventura Publisher One version of Ventura Publisher (VP) has problems working with NCACHE. The problems only occur with version 2.0 of the VP Standard Edition. Users of that version may encounter machine lock-ups during loading or "Internal Error 19" dialog boxes.

There are a number of ways to work around this problem. If you are loading NCACHE from the AUTOEXEC.BAT file or from the DOS command line, try loading it from CONFIG.SYS instead. If that doesn't work, try loading NCACHE before any other TSR's you are using. If you aren't using any TSR's, try loading an additional copy of COMMAND.COM after NCACHE and before VP.

If none of these changes solves the problem, you'll have no choice but to avoid running VP when NCACHE is loaded. Xerox Software actually recommends that you run VP Standard Edition on a machine by itself, with no extra drivers or TSR's. Future versions of VP (greater than 2.0) will have a different memory management system that should solve many driver/TSR problems.

Norton Disk Doctor II
The following switches are not mentioned in the manual:

/REBUILD   Rebuilds an entire disk that has been destroyed.
/UNDELETE   Undelete a DOS partition that was previously skipped.

SpeeDisk
The DOS CHKDSK report and SpeeDisk's Disk Information do not always agree on the number of files and directories on a disk, when in fact both are correct. The reasons are as follows:

- CHKDSK reports the number of hidden files and the number of user files separately; and the total of the sum of these will equal the number reported by SpeeDisk.
- CHKDSK reports the number of subdirectories on a disk but does not count the Root directory. SpeeDisk counts the Root as a directory, so it will always report one more directory than CHKDSK.

- CHKDSK reports the volume label as a hidden file of 0 length. SpeeDisk doesn't include the volume label as a file.

System Information

The following switches are not mentioned in the manual:

/AUTO	Unattended scrolling through and repeatedly displaying of ALL the System Information screens
/DEMO	Unattended scrolling only through the System Information Benchmark screens
/SUMMARY	Causes SysInfo to print the same information as SI v4.5 in a TTY display

UnErase

When in the View File window,

Scroll Left—CTRL+LEFT ARROW Key
Scroll Right—CTRL+RIGHT ARROW Key

WipeInfo

FileSave and DiskMon are automatically disabled when you use WipeInfo.

Compatibility Issues and Additional Considerations

Multitasking with MS-WINDOWS, DESQVIEW, etc.

In general, applications or commands that modify the file allocation table can cause unpredictable results when run under multi-tasking environments.

The following applications can be run directly from the DOS prompt:

Batch Enhancer
DiskEdit (should be run in read-only mode)
DiskReet (For NDisks to work properly the password prompting option must be set to manual open.)

When running under DESQVIEW or WINDOWS, you should:

- Make all NDisks manual-open only.
- Disable Quick Close.
- Disable Auto Close Timeout.
- Disable Screen Clear and Keyboard Lock.

In addition,

- Filefix may cause problems when unzapping a dBASE file

- As a general rule, FileSave should be turned on before loading Windows. Advanced users can manipulate drives independently from within separate instances of COMMAND.COM.
- Under Windows, NCC only affects the current instance of COMMAND-.COM.
- NCD only affects the current instance of COMMAND.COM System Info.
- Image should be run before loading Windows or Desqview.

Networks

This copy of the Norton Utilities is licensed for use by a single user on a single machine. For information on network and site licenses, please call the Peter Norton Computing sales department.

Manual Corrections and Changes

User's guide

Page 18, Paragraph 1

"By default, 11 of the programs are specified..." should be "By default, none of the programs are specified..."

Page 93, (Append to...)

Append to reads "Add the contents of the tagged file to another file you specify."

This is incorrect. Instead, it starts a Manual Unerase operation on the existing file (pre-adding the clusters in the file's allocation chain), adding new clusters to the file.

Page 158, Paragraph 1

There is incorrect information in the last sentence of the paragraph that reads "Also, with the system area protected, WipeInfo could not wipe an unused cluster without your permission." Actually, WipeInfo disables Disk Monitor, so any cluster can be wiped.

Pages 159–160

Disk Monitor refers to an option called "Allow Floppy Format" that should actually be "Allow Floppy Access."

Page 161, Paragraph 2

If a protected write occurs while the screen is in graphics mode—for example, while you are working with Windows—Disk Monitor can't pop up the dialog box. Instead, it automatically rejects the write operation. All you will hear is a beep. The application that was attempting the write should issue a "write-protect" or "access denied" error message.

Page 253, (NCD Function Keys)

F9 and F10 do not do what is described at the bottom of this page. They both simply access the menu bar.

Disk Explorer

Page 167 List at the Bottom of the Page

"DOS 4.xx" should be "DOS 4.xx and higher."

Problems, error messages, and solutions

In general, if things are not working the way you expect, check your AUTOEXEC.BAT. Some programs install a second path statement instead of correctly modifying the first one. Also, check that the NU and/or Norton environment variables are set to the directory where Norton Utilities 5.0 is installed. Many "strange" errors can occur if these variables are set to the wrong directory. Finally, check both AUTOEXEC.BAT and CONFIG.SYS for statements that you don't recognize or that look out of place.

Message: "Error obtaining directory information, insufficient memory."
Solution: Remove (unload) TSR's to free up RAM space. Remove some files from the directory (e.g., move files to another directory).

For lap top users

To improve the viewing quality of an LCD lap-top screen, you may type NORTON /LCD at the DOS prompt. The INSTALL program, however, will allow you to configure all the Utilities to automatically operate on LCD displays.

25
CHAPTER

Questions & answers

Questions on new edition

Some of the files on the distribution diskettes are compressed while others aren't. Why?

The Utilities that aren't compressed are the ones you might need during a recovery operation when you are denied access to your hard disk.

Three megabytes of disk space seems like a lot. Is it necessary to keep all of the Utilities on-line all of the time?

No. You will not need all of the Utilities all of the time. The Utilities on the first three diskettes are not compressed, and you can make copies which are immediately usable. Some of these Utilities need to be on-line all of the time. Some of the

Utilities which are compressed can also be copied to a diskette and kept in readiness that way. If you aren't going to keep all of the Utilities on-line, I'd recommend the following be kept on diskettes:

> CALIBRAT.EXE
> SYSINFO.EXE
> WIPEINFO.EXE
> NCC.EXE (Norton Control Center)
> FILEFIX.EXE (unless you are a database user)
> DISKREET.EXE (if you don't need encrypting)
> DISKMON.EXE (if you only run distribution diskettes)
> NCACHE-x.EXE (the cache Utility you aren't using)

The space savings is only about 1 megabyte, but that might make it easier to keep from running out of disk space so soon.

Some of the Utilities in the last version aren't in this new version. Can I still keep them and use them?

Yes. The INSTALL program will not delete or overwrite the Utilities that aren't in this new version. Utilities like Undelete Directory (UD) may not be worth saving, while LinePrint (LP) may. It depends largely on which of the older Utilities you've found to be most useful.

Will it be necessary for me to make any changes in my Batch Enhancer (BE) batch files with this new version?

No. All of your existing BE batch files will be able to run unchanged with this new version. The only changes you might want to consider are those which will allow you to use the new enhancements.

Will there ever be a time when all of the Utilities will run on a network as multi-user programs?

I really don't know. Most developers have different licensing arrangements for single-user versus multi-user versions of their programs. We can only wait and see what happens.

If I have both DOS and UNIX on the same machine, will I need both versions of the Utilities?

If you want to be able to use the Utilities on your DOS partition and on your UNIX partition, you will need a copy of each version.

Questions from earlier editions

Just how much or how little can be recovered or changed using one of the Norton Utilities?

With FR (Format Recover), it's possible to recover everything on a hard disk regardless of size. Using UD (Unremove Directory), it's possible to recover an entire subdirectory. QU (Quick UnErase) can usually recover every file that hasn't been overwritten. When all else fails, NU (Norton Utility) can recover or restore every bit by byte.

I need to recover a large group of files. What is the best way to do it? None of them have been overwritten.

Try QU first. If the only thing missing is the first letter of the filename, you should be able to recover the files almost as fast as they were deleted. If any of the files are corrupted, you may have to use the slower technique of recovery using NU.

After reformatting my hard disk, I can't get it to boot the system.

Try booting from a floppy in the A drive, and then run NDD. Your problem could be attributed to a few things. First, the necessary system files may not be on the hard disk. Second, one of the files may have been corrupted in some way. NDD will diagnose the problem and provide a recommendation or solution for most of the more common problems.

My list of directories and subdirectories is so long that it runs off the screen.

Using the /Wide switch with the DOS DIR command will compress the listing by a factor of 4 by displaying it 5-wide rather than 1-wide. You can also use the /Pause switch; then the system will wait after each full screen of listing until you press a key. If your directory structure doesn't change too often, you might want to make a hardcopy using the DOS TREE utility or LD (List Directories).

I can't remember where all of my files are stored. Also, I'm not sure if I have duplicated filenames in different subdirectories. Is there any way I can find everything?

The FF (FileFind) Utility with *.* as the filename and the /All switch active will display everything. Also, you can redirect the output to your printer and have a hardcopy of every file in every subdirectory on all of the drives in your system. Be warned that this procedure will take a bit of time, though.

My disks are getting full. I need some way to make sure that I'm getting the most out of the space. Also, is there an easy way to download selected files to a floppy for storage?

SD (SpeeDisk) will remove all fragmenting so that the slack space is minimal. If you have a backup utility program, you can use FA (File Attributes) to turn the ARCHIVE flag on or off so that you can sort the files by name or extension as you download. The DOS BACKUP utility program is always available if you have nothing else. Just remember that all of the backup utilities use a format that prohibits running that file from the floppy. The file must be restored before it is run again. In some ·cases, a compression utility like ARC or PKZIP can be used to reduce the space needed by the files to be downloaded.

Will TS (Text Search) find any text I want to look for?

Yes, with qualifications. TS isn't case-sensitive, so the capitalization isn't necessary. It is context-sensitive, however, which means that you will have to enter the exact wording or use the DOS wildcard characters. When you use the wildcards, you may find more than one match. I'd also recommend that you try to keep the search string short. The longer the string, the longer it will take to search all of the files. One other limitation: the search string must be in ASCII format if you enter an ASCII-format string.

What tests can I run on a diskette before I use it to ensure that I can recover all of the data that I copy onto it?

I'd recommend that you first run WipeDisk on that diskette and then format it using the SF (SafeFormat) utility. This should give you the best possible conditions for safely storing. Just don't think that it will be there forever, regardless of how carefully you protect the diskettes.

How can I keep SD (SpeeDisk) from moving every file every time I run that Utility?

Within SD, there is an option for you to list the way you want the files ordered when SD runs. If you are going to use this option, don't also use the DS (Directory Sort) Utility as a part of your AUTOEXEC.BAT file that runs when you boot up.

If you have both program and data files in the same subdirectory, you might want to force all of the program files (*.EXE, *.COM, etc.) to the top of the directory. This will allow them to remain unfragmented.

If I send a friend a disk, could he discover what I've been using it for?

Maybe. If he has the Norton Utilities and if he wants to take the time, he could recover every byte that hasn't been overwritten by the files you downloaded to send him. One sure way to prevent anybody from ever being able to recover anything from one of your discarded disks is to run WipeDisk on it. You cannot recover data from a diskette that has been wiped.

Why have a WipeDisk and a WipeFile Utility?

WipeDisk removes everything from the diskette, including the format. WipeFile removes only the data, but the format is left intact. Also, if you have only one file to erase, it seems a shame to have to wipe out everything, assuming that there were only the WipeDisk Utility.

What other useful information (beyond a speed comparison) can I get by running SI (System Information)?

Along with the type and copyright date of the processor and coprocessor (if present), SI displays the addresses of the various portions of memory present. You can also discover how many logical drives that system will support. I've seen from 3 to 6 logical drives on various PCs over the years.

Why have the LP (LinePrint) Utility?

Before the days of sophisticated compilers, printouts of code were less than elegant. Even today, much of the text downloaded from bulletin boards hasn't been formatted for printing. LP makes that chore easier, especially when you want to put the printout in a binder or loose-leaf notebook.

If I don't use VL (Volume Label) to delete the label on a disk, is there any other way to get rid of it?

Yes. You can use NU (Norton Utility) and delete it. VL is by far the easier and safer way to do it.

Do I have to write a batch file to use one or more of the stopwatches available?

No. You can start, read, and stop any or all of the stopwatches with a single command-line entry. This information can also be redirected to a disk file or the printer if it would be more useful there.

If I set a background and a foreground color for my system, will all of the programs I run keep that combination?

I'd guess that few, if any, will use your choice of colors. Many programs have their own color change routines in the setup portion of the program. If they don't, you may have to live with the programmer's choice of colors.

I don't want the last screen of figures left on display when I finish one project. How can I prevent this?

Write a short .BAT file to clear the screen when that program is done. You could also add a few lines and have BEEP notify you that the end has arrived.

If something happens to my hard disk, is all of my data lost?

Depending on the circumstances, you have the possibility of recovering from 0 to 100% of the data. Begin your recovery attempt by booting from a floppy copy of DOS, and then run NDD. Complete your recovery attempt by using NU to gather the last bytes up. One of the best ways to keep the cost of hard-disk crashes to a minimum is to back all of your data up at very regular intervals.

Can I use the Norton Utilities on my Bernoulli box disks?

Yes. The Norton Utilities are fully Bernoulli box compatible, as of version 3.1.

Are the Norton Utilities hard to install?

They shouldn't be. There is an INSTALL program present on the distribution disk that takes all of the pain and most of the problem out of installing the Utilities. This began with version 4.0 and continues.

Can I get the Norton Utilities on any other media?

Yes. They are distributed on both 360K/5.25″ and 720K/3.5″ diskettes.

Is there any difference in the operation of the Utilities with different monitors?

The Utilities operate the same regardless of the monitor. If the monitor is monochrome, you may not see some of the differences in color, but you will still be able to distinguish the bold letters. You may also get a black and white display on a color monitor of a Utility if it is unable to locate a copy of ANSI.SYS when it initializes. ANSI.SYS is the DOS utility which provides the color drivers to the various programs.

If ">" and "> >" will redirect the Utility's output to the printer, why should I use the /LOG or /REPORT switch?

Redirecting the screen display to the printer doesn't add the linefeed and carriage return characters to some lines. Thus, they overprint, sometimes making it impossible to read any of the characters.

How long after a file has been deleted can you still expect to recover it?

As long as the data remains on the disk, it can be recovered. Even if other files have been written to that disk, you may be able to recover data. Time isn't as much a factor as what activity has occurred. I still have a few floppies that I am not using that have fully recoverable files on them, although the files were deleted over a year ago.

DOS lets me rename files. Can I also rename subdirectories?

Yes, you can; but not with the DOS rename command. Use NCD and press F6 when you have the highlight bar over the subdirectory name you want to change. NCD also makes it much easier to move between subdirectories as well as to make or delete them.

Can the C > prompt be eliminated completely?

Yes. Using the BE ASK shell Utility, it is possible to eliminate the DOS prompt until you want it. This technique is often used where there are less qualified operators using the systems. By developing a good shell program, you can keep the need for computer training to a minimum and concentrate on the training they need to get the work done.

Another aspect of using a shell is that you can prevent the operator from making major mistakes. The shell doesn't allow copying or deleting of any files and can also restrict the access to others. Data security is in many ways more important than the physical security of the equipment.

Be sure to consider ease of operation when planning to use workers of low skill levels. You want them to get the work done quickly, but you don't want them to be able to make mistakes that will cost hours to correct. You also don't want much of the information carried out of the office on paper, disk, or brain.

Is there any need to use SD (SpeeDisk) on a floppy?

The need is a function of how the data is placed on the disk. If you copy the data from another disk (hard or floppy), it has been unfragmented. If you use DISKCOPY to make the copy, then any fragmentation present on the first disk is present on the second one. If it is a data file that is being used and changed regularly, then SD will improve things. Using SD will also allow you to organize the files so that fragmenting is kept to a minimum.

Can any of these techniques be used on a system with only two floppy drives?

Yes. With a little thought and planning, you can use most of them. I have "start-up" diskettes for those applications which I still run on a double-floppy system. Each diskette is bootable and contains a .BAT file to prepare the system for that application. While it may not be the most efficient way of doing things, it has worked for me for a long time now.

26
CHAPTER

The dissected disk

Discussing the dissected disk

Now that the Norton Disk Doctor (NDD) program checks many things automatically, you need to know more about your hard disk. Then you can use the Norton Utility (NU) more efficiently to correct problems that were discovered but not corrected by NDD. In order to help you, I'm going to build a simple hard disk. It will be simple because it will consist only of word pictures—no chips, no wires, and no software.

A 40 megabyte hard drive is common enough, so I'll use that size. The 5.25″ form factor is still the most common, so I'm going to choose that size also. 5.25″ floppy disks come in five configurations; 160 kilobytes, 180 kilobytes, 320 kilobytes, 360 kilobytes, and 1.2 megabytes. Their capacity is dependent upon their physical characteristics and the hardware or software doing the reading or writing.

The first difference between an individual floppy disk and a hard-disk drive is the material being coated. The basic material in a floppy disk is a thin sheet of

Mylar. For a hard disk, this changes to a somewhat thicker sheet of metal. Next, the number of disks in the drive changes. Floppies are inserted and used one at a time, while a hard drive has a number of disks in it. I'm going to assume that there are four disks in our drive. These disks are mounted on a shaft that has a bearing at one end and a motor at the other. Spacers between the disks provide room for the read/write heads to move over the disk. The read/write heads are attached to arms, for which there is one for each side of each disk. These heads actually ride on the media of a floppy disk. On a hard disk, they remain a very, very short distance above the media. This distance is usually measured in microinches (with 1.001″ being one microinch). In more visible terms, the distance is about the thickness of one very fine baby hair.

A floppy disk spins at 300 RPM (revolutions per minute), so there isn't too much heat buildup or wearing of the media or head. Hard disks normally spin at 3,600 RPM, however; and at this speed, the wear and heat caused by friction become very significant problems.

$5.25'' \times 3.14159 \times 300RPM = 4{,}948.008''/min$ at the rim.
This is just over 4.6 MPH (miles per hour).

$5.25'' \times 3.14159 \times 3600RPM = 59{,}376.101''/min$
This is just over 56.2 MPH.

Disk wear might be one of the problems you come across when running one of your favorite programs from a floppy disk. The surface speed under the head decreases as the head moves closer to the hub. If I assume that the head is about 1″ from the center at its nearest point, then the disk is still traveling over 21 MPH. Perhaps this is why when a head comes in contact with the disk, it is said to have "crashed." Personally, I wouldn't want my head to come in contact with anything traveling at that speed.

Friction isn't the only source of heat in a hard drive. The motor that spins the disks also creates quite a bit of heat. By keeping the motor and the disks separated, the heat can be carried away by the system fan. All materials tend to expand as they are warmed, which means that the disks, the heads, and the arms holding the heads will increase in size as they get hotter. This would be less of a problem if they were all made of the same material; but because they aren't, they expand by different amounts for each degree of temperature change.

All of this should give you some indication of the complexity of a hard-disk drive. Part of the cost of making these drives goes to pay for the "clean room" which is required. This clean room is a special environment that contains almost no dirt of any kind. Because people are in the room, however, and because they breathe, the room is never "absolutely" clean. Just one of the filters used to try to keep the air in this room pure can cost over $400.00. In addition, these are throwaway filters that must be changed regularly.

So far, my hard disk drive consists of 4 metal disks inside a metal box with a motor to spin them at 3,600 RPM, 8 read/write heads mounted on movable arms held very close to the metal disks, and a coating on both sides of each disk which can be magnetized. This coating is in reality more than just a fine powdered rust, but that description will do for now. Still necessary are the means to write and read information to this disk system.

How do you write to a rust-covered metal disk spinning at 3,600 RPM? One answer might be "very carefully." The more correct answer is magnetically. What form does this magnetic writing take? Letters or numbers are out of the question. About the best we can hope for are little spots of magnetized material separated by small spots of unmagnetized material. If the unmagnetized spots equal zeros and the magnetized spots equal ones, binary information can be written to the disk. Once written there, how can it be found again?

Maybe you have already guessed. This is where formatting comes into play. Before using the DOS FORMAT command or the Norton Utility Safe Format program, the disks must be prepared. There are a number of programs which do a low level format/initialization of a hard disk. HFORMAT, WFORMAT, etc., along with separate floppy disk program packs like Disk Manager prepare the disk to accept data. So what do these programs do?

They magnetically define the tracks and sectors on each disk face. A *track* is a thin circle around the disk which will accept the information to be written. Each track is a concentric circle. The first, or 0, track is near the outside edge of the disk. There is a 0 track on each side of each disk. To distinguish these tracks, the sides are numbered 0 and 1. This means that the first disk has a side 0/ track 0 and also a side 1/ track 0. A *sector* is a portion of a track with its own address. The number of sectors per track varies; floppy disks have 8 or 9, but most hard disks have 17. All of the sectors in the 0 tracks on all of the disks form a *cylinder*. My hard disk has a total of 733 cylinders between the rim and the hub.

With a capacity of 512 bytes per sector, I can calculate the total capacity of this hard-disk drive (733 cylinders × 17 sectors × 512 bytes = 6,380,032 bytes). This value describes a single side of a single disk. There are 7 sides available on the disks of this drive, so 6,380,032 bytes × 7 sides = 44,660,224 bytes total (44 megabytes in round numbers). The eighth side is part of the arm-positioning system; with over 400 tracks per inch (TPI), there is very little room for positioning error.

For this discussion "hard drive," "hard disk," "fixed disk," "hard disk drive," and "fixed disk drive" are used interchangeably. Their strict definitions do separate them, but that's a bit too technical for us right now. At 512 bytes per sector, a 44,660,224 byte hard drive has 87,227 sectors (17 sectors × 7 sides × 733 tracks = 87,227). This requires 87,227 addresses if each sector is to be located/relocated. At one time, DOS had a limitation of 65,535 addresses, which limited the size of a fixed disk to 65,535 addresses × 512 bytes or 33,553,920 bytes. Now you know the real reason why there was a 32 megabyte limit for DOS hard drives. Attempting to keep a record of every sector's contents creates a burden on the system. Also, it takes time to find an address, read the information, get another address, read that information, etc. Rephrased, the heads have to move from an address directory to that location and back for every 512 bytes to be read/written. This back and forth movement could be halved if two sectors were grouped into one entity. A *cluster* is that entity and may be 2 or more sectors in length. The larger the cluster, the more bytes per address.

This may sound like a great idea for getting more disk space without having to solve the addressing problem. In a way it does get more space. However, what happens if a file isn't as big as the cluster? Assume that the cluster is eight sectors (4,096 bytes) long. An AUTOEXEC.BAT file of 128 bytes is written to this disk and is placed in the first available cluster. Another .BAT file of 100 bytes is then added. The next address is the next cluster, so it is written into that location. A quick review of what has just happened will reveal one of the problems faced by users of hard disks with large cluster sizes. A total of 228 bytes of information have been written to the disk and a total of 8,192 bytes of storage space have been used. Agreed, a file of up to 4,096 bytes will occupy one cluster and a file of 4,097 to 8,192 bytes will occupy two clusters.

The unused space in each cluster is the "slack" space that is reported by File-Size. This is not the same information reported by SpeeDisk in its Disk Statistics screen under "number of fragmented files." Fragmentation is the separation of the clusters belonging to one file from each other. They don't physically move; there just wasn't any space immediately available for more information when it was added. DOS writes information to the disk one cluster at a time and always writes to the next available cluster.

Ways and means of placing more information on a disk are being researched continuously. Some of the ideas being considered are ways to maintain the data density at a constant level from hub to rim. On a 5.25″ disk, the sector at the rim is about 2.33 times the length of a sector near the hub. A change in the speed of rotation or the speed of information transfer could be used to maintain a constant data density. Changing the track width and reducing the width of the blank space between tracks could also increase a disk's capacity. Technologies like lasers are making giant strides toward very high density disks.

My verbal hard drive now has the capacity to hold just over 40 megabytes of information, and I have a plan which will allow me to locate all of these bytes on the disk. With the disks sealed in a metal, there is no way that I can physically mark off and number each of the sectors. You can do this electronically, however, with a formatting program. FORMAT does more than just number the sectors.

At the very beginning of the disk, sector 0 on side 0, FORMAT establishes what operating system format is being used and whether or not the physical disk has been divided logically. If there is a division, then the user will see more than one disk drive when using the system. These are logical drives rather than multiple physical pieces of hardware. The number of logical partitions available is dependent upon the physical capacity of the hard drive and the programming available in the O/S. This first information area of the disk is known as the *Partition Table*. Floppy disks do not have Partition Tables.

Even when space isn't a consideration, partitioning may be desirable. Many computer systems can use more than one O/S. For more reasons than I fully understand, it is necessary to keep operating systems and their associated programs and files separated. Therefore, a partition is established for each type of O/S being used. Partitioning within an O/S area is also possible if there is adequate space on the physical drive. Given the need and the hardware, it would be possible to have UNIX, MS-DOS, and O/S2 all loaded into one hard drive.

Immediately following the Partition Table is the area known as the *File Allocation Table* (FAT). The FAT is the road map to the information stored on this disk. As each file is written onto the disk, the cluster addresses/numbers used are written into the table. For security reasons, DOS writes a second copy of the FAT on the next section of the disk. This second copy of the FAT may be useful during data recovery operations. Norton Disk Doctor (NDD) compares the FATs as one of its tests.

Following the FATs is the directory area. A portion of the information contained in this area is displayed when the DOS command DIRECTORY (DIR) is used. All of the information kept in this area may be viewed by using the Norton Utility (NU). After the directory area comes the file storage area. This area is the balance of the space available on the disk(s).

Before too much information is written onto this hard disk, I'd better make sure there is a way to check for errors. The errors I'm most interested in are information errors. Along with the 512 bytes of information and the address of the sector, each sector also has space for a *Cyclic Redundancy Check* (CRC) number, which is a calculated value based on the value of all of the bytes written to that sector. Remember that all of this writing and reading is being done in binary form. A way to develop a CRC number would be to count up the number of "1s" that are in the sector. Each time the information in that sector changes, the CRC number will change. The CRC checksum number is used for more than just error checking during data transfers. The /V in conjunction with the COPY command or the FORMAT command uses the CRC to verify instead of checking every bit/ byte.

It is possible to develop the same CRC checksum from two different strings of binary information. This being true, it is then possible to have incorrect information in a sector with a correct CRC checksum. The probability of this happening is very remote, however. The fact that it can be done, though, should be warning enough to those who work with sensitive data.

Why worry about all of this stuff? Why complicate things when the real desire is to be able to store information on a hard disk and use it whenever necessary? Knowing how things can go wrong and where to look for the broken parts makes recovering from an accident easier. Remember, disk drives are mechanical devices. Mechanical and electrical components are very seldom perfect and are made within a tolerance. A *tolerance* is the amount over or under size that the part is allowed to be and still work properly with the other parts or components. The electrical power that comes into our homes and offices also has tolerance. Combining all of these variables means that errors and accidents are possible. Error-checking and backup copies together with recovery techniques help to reduce the damage done when trouble strikes. The most necessary ingredient for recovery can't be purchased or imparted. It is called patience: patience to learn, to follow directions, and to take one step at a time.

Version 5.0 update

The number of significant changes that have been made in the way hard disks operate are very few. For the most, these changes have been confined to improving the quality of the hardware. The software changes have made the way we see hard disks somewhat different. We have no more 32 megabyte barrier to disk size, and the number of physical/logical disks has been increased.

All of these changes tend to make it easier to forget that the basics are unchanged. The mechanical and electrical components are still imperfect and they still fail. Failures are still "when" situations, which makes a strict backup program an even greater necessity today.

There are a few hard disk management schemes that the Utilities do not "read through," which can mean that when a crash occurs, the information on that portion of a logical disk or the entire physical disk will be lost. The data recovery services are still alive and doing well. They continue to thrive because of users and manager who do not back up their disks. I don't begrudge recovery services their livelihood but just feel that they are becoming more necessary than should be expected.

One of the newer developments which may make a number of changes in data storage is the new line of read/write optical disks. When information is written to these disks, it is much less susceptible to damage than any magnetic media. The write-once read-many (WORM) optical disks should continue to function as archives and for the distribution of copyrighted reference material. Combined with the newer technology, the total amount of on-line storage can become more than most users will need or be able to index. Based on a "round" number of 600 megabytes per disk and the possibility of having 20 of these disks connected, the on-line storage figure becomes 12,000,000,000 bytes. Twelve gigabytes of information to maintain can become a full-time task in itself.

Also, the usual newer and faster computers are being introduced everyday. Like hard disks, their basics remain similar. Their increased power does provide users with an expanded capability where needed. The introduction of optical busses promises to change some of those basics. I would also expect some changes in the basics of microprocessors before the end of this new decade. The "mainframe on a desk" concept is almost a reality today. The "supercomputer on a desk" is only a matter of time.

The increases in the interconnection of computers will continue, as will the need for information security and the amount of personal information available on computer. Unfortunately, the possibilities for abuse of this information will also increase.

Only one aspect of computing seems to be decreasing: the amount of personal interaction. By this, I mean the need to come face-to-face with other people. While doing some research on another project, I totaled the number of people I meet with physically and the number of people I meet electronically. The electronic acquaintances are outnumbering the physical ones. The only redeeming feature of this is that the number of physical acquaintances is still increasing. There are those who are letting their face-to-face relationships die in favor of electronic relationships. Isolated humans do not thrive over time; we require the physical presence of other humans to live. Our survival may well depend on our ability to balance the increased efficiency of computer interconnectedness with the requirement for interpersonal relationships.

The other danger of becoming too computer-dependent may come in the form of having too much time to do other things but not knowing what to do. Vacations and leisure time are not luxuries but necessities. Still, too much of anything, even something good and necessary, is just as bad as not enough. It may soon be proven that too much leisure time is more harmful than helpful.

Chromatic scale

Note	Octave	Frequency	Note	Octave	Frequency
C	1	33	C	3	131
C#	1	35	C#	3	138
D	1	37	D	3	147
D#	1	39	D#	3	156
E	1	41	E	3	165
F	1	44	F	3	175
F#	1	46	F#	3	185
G	1	49	G	3	196
G#	1	52	G#	3	208
A	1	55	A	3	220
A#	1	58	A#	3	233
B	1	62	B	3	247
C	2	65	C	4	262
C#	2	69	C#	4	277
D	2	73	D	4	294
D#	2	78	D#	4	311
E	2	82	E	4	330
F	2	87	F	4	349
F#	2	93	F#	4	370
G	2	98	G	4	392
G#	2	104	G#	4	415
A	2	110	A	4	440
A#	2	117	A#	4	466
B	2	123	B	4	494

Note	Octave	Frequency	Note	Octave	Frequency
C	5	523	C	7	2093
C#	5	554	C#	7	2217
D	5	587	D	7	2349
D#	5	622	D#	7	2489
E	5	659	E	7	2637
F	5	698	F	7	2794
F#	5	740	F#	7	2960
G	5	784	G	7	3136
G#	5	831	G#	7	3322
A	5	880	A	7	3520
A#	5	932	A#	7	3729
B	5	988	B	7	3951
C	6	1047	C	8	4186
C#	6	1109	C#	8	4435
D	6	1175	D	8	4699
D#	6	1245	D#	8	4978
E	6	1329	E	8	5274
F	6	1397	F	8	5588
F#	6	1480	F#	8	5920
G	6	1568	G	8	6272
G#	6	1661	G#	8	6645
A	6	1760	A	8	7040
A#	6	1865	A#	8	7459
B	6	1976	B	8	7902

Epilogue

If you have a modem, you are already familiar with the fantastic and expanding world of electronic communications. For those of you who haven't taken the plunge yet, give it serious consideration.

Almost everything you might want to know is accessible via a modem. Direct links to home, office, a university, friend, or a bulletin board can put you in touch with the world. Of these, free and subscription bulletin board services provide the greatest variety of information. I have been a regular participant on the DELPHI system for over 7 years. Although I have written portions of the manual used by other Information Providers, SIG Managers, or SYSOPs, I continue to discover new features.

As I have mentioned earlier, I am a member of DELPHI. My username is ELLISCO, and I'm on-line almost every evening. If you have any questions, comments, constructive criticisms, etc., just leave me a mail message. If no response is required, I will at least acknowledge receiving your message.

Index

A

archived files, 2, 3, 101, 103, 310, 320
ASCII files
  string search, TextSearch (TS), 126
  view file, DiskEdit, 59
ASK, Batch Enhancer (BE), interactive batch files, 16-26, 40, 323
attribute changes to files
  ATTRIB.COM, 100
  DiskEdit, 60
  File Attribute (FA), 100-104
AUTOEXEC.BAT, 314-315
  contents of file, System Information, 253-254, 264
  customization procedure, 309
  editing, 4, 7

B

backup schemes, 1-3, 91-92, 200, 278-279, 320
bad clusters/sectors
  DiskTest (DT), 199
  Disk Tool, 90
  SpeeDisk, 225, 232
Batch Enhancer (BE), 15-40, 304, 318
  ASK, interactive batch files, 16-26
  BEEP utility, 27-28
  BOX utility, 28-30
  GOTO command, 15-16

Screen Attributes Utility, 31-38
batch files
  command definitions, 19
  editing, Save/Discard option, ASK, 26
  filename directory, 19
  interactive, ASK, Batch Enhancer (BE), 16-26
  nested, 20-22
  renaming, 19
  view characters, Explore Disk option, ASK, 22-26
BEEP utility, 27-28, 38-39, 322, 333-334
Bernoulli box use, 322
boot record, view, DiskEdit, 59
bootable disks, creation, Disk Tool, 89
BOX utility, Batch Enhancer (BE), 28-30, 40
  clear screen (CLS), 29
  cursor position (ROWCOL), 30
  DELAY, user-set, 29, 304
  repeated characters (PRINT-CHAR), 29-30
  text inside, 39-40
  WINDOWs, 30
bulletin-board systems, 79

C

cache programs, 9, 311-312
  Calibrate Utility usage, 45
  Disk Cache, 177-183
Calibrate Utility, 9, 41-50, 307

cache programs warning, 45
command-line switches, 41-42
compatibility with hardware/software, 42-43
drive-exclusive test, 42-44
error messages, 46
interleave test, 48-49
low-level format, 42, 47-48
monitoring test processes, 45
network use, 42
optimizing speed of hard disk, 42-43
order of tests, 50
pattern test, 42, 47-49
report generation, 42
seek tests, 41, 46
selecting individual tests, 50
speed of hard disk test, 46-47
surface test of hard disk, 49
CHKDSK, 312
chromatic scale, tonefiles, 333-334
clear screen (CLS), 29, 304
clock setting, (NCC), 158, 163-164, 171-173, 321
CLS, Batch Enhancer, 29, 304
clusters
  bad clusters/sectors, 90, 199, 225, 232
  Disk Information (DI), 271
  hard disk management, 328
CMOS value panel, System Information, 246-247, 261
color selection, 4, 6, 321

color section (*con't.*)

Norton Control Center (NCC), 159-160, 168-169

Screen Attributes, 31-38

comments added to filename, File Information (FI), 112-116

compatibility issues, 42-43, 186, 313

compressed utilities, 2, 3, 10-11, 317-318

CompuServe, 79

computer requirements, 11

CONFIG.SYS, 314-315

contents, viewing, 254, 264

customization procedure, 309

editing, 4, 7

copying Norton Utilities, 1-3

corrupted files

recovery (Disk Tool), 89

recovery (FileFix), 9, 127-129

country information setting, 164

CPU processing speed, System Information, 250-252, 255

crash recovery (*see* hard disk management)

cross-linked files

prevention, WipeDisk, 297

recovery, Quick UnErase, 282

cursors

appearance, Norton Control Center (NCC), 159, 167

position, ROWCOL, BOX utility, 30

cyclic redundancy check (CRC), hard disk management, 329

cylinders, hard disks, 327

D

date stamps (*see* time/date stamps)

dBASE files

corruption recovery, 9, 127-129

erasure recovery, 8

DEC encryption, 10, 81

DELAY, 29, 304

DELPHI on-line service, xii, 79

DEMO programs, 7

DESQVIEW, multitasking/ compatibility, 313

device drivers list, System Information, 262

DIR command, 89, 200-202, 319

directories/subdirectories, 319

change and edit, DiskEdit, 57

change and edit, Norton Change Directory, 147-155

comments after filenames, 116

complete file erasure (Wipe-Disk), 291-302

complete file erasure (WipeInfo), 10, 291-302

damage-repair, Norton Utility (NU), 64

delete/undelete, Norton Change Directory (NCD), 153

delete/undelete, Norton Utility (NU), 154

diagnosis and analysis, Norton Disk Doctor, 194

DIR will not list files, 89, 200-202

erased, recovery (Unremove Directory), 283

hidden subdirectories, 104, 151

list, List Directory (LD), 120-124, 319

Quick UnErase, 280-282

rename, 323

reordering, SpeeDisk, 229, 233, 234

root directories, 66-67, 109-110, 271

slack space reduction, 118-119

sorting, Directory Sort (DS), 236-241

space occupied by files, File-Size, 116-120

subdirectory deletion, Norton Change Directory (NCD), 151

subdirectory-only view, File-Find, 110-111

tree structure, Norton Change Directory (NCD), 149-150

UnErase files, 275-283

utility listing, Norton Integrator, 207-210

version comparison, 4.0, 4.5, 5.0, 11-13

Directory Sort (DS), 236-241

Disk Cache, 177-183

BUFFERS configuration settings, 182

command line format, 178

FASTOPEN configuration settings, 182

network use, 181

parameters, 178-181

Disk Doctor, 185-202

command line format, 185

compatibility, 186

DIR will not list known files, 200-202

Disk Doctor II, 186-191

DiskTest (DT), 197-200

installation, 185

limitations, 186

network usage, 186

Norton Disk Doctor (NDD), 191-197

switch options, 186

Disk Doctor II, 8, 11, 13, 186-191

message transmittal, Custom Message option, 188-189

skipping tests, 189-199

surface test, 188

test display screen, 190

test procedure, 187-188, 187

test results screen, 191

Disk Explorer, 314

Disk Index (DI), 265

Disk Information (DI), 65-66, 270-274

Disk Monitor (DM), 75-80

Disk Tool, 9, 11, 13, 87-92

backup copies, 91-92

bad clusters, 90

bootable disk creation, 89

command line format, 87

corrupted file recovery, 89

DOS unreadable files, recovery, 89

network use, 87

Rescue Diskette creation, Disk Tool, 90-91

tools selection, 88

DiskEdit, 11, 13, 51-74

attribute changes, Set Attributes, 60

boot record viewing, 59

command line format, 52

comparing objects, 61

default option selection, 54-55

directory editing, 57

File Allocation Table (FAT) viewing, 58

linking feature, 53-54

map of clusters used, 59

network use, 52
Norton Utility (NU), version
  4.0 and 4.5, 61-74
objects to view/modify, 52
Partition Table viewing, 59
quitting, 61-62
saving corrections, 56
time/date stamps, 60
Tools Pull-Down menu, 59
viewing options, hex vs.
  ASCII, 56-57, 59
WordStar files, 55
diskettes
  backup copies, 1-3, 91-92,
    200, 278-279, 320
  bad clusters/sectors, 90, 199,
    225, 232
  bootable disk creation, Disk
    Tool, 89
  capacity setting, Norton Disk
    Doctor (NDD), 196-197
  care and handling, 200
  complete erasure (WipeDisk;
    WipeInfo), 10, 291-302
  defective, repairing (Disk
    Tool), 9, 87-92
  defective, repairing, Norton
    Disk Doctor, 195-196
  error corrections (DiskEdit), 9,
    51-74
  formatting errors, Format
    Recovery, 287-290
  formatting errors, FRECOVER,
    286-290
  formatting errors, SafeFormat,
    10, 13, 211-217, 273-274,
    286, 320
  formatting errors, UnFormat,
    285-290
  space occupied by files, File-
    Size, 116-120
  SpeeDisk use, 323
  test for damage, DiskTest (DT),
    197-200
  Volume Labels (VL), 153-155
DiskReet, 10, 81-86
  audible (tones) prompt, 309
  command line format, 82
  Compaq reserved memory
    support, 309
  Extended Memory Specifica-
    tion (XMS) support, 308
  keyboard lock, 85-86

NDisks, 83-86, 309
  network use, 82
  passwords, 82-83
  switches, 307-309
DiskTest (DT), 197-200
  CHKDSK vs., 199
  command line format, 198
  switches and options, 199-200
DOS interface, xi-xii
DOS System Area, System Information, 250, 251, 262

E

editing, 4,6
electronic data transfer, 79
encryption utility (DiskReet), 10,
  81-86
environment settings, 321
  AUTOEXEC.BAT, 4, 7, 253-
    254, 264, 309, 314-315
  clock time, 158, 163-164, 171-
    173
  CMOS value panel, 246-247,
    261
  colors selection, 4, 6, 31-38,
    159-160, 168-169
  CONFIG.SYS, 4, 7, 253-254,
    264, 309, 314-315
  country, 164
  CPU processing speed, System
    Information, 250-252, 255
  cursor, 159, 167
  device drivers list, System
    Information, 262
  DOS System Area, 250, 251,
    262
  graphics selection, 4, 6-7
  hardware interrupts, System
    Information, 245-246
  keyboard speed, Norton Con-
    trol Center (NCC), 161-162,
    170
  memory usage summary, Sys-
    tem Information, 250, 251,
    261
  mouse speed, Norton Control
    Center (NCC), 161-162
  Norton Control Center (NCC),
    10, 157-175
  partition table, System Informa-
    tion, 248-249, 264

serial port selection, Norton
  Control Center (NCC), 161,
  170-171
software interrupts, System
  Information, 246-247
TSR programs list, System
  Information, 262
video card, System Information, 244-245, 257-261
video mode selection, Norton
  Control Center (NCC), 161,
  170
erased file recovery, 319, 323
  protect from overwrite (File-
    Save), 9, 131-135
  Quick UnErase (QU), 280-282
  UnErase, 8, 61-74, 275-283,
    275
error messages, 314-315
Extended Memory Specification
  (XMS) support, DiskReet, 308
extraction errors, archived files,
  310

F

file allocation table (FAT)
  Disk Information (DI), 271
  hard disk management, 329
  lost chains/sectors, Norton Disk
    Doctor (NDD), 194
  view, DiskEdit, 58
  view, Norton Utility (NU), 73-
    74
File Attributes (FA), 93, 100-104,
  320
  archived files, 103
  command-line options, 101
  Norton Utility (NU) vs., 104
  read-only attribute, 102
  System attribute limitations,
    103-104
File Change option, 4
File Information (FI), 112-116
  command line options, 112
  deleted filenames, comments
    recovery, 116
  switches, 112-113
FileDate (FD), 93, 105-108
FileFind (FF), 10, 93-126, 319
  command line format, 93-95
  command-line options, 94, 108

FileFind (FF) *(con't.)*
  File Attributes (FA), 100-104
  File Information (FI), 112-116
  file transfer, disk space available, 98-100
  FileDate (FD), 105-108
  FileSize (FS), 116-120
  hidden files, 109, 110
  List Directory (LD), 120-124, 319
  listing files, sort order, 98-100
  network use, 95
  search limits, 94
  subdirectory-only display, 110
  switches, 94-95, 108
  system files, 109
  TextSearch (TS), 124-126
  time/date stamps, 96-98
FileFix, 9, 13, 127-129
filenames
  comments added to name, File Information (FI), 112-116
files
  archived, 101, 103, 310, 320
  ASCII view, DiskEdit, 59
  attribute changes, DiskEdit, 60
  attribute changes, File Attribute (FA), 100-104
  backup copies, 1-3, 91-92, 200, 278-279, 320
  comments added to filename, File Information (FI), 112-116
  comparison, DiskEdit, 61
  complete erasure (WipeDisk; WipeInfo), 10, 291-302
  corruption recovery (Disk Tool; FileFix), 9, 89, 127-129
  cross-linked, recovery, Quick UnErase, 282
  cross-linked, prevention, WipeDisk, 297
  delete, Norton Utility (NU), 154
  DIR will not list files, 89, 200-202
  Directory Sort (DS), 236-241
  disk space available for transfer, FileFind, 98-100
  disk space available for transfer, FileSize (FS), 119
  erasure recovery, 8, 9, 61-74, 131-135, 275-283, 319, 323

hexadecimal view, DiskEdit, 56-57, 59
hidden, 101, 103, 104, 109, 110, 120, 151
listing, sort order, FileFind, 98-100
lost chains/sectors, Norton Disk Doctor (NDD), 194
overwritten, 9, 131-135, 298-302, 320
print text files, LinePrint, 139-146
purging, FileSave, 134-135
read-only, 101, 102
searching (FileFind), 10, 93-126
size, space occupied, FileSize (FS), 116-120
string search, TextSearch (TS), 124-126
system, 109, 120
time/date stamps, 60, 96-98, 105-108, 158, 163-164, 171-175
utilities listing, Norton Integrator (NI), 207-210
FileSave, 9, 131-135, 277-278
  command line format, 131
  network use, 132
  options for use, 133
  purging deleted files, 134-135
  switches, 131-132
  UnErase use, 132
FileSize (FS), 93, 116-120
  command line options, 117
  directories, slack space, 118
  hidden and system files, 120
  unfragmented disks, 118
floppies *(see diskettes)*
Format Recovery (FR), 8, 287-290, 319
formatting errors, 319, 327, 328
  Format Recovery (FR), 8, 287-290, 319
  FRECOVER, 9, 137, 286-290
  prevention (SafeFormat), 10, 13, 211-217, 273-274, 286, 320
  recovery, UnFormat, 285-290
fragmentation, 227-229, 328
FRECOVER *(see also* Image), 9, 137, 286-290

G

GOTO command, Batch Enhancer (BE), 15-16
graphics selection, 4, 6-7

H

hard disk management, 325-331
  addressing, 327-328
  backup copies, 1-3, 91-92, 200, 278-279, 320
  bad clusters/sectors, 90, 199, 225, 232
  Bernoulli boxes, 322
  bootable disk creation, 89
  boot record viewing, 59
  caching programs, 177-183
  Calibrate, 9, 41-50
  capacity, 327
  clusters, 328
  complete file erasure (WipeDisk; WipeInfo), 10, 291-302
  corrupted file recovery, 89
  crash recovery, 322
  cyclic redundancy check (CRC), 329
  diagnose disk problems, Norton Disk Doctor, 192-194
  Disk Cache, 177-183
  Disk Doctor, 185-202
  Disk Doctor II, 8, 11, 13, 186-191
  disk drive summary/listing, System Information, 246-248
  Disk Explorer, 314
  Disk Index (DI), 265
  Disk Information (DI), 65-66, 270-274
  Disk Monitor (DM), 75-80
  Disk Tool, 9, 11, 13, 87-92
  DiskEdit, 11, 13, 51-74
  DiskTest (DT), 197-200
  DOS unreadable files, recovery, 89
  error corrections (DiskEdit), 9, 51-74
  File Allocation Table (FAT), 58, 329
  formatting errors, 211-217, 285-290, 319, 327, 328
  fragmentation, 328
  heat damage, 326
  interleave test, 48-49

low-level format, 42, 47-48
magnetic media, 327
map of clusters used, 59
Norton Utility (NU), version
    4.0 and 4.5, 61-74
optical disks, 330-331
optimization procedures, 9, 42-
    43, 219, 241, 310, 320, 326-
    327
partition tables, 59, 329
pattern tests, 42, 47-49
performance analysis, 9, 41-50,
    252-253
physical configuration of disks,
    326-327
Rescue Diskette creation, Disk
    Tool, 90-91
SafeFormatted disks, 273-274
seek test, 41, 46
slack space, 328
space occupied by files, File-
    Size, 116-120
speed test, 46-47, 326-327
surface test, 49, 188
test for damage, DiskTest (DT),
    197-200, 197
tolerance figure, 330
tracks, sectors, cylinders, 327
Volume Labels (VL), 153-155
wear, friction, 326
WORMs, 330-331
hardware interrupts, System
    Information, 245-246
Hardware option, 4
head-parking utility, 10
help (F1), 14
Hexadecimal view of file, DiskE-
    dit, 56-57, 59
hidden files, 101, 103, 104, 109,
    110, 120, 151
hidden sectors, Disk Information
    (DI), 272
hidden subdirectories, 104, 151

I
Image, 9, 13, 137-138, 285, 286
installation procedures, 2-8, 185,
    309-311, 322
interactive batch files, ASK,
    Batch Enhancer (BE), 16-26
interleave factor, 48-49
interrupts, System Information,
    245-247

K
keyboards
    lock, DiskReet, 85-86
    speed adjustment, NCC, 161-
    162, 170

L
lap-top users, special information,
    315
LinePrint, 139-146, 321
    command line format, 139
    condensed print, 142-143
    control codes, setup files, 144-
    145
    double-spacing, 142
    header formats, 143-144
    page numbers, 142
    README files, 141, 145
    switches, 140-141
List Directory (LD), 120-124,
    319
lost chains/sectors, 194
Lotus files
    corruption recovery, 9, 127-129
    erasure recovery, 8
    LinePrint use, 144
    string search, TextSearch (TS),
    126

M
mapping disk space usage,
    SpeeDisk, 224-226
media descriptor, Disk Informa-
    tion (DI), 271
memory/memory requirements,
    11, 13, 250-251, 261
menu expansion/modification,
    Norton, 204-207
monitors, 322
mouse speed, Norton Control
    Center (NCC), 161-162
MS-WINDOWS, multitasking/
    compatibility, 313
multitasking, 313

N
NDisk, DiskReet, 83-86, 309
nested batch files, 20-22
networks, 313, 318
    Calibrate Utility use, 42
    Disk Cache use, 181
    Disk Doctor use, 186
    Disk Tool use, 87

DiskEdit utility use, 52
encryption, DiskReet use, 82
FileFind use, 95
FileFix use, 128
FileSave use, 132
Image use, 138
Norton Change Directory
    (NCD) use, 148
Norton Control Center (NCC)
    use, 159
Norton use, 204
SafeFormat use, 212
security, Disk Monitor (DM),
    76-80, 76
SpeeDisk use, 220
System Information use, 244,
    253
UnErase use, 275
UnFormat use, 285
WipeInfo use, 292
Norton, 203-210
    command line format, 203
    menu expansion and modifica-
    tion, 204-207
    network usage, 204
    Norton Integrator (NI), 207-
    210
    switches, 203-204
Norton Cache, 311-312
Norton Change Directory (NCD),
    147-155
    command line format, 147, 148
    cursor movement, 153
    deleting/undeleting directories,
    153
    hidden subdirectories/files, 151
    network use, 148
    subdirectory deletion, 151
    switches, 147-149
    toggling between directories,
    153
    tree structure, 149-150, 153
    Volume Label (VL), 153-155
Norton Control Center (NCC),
    10, 157-175
    active key summary, 167
    color selections, 159-160, 168-
    169
    command line format, 157, 164
    command-line options, 164-166
    country information settings,
    164
    cursor adjustments, 167

Norton Control Center *(con't.)*
keyboard speed, 161-162, 170
mouse speed, 161-162
network use, 159
parameters, configurable, 166
serial port selection, 161, 163,
170-171
switches, 158, 163-164, 171-
173
TimeMark (TM), 173-175
video mode selection, 161, 170
Norton Disk Doctor (NDD), 191-
197, 272, 305-306, 319, 322,
325, 329
command line format, 191
DIR will not list known files,
200-202
directory structure analysis, 194
diskette capacity setting, 196-
197
switches and options, 191
undoing changes, 196-197
Norton Disk Doctor II, 8, 71
Norton Integrator (NI), 207-210
Norton Utility (NU), 61-74, 272,
319, 325
command-line switches/options,
63
deleting/undeleting directories,
154
directory damage-repair, 64
Disk Information, 65-66
editing, HEX vs. text mode, 70
File Allocation Table (FAT)
viewing, 73-74
help, 64, 67-70
menu selection, 64
Norton Disk Doctor vs., 71
Partition table viewing, 72-73
root directory capacity, 66-67
NU5_ARC?.EXE, 2, 3

O

objects, DiskEdit, 52
offset, Disk Information (DI),
272
optical hard disks, 330-331
optimization procedures, 9, 42-
43, 219-241, 310, 320
overwritten files, 9, 131-135,
298-302, 320, 321

P

partition tables, 59, 72-73, 248-
249, 264, 273, 329
passwords, 4-5, 82-83, 310
performance analysis, hard disk
(Calibrate), 9, 41-50
Performance Index, System Information, 252-253, 256
PKZIP compression utility, 2-3
PNCI encryption, 10, 81
printing text files, LinePrint, 139-
146
printouts, 322

Q

Quick UnErase (QU), 280-282,
319

R

read-only files, 101, 102
README files, 141, 145, 303-
315
repeated characters, PRINT-
CHAR, BOX utility, 29-30
Rescue Diskette, Disk Tool, 90-
91
root directories, 66-67, 109-110,
271
ROWCOL, BOX utility, 30

S

SafeFormat, 10, 13, 211-217,
273-274, 286, 320
command line options, 214-216
command line syntax, 211
modifiable configuration
parameters, 216-217
network usage, 212
progress monitoring, 217
switches and options, 211-212
WipeDisk usage, 214
Screen Attributes Utility, Batch
Enhancer (BE), 31-38
screen color *(see* color selection)
sectors, 327
bad clusters/sectors, 90, 199,
225-232
Disk Information (DI), 271
security
backup copies, 1-3, 91-92,
200, 278-279, 320

encryption, DiskReet Utility,
10, 81-86
overwriting files, WipeFile,
298-302
passwords, 4-5, 82-83, 310
system, Disk Monitor (DM),
75-80
self-extracting archives, 2, 3
serial port selection, (NCC), 161,
163, 170-171
settings *(see* environment settings;
Norton Control Center)
slack space, hard disks, 328
software interrupts, System Information, 246-247
SpeeDisk, 9, 13, 219-241, 286,
304, 312, 320
aborting operations, 234
bad sectors/clusters marked,
225, 232
CHKDSK vs., 312
command line format, 220, 230
copy protection compatibility,
230
directory reordering, 229, 233,
234
Directory Sort (DS), 236-241
Disk Information displayed,
224
disk size limitation, 235
diskette use, 323
drive selection, 220-222
error window, 231-232
exiting, 234
file order/priority, 227-229
fragmentation correction, 227-
229
network usage, 220
optimization-type selection,
222-223
pausing operations, 231-232
sensitive, security files, 223
statistics on disk, 226-227
switches and options, 219-220,
230
verification, 223, 233
Walk Map, 224-226
"X" blocks or signature files,
236
stop-watches *(see* clocks)
strings, search for, TextSearch
(TS), 124-126

subdirectories (*see* directories/ subdirectories)

support/assistance, xii, 11, 112, 314-315

surface tests, hard disk, 49, 188

system files
  finding, FileFind, 109
  size, space occupied, FileSize, 120

system ID, Disk Information (DI), 270

System Index (SI), 265-267

System Information, 10, 243-274, 312, 321
  AUTOEXEC.BAT contents, 253-254, 264
  CMOS value panel, 246-247, 261
  command line format, 243, 264-265
  CONFIG.SYS contents, 253-254, 264
  device drivers, 262
  disk characteristics, 263-264
  disk drive summary/listing, 246-248
  Disk Index (DI), 265
  Disk Information (DI), 270-274
  DOS System Area, 250, 251, 262
  hardware interrupts, 245-246
  memory summary, 250, 251, 261
  network usage, 244, 253
  partition table, 248-249, 264
  Performance Index, 252-253, 256
  processing speed, 250-252, 255
  report generation, 253, 255-264
  selecting options, 267-270
  skipping tests, 267-270
  software interrupts, 246-247

switches and options, 243-244, 265

System Index (SI), 265-267

TSR programs list, 262

video card settings, 244-245, 257-261

system requirements, 11
  compatibility, 42-43, 186, 313
  Rescue Diskette creation, Disk Tool, 90-91

T

TELENET on-line service, xii

Text Search, 320

TextSearch (TS), 93, 124-126

Time Mark (TM), 158, 173-175

time/date stamps, 60, 96-98, 105-108, 158, 163-164, 171-175

TIMEOUT, 40

tolerance, hard disks, 330

tonefiles, 27-28, 38-39, 333-334

tracks, hard disk, 327

TREE, 149-150, 153, 319

TSR programs, 10, 76, 262

TYMNET on-line services, xii

U

UNDO logs, 9

UnErase, 8, 11, 13, 275-283, 313
  automatic vs. manual operations, 277
  command line format, 275
  display options, 277, 279
  FileSave use, 132, 277-278
  network usage, 275
  Quick UnErase (QU), 280-282
  search for file data, 277
  Unremove Directory (UD), 283

UnFormat, 8, 11, 285-290
  command line format, 285
  Format Recovery (FR), 287-290

network usage, 285

UNIX operating system use, 318

Unremove Directory (UD), 283, 319

user interfaces, xi, 17-19

utilities listing, Norton Integrator (NI), 207-210

V

video card settings, System Information, 244-245, 257-261

video mode selection, Norton Control Center (NCC), 161, 170

virus protection, 10

Volume Label (VL), 153-155, 321

W

WINDOW, BOX utility, 30, 39-40

WipeDisk, 79, 199, 295-298, 320, 321

WipeFile, 298-302, 321

WipeInfo, 10, 13, 79, 291-302, 313
  command line format, 291
  configuration of default values, 294-295
  file selection for wiping, 292-294
  network usage, 292
  switches, 291-292
  WipeDisk, 295-298
  WipeFile, 298-302

WordStar files
  DiskEdit use, 55
  LinePrint use, 145

WORMs, 330-331

X

XMS support, DiskReet, 308